The Struggle for Natural Resources

Diálogos Series

Understanding Latin America demands dialogue, deep exploration, and frank discussion of key topics. Founded by Lyman L. Johnson in 1992 and edited since 2013 by Kris Lane, the Diálogos Series focuses on innovative scholarship in Latin American history and related fields. The series, the most successful of its type, includes specialist works accessible to a wide readership and a variety of thematic titles, all ideally suited for classroom adoption by university and college teachers.

Also available in the Diálogos Series:

Viceroy Güemes's Mexico: Rituals, Religion, and Revenue by Christoph Rosenmüller

At the Heart of the Borderlands: Africans and Afro-Descendants on the Edges of Colonial Spanish America edited by Cameron D. Jones and Jay T. Harrison

The Age of Dissent: Revolution and the Power of Communication in Chile, 1780–1833 by Martín Bowen

From Sea-Bathing to Beach-Going: A Social History of the Beach in Rio de Janeiro, Brazil by B. J. Barickman

Gamboa's World: Justice, Silver Mining, and Imperial Reform in New Spain by Christopher Albi

The Conquest of the Desert: Argentina's Indigenous Peoples and the Battle for History edited by Carolyne R. Larson

From the Galleons to the Highlands: Slave Trade Routes in the Spanish Americas edited by Alex Borucki, David Eltis, and David Wheat

A Troubled Marriage: Indigenous Elites of the Colonial Americas by Sean F. McEnroe

Staging Frontiers: The Making of Modern Popular Culture in Argentina and Uruguay by William Garrett Acree Jr.

A Woman, a Man, a Nation: Mariquita Sánchez, Juan Manuel de Rosas, and the Beginnings of Argentina by Jeffrey M. Shumway

For additional titles in the Diálogos Series, please visit unmpress.com.

UNIVERSITY OF NEW MEXICO PRESS ALBUQUERQUE

the STRUGGLE for NATURAL RESOURCES

Findings from Bolivian History

Edited by Carmen Soliz and Rossana Barragán

 Published 2024
Printed in the United States of America

ISBN 978-0-8263-6616-0 (cloth)
ISBN 978-0-8263-6617-7 (paper)
ISBN 978-0-8263-6618-4 (ePub)
ISBN 978-0-8263-6640-5 (webPDF)

Library of Congress Cataloging-in-Publication data is on file with the Library of Congress.

Founded in 1889, the University of New Mexico sits on the traditional homelands of the Pueblo of Sandia. The original peoples of New Mexico—Pueblo, Navajo, and Apache—since time immemorial have deep connections to the land and have made significant contributions to the broader community statewide. We honor the land itself and those who remain stewards of this land throughout the generations and also acknowledge our committed relationship to Indigenous peoples. We gratefully recognize our history.

Cover illustration by Alejandro Salazar, Bolivian artist
Designed by Isaac Morris
Composed in Athelas and Kristal

CONTENTS

ILLUSTRATIONS

MAPS

TABLES

ACKNOWLEDGMENTS

The idea for this book arose two years ago, amid the pandemic. During a talk in lockdown, we complained that despite the richness of Bolivian historiography of recent decades, general history books were once again focused on a classic narrative centered on the nation-state and ordered by successive, well-defined political periods. We wondered how to write a history of Bolivia that highlighted what traditional political narratives have overlooked: the connections and intersections between local, regional, national, and transnational actors, and how these interrelationships have shaped history. Using our research on land and mining as an anchor, we began to frame this project. We are grateful and fortunate that our colleagues Thomas Grisaffi, Sarah T. Hines, José Orsag Molina, and Kevin Young enthusiastically joined this project by bringing to the table their recent research on coca, water, rubber, and oil.

We appreciate the generosity and support of Kris Lane, editor of the Diálogos Series, and Michael Millman, senior editor of the University of New Mexico Press. Both provided their extensive expertise and supported and encouraged our project. We sincerely want to thank Professor Sinclair Thomson for his insightful and detailed comments and the time he took to read the manuscript.

We also thank Myrna Santiago, professor at Saint Mary's College of California, and Ulbe Bosma, senior research fellow at the International Institute of Social History in Amsterdam (IISH), for joining this project and writing the epilogues to this volume. Myrna Santiago offered her vast experience in Latin American and environmental history to think of Bolivia as "El Dorado" and to highlight the histories of extractivism in Bolivia. Ulbe Bosma provided his expertise in plantations and the "making" of peripheries to examine the Bolivian case.

Finally, we are grateful for the continuous support of family and friends without which this project would not have been possible, and the support of our institutions: The University of North Carolina at Charlotte, the International Institute of Social History in Amsterdam, and the University of San Andrés in La Paz (CIDES-UMSA) research and postgraduate center.

—Carmen Soliz and Rossana Barragán

Introduction

A MULTILAYERED APPROACH TO ANALYZE STRUGGLES OVER NATURAL RESOURCES

Rossana Barragán and Carmen Soliz

In November 2019, Bolivia underwent a dramatic political crisis that culminated in the resignation under intense pressure of President Evo Morales after thirteen years in power. Morales assumed the presidency in 2006 with massive support and a loaded political agenda. Among his top goals were "to recover effective control of the country's natural resources and to ensure that they were at the service of Bolivians' welfare."[1] He also wanted to assert Bolivia's economic independence from global powers, especially from the United States.

Since Morales's departure, much heated debate has focused on his decision to run for a fourth term in the 2019 election and the political crisis that led to his ouster. Discussion seemed reduced to analysis of the immediate political events, led by two camps: Evo Morales's supporters and his detractors. Sidelined was the complex and often contradictory agenda of Bolivia's distinct social and economic groups: lowland Indigenous peoples, peasant migrants, coca leaf producers of the Yungas and Chapare districts, mine workers, mining cooperatives, Santa Cruz's big landowners, and urban dwellers. The political debate also left unresolved critical policy debates that engulfed the country during Evo Morales's presidency. For example: What has been the net effect of Morales's gas nationalization policy initiated in 2006? What has been the effect of the third agrarian reform enacted under the Morales government? What happened to the much-hyped lithium industrialization project? What is the story with the coca leaf economy? To what extent did the Morales government constitute a rupture or a continuation of past political-economic processes and policies? These questions prompted us to dig into the quest for commodities in Bolivia over the *longue durée* and to engage Bolivia's history through struggles over ownership and use of the country's critical natural endowments. We examine possession and management of specific natural resources; the roles played by local, national, and transnational elites; and the insertion and agency of popular sectors in these areas. We analyze these topics through six commodities: land, minerals, rubber, water, fossil fuels, and coca/cocaine.

All are crucial to understanding Bolivia's overlapping waves of exploitation of natural resources and their role in the complex process of capitalist expansion.

The Struggle for Natural Resources examines Bolivia's land and commodity disputes from a historical perspective, exploring the intertwined relationships between structure and agency that global history approaches tend to overlook. We are also keen to make sense of the multidimensional relationships between imperial and transnational groups connected with regional and local elites and popular sectors. We are critical of perspectives that assume subaltern/elites as monolithic categories, getting beyond simple elite/subaltern binaries. Although there may be critical moments of confluence, neither the subaltern nor the elites always constitute unified, oppositional blocs when it comes to resource management.

This book offers a multilayered analysis of struggles over Bolivian resources from the local, regional, national, and global perspectives. We believe paying attention to the participation of multiple actors in the exploitation of natural resources will enrich the analysis and reading of other realities beyond Bolivia. Our exploration of the Bolivian case invites dialogue and comparison with other parts of the world, particularly regions and countries of the so-called Global South.

EXTRACTIVISM AND COMMODITY FRONTIERS

In the last two decades, debates over natural resource extraction in Latin America have centered on two terms, or concepts: *extractivism* and *commodity frontiers*. The term "extractivism" has a long history. Latin American scholars, in particular, have long linked extractivism to a country's specialized production of a primary natural resource for the global market. In the mid-twentieth century, economists Raúl Prebisch and Hans Singer, precursors of Dependency Theory, used this term to explain unequal economic exchange relations between industrial centers and peripheral economies.[2] Yet the term "extractivism" gained most popularity in the 1990s, often associated with analysis of the Brazilian Amazon. Stephen Bunker's work was pivotal in disseminating this term. One of Bunker's most important contributions was to highlight the difference between modes of extraction and modes of production, plus the unbalanced flows of energy and matter from extractive peripheries to the productive core.[3] The term "extractive" indicated the "overexploitation of nature (human labor and non-human resources) to such an extent that it undermines its conditions of existence over time."[4]

Since about the year 2000, Alberto Acosta, Maristella Svampa, and Eduardo Gudynas have placed the terms "extractivism" and "neo-extractivism" at the center of political debate in Latin America. This academic trio, all very critical of Latin America's neoliberal past, also criticized the "post-neoliberal" governments of post-2000 Argentina, Bolivia, and Ecuador. Alberto Acosta headed Ecuador's Mining and Energy Department and served as president of the Constituent Assembly under President Rafael Correa (2007–2017). In "Colonialism in the Twenty-First Century" (2011), Acosta argued that extractivism is a form of accumulation in contemporary capitalism.[5]

In 2013, Argentine sociologist Maristella Svampa coined the term "commodity consensus," a reference to the Washington Consensus of the 1990s, to describe the new economic, political, sociological, and ideological order installed in Latin America at the turn of the twenty-first century. Svampa argued that, beyond a government's ideological alignments, the general rise in international commodity prices led the region to export raw materials on an unprecedented scale. A consequence of this economic boom was the "reprimarization" (understood as the expansion of activities associated with the primary sector, such as mining, oil drilling, cattle ranching, and soy farming)[6] of most Latin American economies based on single-commodity exports, overexploitation of non-renewable resources, and the expansion of new extractive frontiers.[7]

Also in 2013, Uruguayan anthropologist and ecologist Eduardo Gudynas argued that in Latin America in the first decades of the twenty-first century, classical ideas of resource-driven development were revived. He noted that 90 percent of Bolivia's exports consisted of oil, gas, minerals, and soy in 2012. Gudynas stated that the term "neo-extractivism" refers to extraction and consumption of natural resources in unprecedented volume and intensity. These commodities are exported "raw," with no, or very limited, industrial processing. This is the case in agriculture, mining, hydrocarbons, forestry, and fisheries. In this sense, extractivism is understood as a non-industry linked to the large-scale export of "natural resources."[8] Also, as Maristella Svampa claims, neo-extractivism is not a completely new phenomenon; its origins date to the colonization of the Americas. But twenty-first century extractivism has its own features, characterized by the quantity and scale of the projects, the types of transnational actors involved, and the intensive use of water, energy, and resources—all while providing relatively few jobs.[9]

Anthony Bebbington and Jeffrey Bury, specialists in extractive industries, environmental studies, and political ecology, analyzed the transformation of natural and social environments amid social and political conflicts in Latin America over the last two decades. They argued that the political ecology of extraction in Latin America in recent decades constitutes a fundamental reorganization of the geopolitical economy in which resources, territory, global production, and the centrality of the state are "co-produced."[10] They stressed that both left and right in Latin America share similar paradigms of development and progress driven by the commodity boom of the first two decades of the twenty-first century, and have similarly bet on the benefits of extractive projects.

In 2014, Henry Veltmeyer and James Petras questioned models of political economy, left and right, that proposed neo-extractivism as a sustainable, viable, and novel model and means of development.[11] As popular forces struggled against neoliberal regimes, Latin America witnessed the emergence of governments associated with the so-called Red or Pink Tide. These left-leaning regimes promised a new world of social justice and sustainable development. Some spoke of a new form of socialism "for the twenty-first century." Yet, citing James Cypher[12], Petras and Veltmeyer argued that, rather than calling for, say, industrial revival or enhanced conservation, "these regimes mostly bet on a predatory capitalism of natural resource extraction."[13] Regarding the Bolivian case, they noted: "Despite the populist rhetoric of resource nationalism (the country's resources and wealth belong to the people) and social inclusion, the relationship of the Bolivian state to global capital under the Evo Morales–García Linera regime had not changed substantially."[14]

The concept of extractivism is then also useful for thinking about even longer historical continuities. Despite ruptures in the structures of power between the colonial and republican periods, or between nineteenth-century liberalism and twentieth-century nationalism, Bolivia's relationship with the world market has centered on export of natural products with varying degrees of industrialization. Such was the case of silver in colonial times, rubber in the nineteenth century, tin and oil in the twentieth century, and lithium today.

The second core concept, "commodity frontiers," is connected to the work of Terence Hopkins and Immanuel Wallerstein (1986), the geographer and ecologist Jason W. Moore, and a group that publishes the journal *Commodity Frontiers*.[15] Immanuel Wallerstein's influential 1974 work *The Modern World-System I*, on the relationship between the economies of the "center," the "semi-periphery," and the "periphery," was one of the cornerstones of this approach.[16] Production processes in different geographical areas as integrated parts of the world economy led Wallerstein and Hopkins to develop the concept of "commodity chains" as a network of labor and production across frontiers. Since then, the term "commodity chain" has been embraced by scholars of global goods movements and value chains.[17]

Steven Topik, Zephyr Frank, and Carlos Marichal's 2006 edited volume, *From Silver to Cocaine: Latin American Commodity Chains and the Building of the World Economy, 1500–2000*, exemplifies the commodity-chain approach, following the history of Latin American products from production to consumption.

Other commodity frontier scholars, influenced by Hopkins and Wallerstein, have analyzed the continuous expansion of resource exploitation with the rise of capitalism and the making of the modern world.[18] This "expanding frontier" approach "explores the history and present of capitalism, contestation, and ecological transformation in the global countryside."[19] Sven Beckert and coauthors of a position paper discuss commodity frontiers in terms of the "processes and sites of the incorporation of resources, land, energy, and raw materials."[20] In contrast to most recent works on extractivism published in Latin America, these scholars foreground historical rather than structural analysis. They are interested in the long history of capitalism, taking into account multiple resource frontiers across time, as experienced by a variety of actors. They also call attention to the environment at local and global scales, pointing to cyclical frictions, contestations, and countermovements, noting how all of these factors changed the world.[21]

The notion of commodity frontiers encourages putting space at the center of historical analysis. More than gross production or export patterns, what has changed in Bolivia is the geography of economic exploitation. Until the mid-twentieth century, Bolivia's productive engine was concentrated in its mineral-rich highlands. Since the second half of the twentieth century, the geography of land exploitation has shifted to the eastern lowlands, the center of hydrocarbon and soybean production. The notion of the commodity frontier also urges us to think about the history of the commodification of nature. For instance, although rubber was known and used even before the colonial period, it was not until the end of the nineteenth century that this resource became an object of high economic value, as José Orsag Molina explains in his chapter in this volume. Similarly, explosive battles over water access in highland Bolivia in the last two decades stem from efforts over several decades to commodify this common resource, one of the last frontiers in the commodification of nature, as Sarah Hines traces in her chapter.

FOUR LINES OF INQUIRY: AN APPROACH TO POLITICAL STRUGGLES OVER NATURAL RESOURCES

Enriched by the extractivism and commodity frontiers approaches to world history, this book treats political struggles over natural resources in Bolivia as long-term processes that outlast immediate political events. We have identified four areas of inquiry to better explore what we see as intertwined relationships between structure and agency. The first line of inquiry pays attention to the processes of appropriation of land, water, and raw materials. The second line of inquiry follows closely by examining the role of key economic, political, and social actors at the local, regional, national, and global levels. Our third line of inquiry studies those moments of economic, social, and political continuity and rupture in the longue durée, and the fourth scrutinizes alliances and splits in the constitution of political blocs and the making of political transformations.

The first line of inquiry is an invitation to analyze the processes of appropriation of organic resources (like timber and rubber), plus land, water, minerals, and labor, from the colonial period up to the present. Colonization's greatest impact was felt in Bolivia's Andean communities and fertile valleys. These appropriative processes did not stop when Bolivia became independent from colonial powers in 1825. Bolivian dependency on mineral extraction continued in the Bolivian highlands with the exploitation of silver (in the late nineteenth century), tin (in the twentieth century), and lithium (today), as described in this volume by Rossana Barragán. With the export of rubber and later oil, described in chapters by José Orsag Molina and Kevin Young, these processes of resource extraction also extended into new geographies, primarily the tropical lowlands.

Following these processes of resource appropriation, our second line of inquiry explores how elite and subaltern economic actors at the local, regional, national, and international levels, including private and state agents, became involved in these extractive economies. Our long-term and multilayered analysis strongly suggests that that binary approaches to elite and subaltern actors as homogenous groups fail to make sense of shifting relationships between imperial and transnational groups connected with regional and local elites and popular sectors. Although one may spot critical moments of confluence, subaltern groups do not always constitute unified blocs opposed to "elites." Rather, one often finds, as in the Bolivian case, shifting coalitions in the struggle for appropriation and distribution of existing resources. We examine, in the words of historical sociologists Alexander Anievas and Kerem Nisanciouglu, the formation and consolidation of capitalisms (in plural) and how diverse economic sectors (including subaltern groups) have resisted but also adapted to, negotiated, and profited from the extraction of natural resources.[22]

Bolivia's history calls special attention to the historical strength of the popular and subaltern sectors, a point driven home by all the chapters presented in this volume. There is no doubt that some of the most important policies for resource nationalization or the approval of new legislation favoring Indigenous, peasant, and workers' rights were the product of long-term, tenacious popular struggles. Throughout Bolivia's three-hundred-year colonial and two-hundred-year republican past, we find numerous cases of Indigenous leaders fighting in the courts for the restitution of their lands as well as of Indigenous revolts and rebellions demanding the right to land. Sparked in part by the five-hundredth anniversary in 1992 of Columbus's first landing in the Americas, Indigenous marches epitomized Bolivian political history. Part of a Pan-American Indigenous movement, these actions were crucial for consolidating territories for the Indigenous peoples of Bolivia's lowlands. As Hines and Young point out in this volume, the nationalization of gas in 2006 and the ending of contracts with transnational companies for the management of water were, in part, the result of widespread popular mobilizations that started in the year 2000 with the so-called Water War in Cochabamba and the Gas War of 2003 in La Paz–El Alto.[23]

Not all popular-sector gains were the result of dramatic social upheaval. Other changes stemmed from day-to-day acts of resistance and adaptation on the part of peasants and mine workers. A prime example of this was the capacity of the mine workers in the colonial period to vie with Spanish mineowners for control over the ore they mined. Barragán demonstrates that the colonial informal economy was more than an appendage of the formal economy and that independent mine workers called *k'ajchas* were fierce economic competitors. This reveals the long-range tenacity of the popular economy in Bolivia in spite of unequal circumstances in which ordinary people have been forced to operate. Indeed, this volume is a testimony to the capacity of Bolivia's subaltern sectors to subvert imposed systems of extraction. It also speaks to the capacity of these sectors to enter and exit the market despite an unwelcoming framework in adverse economic conditions. In more recent decades, popular sectors have responded to scarce urban opportunities and to privatization of mines and state enterprises by migrating to the lowlands, producing coca, and organizing small cooperatives circumventing environmental or labor laws. In other words, the extractive economy has organized the economic strategies of both elites and subaltern sectors in times of economic boom as well as in times of crisis.

A third line of inquiry examines continuities and ruptures within Bolivia's economic, social, and political cycles over the longue durée. It is only through historical analysis of long-term cycles that we can make sense of critical events of the present. As Sarah Hines argues, we cannot understand protesters' success in overturning Cochabamba's water privatization in the year 2000 without tracking their many years of political organization and their deep knowledge of water sources, systems, and management accumulated over a century of struggle. It is also only in the shadow of the longue durée that we can grasp the historical importance and density of current political agendas. For instance, we cannot fully comprehend the political significance of President Evo Morales's decrees on gas nationalization if we do not understand how deeply rooted this policy was in the political memory of Bolivians who saw nationalization as an expression of national sovereignty against foreign interests.

It is also only in the long view that we see the historical construction of categories such as "elites" and "subalterns," as well as the multiplicity of their competing and sometimes overlapping objectives. As an extensive Bolivian historiography has shown, the concepts of subaltern or "Indian" bring together diverse subjects with distinct histories of political struggle and insertion into markets, and, in some cases, rival agendas. For example, Soliz analyzes the growing rivalry between lowland

Indians and peasants who had migrated from the highlands to the lowlands, the so-called *colonizadores*. The two groups espouse different notions of property and economic development. Thomas Grisaffi's work on coca production also points to the ongoing conflict between producers of coca leaf in the Yungas of La Paz and those from the Chapare in Cochabamba. The history of mining analyzed by Rossana Barragán reveals the conflicting interests of salaried miners, cooperative members (*socios*), and cooperative laborers. Sarah Hines's study of water exposes the complicated relations between peasant and irrigators' associations, residents of neighborhoods on city outskirts, and core urban water customers in Cochabamba. These examples demonstrate how generic, overlapping categories such as subaltern/peasant/Indian can blur significant economic differences within these groups and hide conflicting political agendas.

Bolivia's "elites" have been no less fractured, constituting distinct groups with diverse agendas. Analysis of colonial history reveals that mining and landed elites competed often against each other to control Indian labor. For example, hacienda owners in need of workers welcomed Indigenous people migrating from their communities to avoid paying tribute and compulsory mine work. In the nineteenth and twentieth centuries, regional elites competed for political power and control of resources. The rivalry between the elites in Chuquisaca (Sucre) and La Paz ended with the Federal War of 1899, favoring the latter. In the second half of the twentieth century, rivalry between the rising economic elites of (lowland) Santa Cruz and (highland) La Paz's political elites intensified. Among other things, access to oil royalties drove a wedge between these geographically separated elites in the 1970s and 1980s.

A fourth line of inquiry considers convergent and divergent agendas and the sometimes-paradoxical alliances and disputes that have arisen among different sectors of Bolivian society. For example, in the nineteenth century, liberal La Paz elites allied with the Indigenous forces of Pablo Zarate Willka against republican elites centered in the south. This short-lived alliance ended dramatically when, after winning the war, the liberal elites lashed out at their former allies, accusing them of waging a race war. Similarly, the revolutionary nationalist movement, the MNR, which took power after the National Revolution of 1952, forcefully battled the mining and landowning elites but surrendered to US pressure by reopening the oil sector to foreign investment, reversing the 1937 oil nationalization. Strange bedfellows and subsequent "divorces" or break-ups have continued to appear. The administration of Evo Morales forged unexpected alliances with the Santa Cruz landowning elites. At the same time, Hines and Young offer examples of cross-class alliances in pursuit of common goals. For instance, Hines demonstrates that the Cochabamba Water War brought together two sectors that had been in conflict: city dwellers and peasant communities who held rights to water sources. Young shows that the agenda of gas nationalization also united different social, economic, and even regional sectors that otherwise shared few interests.

CONTINUITY AMID CHANGE: A BRIEF "EXTRACTIVE" HISTORY OF BOLIVIA

As Myrna Santiago points out in the first epilogue to this volume, *El Dorado* is a metaphor and reality of extractivism that seems to encompass the entire history of Latin America. El Dorado implies plunder and desolation, not development. Echoes of El Dorado persist, as Ulbe Bosma underscores in the second epilogue to this volume: Latin American extractivism has entailed processes of limited industrial processing and reduced added value. This historical process of exploitation of natural resources across more than five hundred years suggests continuity: extraction leads to underdevelopment rather than its desired opposite. As Bosma reminds us, the new extractivism simply reinforces commodity regimes' links to the configurations of global capitalism. In such a scenario, the main political struggles defined within Bolivia's national borders were and are around, in the words of sociologist René Zavaleta Mercado, "struggles for surplus" (*querella del excedente*).

As the following brief historical overview of struggles over the appropriation of land, minerals, water, rubber, oil, and coca leaf reveals, the persistence of extractivism in Bolivia challenges scholars who underscore clear breaks between different historical phases, such as colonialism, liberalism, nationalism, neoliberalism, or post-neoliberalism. It also challenges marked differentiations between preindustrial, industrial, and neoliberal regimes. These cycles, which may be more helpful in understanding North Atlantic economies, work less well in the Bolivian case, where industrialization was meager.

In the early sixteenth century, the Spanish Crown claimed most American lands as its own, incorporating them into the global economy. This was a process of land grabbing on a continental scale. Spanish interest in the Andes grew tremendously after the 1545 "discovery" of Potosí, one of the largest silver mining camps of the colonial period. Yet the Spaniards realized the mines had little value without labor to exploit them. Andean communities agreed to furnish tribute in labor and cash in exchange for Crown protection of their land base and local political autonomy. This hierarchical and unequal relationship between the Crown and Andean communities allowed Indigenous populations to survive in exchange for their work in the mines plus payment of cash tribute. The most densely populated communities were concentrated in the corridor that stretches between Lake Titicaca and what is today the southern portion of the department of Potosí. These Indigenous communities were henceforth part of what historian Carlos Sempat Assadourian called the "Andean colonial space," which was almost instantly articulated to the emerging global market.[24]

After congregating Indigenous communities into more densely populated town districts (called *reducciones*), the Crown auctioned off lands it considered vacant to Spaniards. This was one of the origins of the hacienda or great landed estate. Haciendas multiplied on fertile lands and developed links to the mining centers where they could sell their produce. It was precisely in response to the demand of the Potosí market as well as other mining and urban centers that the coca leaf trade emerged. Although it is true that coca continued to be crucial in ritual offerings, in reciprocal relations, and in the socialization of workers during the colonial period, coca became one of the staple products of consumption among mine workers, as Thomas Grisaffi discusses in his chapter. Initially, most coca came to Potosí from the Cuzco area and the trade involved various actors, including Indigenous women.[25]

In the seventeenth century, the frontiers of production and exchange continued to expand with the emergence of new mining centers, although not of the magnitude of Potosí. In the eighteenth century, Potosí silver production peaked once again, as discussed by Rossana Barragán in chapter 2. This second boom encouraged the opening of new frontiers for coca production in Yungas, a subtropical ecoregion northeast of the city of La Paz. Coca production in these warm lowlands led to the creation of new fortunes for local and regional elites.

In the early nineteenth century, as part of the Atlantic Age of Revolution, local elites, with uneven support from Bolivia's Indigenous populations, rebelled against Spanish colonial power and won their independence. After independence was secured in 1825, this south-central portion of South America formerly ruled by a distant king adopted a new political system based on the sovereignty of the people and the election of representative authorities.[26] Although military regimes and constitutional ruptures plagued these representative systems in Bolivia's first decades as a free country, they constituted advanced political projects in their day, especially when compared to the monarchical system that still ruled Europe.[27]

The formation of republican nation-states involved the drawing of national borders. In the Bolivian case, the outlines of the new republic were set, in part, following the jurisdictional limits of the Audiencia de Charcas (the royal court of Charcas was until 1776 subordinate to the Viceroyalty of Peru and after 1776 under the Viceroyalty of Río de la Plata). The final drawing of Bolivia's boundaries entailed tense political relations with neighboring Peru, Argentina, Brazil, and Paraguay. For much of the nineteenth century and even the twentieth, the Bolivian government's control over its territory was more nominal than real. As in the colonial period, political and economic power, along with the majority of the population, remained concentrated in the highland geographical corridor between Lake Titicaca and southern Potosí.

In the republican context, elites sought to establish, in the spirit of European liberalism, a new tax system based on private property. At first this political project failed because imposing it would have implied sacrificing the revenues the state obtained from Indigenous communities. Since more than 50 percent of national income came from Indigenous tribute after independence in 1825, governing elites postponed change. However, in the 1860s and 1870s, these same elites enacted new laws that finally consolidated the privatization of land. As with the prior retention of colonial-style tribute, this privatization policy was to the detriment of Indigenous peoples, suddenly eroding communal property.

Continuity persisted amid change. Mining (the "old extractivism") continued to be the engine of the Bolivian economy across most of the nineteenth and twentieth centuries. At the turn of the twentieth century, the geography of mining widened with the search for a new global commodity: tin. This metal was essential for the development of the canning industry, which became particularly important in the era of the world wars. The Bolivian tin industry was dominated by three big companies, owned by Simón Patiño, Moritz Hochschild, and José Avelino Aramayo. Bolivia's three "tin barons," as they were known, controlled almost 80 percent of tin mining in the country. Their success was based on control over extraction, processing, and export of the raw mineral to European and North American markets. Control of a precious resource by Bolivian nationals rather than foreign enterprises was significant, but outsized economic strength gave the three tin barons enormous political influence, leading to tense relations between them and the Bolivian state, which was chronically in debt.

The quest for new commodity frontiers or extractive opportunities did not cease. At the turn of the twentieth century, rubber and petroleum gained importance in the world market. Demand for these commodities was unlike demand for tin in that it ended up mapping Bolivian state expansion onto the expansion of resource frontiers. Natural rubber was found in the Amazon and petroleum in the southeast of Bolivia, in the Chaco Basin. The Bolivian state considered the Indigenous inhabitants of these areas to be "barbaric" and thus ignored their territorial claims. As suggested by José Orsag Molina, the rubber economy enveloped the territories of those Indigenous groups deemed "savages." This extractive regime developed after the appropriation of extensive forests deemed "vacant." Vast state-claimed spaces were transformed overnight into private or nationalized lands. Nationalist historiography charted these changes by celebrating lowland colonization and Indigenous disinheritance and displacement as the nation's birthright and as a "civilizing" process.

Extraction continued. In the early twentieth century, Bolivia's mostly lowland petroleum sector surfaced with great dynamism. In chapter 5, Kevin Young shows that the earliest economic nationalist discourses focused on this industry. Unlike mining, which was in the hands of local entrepreneurs, oil was in the hands of the transnational Standard Oil Company of New Jersey. In 1920s Bolivia, Standard Oil benefited not only from favorable state concessions but also from tax evasion, enabled by local bureaucrats who took illegal payments. After Bolivia's bloody war with Paraguay (1932–1935), popular resentment against the national and transnational elites grew due to the magnitude of the war's human toll and postwar political and economic crisis. In this context, renewed enthusiasm among intellectual middle classes for leftist ideas led to the first nationalization of petroleum reserves and exclusion of a foreign oil company in Latin America. Bolivia beat Mexico to the punch in 1937.[28]

A second wave of resource nationalization occurred during the 1952 revolution. Bolivia's Revolutionary Nationalist Movement (Movimiento Nacionalista Revolucionario, MNR) confiscated the mines of the three tin barons. After nationalization, the government created the state-run Mining Corporation of Bolivia (COMIBOL). Under intense US pressure, later governments backed off from nationalization, authorizing private companies to operate mines. Indeed, it is impossible to understand Bolivian political and economic dynamics during the twentieth century without recognizing the overbearing role of the United States. Beginning in the 1930s, the US government, following US corporate interests, dictated, shaped, or constrained Bolivian national decisions. Several chapters in this volume offer examples that expose the ways in which the United States meddled in Bolivia's economy and politics. In discussing the 1950s, Kevin Young highlights how the nationalist revolutionary government approved a new oil code in 1956 to reopen the hydrocarbon sector to foreign investment because of US pressure.[29] The primary new concessionaire was Gulf Oil. Yet political winds blew both ways, even as the Cold War progressed. In 1969, General Alfredo Ovando nationalized hydrocarbons once again, turning the tables and angering the United States. Thus, the economic history of the twentieth century was marked by several cycles of nationalization and privatization that do not map neatly onto right versus left governments.

It was also in the revolutionary context of the 1950s, as Carmen Soliz discusses, that Bolivia enacted one of the most radical agrarian reform policies in Latin America. The agrarian reform of 1953 put an end to the latifundia or great estates, eliminated the personal service of peasants on haciendas, and distributed land among peasants. This agrarian reform, as Sarah Hines explains, also helped democratize access to water by redistributing sources previously controlled by hacienda owners. Agrarian reform was most transformative in Bolivia's highlands and valleys. In the lowlands, however, latifundia slowly began to emerge in recently opened or "homesteading frontier" lands. It was particularly during the military regimes of the 1970s and 1980s that a new landowning elite seized enormous expanses of land for cattle ranching, exotic hardwood exports, and soybean production. This new landowning elite displaced and marginalized lowland Indigenous populations.

The United States government's influence in Bolivia grew in the second half of the twentieth century, when it exerted financial and political pressure either directly on governments or through international organizations like the United Nations. As Thomas Grisaffi notices, a 1950 UN report declared the traditional coca leaf (not just cocaine) to be a drug. In the 1970s and 1980s, coca leaf production in South America's producing countries grew sharply in response to the increasing demand for cocaine in the North Atlantic countries. The prices offered for this drug made exports soar.

In the 1980s, Bolivia confronted an unusually severe economic crisis characterized by hyperinflation and foreign debt. As Barragán outlines, this was the moment when the Bolivian government implemented structural adjustment policies that culminated in the laying off more than 23,000 workers from the formerly state-run mining centers. Much of the dismissed mining labor force moved to the lowland tropical Chapare region in eastern Cochabamba to plant coca, a product that promised enormous income. In what some called a "white gold rush," thousands of mining families, including that of Evo Morales, became coca growers in the Chapare. As Grisaffi points out, the population of the Chapare, which did not exceed 25,000 in 1967, grew to more than 350,000 by 1989. This brought about a sea of change in the geography of economic production in Bolivia oriented to the global market. As the geography of coca and cocaine production expanded, the United States intensified its drug war policy in Colombia, Peru, and Bolivia, which in turn encouraged targeted coca growers to organize unions. Evo Morales, the leader of the Chapare peasant unions, won election to the national assembly in 1997. From this platform, coca growers' unions built a strong political party, enabling Morales to win the presidential election of 2005. Early in his presidency, Morales legalized cultivation of a small plot of coca leaf per family in specific parts of the Chapare.

There were more changes amid resource-export continuity. Beginning in 1985, Bolivian governments began to abandon the statist economic model to adopt instead a neoliberal one. Following, in part, the World Bank's agenda that promoted the commodification of land, the government passed a new agrarian reform law in 1996. Yet, using one of the transitory provisions of the law, lowland Indigenous peoples, who had been displaced by the new landowning elite, were able to consolidate approximately eight million hectares as autonomous territories. At the same time, small, medium, and large properties oriented mainly to soybean production consolidated about four million hectares in the most fertile lowland regions of the country.

In the 1990s, following neoliberal Washington Consensus policies, the Bolivian government reprivatized oil and mineral resources as well as vital services and utilities such as social security, electricity, and telecommunications. The government also contracted transnational corporations to administer water supply systems in the cities of La Paz and El Alto in 1997 and Cochabamba in 1999. Until then, both had been administered by municipal companies and water user collectives. This policy change led not only to increased water rates for municipal customers but it also entailed dispossession of water sources and systems owned, built, maintained, and administered by water users themselves. As a result, revolts broke out against water privatization, first and most dramatically in Cochabamba's 2000 Water War, in which broad and heterogeneous sectors of the population mobilized.

Deprived of oil and mining revenues by 2003, Bolivia faced a deep crisis that culminated in a massive revolt later called the Gas War. The tide turned once again toward national control of natural resources, aligning with popular demand for broad social change. Evo Morales was swept into power. One of the first actions of the Morales administration was the nationalization of hydrocarbons in 2006. This measure, which responded to the clamor of the population, was also part of a historical tradition of the Bolivian state to assert national sovereignty. One of the Bolivian government's toughest negotiations in 2006, amid the Morales government's gas nationalization, involved not the Spanish company Repsol but the state-owned Brazilian company Petrobras.[30] Something of a historical irony, here was an apparently Indigenous-led struggle over natural resources that pitted state against state, leftist neighbor against leftist neighbor—with a former colonial player in the mix as well.

Others joined the twenty-first century's "Great Game." Since 2005, China has steadily replaced the United States as Bolivia's most powerful customer for frozen meat, concentrated mineral ores, and tropical lumber, creating close economic ties. Some have argued that soaring Chinese (and other Asian) demand for primary materials has largely enabled "new extractivist" regimes to flourish regardless of political persuasion. Bolivia appears to be no exception. During the Morales administration, the reprimarization of the economy (understood as the expansion of activities associated with the primary sector) intensified due to the growing export of minerals, soybeans, timber, and cattle to China.[31] Alicia Gómez argues that "between 2000 and 2014, annual bilateral trade between China and Bolivia increased from $75.3 million to $2.25 billion. In 2015, the Bolivian government owed more than $600 million to Chinese banks (primarily the Export-Import Bank of China and the Chinese Development Bank), constituting 9.2% of the country's total foreign debt." With China's assistance, Morales boasted, Bolivia achieved independence from

US-dominated financial institutions like the International Monetary Fund and the World Bank. However, Gómez argues that "behind the discourse of financial sovereignty, the reality is one of greater dependency on extractivism and foreign capital," effectively "substituting one imperialism for another."[32]

To conclude this historical overview, it is important to underline the sometimes contradictory role played by the Bolivian state. On many occasions, the central government worked hand in hand with local, regional, and global interests to expand the geography of capitalism. As Orsag Molina points out, this is particularly evident in the state's incursions into the Amazon amid the rubber boom. Yet there were other occasions when the national government provided the tools that social movements needed to limit the power of corporations and multinationals. In such cases, the state nationalized resources precisely when social movements were demanding control over them. However, the authors also point to the fragility of these political victories. There were repeated instances when the Bolivian state, after years of political mobilization and revolutionary transformation, enacted laws to nationalize strategic natural resources only to see these efforts diluted when subsequent governments came to power and signed contracts, agreements, or laws that changed the rules of the game once again.

Thus, the history of Bolivia in the twentieth and twenty-first centuries has followed the path of a boomerang, defined by cycles of nationalization and privatization. Revolutionary and reformist Bolivian governments loudly celebrated moments of resource nationalization as grand popular conquests. By contrast, policymakers silently privatized resources, as Sarah Hines points out, amid acute economic and political crises. The expansion of commodity frontiers to encompass much of Bolivia's expansive geography mirrors the expansion of global capitalism. This history of "commodity continuities" amid whip-saw political changes is essential to make sense of the Bolivian past in order to assess its present dilemmas and future promise.

A DEEP HISTORY OF NATURAL RESOURCES: THE BOLIVIAN CASES

This book begins by examining three Bolivian resources at the center of political dispute since the early colonial period, namely land, water, and minerals. Soliz, Barragán, and Hines show that, as in the colonial and early republican past, these resources have remained the focus of political contention to the present day. Until the end of the nineteenth century, Bolivia's battle over natural resources was primarily concentrated in the highlands and inter-Andean valleys. Beginning in the 1860s, the bicycle and soon the automobile industry triggered demand for natural rubber found in the heart of the Amazon. Orsag Molina analyzes the impact of this extractive economy at the turn of the twentieth century. The book concludes by examining two resources that are central to understanding the last century of Bolivia's history. Young examines fraught business of hydrocarbons and Grisaffi, the coca/cocaine circuit. Extraction of each commodity shaped its own peculiar geographical space and social structure, and terms of conflict, even as each took on national dimensions, shaped the broader discourse of dependency versus development.

In chapter 1, Carmen Soliz explores three waves of land concentration that displaced Indigenous people and small farmers from the colonial past to the present (colonialism, liberalism, and dictatorship). The chapter also examines critical moments of Indigenous and peasant political struggle that successfully reversed some of the effects of Indigenous displacement and political marginalization. In particular, Soliz discusses the three agrarian reform programs that took place in Bolivia in the twentieth and twenty-first centuries (1953, 1996, and 2006), all aimed at guaranteeing fairer distribution of land.

The chapter advances three arguments. First, the liberal oligarchic period from the late nineteenth to early twentieth centuries witnessed the greatest waves of land dispossession at the expense of Indigenous communal property after independence. Second, in the second half of the twentieth century following a revolution, two distinct trends emerged. One trend saw Indigenous and peasant communities successfully obtaining a favorable redistribution of land in both the highlands and valleys. The other trend saw elites expanding their landholdings in the lowlands. Third, during Evo Morales's tenure as president, pressure from elite landholders forced his government to make concessions in order to maintain political stability. This partnership between his administration and powerful landowners significantly hindered the ability of Indigenous peoples to gain access to land and win representation in politics.

In Chapter 2, Rossana Barragán analyzes Bolivia's long history of mineral extraction in Potosí, the emblematic center of silver production. Incredible as it may seem, the Cerro Rico or Rich Mountain is still in active exploitation after more than five hundred years of short booms and long crises. Barragán argues first, that minerals destined for the global market expanded the commodity frontier from one mineral to another, enlarging the geography of mining. Second, that a process of "de-industrialization," understood, in this context, as a rupture between extraction and refining processes, took place with the shift from silver to tin production. Third, that there is no continuity among mining elites across time. Barragán begins with the first silver boom that lasted from the sixteenth to the end of the eighteenth century. The tin boom is next, from the first half of the twentieth century through nationalization of the mines in 1952 to the bust of the 1980s. Afterward comes the boom of the 1990s, characterized by the proliferation of cooperatives, the arrival of transnational companies, and the return to Potosí of the state-run Mining Corporation of Bolivia (COMIBOL). Finally, Barragán examines the opening of a new geographical frontier with the exploitation of lithium. Key actors are considered in her chapter: the Spanish Crown and later the nation-state with its policies regarding property rules and relations with capital and transnational firms; the private entrepreneurs, the owners of the mines and the refineries; and the multiple types of workers from the colonial period to the late formation of the proletariat and up until the consolidation of independent artisanal mine workers and cooperatives. Particularly relevant in her analysis are the workers' individual and collective struggles and their politics of resistance, the internal divisions and rivalry between their organizations, and the peculiar power dynamics that emerged in each historical period.

In chapter 3, Sarah Hines studies the fraught history of water in Bolivia. Her chapter constitutes a pioneering contribution to Bolivia's environmental history. Hines analyzes water management and ownership claims across four broad periods: the Inca and Spanish Empires (ca. 1400–1825); the early Bolivian Republic (1825–1935); the era of reform, revolution, and dictatorship (1935–1982); and the neoliberal era, with its "water wars" and their aftermath (1982–2019). Focusing on the Cochabamba region, Hines demonstrates that one of the worst moments of water dispossession for Indian communities took place in the late nineteenth century under the halo of liberalism and a second occurred almost a century later, under neoliberalism. Hines argues that although land appropriation was more visible, water appropriation was more extreme. Her analysis of the twentieth century demonstrates the importance of the military socialist regimes and the 1952 revolution for democratizing water access. The neoliberal reforms of the 1990s sought to privatize water and other critical resources, sparking mass protest.

Led by peasants, irrigators, and city dwellers, Cochabamba's 2000 Water War put an end to neoliberal water policies. Rather than an isolated event, Hines asserts that the 2000 showdown resulted from a long history of social struggle over water management and property rights. She argues that users gained increasing control over water resources and infrastructure in the twentieth and early twenty-first centuries through their labor, expertise, mobilization, and steady demands for state and international financial and institutional support for what she calls "vernacular hydraulic development."

In chapter 4, José Orsag Molina treats the history of rubber, beginning with the arrival of the nation-state and commercial interests to the Indigenous territories of Araona, Pacaguara, and Ese'ejja at the end of the nineteenth century. Orsag Molina argues that the state's ability to dominate the rubber-bearing territory and to build infrastructure has been the standard metric by which to measure development, progress, or failure. This developmentalist narrative obscures the violence of the conquest and colonization of Indigenous territories, a precondition for capitalist expansion and the formation of the state. From this perspective, the rubber boom appears as one of the most catastrophic phases of extermination of Bolivia's diverse Indigenous population.

In chapter 5, Kevin Young discusses the three episodes of hydrocarbon nationalization that took place in 1937, 1969, and 2006, arguing that nationalization united a variety of social sectors that otherwise shared few common interests. Young argues that nationalization has helped mitigate regional, ethnic, and class frictions while also reducing the government's incentive to pursue other reforms such as a progressive income tax that would directly target wealthy Bolivians. There were also contradictions between discourse and economic policy. Young notes, for example, that while it was the nationalist MNR that privatized oil in 1955, the right-wing dictator General Hugo Banzer kept hydrocarbons under state control. The Bolivian government then turned to gas and oil privatization under democratic regimes starting in the 1990s. Finally, Young analyzes the hydrocarbons policy of the Evo Morales government. Morales's higher taxation of gas companies enabled the state to capture a larger share of the profits generated from gas exports. While not a "nationalization" in the classic sense, this policy did provide new revenues for poverty reduction and public investments. Government figures suggest an impressive decline in poverty: The poverty rate has fallen from 60.6 percent in 2006 to 35 percent in 2019, and the extreme poverty from 37.7 percent to 15.2 percent over the same period.[33] Despite this unquestionable success, Young points out how the government marginalized the voices of Indigenous leaders and environmental groups that questioned hydrocarbon exploitation in Indigenous and protected forest areas. Morales also silenced left-leaning groups that demanded that the government create economic alternatives to oil and gas exports.

In chapter 6, Thomas Grisaffi examines the cultural, economic, and political dimensions of coca production. He argues that in Bolivia the coca leaf is not just a commodity but also a marker of Indigenous identity and a sacred substance according to many Andeans who consume it. The production of coca leaves, more than any other commodity, has strained relations with the United States, and thus it is not surprising that anti-imperialist sentiments are most deeply rooted among coca producers.

The production of coca leaf and cocaine trafficking has lubricated Bolivia's economy. In the middle of the country's worst economic crises, hyperinflation in the 1980s and structural reforms in the 1990s, the coca and cocaine trades revitalized the Bolivian economy and prompted a construction boom in the cities, where office buildings, roads, and houses went up at an unprecedented rate. Grisaffi argues that the illicit cocaine trade provided a safety net for those workers and peasants impoverished by neoliberal structural adjustment. After more than a decade of forced eradication and police repression, the Morales government, under the slogan "Coca yes, cocaine no," petitioned the UN to remove coca from the list of globally banned substances, and, despite US opposition, successfully gained an exception in 2013, allowing for traditional uses of the leaf in the country. The amendment was an important international victory, yet not all sectors in Bolivia have been equally pleased with Morales's victories on this matter. Indigenous lowland groups have struggled against the incursion of coca growers into Indigenous territories.

Finally, Myrna Santiago and Ulbe Bosma provide the volume with separate epilogues. Santiago, who specializes in the environmental history of Mexico, and Bosma, one of the leading voices of the commodity frontier approach to global political economy, highlight the role that extractivism has played across different political and economic historical phases. Both underscore the role that extractivist regimes have played in the construction of capitalism. Overall, this volume tells the story of the commodification of natural resources and the incorporation of complex, often Indigenous geographies into the global market. The book illustrates how policy makers, elites, workers, and other subaltern groups struggled to control valuable natural resources. Going back to colonial times, they forged conjunctural alliances in order to do so and developed strong political cultures featuring their claims to rights and sovereignty.

The history of Bolivia, seen through the lens of specific natural resources converted into commodities, helps us situate land, metals, rubber, oil, water, and coca in a network of transnational and global relations and connections that defies national borders. Narratives that revolve around the nation-state and the role of local elites and popular groups can obscure the persistence of transnational corporations and their adeptness at circumventing local-level shifts. Focusing on extractivism and commodity frontiers also highlights the fierce struggles and competition for key resources that have developed between countries and regions, as well as the competition for their appropriation, industrialization, commercialization, and consumption. Bolivia's long and troubled "extractive history" also reminds us that technological changes are another crucial and strategic part of the story, sometimes shuffling market positions overnight. Indeed, technologies often develop at lightning speed, rapidly upending upstream and downstream flows and linkages, and remaking global extractive geographies. The struggle for natural resources in Bolivia, as elsewhere, shows no signs of letting up.

NOTES

1. Movimiento al Socialismo, "Programa político: Nuestros principios ideológicos," 2006.
2. Frakenhoff, "The Prebisch Thesis." See also Ferraro, "Dependency Theory: An Introduction."
3. Bunker, "Exchange, and the Progressive Underdevelopment of an Extreme Periphery," 1018.
4. Sonja-McKibbin and Zalik, "Rethinking the extractive/productive binary under neoliberalism," 538.
5. Acosta, *Colonialismos del siglo XXI*.
6. Coney, "Reprimarization: Implications for The Environment," 553.
7. Svampa, *Las fronteras del neo-extractivismo*.
8. Gudynas, "Neo-extractivismo y crisis civilizatoria," 32.
9. Svampa, *Las fronteras del neo-extractivismo*, 15.
10. Bebbington and Bury, *Subterranean Struggles*, 10–21.
11. Veltmeyer and Petras, *The New Extractivism: A Post-Neoliberal Development Model or Imperialism of the Twenty-First Century?*
12. Cypher, "South America's Commodities Boom," 635–62.
13. Veltmeyer and Petras, *The New Extractivism*, 21.
14. Veltemeyer and Petras, *The New Extractivism*, 39.
15. Moore, *Capitalism in the Web of Life*.
16. Wallerstein, *The Modern World-System I*. Two volumes followed.
17. See Terence Hopkins and Immanuel Wallerstein, 1986, 156. In the words of Jonoko Lee, the commodity frontier approach seeks "to explain the social and organizational structure of the global economy and its dynamics by examining the commodity chains of a specific product or service." Lee, "Global Commodity Chains and Global Value Chains."
18. Moore, "The Modern World System as Environmental History?" i–iii.
19. "Journal Mission Statement," *Journal of Global Commodity Frontiers*, accessed October 2, 2021, https://commodityfrontiers.com/journal/#:~:text=Mission%20Statement&text=Edited%20by%20a%20group%20of,transformation%20in%20the%20global%20countryside.
20. Beckert et al., "Commodity Frontiers," 466.
21. Beckert et al., "Commodity Frontiers," 469.
22. Anievas and Nisanciouglu, *How the West Came to Rule: The Geopolitical Origins of Capitalism*, 9; Marques, "Colonial America and Commodity History."
23. In Bolivia recent conflicts have been referred to as "wars," a term that describes a series of widespread mobilizations. The violence resulting from the protests, blockades, and police repression led to seven deaths in Cochabamba and sixty in La Paz and El Alto.

24. Sempat Assadourian, *El sistema de la economía colonial.*
25. Numhauser, *Mujeres indias y señores de la coca.*
26. Sábato, *Republics of the New World.*
27. Sanders, *The Vanguard of the Atlantic World*, 6–8.
28. Latin American historians usually recall the nationalization of oil by Mexican President Lázaro Cárdenas in June 1938. The first experience of oil nationalization took place in Bolivia in March 1937.
29. Paz Estenssoro enacted the Decree Law 4210 on October 26, 1955. Congress signed it into law a year later.
30. Martín Cúneo, "Andres Soliz Rada: El presidente más habiloso para hacer daño a los países chicos de América Latina fue Lula, te metía el puñal mientras te sonreía," *Observatorio de Multinacionales en América Latina*, November 1, 2011, https://omal.info/spip.php?article590. See also "Bolivia dice Petrobras entraba nacionalización gas," *Electricidad, La revista energética de Chile*, August 16, 2006, https://www.revistaei.cl/2006/08/16/bolivia-bolivia-dice-petrobras-entraba-nacionalizacion-gas/.
31. Webber, *The Last Day of Oppression*, 28.
32. Gómez, "Financial Sovereignty or A New Dependency?" For a portrait of the Chinese presence in Latin America, see Svampa, *Las fronteras del neo-extractivismo*, 90–103.
33. Arauz et al., *Bolivia's Economic Transformation.*

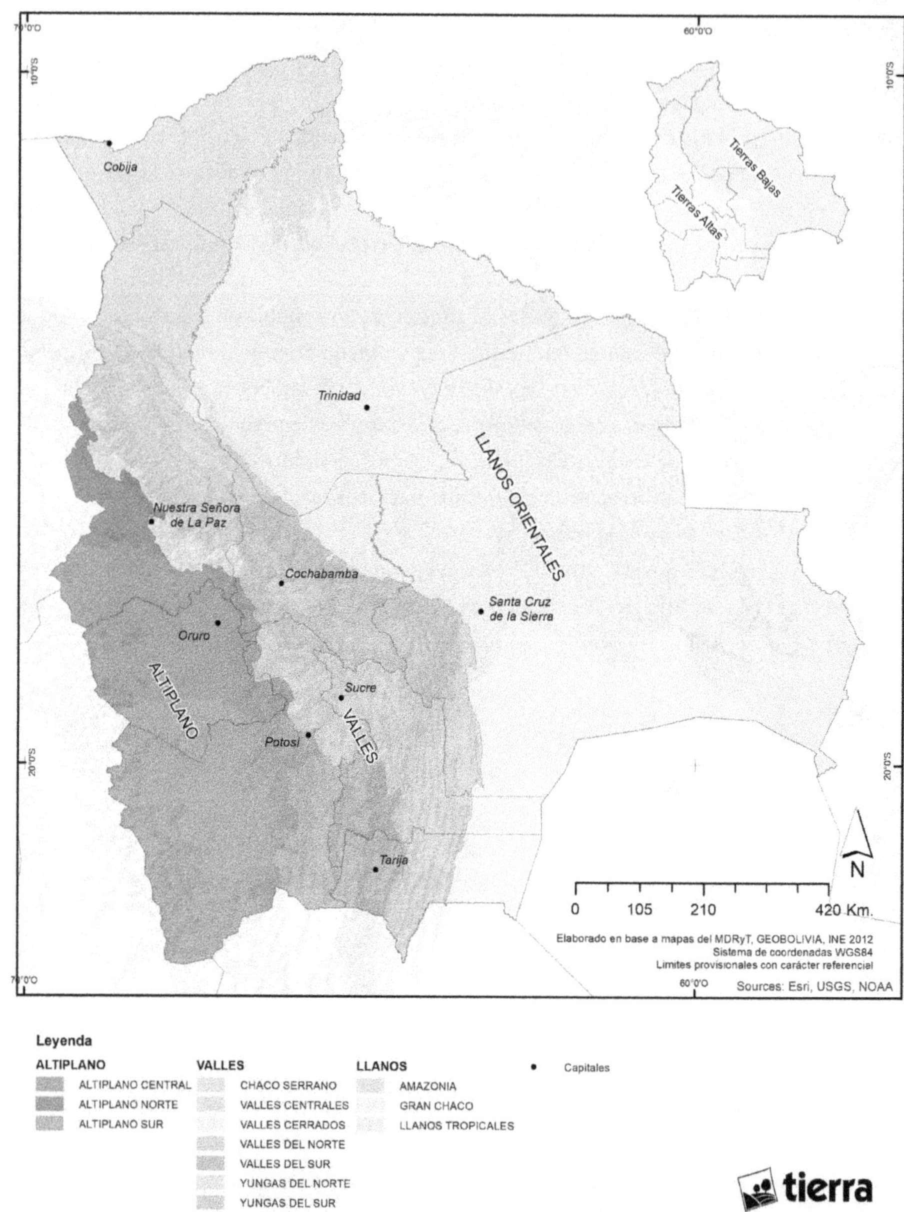

Map 1.1. Geographic differences between Bolivian highlands, valleys, and lowlands. Map courtesy of Fundación Tierra.

Chapter One

FIVE HUNDRED YEARS OF LAND STRUGGLE

Carmen Soliz

INTRODUCTION

Land has long been at the center of political struggle in Bolivia, making it impossible to understand Bolivia's colonial and postcolonial history without delving into processes such as land grabbing, rural migration, Indigenous and peasant politics, and agrarian reforms. While it is hard to capture such a long and complicated history of about five hundred years in just a brief review, this chapter examines on the one hand, three waves of land dispossession suffered by Indigenous populations under colonial, liberal, and dictatorial rule. On the other, it examines critical moments of subaltern struggle for land redistribution. These waves of land dispossession that led to the marginalization and exclusion of Indigenous peoples and to the currently unequal distribution of land are important for understanding the history of dispossession of Indigenous populations in Latin America more broadly.[1]

The first wave of land dispossession in the Andes started in the sixteenth century. Spanish colonialism brought about a far-reaching process of restructuring Andean communities. The second wave took place under liberal regimes decades after Bolivia became an independent republic in the early nineteenth century. Many of the Indigenous communities of the Bolivian highlands that continued holding communal lands during the colonial period lost them when liberal elites pushed for the privatization of communal property and opening the land market. The third wave of land dispossession, which started in the 1950s but accelerated under the dictatorial regimes of the 1970s and early 1980s, targeted a different geography and a different group: the Indigenous peoples of the eastern lowlands. From colonial times until the 1950s, land conflicts had been concentrated in the highlands, in the western part of the country. From the second half of the twentieth century to the present, Bolivia's most serious territorial conflicts were centered in the lowlands.

Bolivian history has been characterized by important moments of Indigenous and peasant political action, government reform legislation, and party-political struggle combating elite land accumulation along with peasant displacement and political marginalization. This chapter discusses the three agrarian reform programs that sought to guarantee fairer land distribution during the twentieth and twenty-first centuries. It also assesses the goals and actual achievements of these policies as well as their limitations. Focused on the years of left-leaning Evo Morales's presidency (2005–2019), it explores the political dilemmas driving Bolivia's land struggle in the lowlands. It examines the competing agendas of three groups: agroindustry, one of the strongest economic and political actors in the region; lowland Indigenous groups demanding recognition of their ancestral territories; and peasant migrants from the highlands who have settled in the lowlands since the 1950s demanding their rights to land.

This chapter makes three sequential historical arguments. First, the liberal oligarchic period between the late nineteenth and the early twentieth centuries was responsible for major dispossession of Indigenous and peasant lands and of land concentration in the hands of the elite. Second, the postrevolutionary period after the mid-twentieth century was marked by two contrasting tendencies, one in which Indigenous and peasant sectors were able to attain a favorable redistribution of land in the highlands and lowlands, and one in which elites were successful in expanding their lowland land holdings. Third, the MAS government under Evo Morales yielded to pressure from landowning elites to guarantee political stability. This unexpected alliance between a left-wing government and large landowners severely compromised Indigenous people's access to land and political representation.

LAND DISPOSSESSION IN THE COLONIAL ERA

The conquest of the Inca Empire marked the beginning of a three hundred–year history of dispossession and marginalization of Indigenous communities. After years of military incursions and skirmishes, the conquistador Francisco Pizarro and his native allies captured and executed Atahualpa in the Battle of Cajamarca in 1532. This was the first step in a long campaign that ended with the colonization of the Inca Empire, which was later called the Viceroyalty of Peru. One of the factors that drew the Spaniards to this area was the discovery of silver in Potosí in 1545. The Spaniards founded the city of Potosí that year and the city of Chuquisaca, the most important administrative and judicial center of the Real Audiencia (royal court) of Charcas, in 1548.[2] The Real Audiencia of Charcas later became the territorial base for the formation of the Bolivian Republic in 1825.

After colonization, Spaniards used and reoriented precolonial institutions and systems of labor and tribute for their own benefit. For instance, Spaniards forced the ethnic groups—the Kana, Kanchi, Lupaqa, Pakasa, Sura, Killaka, Kallanka, Charka, and Qulla—in the region called Upper Peru (now Bolivia) to pay the tribute that they used to pay to the Inca.[3] During the first two decades after conquest, encomenderos or ex-conquistadors accumulated most of the tribute. In compensation for their service to the Spanish Crown, the conquerors were granted encomiendas or rights over Indian labor and taxes. The encomiendas were reserved for a small group of Spaniards and served as one of their most crucial wealth sources in the sixteenth century. Some persisted. Herbert S. Klein notes that by 1650, there were about eighty-two encomiendas in Upper Peru, twenty-one of which had more than one thousand Indians each.[4] Although peasant communities were well accustomed to paying tribute, historians have calculated that the amount demanded increased significantly during the colonial period. Bridikina et al indicate an increase of some 880 percent.[5] Encomenderos exerted pressure and even inflicted violence on ethnic authorities to extract tribute. For instance, Alonso de Montemayor, encomendero of the Sacaca community between 1549 and 1556, held the *mallku* (Indigenous authority) Alonso Ayaviri as a prisoner in Potosí for almost six months, threatening to hang several caciques (other Indigenous leaders) if he did not receive tribute payment.[6]

By the mid-sixteenth century, the encomienda system started to decline. The encomenderos were certainly interested in preserving these grants for their heirs, but the Crown began to recover the wealth it had endowed to the encomenderos. Viceroy Francisco de Toledo, who ruled the Viceroyalty of Peru between 1569 and 1581, broke the power of the encomenderos and limited the encomienda patrimony to three generations. Toledo pressed for the return of the encomiendas to the Crown and the establishment of a direct relationship between the Spanish Crown and Indigenous communities. The king's interest in directly accessing tribute revenues drove the Crown to protect the integrity of Indigenous communities and their traditional system of authorities. Enrique Semo's classic study of colonial Mexico indicates that the Crown's protection of communal property and the collection of tribute were two sides of the same coin. It was a system of exploitation of communities, not individuals.[7] Tristan Platt named this system the colonial tributary pact. Indian communities in the Andes were able to maintain communal control over land and a margin of local political autonomy for much of the colonial period in exchange for tribute in cash and labor.[8]

It was also on Toledo's watch that Indigenous communities faced dramatic territorial restructuring. To offset sharp decline of the Indigenous population due to labor overexploitation and European epidemics, Toledo relocated Indigenous communities by following the model of Spanish towns. These new units called *reducciones* forced Indians to live in villages established around a square, a church, and a town hall. Until then, Indigenous communities had extended control of their territories and access to different ecological zones. "Reduction" gave priests and colonial authorities more control over Indigenous groups. Under Toledo, 129,000 Indians were congregated in forty-four villages in Upper Peru.

To guarantee labor for the mines, Toledo also reimposed the mita—an Inca labor system that required people to perform a multiplicity of tasks in favor of the empire. The system forced one-seventh of all adult men of every community to work in the mines once every six years. Each year, the mita mobilized over eleven thousand Indigenous people from the highland provinces between Potosí and Cuzco. Sustaining the mita was another factor that helps explain the Spanish Crown's interest in protecting Indigenous communal land ownership.

In the precolonial period, *mitayos* or Indigenous workers received support from the state and compensation in goods. The Spaniards also set a ridiculously small salary for each mitayo. Thus, mita service plus the tribute that Indigenous communities were already paying the Crown in cash constituted the two heaviest burdens on Indigenous workers for much of the sixteenth and seventeenth centuries. In the eighteenth century, the Crown imposed new burdens on Indians, such as the *repartimiento* (the distribution of goods that communities were forced to buy whether they needed them or not) and taxes on locally traded goods.

The hacienda was a new feature of the colonial landscape. Due to the demographic collapse and forced relocation (*reducción*) of Indigenous communities, many lands that previously belonged to these communities became available. Starting in the second half of the sixteenth century, the Crown started to sell those allegedly "empty" lands to wealthy Spaniards in a process called the *composición de tierras*. Haciendas developed largely in the temperate valleys of Chuquisaca, Tarija, and Cochabamba, where they produced large quantities of corn, wheat, cereals, and coca leaves. The Catholic Church became the single largest hacienda owner during the colonial period.[9] Most of this production found a buoyant market in Potosí.[10] The fertile soil, mild climate, and proximity of these regions to the mines made them a prime site for expansion of the hacienda. The hacienda landowner became a serious competitor to the Crown and mineowners for Indigenous labor. Members of Indigenous communities were willing to migrate to a hacienda and eventually lose their access to communal land just to avoid paying tribute and working in the mines.

The number of haciendas and workers on them grew significantly between the sixteenth and seventeenth centuries. According to Thierry Saignes, there were 5,500 Indians working on 374 haciendas in 1574 and 8,000 Indians working on 1,200 haciendas in 1609.[11] Despite the profound restructuring that Indigenous communities faced in access to territory and their work systems, Klein argues that the boundaries between communities and haciendas began to stabilize by the end of the seventeenth century. Population in the rural communities had also begun to recover. The eighteenth century was marked by a crisis in the mining industry. Since most of the haciendas' production was destined for the mining centers, the hacienda also plunged in value, reducing pressure on Indigenous communities. In fact, populations grew in the communities in the 1700s.[12]

LAND ENCROACHMENT IN THE LIBERAL ERA

Despite three centuries of profound economic and political change during the colonial period, Indian communities continued to control about two-thirds of all cultivable land. Another serious threat to Indigenous communal property started during the republican period in the second half of the nineteenth century.[13] Shortly after Bolivia achieved its independence, the ruling elites, seduced by liberal ideology like many of their counterparts in Latin America, began to promote a land ownership system based on individual private property. It took decades for local elites to implement this project in the countryside, which led to the gradual dismantling of the Indigenous communal land-base. In 1824, Simón Bolívar, the hero of South America's wars for independence and Bolivia's first president, abolished the colonial tribute paid by Indigenous communities, something he considered one of colonialism's most repugnant legacies. His efforts to create an individual property system, however, were short-lived. Two years later, President Antonio José de Sucre, another hero of the independence, was forced to reinstate the Indigenous tribute. After fifteen years of war, the mining industry and commerce were in ruins, and the new republic had no alternative source of income. In that chaotic economic context, the Indigenous tribute, which was rebranded as an "Indigenous contribution," represented the state's most important income source until the 1860s. The payment of the tribute illustrated the state's implicit recognition of communal property. Tristan Platt's research shows that, contrary to what one might assume, Indigenous communities willingly paid the tribute to guarantee their territorial control. This fiscal pact between the state and Indigenous communities lasted for approximately four decades.[14]

In the second half of the nineteenth century, once state revenues began to rise again from mining exports, Bolivia's elites became less dependent on Indigenous contributions. In this new context, the ruling elites resumed the old project of land privatization. In 1866, President Mariano Melgarejo (1864–1871) launched a brutal attack on Indigenous communal lands. Melgarejo declared the state to be the owner of all communal properties. All Indians residing on state-owned lands were now required to purchase individual titles within a sixty-day period.[15] If they were unable to pay that sum, the land had to be sold at public auction.[16] Unable to pay these fees, the Indigenous people lost their communal land.[17] Historian Laura Gotkowitz writes that "between 1866 and 1869, government auctioneers sold the lands of 356 communities to private bidders." This took place in the most densely populated provinces of Omasuyos, Pacajes, Ingavi, Sicasica, and Muñecas.[18]

Melgarejo's decree triggered a series of Indigenous uprisings that culminated in his overthrow in 1871. President Tomás Frías (1874–1876), who took power after Melgarejo, promised to return the property to the Indians and cancel all auction sales.[19] Yet, in 1874, he signed the so-called De-Entailment Law (Ley de Exvinculación), a more refined attempt to abolish Indigenous communal property. In contrast to Melgarejo's decree, Frías guaranteed that the process of dividing individual plots among Indians could only take place with the consent of community members. The privatization policies of the late nineteenth century and the first decades of the twentieth century had severe effects on Indigenous communities' control over land. In 1825, Indigenous communities controlled two-thirds of cultivable land, but by the 1950s, they only held roughly one quarter of the land.[20] Table 1.1 shows the structure of property in 1950. Landlords held 44 percent of cultivable land, Indigenous communities held 26 percent of the land, and 18.8 percent of lands belonged to independent farmers. These small independent farmers were primarily located in the valleys of Cochabamba and the Yungas of La Paz.

Land privatization in the second half of the nineteenth century and the first half of the twentieth century was not only a Bolivian phenomenon. After independence and until the mid-nineteenth century in much of Latin America, most cultivable land continued to be in the hands of Indigenous people and small owners. Talking about El Salvador, for example, William C. Thiesenhusen highlights that nineteenth-century visitors "spoke of the absence of extreme poverty . . . All residents seem to enjoy access to land; the hacienda existed but did not seem to monopolize the rural economy."[21] Beginning in the 1850s, the ruling elites' desire to boost exports and railroad construction made rural areas much more attractive to private national entrepreneurs and international companies. In Mexico, for example, President Porfirio Díaz encouraged the privatization of state land by inviting foreign entrepreneurs to invest in Mexican agriculture. During the Díaz regime, thirty-nine million hectares of untitled communal land were converted into private property, about a fifth of Mexico's total land area. Luis Terrazas, the Chihuahuan magnate and perhaps the largest landowner in all of Latin America, owned roughly fifty haciendas and ranches, totaling nearly three million hectares. The Richardson Construction Company in Los Angeles owned 547,000 hectares in northern Mexico, and the newspaper publisher William Randolph Hearst acquired a large estate measuring 350,000 hectares in Chihuahua.[22]

Table 1.1. Structure of property according to the 1950 Agricultural Census

	HECTARES	%	CULTIVATED HECTARES	%
Farmer	9,526,421	29.1	123,328	18.85
Farmer with colonos	12,701,076	38.8	290,165	44.35
Renters (*arrendatarios y medieros*)	2,365,879	7.2	49,673	7.59
Indigenous communities	7,178,448	22	170,106	26
Other	978,023	2.9	20,986	3.21

Source: Ministerio de Asuntos Campesinos y Agropecuarios, Censo Agropecuario 1950, ii.

The privatization of communal property in Latin America ended with the massive transfer of land into a few hands. Many communities fell within the property of a single owner, and their inhabitants became dependent estate laborers on the new hacienda. National and international elites used their political power to seize Indigenous land. This was the case, for example, with Bolivian President Ismael Montes (1904–1909), who used his time in office to confiscate the lands of the Taraco community for himself. The hacienda's most significant expansion was the product of a republican and liberal regime rather than a colonial one.

Privatization of Bolivia's best farmland and concentration in a few hands did not occur without resistance. Beginning in the late nineteenth and early twentieth centuries, Indigenous leaders fought illegal encroachment by the hacienda system. In 1899, Indigenous leader Pablo Zárate Willka led one of the nineteenth century's largest Indigenous rebellions, demanding the restitution of communal land. In the context of the Federal War (1898–1899) in which liberals fought conservatives, Zárate Willka pledged his support to the Liberal Party in exchange for the promise of restitution of communal lands. This pact between the Liberals and Indigenous forces was established between Zárate Willka and José Manuel Pando, who would later assume the presidency of the republic.[23] However, the pact was broken when Liberal troops were killed by "hostile Indians" as they passed through the town of Mohoza. It is unclear what happened that night, but some historians claim that the Indians mistook the Liberal soldiers for Conservatives. The "Mohoza Massacre" brought about the end of the pact, and Zárate Willka was directly charged with responsibility for the events and tortured during his time in jail. The elites who followed the trial, steeped in the Social Darwinist ideology of the late nineteenth century, insisted that the Indians had decided to start a race war against the whites and tried to eliminate all traces of the old pact.[24]

Despite this repression, in the first two decades of the twentieth century,

Indigenous communal representatives (called *caciques apoderados*) organized a broad movement that compiled official documents to demonstrate legal ownership of lands that had been violently seized by private landowners. The caciques apoderados traveled to the historical archives of Lima, Peru, and Sucre, Bolivia, to obtain copies of land titles and then traveled to La Paz to represent their communities in court.[25] Along with this legal mobilization, there were violent Indigenous rebellions in Jesús de Machaca (La Paz) in 1921 and Chayanta (Potosí) in 1927, demanding restitution of communal lands.[26] In these protests, Indians clearly stated that their subjugation had not ceased after independence. Aymara historian Roberto Choque found that a manifesto published in 1929 entitled "La Voz del Campesino" (The Peasant's Voice) vehemently denounced Indigenous marginalization: "For more than a century and thirty years we have been suffering the most iniquitous slavery that could happen in the republican hour that independence offered us, that cost us Indian life and blood to free us from the Spanish yoke that made us groan for more than four hundred years or four centuries. The cudgel danced marvelously, [we felt] the kicks in our backs in those years of barbarism and today the brutality is repeated with more force amid a century of freedom."[27] These attempts at resistance largely failed because the landowning elites also controlled political power. Beyond the promulgation of some decrees that encouraged public officers to comply with the law, the result was a considerable transfer of land from Indigenous communities to private hands.

As the Indigenous and peasant struggles continued in rural areas during the first decades of the twentieth century, left-leaning intellectuals began questioning the extreme concentration of land in a few hands and the exploitative system of work that the *colonos* (dependent estate laborers) faced on the haciendas. Klein notes that in the 1920s, Bolivian youth started enthusiastically reading Karl Marx and José Carlos Mariátegui's *Seven Interpretive Essays on Peruvian Reality*.[28] The most prominent and radical voice of this generation was Tristán Marof, who led the group Túpac Amaru.[29] The group argued for a revolution that would eliminate the latifundio and rural feudal relations. Marof stated, "Indian liberation will only happen when Indigenous people recover the lands usurped by the whites and the Creoles from the colonial period to the present."[30] Yet Klein points out that in the first decades of the twentieth century, these radical ideals were only embraced by a minority of intellectuals and had a limited impact on the mainstream political parties.[31]

It was only in the late 1930s that the ruling classes in Bolivia began to discuss important legal changes in favor of Indigenous communities. Between 1932 and 1935 Bolivia experienced a devastating conflict—the Chaco War—with neighboring Paraguay. After Bolivia's defeat, a large number of veterans, many of them Indigenous forced conscripts, returned from the war ready to condemn the nation's leaders for Bolivia's defeat. They also criticized the economic and political system that had systematically excluded them. It was after the war, and as a result of the economic crisis that shook the country, that Bolivia's elites were forced to rethink the liberal project consolidated at the end of the nineteenth century. It was in this context that the self-proclaimed socialist and military officer Germán Busch (1937–1939) seized the presidency and called a constitutional convention to revise the liberal constitution that had structured the country since 1880.

As historian Rossana Barragán states, one of the most important outcomes of the convention was an opportunity to publicly rethink the role that the state should play in the economy and in guaranteeing workers' economic rights.[32] This political reconsideration of nineteenth-century liberalism was not new in Latin America. In the 1930s, many countries rewrote their constitutions to assign a more significant role to the state in the economy. Beginning with the Mexican Constitution of 1917, "Latin American states wrote detailed chapters on the social responsibility of capital, the economic rights of the worker, and the state responsibility for the protection and security of all its citizens."[33]

The agrarian question was subject to fierce debate during the Bolivian National Convention of 1938. Representatives Gregorio Balcazar, Eguino Zaballa, Víctor Paz Estenssoro, and Walter Guevara Arce proposed a new constitution that required rural landed property to fulfill a "social function." This principle followed Mexico's 1917 constitution and challenged Bolivia's liberal constitution of 1880, which prescribed the sacredness of private property. After an intense debate, the proposal was approved, dealing a hard blow to rural landholders.[34] Bolder options were on the table, as when future National Revolutionary Movement (MNR) party leaders Paz Estenssoro and Guevara Arze proposed dismantling the latifundio system, a plan severely criticized and rejected.[35] Representatives from the Bolivian lowlands denied that Bolivia's problem was a lack of land.[36] They argued, "There is plenty of land in Bolivia. The problem is that we do not have the resources to occupy (colonize) and to make the vast lowlands suitable for agriculture."[37] The 1938 constitution for the first time legally recognized and guaranteed Indigenous communal land rights. This was a great departure from the 1880 constitution which only recognized private property. At the same time, President Busch passed labor legislation that granted the right to unionize to workers in cities, mining centers, and the countryside. This opened an unexpected opportunity for peasants working on haciendas to negotiate with landowners as a union.

However, many of the changes remained as unenforced constitutional principles. Unable to handle mounting political pressure, the young President Busch committed suicide in 1938. After Busch's dramatic death, conservative presidents

Lieutenant Colonel Carlos Quintanilla (1939–1940) and General Enrique Peñaranda (1940–1943) strived to dismantle many of his reforms. President Quintanilla, in an effort to curb mobilization in the countryside, prohibited the unionization of colonos on the haciendas.[38] Later, President Peñaranda exiled dozens of peasant leaders to the recently created penal colonies of Coati Island, Todos Santos, and Ichilo after landowners reported generalized sit-down strikes on their haciendas.[39]

After five years of conservative governments ruling the country, nationalist Colonel Gualberto Villarroel took power in December 1943. The government of Villarroel represented a new attempt to realign power relations in rural areas. The government convened 1,200 Indigenous representatives from across the country to the First National Indigenous Congress in May 1945 to discuss the problems they faced in the countryside.[40] At the conclusion of the Indigenous Congress, Villarroel signed four executive decrees to regulate labor relations between hacendados and colonos in the countryside. The new legislation ordered that colonos could not be forced to perform any services other than agricultural tasks, unless landowners and colonos agreed to some form of fair economic compensation beforehand. It decreed that colonos owned their harvest production, which they could either use or sell. Additionally, landowners could not force colonos to pay property taxes; landowners or hacienda administrators could not use physical violence against colonos; and landowners had to erect schools for colonos' children on their properties.[41] These decrees demonstrate that the government—rather than tackling the structure of property—concentrated on regulating labor relations by limiting the power of the landowners over resident colonos.[42]

Villarroel's decrees would not be executed. In 1946, a coalition of right- and left-wing parties overthrew the president. This represented a radical move by mining and landowning elites to regain political power (with the unusual support of the left against a nationalist regime). Although the ensuing conservative presidents Tomás Monje Gutiérrez (1946–1947), José Enrique Hertzog (1947–1949), and Mamerto Urriolagoitía (1949–1951) did not dare to repeal Villarroel's 1945 decrees, all of them cracked down on peasant leaders' attempts to actually implement them in the countryside. Indigenous uprisings spread across the Altiplano in the departments of La Paz, Oruro, western Cochabamba, and northern Potosí. To pacify the country, President Hertzog sent troops to arrest, jail, and even torture hundreds of peasant leaders as well as leaders of the workers' federation, the Federación Obrera Local, which allegedly supported and gave weapons to the peasants, as well as members of the Partido Obrero Revolucionario and the MNR, which had supported Villarroel's regime.[43]

AGRARIAN REFORM AND REVOLUTIONARY NATIONALISM

From the beginning of the twentieth century, Bolivia witnessed growing competition between progressive forces and the conservative parties and landowning elites. Indigenous community leaders developed a wide range of strategies to demand the restitution of their lands plus better living conditions for those working on haciendas. However, the landowners, deeply connected to the political elites, had managed to block any attempts at reform. This tension finally erupted in April 1952 when urban workers with the support of mine workers overthrew the government.

During the 1951 elections, MNR's party leader Víctor Paz Estenssoro won the election, despite the banishment of most MNR leaders. President Urriolagoitía, unwilling to transfer power to Paz Estenssoro, incited a coup d'état against his own government and granted power to the army. Bolivia's politics then took a radical new turn, when in April 1952, a three-day popular insurrection led by armed worker militias defeated the army and overthrew the military junta headed by General Hugo Ballivián. MNR leader Hernán Siles Zuazo took provisional power and then granted the presidency to Paz Estenssoro, who was at the time exiled in Buenos Aires. The MNR governed Bolivia for twelve years until another military coup led by General René Barrientos toppled the government.

In its first two years in power, the nationalist MNR enacted three reforms that changed the course of Bolivian history. Paz Estenssoro nationalized the mines, which were under the ownership of three local families prior to the revolution; he decreed universal suffrage, which allowed women and the majority Indigenous population to vote; and he passed agrarian reform legislation that abolished the latifundios and eliminated the obligatory unpaid labor that had forced Indigenous people into servitude on the haciendas.[44] The MNR government shuttered the Bolivian Rural Society, the institution that represented the interests of landowners at the national level, and at the local level it legalized and empowered peasant unions, which had been illegal since 1942. Each of these measures represented a radical departure from the past and resulted from the culmination of decades of political struggle and activism.

Although the mine nationalization policy had clearly been part of the MNR's political agenda since the 1930s, it is less clear to what extent the party was committed to initiating a comprehensive land reform program. It is worth mentioning, for example, that in 1952 the MNR rushed to implement the decrees approved by President Villarroel in 1945. President Paz Estenssoro hoped that the reinstitution of Villarroel's decrees would end colonos' personal servitude on the haciendas without challenging the existing property structure. Yet research shows that colonos stubbornly refused to sign contracts with the landowners and pressured the government to order the expropriation of haciendas.[45]

To curb the growing social upheaval emerging in the countryside, the president convened an agrarian reform commission to draft new legislation. After seven months of intense debate, the commission presented a bill that Paz Estenssoro signed in the rural town of Ucureña in front of 100,000 peasants. The historic decree abolished all forms of servitude and forced labor on the haciendas, obliged landowners to pay salaries in exchange for any type of work, ordered the expropriation of all latifundios or large unproductive estates to be distributed among their colonos, and ordered the restitution of property to Indigenous communities whose lands were usurped after 1900. The decree also sought to stimulate greater productivity and commercialization of agriculture, to preserve the country's natural resources, and to promote migration of a population excessively concentrated in the inter-Andean zone to settle in areas like the eastern lowlands.[46]

The multiparty commission that drafted the Agrarian Reform Decree was convinced that while it was important to abolish the latifundios, the law had to protect medium-sized property owners. Therefore, the decree outlined in detail the characteristics of medium-sized properties in contrast with what would be considered a latifundio. Given the striking geographical differences in Bolivia, the maximum limit of a medium-sized property varied considerably from one ecological zone to the other. While the maximum size of a small estate in the grain-growing areas in the valleys of Cochabamba was set to three hectares, in the dry area of the Chaco, closer to the border with Paraguay, it was eighty hectares.

Initially, MNR leaders assured medium-sized landowners that expropriation would only target large unproductive estates. The government promised it would guarantee the property rights of those who could prove investments, personal involvement in hacienda production, and a production model oriented to the market—the signs of modern agricultural development.[47] Despite the MNR's assurances, analysis of agrarian court cases shows the colonos sought and found ways around these apparent protections for some landowners. They demanded the expropriation of haciendas where they served as colonos, whether or not those properties fit within the parameters for property size, investments, and productivity allowed by law.[48] In their petitions for land expropriation, the peasants emphasized the landowners' practices of *pongueaje* and *colonato*, both types of forced labor, prior to the revolution. Since unremunerated servile labor was banned by the Agrarian Reform Decree, peasants urged the government to grant them all the land in question, even if it was a productive estate, one in which the owners had invested capital, or one that fell within the allowable size. Claims about abusive working conditions and lack of pay became pivotal points in fighting back against the landowners in the courts. The landowners who had lost most of their political power after the revolution saw the courts as their last opportunity to consolidate and retain at least a portion of their former properties using—and stretching—the parameters of size and investments inscribed in the law.

The actual implementation of the 1953 Agrarian Reform Decree took place in local and national courts, in which landowners and colonos drew upon different established legal and technical criteria to demand the government enforce the law. In the hands of different actors, the law became an effective instrument to pressure state officials and shape their decisions. In the politically mobilized Altiplano regions, successful cases for land redistribution illustrate the power of peasant unions to pressure state authorities to consolidate their access to land, regardless of the landlord's compliance.

Another fundamental aspect of the 1953 decree was that it allowed for the restitution of community lands to ex-*comunarios*. These were former members of Indigenous communities who had lost their land to the expansion of the hacienda and who had become a dependent labor force on the land they used to own or on neighboring haciendas. Basing their demands on the Agrarian Reform Decree and the Land Restitution Decree, ex-comunarios of the province of Omasuyos successfully obtained restitution of their communal lands by showing the land titles they obtained from the Revisita of 1883, a land titling procedure, as proof that their parents lost lands after 1900. Remarkably, because of pressure from below, local and national authorities were willing to accept this type of argument and dictate restitution in favor of the comunarios.[49]

In addition to the colonos, other groups of peasants who temporarily worked on the hacienda embraced the Agrarian Reform Decree, seeking to consolidate plots for themselves. Depending on region and type of work and living conditions, they were called variously *arrimantes*, *yanaperos*, *utahuahuas*, and *sitiajeros*. The archives show that, in general, presidential rulings on agrarian court cases ended up yielding to these groups' demands, thereby amplifying the redistributive character of the reform. A review of the agrarian reform files indicates that the signing of the decree was a starting point for a much more complex political negotiation process.[50] These files reveal that, although each of the state authorities claimed to be governed by the technical criteria inscribed in the law, in practice, all decisions were affected by deep political considerations. This political influence becomes evident when we observe that similar cases yielded different verdicts. There were many landowners who faced expropriation without compensation; others retained smaller plots of land; and there were some who sought and obtained direct compensation from the state due to their own legal and political maneuvers.

Despite the chaotic administrative and legal process of agrarian reform, a clear pattern was established: peasants continuously forced land redistribution well beyond the agenda initially set by the MNR, arguing that they had long been subject to servile labor conditions.[51] Because of peasant pressure, authorities expropriated productive large, medium, and even small properties. The novelty and significance of this process cannot be overstated. Prior to the revolution, few political parties (including the Trotskyist POR) insisted on carrying out a reform that would entail expropriation without economic compensation to previous landlords. Although most parties (including the moderate MNR and the PIR) rejected such a principle, in practice peasants took control of land without title holder indemnification. Yet, in contrast to what the POR proposed, the state had little control over expropriated farms. Peasant unions took control of the process of land distribution. The diverse forms that rural property took after the revolution exposed how social practices shaped the final outcome of the agrarian reform and challenged the state's modernizing project.

The revolution swept away traditional structures of power, opened new mechanisms for political representation, and reshaped the role of peasants who made up the majority of the population within Bolivian society. Soon after the revolution, the newly organized peasant unions began to appoint rural authorities, becoming a major voice within local political affairs and gaining a type of representation that, prior to the revolution, was the exclusive privilege of the small circle of citizens organized in neighborhood councils. The elimination of these neighborhood councils and of their ability to elect representatives to positions of power offered colonos and comunarios unprecedented access to local political power. The feverish organization of hundreds of unions across the countryside in the first two years of the revolution does not point to the strength of the MNR in the countryside but, rather, to the power of the peasants. Given the historical fragility of the government and the state in Bolivia, it is hard to imagine that the MNR could have organized hundreds of unions solely on the basis of a decree. Peasant unions grew from existing organizations: colonos and comunarios organized unions based on the contours of haciendas and Indigenous communities, maintaining previous territorial boundaries. The peasant unions elected their representatives following the Andean system of rotation of authorities: union leaders were selected for one year and their positions alternated among all union members. All of these factors reflect the strength of Indigenous forms of political representation rather than the separate strength of the state or of the MNR. In other words, syndicates were not an artificial creation from the top down; instead, these territorialized unions solidified and gave visibility to economic, social, and political units that had formed and operated before the revolution.

Reexamining agrarian reform in Bolivia illuminates the relationship between state and peasantry. Merilee Grindle has shown that land reforms gave states an opportunity to assert their presence in the countryside. She argues that, once landlords' economic and political power in the countryside weakened, the state became the new mediator of local conflicts.[52] This was the case in the paradigmatic reforms of Mexico, Peru, and Cuba, where radical policies undermined rural elites and extended state control in the countryside. In Bolivia, by contrast, when elite power structures fell apart it was not the state but rather peasant unions and the Indian communities that filled the void. Once landlords fled the countryside, peasant unions became conflict mediators in other political conflicts. After the reform was instituted, the state had few means to regulate the numerous disputes that arose among peasants—over territorial boundaries, over the rights to pasturelands or water, or even over family and personal affairs such as inheritance or theft. In the new political scenario, the unions as well as traditional community authorities performed a critical political and legal role.

Today, Bolivia's Altiplano and inter-Andean valleys remain predominantly in the hands of Aymara and Quechua peasants organized in unions and Indigenous communities. These institutions continue to play a leading role in determining issues concerning landed property as well as schooling, water access, and political organizing. Implicit rather than written rules encourage small-scale property owners to be involved in the union in order to secure access to land and be recognized as part of the community. Participation in the union requires families' labor, monetary contributions, and involvement in local festivities. These now-entrenched features demonstrate that a profound transformation in rural property relations has taken place in Bolivia since 1952. Land indeed has been conceived in terms of its social function, as many constitutions in Latin America have mandated. Perhaps nowhere more so than in Bolivia, however, have peasant organizations seized on that principle and taken advantage of it.

NEOLATIFUNDIO, DICTATORSHIP, AND THE BIRTH OF A NEW AGRARIAN REFORM LAW

The 1953 Agrarian Reform Decree had a profoundly redistributive effect in terms of land tenure in the Bolivian highlands (La Paz, Oruro, and Potosí) and valleys (Cochabamba, Tarija, and Chuquisaca). But its effects were not the same in all regions. In the lowlands (Bolivian plains and Amazon, northern La Paz, eastern Cochabamba, Chuquisaca, Tarija, and the extensive departments of Santa Cruz, Beni, and Pando), the MNR's agrarian policy differed little from the civilizing mindset of the nineteenth-century elites.

The 1953 Agrarian Reform Decree conceptualized lowland Indigenous peoples differently from highland Indigenous peoples. While the MNR promoted the distribution of land to peasants in the highlands, the nationalists—resembling the conservative elites of the nineteenth century— thought that the lowland Indians were unfit to hold property and needed to be subject to tutelage. Article 129 of the Agrarian Reform Decree stated, "Lowland groups . . . that are in a wild state and have a primitive organization are under the protection of the State."

The civilizing ethos inherent in the Agrarian Reform Decree was not uncommon. International conventions shared very similar attitudes. In 1957, Convention 107 of the International Labor Organization (ILO), undoubtedly the most relevant international document on the rights of Indigenous peoples, recommended that nation-states "promote the integration of tribal and semi-tribal populations into the national community." Since the MNR assumed that the lowlands were unoccupied territories because only "savages" lived there, the government promoted their colonization by relocating peasant populations from the highlands to the lowlands. Colonization by state-sponsored "homesteading" brought about the gradual marginalization or outright expulsion of Indigenous populations from their former territories. Although Bolivia's ambition to occupy the lowlands began decades before 1952, colonization only took off after the government finished the Cochabamba–Santa Cruz highway in 1954. Road construction increased land values in Santa Cruz and made the lowland colonization project attractive to private landowners.[53] At the same time, the Ministry of Agriculture, with the support of the Inter-American Agricultural Service, promoted development of the sugar industry in Santa Cruz.

The most extensive process of land occupation and accumulation in the lowlands took place in the 1970s and early 1980s under the dictatorships of General Hugo Banzer Suárez (1971–1978) and General Luis García Meza (1980–1981). Both conceded large land grants to private parties to repay political favors. The stakes were huge and consequences lasting. Anthropologist Nancy Postero notes that General Banzer granted about ten million hectares to private individuals in the department of Santa Cruz alone.[54] In contrast to the land policies in the highlands where peasants and small farmers were granted plots of five hectares, in the lowlands 72 percent of the land was made up of properties of more than one thousand hectares each.[55] As Jean-Pierre Lavaud points out, Bolivia's land policy in the 1970s, instead of stimulating economic growth, spawned financial and speculative activity and neolatifundio property accumulation.[56]

Ximena Soruco et al. state that governmental policies such as building new roads and granting and forgiving loans fostered the creation of a new landowning elite in Santa Cruz. In the 1970s, Santa Cruz landowners received generous loans through the Banco Agrícola de Bolivia. Santa Cruz received 37 percent of the loans that Bolivia obtained from the United States between 1955 and 1984.[57] During the inflationary crisis of the early 1980s, the government pardoned those who were unable to pay their debts.[58] This allowed the agricultural sector to continue receiving renewed credits. The Santa Cruz elite also benefited from tax exemptions on industrial goods, gas subsidies, and favorable prices for their products from neighboring countries.

This policy of favoring the new landowning elites continued into the 1980s even after the end of the military cycle. Bolivia returned to democracy in 1982 and in 1985 Paz Estenssoro was reelected president for the fourth time. In 1985 the government, with the support of the World Bank, gave out grants with a value of $35 million for the growth of agribusiness. This project was part of Paz Estenssoro's Nueva Política Económica (New Economic Policy) aimed to finance soy exports. This process accelerated the expansion of the agricultural frontier in the Amazon and the continuing expulsion of Indigenous peoples from their lands.[59]

In the second half of the 1980s, migration to the lowlands intensified. After the government of Paz Estenssoro privatized the mines, hundreds of former mine workers migrated to Santa Cruz, northern La Paz, and the Chapare in Cochabamba. Most former mine workers turned to the cultivation of coca leaves, one of the most attractive products on the market.[60] These various waves of migration from the highlands to the lowlands accentuated the displacement of Indigenous groups from their original territories.

After decades of land grabbing and displacement, lowland Indigenous groups began to organize to defend their territorial rights. In 1982, they created the Confederation of Indigenous Peoples of Eastern Bolivia (CIDOB), representing thirty-four Indigenous and peasant groups living in eastern Bolivia. During their first two annual meetings in 1982 and 1983, they demanded implementation of the 1953 Agrarian Reform Decree in their territories. They asked the government to endow plots of land mirroring the rights that peasants had gained in the 1950s and 1960s in the highlands. Yet, in 1984, the CIDOB came up with a new and more radical proposal. They demanded the government enact a new agrarian law to recognize Indigenous rights related to their territories, not just individual plots of land. This change took place after CIDOB leaders participated in the Ninth Congress of the Instituto Indigenista Interamericano and the First Congress of the Coordinator of Indigenous Organizations of the Amazon River Basin (COICA), both of which were held in 1984. The participation of the CIDOB in these international meetings along with the commitment of the ILO to "provide material and human resources to help this grassroots organization" were fundamental to rethinking Indigenous demands in the Amazon. Thus, CIDOB's demands for territory took on a new dimension in the early 1980s in dialogue with other lowland Indigenous organizations in Peru, Ecuador, Colombia, and Brazil, and with the support of various international organizations. Since 1985, the newly formed CIDOB has received support from nongovernmental organizations such as the Apoyo para el Campesino-Indígena del Oriente

Boliviano (APCOB) and the ILO. Since 1990, the Centro de Estudios Jurídicos e Investigación Social (CEJIS), the Asociación Latinoamérica-Suiza (ALAS), and the Centro de Investigación y Documentación para el Desarrollo del Beni have helped channel the demands of Indigenous peoples toward the national public agenda.

The growing demands of Indigenous peoples in the lowlands and reconstitution of the latifundios since the late 1980s, plus extreme land fragmentation in the highlands and the shadowy land distribution operations of the National Council of Agrarian Reform (CNRA), signaled the end of the agrarian reform process that began in Bolivia in 1953. In 1990, the CIDOB led Bolivia's first nationwide Indigenous mobilization, called the "March for Territory and Dignity." This historic march led by Indigenous groups of the lowlands started in the city of Trinidad and reached La Paz thirty-four days later. Anthropologists Ricardo Calla and Ramiro Molina argue that the march had a profound impact on national politics since it transformed the parameters of the political discourse around Indigenous demands: "The march challenged the state and the society as a whole, showing that a large part of the population had been marginalized from national processes. The march defied legal norms that were considered unquestionable, such as to talk about Indians' collective territories and collective rights."[61]

In response to the 1990 march, President Jaime Paz Zamora (1989–1993) signed three iconic decrees that recognized, for the first time, the rights of lowland Indigenous peoples to their territories.[62] Only a year later, Bolivia's congress ratified the ILO Convention Concerning Indigenous and Tribal Peoples, 1989 (No. 169), which recognized Indigenous rights to "exercise control over their own institutions, ways of life and economic development, and to maintain and develop their identities, languages, and religions."[63] These two events demonstrated that in the 1990s there was a new political model for understanding Indigenous demands at both the national and international levels. It is important to note that many other countries in Latin America, including Colombia, Costa Rica, Ecuador, Guatemala, Nicaragua, Honduras, Mexico, Paraguay, and Peru, also ratified the 169 ILO Convention.[64]

The final event marking the end of Bolivia's first agrarian reform took place in 1992, when President Paz Zamora closed the two national agencies in charge of handling land titling, the CNRA and the National Institute of Colonization (INC). Paz Zamora made that decision in response to continuous and growing allegations of corruption in the land distribution process, some of them directly leveled against members of his cabinet. Paz Zamora's decree reads: "Considering . . . that these institutions do not [have] statistics . . . that show with certainty the degree of distribution of the lands, which [has] caused duplication of demands, overlapping of endowments and adjudications, anomalies in the land titling, latifundios, and illegal commerce of land . . . the government declares the intervention of [INC and CNRA]".[65]

With this decree, the government ordered the suspension of all processes of land endowment or new adjudications, and the cessation of all agrarian processes.[66]

In the midst of this severe institutional crisis, President Gonzalo Sánchez de Lozada (1993–1997) called for the drafting of an agrarian law that addressed Bolivia's new situation. In February 1995, the government convened three economic and social sectors to discuss the new legislation: agroindustry represented by the Chamber of Industry and Commerce, which brought together cattle ranchers and landowners from the departments of Santa Cruz, Pando, Beni, and northern La Paz; the peasant communities of the highlands and peasant migrants of the lowlands called *colonizadores* represented by the Confederation of Peasant Workers of Bolivia (CSUTCB); and thirty-four Indigenous groups of the lowlands represented by the CIDOB.

According to the government, one of the most important objectives of the bill was to implement a national land registry that would identify overlapping lands or illegal land occupation. Remarkably, the three sectors (agroindustry, peasants, and Indigenous peoples) opposed the bill, though each for different reasons. Landowners feared that a new titling process would reexamine the ownership of lands they had illegally acquired in the 1970s. Many feared losing fallow lands that were not fulfilling an economic function, as established in the constitution.[67] Finally, many were afraid the government would seize the property of those who had not paid taxes for more than two years. The peasants and colonizadores opposed the bill because they saw it as the government's new attempt to privatize communal land. Román Loayza, a CSUTCB leader, argued that opening land to the market would undermine Indigenous peoples' and peasants' livelihoods. The colonizadores also demanded recognition and legalization of the properties they had been occupying for more than twenty years in the lowlands. Finally, Indigenous groups of the lowlands rejected the government's bill because it did not include a clause about Indigenous territories, which had been recognized under Paz Zamora's government.

Considering the divergent demands of each sector, the government summit convened to review the new legislation soon became a battleground, and alliances between the three sectors changed radically during eighteen months of negotiation. Initially, the CSUTCB and CIDOB came to the negotiating table as allies; both denounced the government's intention to approve a law that favored private enterprises' access to land at the expense of peasants and Indigenous people. To stop the government's bill and make demands, they organized a march from the city of Santa Cruz to the seat of the government in La Paz. However, the initial alliance between the CSUTCB and the CIDOB broke down when CIDOB representatives found out that the government and even agribusiness were more willing to agree to the demands of the lowland Indigenous groups. Agribusiness representatives understood that endowing territories for the scarce Indigenous population of the lowlands was an indirect way to stop the incessant migration of peasants from the highlands. The colonizadores and landowners also discovered that they had some demands in common. Both sought legalization of their settlements, many of them in forested areas and national parks in the lowlands.

After eighteen months of intense wrangling, the government enacted the Law of the National Institute of Agrarian Reform (Ley del Instituto Nacional de Reforma Agraria, or INRA) in October 1996. The fundamental objective of the INRA law was to consolidate a national land registry to address overlapping land claims. The law also made some important concessions to the Indigenous groups of the lowlands and to agribusiness. This new law recognized the collective territories of Indigenous people, called Tierras Comunitarias de Origen. This was a remarkable achievement for the CIDOB. The government also granted crucial benefits to agroindustry by cutting taxes in half for rural landowners and implicitly legalizing settlements in existence since the 1970s and 1980s. All they had to do was prove their properties fulfilled an Economic and Social Function (FES, Función Económica Social).[68] The new law offered no concrete policies to peasants living in the highlands and valleys. Nor did it offer anything concrete to colonizadores, including coca growers, demanding the legalization of their settlements in the lowlands.[69]

Upon approval of this new law on agrarian reform, the government expected to finish the process of land titling in about ten years. However, a report published by Fundación Tierra in 2016 revealed that the INRA had only completed 11.7 percent of title requests. Another 14.9 percent of claims were still in process, and 73.3 percent remained untitled.[70] Of the total land area titled, 64 percent (around eight million hectares) had gone to Indigenous people of the lowlands.[71] Between 1996 and 2006, the land titling process had mainly benefited Indigenous populations of Bolivia's vast lowlands yet there was very little progress in titling and reversing the latifundio system.[72] How can we explain this result? Most of the funding that the INRA received to work on land titling was expressly allocated to process the demands of Indigenous groups of the lowlands. The World Bank, the United Nations, and the Danish Cooperation for Environment and Development granted external loans to the national treasury for this specific purpose.[73] Additionally, several nongovernmental organizations such as OXFAM Bolivia (Oxford Committee for Famine Relief), APCOB (Apoyo Para el Campesino-Indígena del Oriente Boliviano), CEJIS (Centro de Estudios Jurídicos e Investigación Social), and ALAS (América Latina Alternativa Social) worked with Indigenous groups in supporting their claims to land.

The process of land titling also benefited medium-sized and especially large companies involved in the production of soybeans. Although Indigenous populations consolidated an enormous amount of territory, little of this territory had agricultural potential. On the other hand, large companies consolidated 1.3 million hectares (corresponding to 10.6 percent of the titled territory) in areas of enormous agricultural potential, which is where soybean and oilseed production had been established. The groups that had clearly been marginalized from the titling process, the migrants from the highlands (the colonizadores) including the *cocaleros* (coca growers), mainly settled in the Chapare region. Starting in the late 1990s, conflicts between Indigenous people and colonizadores intensified in northern La Paz, eastern Cochabamba, and the departments of Pando and Santa Cruz.

THE NEW LEFT AND NEO-EXTRACTIVISM

Partial implementation of the INRA law did not solve the issue of land access for the majority of Indigenous peoples and peasants, and the latifundios continued. The colonizadores, especially the coca growers, had not legalized their settlements either. Moreover, as Thomas Grisaffi points out (p. 213), since 1997 and under increasing pressure from the Drug Enforcement Administration, the Bolivian government tightened its coca leaf eradication policies. These policies resulted in the deaths, abuse, sexual assault, and serious injury of dozens of coca growers. It also led to the burning of farms and the imprisonment of thousands of people.[74] In the 1990s, the coca farmer and union leader Evo Morales became one of the most critical voices in the country denouncing the violent policies of coca leaf eradication and US interference in Bolivia's national politics. His criticisms resonated not only among coca growers, but also among the urban middle classes as well as leftist and nationalist intellectuals.

Widespread mobilizations at the beginning of the century culminated in the so-called Water War in 2000 and Gas War in 2003. These placed the political system in crisis, and Evo Morales was elected president in 2005, taking office in 2006. His anti-imperialist and environmentalist rhetoric guaranteed him the support of left-leaning social and political movements, Indigenous organizations from the highlands and lowlands, colonizadores, cocaleros, and the urban middle class. Morales's first land policies sought to meet the demands of the different social forces that had brought him to power: peasants, Indigenous people, and colonizadores. During his first year in office, President Morales enacted the Communal Redirection Law or Ley de Reconducción Comunitaria, which made important changes to the INRA law.[75] It replaced the term Tierra Comunitaria de Origen with Territorio

Indígena Originario Campesino (TIOC).[76] By combining the terms "Indigenous," "original inhabitant," and "peasant," the TIOC gave colonizadores and cocaleros the opportunity to make land claims on the same footing as Indigenous people from the lowlands.[77] The law determined that available public lands could only be endowed in favor of Indigenous and peasant communities, including the colonizadores.[78] In the words of Vice President Álvaro García Linera, the new constitution (promulgated by President Morales on 7 February 2009) plus the new agrarian reform law sought to erase the artificial distinctions that had been made by the NGOs between lowland Indians and peasants from the valleys and highlands. For him, this dualism was a caricature created by the landowners to feed antipeasant xenophobia and stop the migration of Indigenous highland peasants.[79] The law also underscored, once again, that rural property should fulfill the Economic and Social Function (FES in Spanish). The law determined that the landowners must demonstrate their compliance with the FES every three years, or potentially face expropriation.[80] During its first four years, the Morales government, under the impetus of Vice Minister of Land Alejandro Almaraz, adopted a more aggressive policy against latifundios. Almaraz publicly announced that fifteen families were seeking title to half a million hectares.[81]

The Morales administration also sought to honor its commitment to the environment. In 2009, Morales signed a new constitution that advocated for sustainable development. Article 33 of the new constitution states: "People have the right to a healthy, protected, and balanced environment. The exercise of this right must allow individuals and collectivities of present and future generations, as well as other living beings, to develop normally and permanently."[82] In 2010, the government also approved Law 071 of the Rights of Mother Earth. The legislation consolidated a new legal framework to protect the rights of Indigenous and peasant peoples and to promote the rights of nature.[83]

But Morales's administration encountered several obstacles when implementing these new laws. One of the most severe conflicts his party faced was a festering dispute with regional lowland elites. The crisis reached fever pitch in 2008, when the governors of five of Bolivia's nine departments—Santa Cruz, Tarija, Beni, Pando, and Chuquisaca—rejected the constitutional project promoted by the president and demanded autonomy. This demand, which was not new in Santa Cruz, allowed local elites to obtain the support of the country's most conservative sectors in an attempt to halt the national government's policies. The call for autonomy masked economic, ethnic, and ideological grievances. For example, local elites wanted control over gas revenues and over the nation's largest hydrocarbon reserves, located in the eastern region. These elites, who identified as white or mestizo, felt threatened by the rise of Indigenous and peasant actors empowered by the Morales government. In short, the agro-industrial elite defended neoliberalism, the economic model the Morales government had set out to tear down.

Morales managed to end the crisis that threatened to break the country in two after offering important concessions to these regional elites. These concessions arguably ended up consolidating and empowering the neoliberal economic model severely criticized by Morales's Movimiento al Socialismo (MAS) party.[84] In 2009, the government made a first concession by approving a new constitution which stated that the limits on landholding size would not be applied retroactively.[85] Later, the Morales government abandoned many of the principles adopted in previous legislation in favor of Mother Earth and the protection of Indigenous and peasant land rights. First, the government established the maximum limit of a medium-size property at 8,000 hectares, instead of the 5,000 hectares that had been established in the 2009 constitution.[86] Second, Morales decided to loosen controls over illegal logging, a widespread practice that has contributed to deforestation. In 2013, Morales approved a new law that exempted deforestation that took place between July 1996 and December 2011 from legal prosecution that could end in the payment of fines or reversion of cleared property to the state. The new law required beneficiaries to pay a one-time fee as an administrative sanction for deforestation without authorization.[87] Each of these decisions shows that Morales managed to regain political control of the country by altering the very essence of "the process of change," the term he used to refer to his government.

The second most significant conflict that Morales faced was during his second term in power. In 2011, Indigenous groups living in the Isiboro Sécure National Park and Indigenous Territory (TIPNIS) began protesting the government's decision to build a highway through their territory. This unilateral decision violated the right to prior consultation that the 2009 constitution had guaranteed to Indigenous people. This move not only ignited a conflict between Indigenous groups living in the area and the government but also between Indigenous people of the lowlands and the cocaleros who lived and produced coca on the outskirts of the park. The cocaleros constituted the president's most solid social base. The cocaleros defended the construction of a road connecting the towns of Villa Tunari (Cochabamba) and San Ignacio de Moxos (Beni) across the national park, whereas lowland Indigenous communities argued that this project would permanently harm the fragile ecosystem of this area.

The MAS government's decision to continue with the construction of the road despite the protests shook public opinion, nationally and internationally. Several analysts criticized the contradiction between Morales's political discourse

Figure 1.1. A pro-MAS Indigenous organization marching in favor of road construction through the TIPNIS, Cochabamba, July 2011. Photo courtesy of Thomas Grisaffi.

of respect for the rights of Indigenous peoples and Mother Earth, which he led or proclaimed internationally, and the undemocratic methods used by his government to silence internal protest. On September 26, 2011, the police violently repressed an Indigenous march, delivering a severe blow to the democratic image of the Morales government.

For their part, government officials defended the project as essential for the development of the nation. The Minister of the Presidency René Martínez argued that it was not right to leave Beni, one of the nation's largest departments, severed from the rest of the country and without roads, "only to protect Mother Earth." He argued that the highway would benefit the Indigenous peoples living in the park and added, "We cannot leave the Indigenous communities isolated, without access to education or health."[88] Strategically, the government discredited the mobilization of Indigenous people of TIPNIS by claiming protesters were being controlled by foreign NGOs and the right-wing political opposition. Although there is no doubt that right-wing groups suddenly assumed an environmental, pro-Indigenous stance to capitalize on the crisis, the argument of manipulation and co-optation of Indigenous groups was used to delegitimize, erode, and block Indigenous demands.[89]

The TIPNIS conflict forced the government to take sides in favor of the cocaleros and against the Indigenous people of the lowlands, dismantling the political support of a segment of the population that brought Morales to power. After that rift, the cocaleros took even more aggressive steps against lowland Indigenous groups. They questioned the volume of land granted by the government to Indigenous groups in the 1990s, calling them the "new landowners."[90]

The two conflicts left a stain on the MAS government and redefined Morales's initial policies on land. By 2011, lowland Indigenous leaders openly questioned President Morales's double standards—a self-proclaimed leader of environmental rights in international forums while continuing to approve policies harmful to the environment and Indigenous territories at home. The TIPNIS conflict also reflects a dilemma that goes beyond Bolivia's borders. The left-leaning governments that emerged in Latin America during the first decade of the twenty-first century faced similar impasses. Despite their initial rhetoric to support and embrace an environmentalist agenda, no government was able to find alternatives to extractivism. The need for immediate revenue rather than long-term planning has continued to guide public policy.[91]

The government of Evo Morales, far from protecting the rights of Mother Earth, promoted the continued expansion of the agricultural frontier and the farming and export of soybeans, while marginalizing and ignoring the rights of Indigenous people. In fact, as Jeffrey Webber states, despite the initial political confrontation with the agro-industrial elite, the dynamism of the soy economy continued to accelerate under Morales's government. Webber shows that industrial crops accounted for 70.1 percent of agricultural production between 2005 and 2006 and 80.4 percent between 2010 and 2011. Essentially, 76 percent of the total volume of growth in agricultural production between 2005 and 2011 was soybeans (40 percent) and sugarcane (36 percent) combined.[92] Valdermar João Wesz adds that the expansion of a soy-based economy in the country had dramatic implications in terms of food sovereignty because the crop expansion was advancing over areas of native vegetation and food crops were being replaced by soy.[93]

Equally aggressive against the environment was legislation approved by the Morales government relating to hydrocarbons. In April 2018, the government approved three contracts for hydrocarbon exploration in the Tariquía National Flora and Fauna Reserve, despite the opposition of the communities living in the area. Experts agree that all protected areas in Bolivia are threatened since Morales opened them to hydrocarbon exploration.[94]

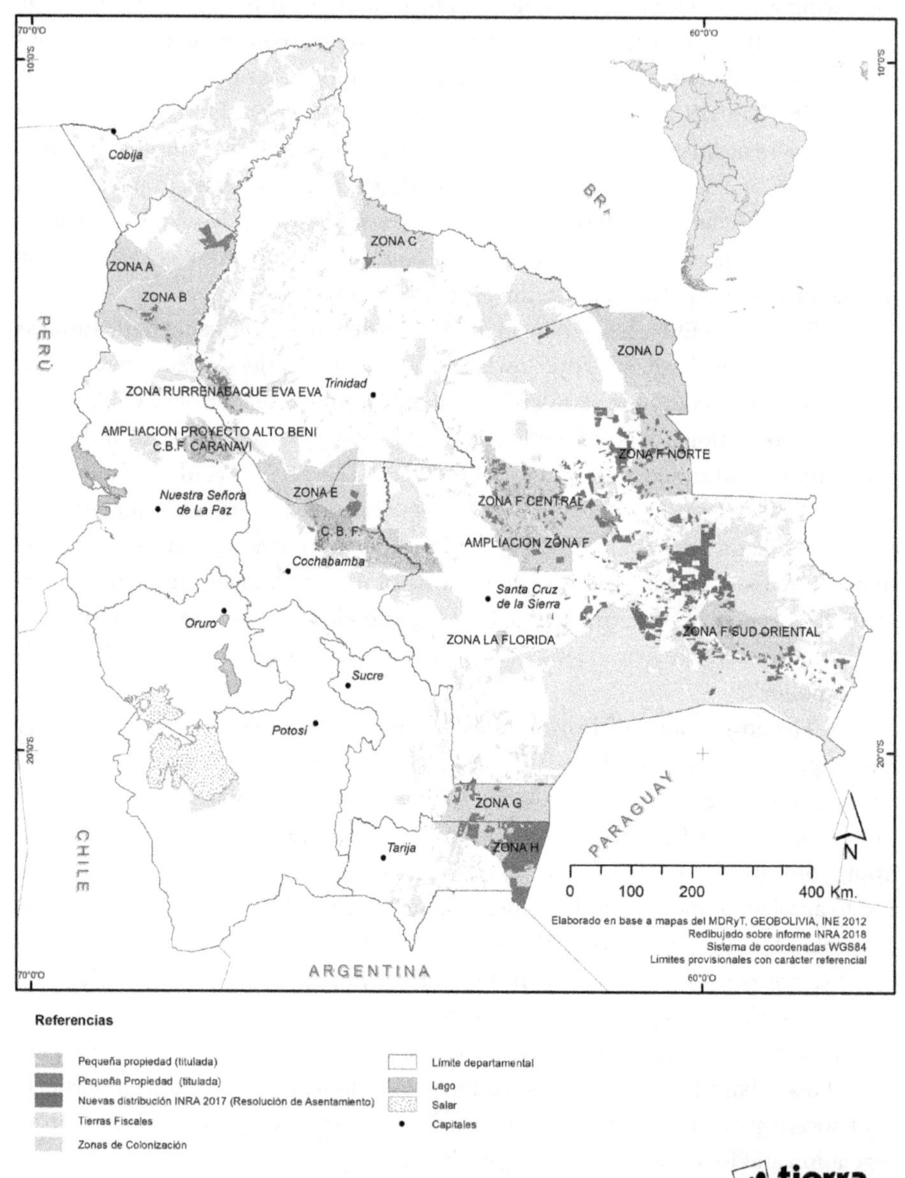

Map 1.2. Zones of colonization in Bolivia, with small peasant properties and titled communities (2010–2017). Map courtesy of Fundación Tierra.

Table 1.2. Zones of colonization in Bolivia, including small peasant properties and titled communities (2010–2017)

DESCRIPTION	AREAS OF COLONIZATION	COMMUNAL PROPERTY	SMALL PROPERTY	TOTAL SURFACE
Ampliacion Proyecto Alto Beni	67,716	10,732	10,567	21,298
Ampliacion Zona F	898,982	125,750	304,702	430,452
C. B. F. Caranavi	334,488	2,332	160,779	183,111
Zona A	815,165			
Zona B	1,664,777	143,455	32,152	175,608
Zona C	947,225	22,967	16,489	39,456
Zona D	1,575,543	9,992	524	10,517
Zona F Central	1,493,988	144,122	234,628	378,750
Zona F Norte	1,182,228	137,208	38,737	175,945
Zona F Sud Oriental	989,311	15,995	81,378	97,373
Zona G	954,264	146,883	51,893	198,776
Zona H	1,001,968	623,058	24,194	647,252
Zona La Florida	50,096	32	7,455	7,487
Zona Rurrenabaque Eva Eva	288,672	81,916	73,439	155,355
C. B. F.	1,478,266	78,430	451,978	530,408
Zona E	1,402,429	10,145	38,820	48,965
Interseccion Zona C. B. F. - Y - Zona E	526,865	61,854	210,777	272,631
Total	14,618,255	1,634,873	1,738,511	3,373,384
INRA land distribution 2010–2017				1,398,938
Total distribution 2018				4,772,322

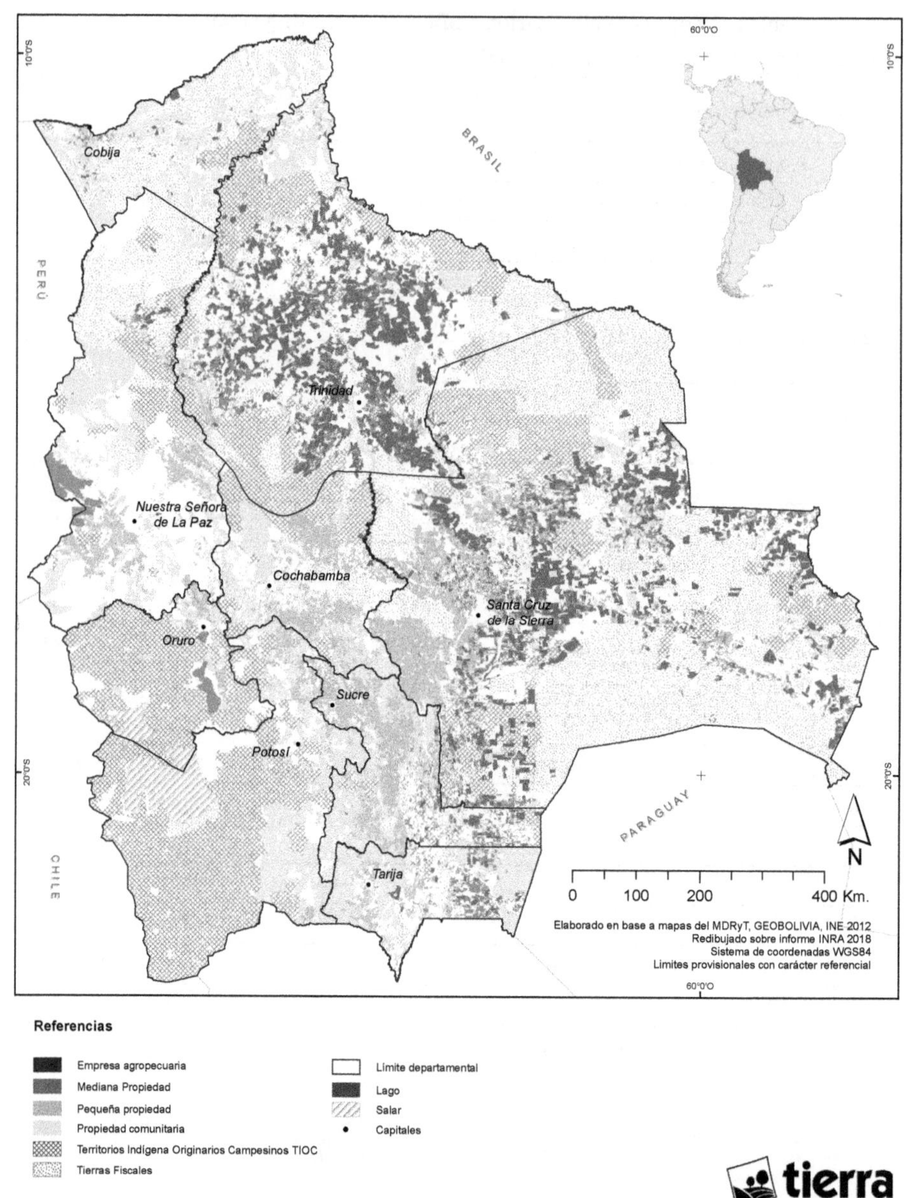

Map 1.3. Types of agricultural property titled as of December 2018, by area in hectares. Map courtesy of Fundación Tierra.

Table 1.3. Types of agricultural property titled as of December 2018, by area in hectares

DESCRIPTION	SURFACE IN HECTARES
Total surface in Bolivia	109,849,100
Urban areas and bodies of water	6,430,328
Areas subject of land titling	103,418,772
Titled areas	85,568,880
Small	8,351,604
Medium-size	4,088,570
Enterprise	7,509,489
Communal land	14,959,517
TIOC	23,929,818
State land	26,541,686
FFAA	66,936
UE	121,259
Surface pending of titling	17,849,892
Surface in the process of being titled	5,800,287
Land in conflict	8,441,590
Land pending of measurement	3,608,015
Total	103,418,772

CONCLUSION

This chapter has analyzed the scope and limits of the three agrarian reform policies that took place in Bolivia in the twentieth and twenty-first centuries. Bolivia's 1953 agrarian reform eliminated the latifundio in the highlands and valleys of Bolivia and turned former hacienda peons into owners of their own plots of land. Unlike other examples in Latin America, the military regimes that took power after the fall of the MNR in 1964 did not dare to challenge the property rights that peasants had consolidated in the Bolivian highlands. To this day, peasant communities own their land, guaranteeing them national political representation. It is almost impossible to win national elections without peasant support.

Since the 1970s, the geography of Bolivia's land conflict has shifted to the east, as state-sponsored migration programs fostered penetration and occupation of the lowlands. During the dictatorial regimes of Generals Banzer and García Meza, landowners obtained illegal concessions, which led to the reconstitution of latifundios. This process of land grabbing displaced Indigenous populations living in these areas. After years of mobilization, lobbying, and demonstrations, the government signed a new agrarian law that recognized Indigenous collective rights to their territories, but implementation of the second law of agrarian reform brought mixed results. Between 1996 and 2009, Indigenous peoples consolidated eight million hectares of land but with little productive capacity. At the same time, the lowland agribusiness sector secured fertile lands that today are primarily devoted to export-oriented soy, sugar, and cattle ranching.

In 2006, President Morales signed a new law for agrarian reform that promised to end latifundio, challenging agribusiness elites. He also promised to protect Indigenous and peasant interests, along with the natural environment. Yet his agrarian policy proved erratic. Especially after 2010, the MAS government's policy toward Bolivia's large landowning elites became much more complacent, and many of the decrees Morales enacted after 2010 intensified environmental damage in the Amazon. When referring to the conflict between Indigenous peoples and colonizadores, Morales's agrarian policy has undoubtedly favored the latter.

In 2019, a right-wing president, Jeanine Áñez, assumed power, buoyed by Bolivia's restive landowning elite. Branco Marinković, one of the country's largest landowners, assumed the portfolio of the Department of Economy. During her short presidency, Áñez used INRA to illegally hand over agrarian titles to medium- and large-sized landowners. The Branco Marincović family got thirty-three thousand hectares.[95] In 2020, Luis Arce, a close associate of Evo Morales, won the national presidential election. Thus far, Arce has been cautious about speaking out on the land conflict or protecting the rights of any of the contending groups. However, INRA is immersed in a new institutional crisis, with widespread allegations of land seizures, illegal titling, corruption, and overlapping plots. As in the past, forces on the ground rather than state-level institutions ultimately define who holds the land in the face of official silence and inaction. The expansion of the agricultural frontier that continues to endanger forests, protected areas, and Indigenous territories jeopardizes the objectives of food sovereignty and the more balanced relationship with the environment once embraced by the self-proclaimed Indigenous and leftist governments of Morales and Arce.

ACKNOWLEDGMENTS

I want to thank Rossana Barragan, Sinclair Thomson, and Kris Lane for their generous comments and insights.

NOTES

I published an analysis of Bolivia's three agrarian reforms in "Agrarian Reform in Bolivia in the 20th and 21st Centuries," *Oxford Research Encyclopedia of Latin American History*, August 2018. In 2021, University of Pittsburgh Press published my book *Fields of Revolutions: Agrarian Reform and Rural State Formation in Bolivia, 1935–1964*, which delves into the 1950s agrarian reform. I have drawn on both to write this chapter.

1. The comparative work of Thiesenhusen studying processes of agrarian reform in the twentieth century shows the devastating effects of the implementation liberalism in the countryside in Latin America. It also examines how dictatorial regimes over the twentieth century deepened peasant dispossession. Thiesenhusen, *Broken Promises*. For Guatemala, McCreery exposes the extent village lands were incorporated into latifundios on a massive scale as a way of getting workers for coffee cultivation, "Coffee and Class: The structure of Development." The works of Klaren, Peru: *Society and Nationhood in the Andes*; Piel, *El capitalismo agrario en el Peru*; and Peloso and Tenenbaum, *Liberals, Politics, and Power* are key to understand this process in the late nineteenth century in Peru. The studies of Grieshaber, *Survival of Indian Communities*; Rivera, "La expansión del latifundio en el altiplano boliviano"; and Gotkowitz, *A Revolution for Our Rights* are key to understand the Bolivian case.
2. Klein, *A Concise History of Bolivia*, 33.
3. Saignes, "Caciques, Tribute and Migration in the Southern Andes," 4.
4. Klein, *A Concise History of Bolivia*, 34.
5. Bridikhina et al., *Bolivia, su historia*, vol. 2, 119.
6. Bridikhina et al., *Bolivia*, 120.
7. Semo, *Historia del capitalismo en México*, 83.
8. Platt, "The Andean Experience of Bolivian Liberalism, 1825–1900s," 307–9.
9. Semo, *Historia del capitalismo en México*, 98. See also Schwaller, *The Church in Colonial Latin America*.
10. Klein, *A Concise History of Bolivia*, 251–52.
11. Klein, *A Concise History of Bolivia*, 254
12. Klein, *A Concise History of Bolivia*, 61–62
13. Larson, *Trials of Nation Making*, 205.

14. Platt, "Simón Bolívar, the Sun of Justice and the Amerindian Virgin," 161.

15. Larson, *Trials of Nation Making*, 216.

16. Law September 28, 1868, art. 1: "Las tierras poseidas por la raza indijenal y conocidas hasta hoy bajo el nombre de tierras de Comunidad, se declaran propiedad del Estado. Art 3: Dichas tierras serán vendidas en pública subasta y con las formalidades prescritas para la venta de los bienes fiscales, con el objeto de cubrir con su producto la deuda interna y gastos del servicio público." For an excellent analysis of Bolivia's Liberal Project, see Laura Gotkowitz, *A Revolutions for Our Rights*, 17–42.

17. Langer, *Economic Change and Rural Resistance in Southern Bolivia*, 18–20. See also Rivera, "La expansion del latifundio en el altiplano boliviano"; Platt, *Estado boliviano y ayllu andino.*

18. Gotkowitz, *A Revolution for Our Rights*, 20.

19. Sanchez-Albornóz, *Indios y tributos en el Alto Perú*, 209–10.

20. Gotkowitz, *A Revolution for Our Rights*, 31. See also Ministerio de Asuntos Campesinos y Agropecuarios, Instituto Nacional de Estadística, *Censo Agropecuario 1950*, II.

21. Thiesenhusen, *Broken Promises*, 140.

22. Easterling, *The Mexican Revolution*, 18.

23. Larson, *Trials of Nation Making*, 231

24. Condarco Morales, *Zárate, el "temible" Willka*. For further research on Zárate Willka's rebellion, see Hylton, "Reverberations of Insurgency"; and Mendieta, *Entre la alianza y la confrontación.*

25. Condori Chura and Ticona Alejo, *El escribano de los caciques apoderados*, 22–55.

26. Choque Canqui and Ticona Alejo, *Sublevación*, 12–14; Forrest Hylton, "Tierra Común: Caciques," 137–42, 170–75.

27. "La voz del campesino, 1929," manifesto cited in Choque Canqui, "República de indios y república de blancos," 250. Translation from Spanish is mine.

28. Mariátegui, *Seven Interpretive Essays on Peruvian Reality.*

29. Klein, *Orígenes de la revolución nacional boliviana*, 148, 165.

30. Schelchkov, "En los umbrales del socialismo boliviano," 6.

31. Klein, *Orígenes*, 123. See also Guillermo Lora, Bolivia's most important Trotskyist leader, who argues that radical ideas in the 1920s had very little impact in mainstream political parties. Lora, *Historia del movimiento obrero boliviano*, vol. 4.

32. Barragán, *Asambleas constituyentes.*

33. Klein, "'Social Constitutionalism' in Latin America," 258.

34. Barragán, *Asambleas constituyentes*, 145–46.

35. Klein, *Orígenes de la revolución nacional boliviana*, 328; Gotkowitz, *A Revolution for Our Rights*, 123.

36. Gotkowitz, *A Revolution for Our Rights*, 126.

37. Román, *Redactores del Congreso* (La Paz, 1938), 255. Similarly, Congressman Lijerón Rodríguez argues that Bolivia is very different from Mexico, thus it cannot replicate Mexican legislation.

38. Antezana Ergueta and Romero Bedregal, *Historia de los sindicatos campesinos*, 74. Aside from the Cliza and Vacas peasant unions, peasants organized several unions in Higuera-Huayco (Tarija), Coca Marco (Arque, Cochabamba), Kochi (Punata), and Iscayachi (Tarija). These unions were all created on municipal or ecclesiastical rural properties.
39. Coati was created under the Supreme Resolution of July 17, 1942. The Supreme Decree of July 18, 1942, ratified the creation of the three penal colonies in Coati, Todos Santos, and Ichilo. Gaceta Oficial de Bolivia. Bolivian legislation from independence in 1825 to the present can be found at the Gaceta Oficial del Estado Plurinacional de Bolivia (hereafter Gaceta Oficial) or on the legal website Lexivox.org.
40. Gotkowitz, *A Revolution for Our Rights*, 193–94. Gotkowitz points out that Mexico and Peru led Indigenous congresses. In these settings, creole intellectuals debated the Indian problem. In Bolivia, the Indigenous congress brought together 1,200 Indigenous leaders from communities and haciendas to discuss the Indian problem.
41. Supreme Decrees 318, 319, and 320, May 1945, Ministerio de Asuntos Campesinos, *Gaceta Campesina*, no. 1 (August 1952), 38–44, Gaceta Oficial de Bolivia.
42. I have shown that in the 1940s and even in the early 1950s the term agrarian reform meant different things to different groups. For some it meant improving the labor conditions of the colonos, for others expropriation, for others restitution, and for others credits and mechanization of the countryside. Soliz, *Fields of Revolution*, 47, 124, 140.
43. Gotkowitz argues that the cycle of rebellion in the 1940s was a "revolution before the revolution." This broader understanding of the period shows that peasants were key actors in the revolutionary process. It powerfully challenges the prior understanding of the revolution as consisting of three days of urban uprisings, in which factory and mine workers had the protagonic role. *A Revolution for Our Rights*, 5–6, 269, 271.
44. In exchange for their work for the landlord, colonos had access to plots that they used to cultivate crops for subsistence and sometimes agricultural produce to sell at the market. *Pongueaje* is the Bolivian name for colonos' obligatory unpaid servitude.
45. Soliz, *Fields of Revolution*, 78–88
46. "Considerando" section, Bolivia: Decree-Law 3464 of Agrarian Reform, 2 Aug. 1953, Gaceta Oficial del Bolivia.
47. Speech by Federico Álvarez Plata, secretario ejecutivo del comité político nacional del MNR, MNR National Convention, "Inauguración de la Convención Nacional del MNR," *La Nación* (La Paz), February, 4, 1953. See also Supreme Decree 3464, arts. 35, 36, and 39, 2 Aug. 1953, Gaceta Oficial del Bolivia.
48. For a definition of latifundio see Supreme Decree 3464, 2 Aug. 1953, art. 12, Gaceta Oficial de Bolivia.
49. Soliz, "'Land to the Original Owners," 259–96.
50. For a detailed analysis of the negotiation process between landlords and peasants (both colonos and comunarios), as well as presidential agrarian court decisions, see Soliz, *Fields of Revolution*, 94–170.

51. For the legal process of agrarian reform, see the introduction by Miguel Urioste and the article of Rossana Barragán in Urioste, Barragán, and Colque, *Los nietos de la reforma agraria*, 93.
52. Grindle, *State and Countryside.*
53. Soruco, *Los barones del oriente*, 31.
54. Postero, *Now We Are Citizens*, 47.
55. Sandóval, *Santa Cruz: Economía y poder*, 46–47.
56. Lavaud, *El embrollo boliviano*, 280–81.
57. Soruco et al. argue that one of the outcomes of the national revolution was the creation of the Santa Cruz elite. Soruco et al., *Los barones del oriente*, 69.
58. See, for example, Supreme Decree 13830 and 12401 signed by Bánzer in June 1976 to take on loans from Banco de Brasil and Banco City.
59. Soruco et al., *Los barones del oriente*, 74.
60. Orozco, García Linera, and Stefanoni, *No somos juguete de nadie.*
61. Calla and Molina, "Los pueblos indígenas y la construcción de una sociedad plural," 26.
62. Supreme Decrees 22609, 22610, and 22611, Gaceta Oficial de Bolivia.
63. The 169 ILO Convention on Indigenous and Tribal Peoples Convention was signed on June 1989 and ratified by Bolivia on December 11, 1991.
64. In the 2000s Argentina, Brazil, Chile, Dominican Republic, and Venezuela also ratified the 169 ILO convention. Overall, twenty-three countries have ratified this convention; fifteen of the twenty-three are Latin American countries.
65. Supreme Decree 23331, 24 Nov. 1992, Gaceta Oficial de Bolivia.
66. Supreme Decree 23331, 24 Nov. 1992, art. 2, Gaceta Oficial de Bolivia.
67. "Los empresarios temen la reversion de tierras," *La Razón* (La Paz), August 22, 1996; "CEPB: Ley INRA es populista e ignora a los empresarios," *La Razón* (La Paz), August 25, 1996; "Exportadores temen funestos efectos de una mala ley INRA," August 30, 1996; "La propiedad de la tierra bajo amenaza" and "Garantías Jurídicas para el sector agropecuario," *La Razón* (La Paz), September 12, 1996.
68. According to the INRA Law, a property is considered to fulfill an Economic and Social Function (FES in Spanish) if the production of a property is oriented to consumption (in the case of small properties and Indigenous community lands) or if the production is oriented to the market (in the case of medium-sized properties or agricultural companies). See "Función Económico Social," Dirección General de Administración de Tierras, January 3, 2023, https://www.inra.gob.bo/InraPb/paginaController?cmd=contenido&id=6649.
69. Loayza, "La visión de un diputado campesino," 50.
70. Colque, Tinta, and Sanjinés, *Segunda reforma agraria*, 154.
71. Colque, Tinta, and Sanjinés, *Segunda reforma agraria*, 137.

72. Fundación Tierra, *Reconfigurando territorios, reforma agraria, control territorial y gobiernos indígenas en Bolivia.*
73. For a detailed explanation of the funding to the institute of agrarian reform see Colque et al., *Segunda reforma agraria*, 142.
74. Grisaffi, "A Brief History of Coca" (chapter 6 in this book).
75. Law 3545 enacted on Nov 28, 2006. The law incorporates principles from Law 1715—Ley del Servicio Nacional de Reforma Agraria (INRA). Gaceta Oficial de Bolivia.
76. Decree 727, December 6, 2010, art. 1, Gaceta Oficial del Bolivia.
77. Chirif, *La normativa sobre territorios indígenas y su implementación en Bolivia*, 37.
78. Constitución Política del Estado, approved February 7, 2009, article 395.
79. García Linera, *Geopolítica de la Amazonía*, 74–75.
80. Colque, Tinta, and Sanjinés, *Segunda reforma agraria*, 163–65.
81. Colque, Tinta, and Sanjinés, *Segunda reforma agraria*, 171.
82. Constitución Política del Estado, Feb 7, 2009, art. 33. The Morales administration sought to promote the rights of Indigenous people and of Mother Earth internationally. In April 2010, the government organized the "World People's Conference on Climate Change and the Rights of Mother Earth" in Tiquipaya (Cochabamba) with the participation of representatives of institutions and social groups from all five continents. In "Acuerdo de los Pueblos del 22 de Abril de 2010 Cochabamba, Bolivia," Universidad Veracruzana, April 22, 2010, https://www.uv.mx/blogs/kaniwa/2010/05/11/acuerdo-de-los-pueblos-cochabamba-bolivia-22-de-abril-de-2010/.
83. Stressing the importance of this legislation, scholars Leandro Vergara-Camus and Cristóbal Kay state that Bolivia (together with Ecuador) introduced notions of good living (Vivir Bien), food sovereignty, and the rights of Mother Earth into their constitutions, which represented a crucial contribution of peasant and Indigenous movements to the transformation of the development model. Vergara-Camus and Kay, *Agronegocio, campesinos, estado y gobiernos de izquierda en América Latina*, 41.
84. Eaton, *Territory and Ideology in Latin America*, 169.
85. Constitución Política del Estado Plurinacional de Bolivia, approved in February 2009.
86. Decree-Law 3973, July 10, 2019. Article 38 of the Constitution limited the medium-sized property to a maximum of five thousand hectares. The law is not retroactive.
87. Law 337, January 11, 2013, Ley de Apoyo a la Producción de Alimentos y Restitución de Bosques.
88. René Martínez, "Ministro de la presidencia arremete contra Mesa por declaraciones sobre el Tipnis," *Los Tiempos* (Cochabamba), August 17, 2017.
89. Postero points out that the MAS and Indigenous leaders moved from a language that focused on decolonization and defense of Indigenous rights to one centered on distributing the benefits of national development. Postero, *The Indigenous State*, 149.

90. Alejandro Almaraz, "El proceso de cambio está corriendo el grave riesgo de agotarse," *Página Siete*, January 18, 2012.
91. In Ecuador, President Rafael Correa faced a similar problem with Yasuní National Park. Initially, the president offered to not drill for oil to avoid carbon dioxide emissions, to safeguard Indigenous rights, and for the conservation of biodiversity. The president hoped that the international community would offer Ecuador financial compensation in exchange for not drilling for oil. But while the Ecuadorian government sought to obtain about $3.6 billion, the compensation fund never exceeded $116 million. As a result, on August 15, 2013, President Correa announced that the government would start drilling in Yasuní. Becker, "The Stormy Relations," 43–62; Wagner, "Defendiendo la biodiversidad," 81–82.
92. Webber, "Evo Morales, 'el transformismo,'" 203.
93. Wesz, "Expansión de la soya en el Cono Sur," 21. See also Webber, "Evo Morales, el 'transformismo,'" 192.
94. "Aprueban ley para exploración petrolera en reserva de Tariquía," *Página Siete*, March 29, 2018.
95. "Pronunciamiento ante el tráfico de tierras en la gestión de Jeanine Áñez," Fundación Tierra, November 3, 2020, https://ftierra.org/index.php/tema/tierra-territorio/964-pronunciamiento-2020-ante-el-trafico-de-tierras-en-la-gestion-de-jeanine-anez.

Chapter Two

FROM SILVER TO TIN TO LITHIUM

Five Centuries of Mining in Potosí

Rossana Barragán

"The laborers have contracts earning . . . by *mita* or round of work per day. There are . . . three mitas each day: two during the day, of four hours each, and one in the night . . . To get the ore out of the mine, [they] have to carry it on their backs, walking for more than forty-five minutes with forty to sixty kilos of ore on their backs, bending over, crouching in the galleries that are not high enough to allow a standing man to pass . . ."
—Jocelyn Michard, *Cooperativas mineras: Formas de organización, producción y comercialización*

"They divided their labor in such a way that some work by day and rest at night, and others work at night and rest by day. The ore is usually very hard and is loosened by blows of a mattock, which is like breaking stone. Then they carry the ore on their backs . . . Each man has a fifty-pound load in a blanket tied over his breast, with the ore it contains at his back . . ."
—Joseph de Acosta, *Natural and Moral History*, 1590

These descriptions of mine work in Potosí, Bolivia, are striking in their similarity and demonstrate the back-breaking nature of the labor required of miners. The opening quote illustrates the work of cooperativists in 2008, and the one that follows describes *mitayo* workers in 1590. In this chapter, I am interested in analyzing how and why these striking similarities relate to the long process of Potosí's mining history. First, I argue that minerals destined for the global market expanded the commodity frontier from one mineral to another in short boom cycles followed by longer periods of decline, enlarging the geography of mining and related extractive processes. Silver was at the center of exports in the colonial period as well as in the nineteenth century. Tin became Bolivia's most important export in the twentieth century, and it seems that lithium will become the new backbone of the Bolivian economy in the twenty-first century. Second, I contend that during the colonial period a sophisticated silver industry developed, integrating extraction and refining. Even with rudimentary technology, producers obtained pure silver. It appears that in the transition from the colonial to the republican period and from silver to tin, there was a process of "deindustrialization," since tin was not locally smelted. There was a split between extraction (mining) and the first phases of processing ores to obtain tin concentrates. Even with modern technologies, Bolivia exported raw material to be refined and smelted in North Atlantic countries. Third, in looking at labor, I claim that *k'ajchas* or independent mineworkers who became important in the eighteenth century morphed into relevant economic and political actors still animating Potosí's mines today.

Over time, three main economic and political actors shaped Potosí's changing economic, social, and political landscape. The colonial and later republican state and its policies defined the rules of property, legitimate access to minerals, and rights to trade and export mineral products on the global market. Entrepreneurial concessionaries of the mines and refineries also proved crucial in their relations with the state and with mine workers. Finally, laborers' defiant economic strategies won better conditions but also prevented formation of a totally dependent waged workforce.

In surveying the history of mining over the course of five centuries, I have chosen to concentrate on four periods particularly relevant for Potosí and for Bolivia. First, I analyze exploitation of silver from the end of the sixteenth century to the end of the eighteenth century. I focus on the importance of the silver industry, and on the emergence and empowerment of the k'ajchas, people claiming their right to mine ore for themselves. In the second period, I examine tin mining during the first half of the twentieth century, when a substantial portion of total production was in the hands of two of Bolivia's famous "tin barons," Simón A. Patiño and Moritz Hochschild. Throughout the first few decades of the new century, important changes took place, particularly after the 1930s. The Bolivian state tightened its control over the mines, and it recognized independent and artisanal workers' (k'ajchas') right to be concessionaries. As seen in the previous chapter, some decades later, in 1952, the Movimiento Nacionalista Revolucionario (MNR) created the Corporación Minera de Bolivia (COMIBOL) and nationalized the mines. The mission of the new institution (COMIBOL) was to explore, exploit, and market the country's minerals. At that point, the Bolivian state divided the exploitation of minerals among the state company, the trade unions of k'ajchas who became cooperativists, and international companies. In the third period, I look at exports of silver, zinc, lead, and tin during the last decades of the twentieth century. Here I am particularly interested in small-scale and artisanal mining carried out by cooperatives that established agreements with the state and with transnational companies. It is important to emphasize that shifting arrangements among these actors mainly affected the exploitation phase, whereas the refining process remained the arena of transnational companies. Fourth, I consider the developing exploitation of lithium, in some ways a "mining of water," that is opening up new geographical and technological frontiers in Bolivia's vast salt deserts, widening again the gaps between different actors' access to technology.

POTOSÍ AS THE CENTER OF WORLD SILVER PRODUCTION

Silver was the main product of the Spanish Empire from the sixteenth century to the eighteenth century, constituting the bedrock of the first wave of globalization. Spanish-American silver, whether from New Spain or Greater Peru, was distributed throughout the world. Flynn and Giráldez, as well as Gunder Frank, argued that a highly integrated global economy dated to the sixteenth century, emphasizing that American silver traveled as far as China.[1] Frank commented that "the wheels of this global market . . . [were] oiled by the worldwide flow of silver." This circulatory system connected, lubricated, and expanded the world economy.[2] Potosí alone produced sixty percent of the world's silver in the second half of the sixteenth century, a testament to its early global significance.[3]

In this section I will show how in the last decades of the sixteenth century, the Spanish Crown, by restricting mine access and allocating labor, divided people into those obliged to work—the mitayos (who came from Indigenous communities)—and those who benefited from their work—mine and mill owners (in most cases Spaniards). Potosí's success relied on the mita labor system that originated in pre-Hispanic times, and I argue that the early silver industry relied on "factories" that drew more than twelve thousand laborers. Finally, I examine how particular groups of workers known as k'ajchas transformed their labor conditions in the eighteenth century to avoid both proletarianization and dependency on mine and mill owners, as part of their struggle to extract and refine ore for their own profit.

Understanding the new global economy entails a close look at Spain's pretentions to sovereignty over land and mined resources in the Indies. The Spanish Crown claimed and exercised political dominion over newly conquered territories,[4] although Indigenous lands remained in the hands of their communities, who held them in usufruct. The Spaniards created a "neo-Inka" system under which hundreds of these communities were obliged to pay a tribute to the Spanish Crown and to deliver a labor subsidy or mita. Drafted workers staffed mines and landholdings and constructed buildings in the main villages and cities, plus roads and wayside lodges (tambos). As far as the mines themselves, the king of Spain was legal owner of all underground treasure and this *jus regale* gave the Crown the right both to award concessions and to claim part of the resulting production.[5] Although in 1574 the Spanish

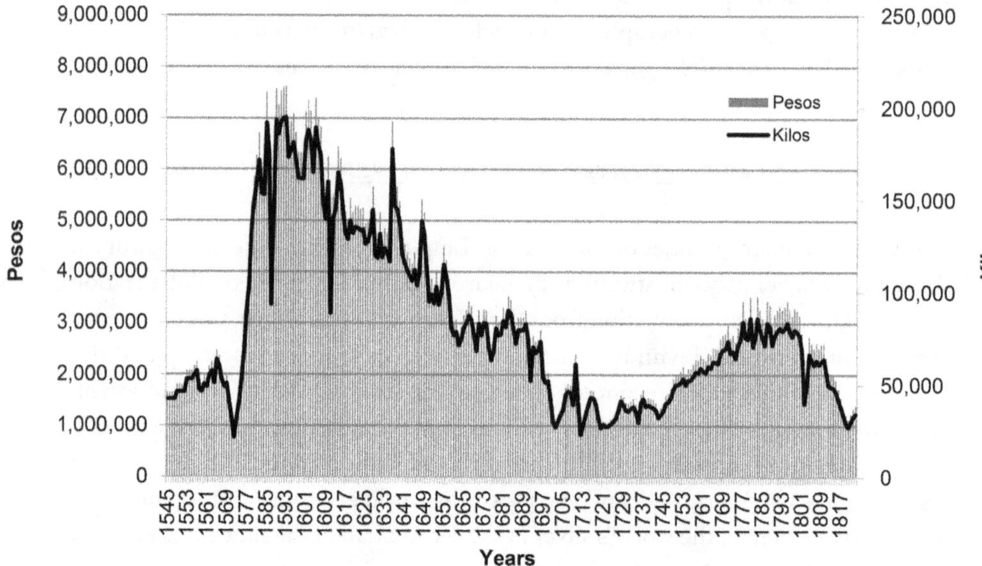

Figure 2.1. Potosí silver production, 1545–1815. Richard L. Garner, https://www.insidemydesk.com/hdd.html, Te Paske Page, Peru Silver dataset. See also TePaske, *A New World of Gold and Silver*.

Crown stipulated that Spaniards, Indians, and foreigners could exploit mines in exchange for a tax on production,[6] few Indians appeared as concessionaries in Potosí in the seventeenth century. Mineowners were mainly Spaniards, while Crown policy supplied coerced Indians to work them. Some Indian authorities, the so-called caciques, received small mining concessions inside the Cerro Rico of Potosí. These grants were meant to help them pay their taxes and mita labor expenses, although at times they were direct payment for work performed.[7] These "royal possessions" granted to Indians served as compensation for the new property regime established by the Crown over all American mines.

Mass deployment of Indian labor to work Potosí's mines along with the implementation of new amalgamation technologies in the 1570s led to an extraordinary rise in silver production for the world market. Potosí became the economic center of South America, and Lima the political center of Greater Peru, a territory that included what is now Colombia, Ecuador, Peru, Bolivia, Chile, Argentina, and Paraguay.[8]

Table 2.1. Urinoca: an example of the mita labor "turn"

Tributary people or males from 18 to 50 years old:	263
Total population:	1,222
Mitayos	42 (16% of the tributary population)

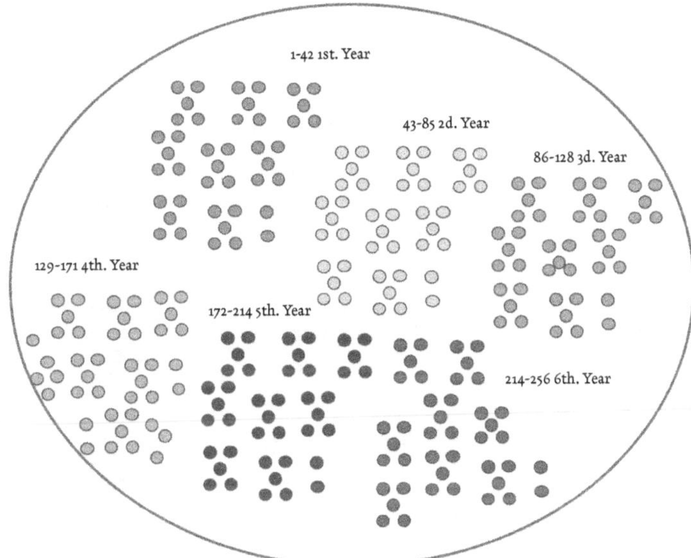

Figure 2.2. The case of Urinoca: an example of the mita labor "turn." Scheme prepared by the author.

Potosí silver production boomed between 1549 and the early 1600s, followed by a deep decline across the seventeenth century. Yet Potosí and other Andean silver mines were not dead, and production climbed once again, rising from the 1720s through the 1790s (fig. 2.1).[9]

Potosí thrived thanks to the mita, by which the Spanish Crown and its authorities guaranteed a continuous flow of drafted workers from the Andean countryside. Indigenous mitayo workers from a dozen or more districts were distributed to just over one hundred private entrepreneurs, including mine and mill owners.[10] Crown dedication to the mita across several centuries, despite considerable protest, demonstrates the close relationship that developed early between the state and the private sector.

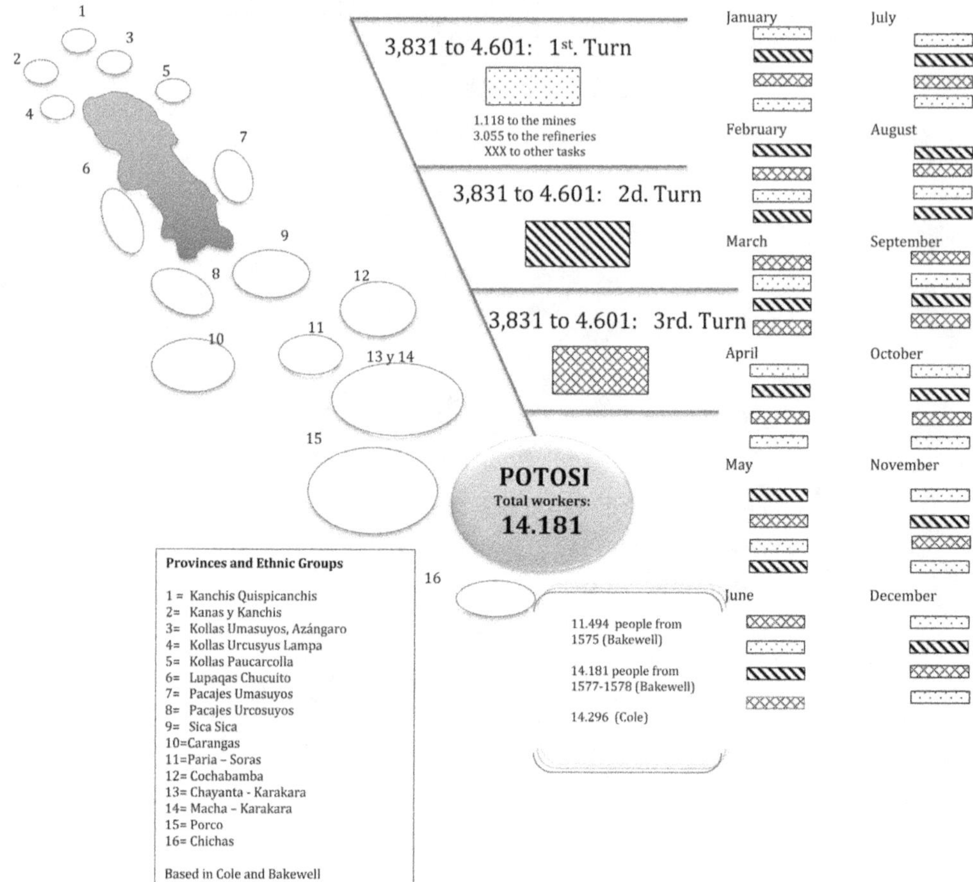

Figure 2.3. The vast region linked to Potosí through the mita. Scheme prepared by the author.

In the Quechua and Aymara languages, the term *mita* means "turn" or work by turn. This "turn" fell upon local communities yearly, and they struggled to fulfill the "delivery" of mita laborers to Potosí. Figure 2.2 shows what this rotation scheme looked like from the communities' perspective. The 263 households had to "deliver" 42 different mitayos every year (each shade of gray is a turn). Every mitayo had to go to Potosí every six years (in theory). Every point is a household.

Between twelve thousand and fourteen thousand male mitayos aged eighteen to fifty were recruited every year based on this system from hundreds of communities in sixteen provinces (fig. 2.3). Many trekked to Potosí with their families, and all told more than forty thousand people arrived in the mining city through the mita system.

The process of extracting and refining silver was very complex (fig. 2.4).[11] Raw ores passed through at least six stages of preparation, some underground and others above ground.[12] First came mining, or ore extraction, followed by selection or grading, milling, amalgamation, washing of mixed minerals, and finally, distillation.[13] All this work was done by Indian mitayos alongside hired workers or free workers called *mingas*. Many mingas were in fact "off-duty" mitayos.[14] After the first phase of extraction, the *ingenio* or millhouse became the key unit of production, giving rise to Potosí's substantial water-powered industrial complex or "industrial belt" (fig. 2.5).[15]

Silver production began to decline during the first decades of the seventeenth century due to demographic decline, but also as a result of incessant worker desertion. The number of mitayos fell from fourteen thousand in the late sixteenth century to no more than four thousand at the end of the seventeenth century. At the same time, a new practice was introduced whereby a proportion of the annual draft of workers was delivered in cash rather than in actual workers. By 1615, as many as 50 percent of mitayos commuted their obligation through cash payments.[16] The process was accelerated by the difference in wages promised mita workers versus hired workers. The latter garnered more (much more), and it was therefore more attractive for Indigenous people to go to Potosí as hired workers and "to pay their way out" of the mita requirement.

The mita crisis prodded royal authorities to tender solutions. In 1689, almost a hundred years after Viceroy Francisco de Toledo organized the mita system, another viceroy, the Duque de La Palata, proposed to increase the number of mitayos by extending the obligation to provinces that had been exempt since 1575. His attempt failed. Not only Indigenous peoples but also landowners and ecclesiastical authorities opposed the change; it challenged their own access to labor. In the end, the mita, although considerably diminished, continued until 1812.

By the mid-eighteenth century, after the Crown reduced severance taxes by half and guaranteed a more regular supply of mercury, Potosí silver production revived.[17] In addition, the Crown set up a bank to purchase silver and to assist producers with low-interest credit and select commodities.[18]

Amid these changes, a new group of actors appeared in the mines. Mineowners and royal authorities labeled them "silver thieves." These were the k'ajchas,[19] a term used to describe people (most of them Indigenous, although some were said to be mestizos and mulattos) who extracted ore from the mines for their

1. Waterwheel with a single milling assembly (*cabeza de ingenio*).
2. Storage rooms for copper, salt, dung, lime, and other materials.
3. Storage rooms for ore arriving from the mountain.
4. Llamas used to transport ore. Second door of the *ingenio*.
5. Shelter for the refiner doing assays for the amalgamation.
6. Small pools or ponds to wash the boxes to obtain the mixture of silver and mercury.
7. Wire screen to sieve the ore after crushing.
8. Mortar where the stamps crushed the ore.
9. Shelter.
10. Furnaces to prepare the ore called *negrillo*.
11. Chapel to celebrate mass.
12. Place where the Indians mix ore in boxes.
13. Place for drying wet ore (*pampear*).
14. Place where ore boxes are prepared.
15. *Buitron*, or place where the Indians remove and mix ore with mercury, using their feet (*repasiris*).
16. Main house of the owner.
17. Main door.
18. Warehouses for silver and mercury.

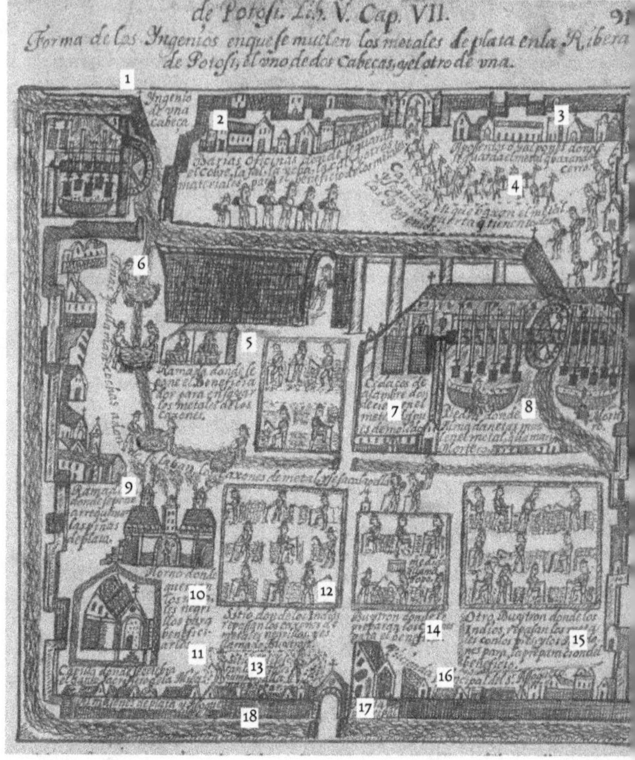

Figure 2.4. Ingenio operations according to Arzans Orsúa y Vela, Historia de la Villa Imperial de Potosí. Brown University Library Digital Repository, https://repository.library.brown.edu/studio/item/bdr:371585/, page-image 201.

own benefit on weekends. The k'acjchas worked underground, in close relationship with mitayos, extracting ore without owning mine concessions. They then refined silver in their own rudimentary mills, called *trapiches*. With the riots in 1751 and 1756, the k'ajchas succeeded in imposing themselves as key actors in Potosí.

Gauging the economic weight of k'ajchas and *trapicheros* (trapiche owners) amid Potosí's eighteenth-century revival changes our perspective on colonial labor and mine production. Scholars long claimed that Potosí's success relied primarily on the work of coerced laborers or mitayos and free hires or mingas. However, my research demonstrates that k'ajchas and trapicheros within the city, together with miners from outside the city, were responsible for fifty percent of all silver produced between 1751 and 1774. Although Potosí's outspoken *azogueros* (prominent mine and

Figure 2.5. The Potosí industrial belt. Figure based on the painting of Gaspar Miguel de Berrío, 1756, Museo Nacional de Charcas. Slow Landscapes, https://slowlandscapes.blogspot.com/2011/01/cerro-rico-potosi.html. CC BY-NC-ND 3.0 DEED.

mill owners) insisted on calling the k'ajchas and trapicheros thieves, it is worth noting that they were paying taxes. In that sense, the k'ajchas' silver production was neither illegal nor entirely informal; they were on the Crown's books.[20] This "extra" circuit of production and commercialization encompassed a broad arena of artisanal miners, small-scale refiners, and petty merchants. Women were quite active, representing 10 to almost 20 percent of all participants registered in local accounts. The same accounts show that women sold between 4 and 7 percent of all "trapiche" silver.

Potosí's k'ajchas and trapicheros together constituted a parallel sphere of silver production, a mining and refining world distinct from the "formal" one of contested mita allotments and big water-powered mills. This independent, popular economy and society operated beyond the reach of the traditional azogueros, who benefited from the support of the Spanish Crown. Workers' growing control of the production and processing of silver ore across the course of the eighteenth century helps explain why Potosí's labor system did not evolve into one characterized either by free wage labor or unfree labor. K'ajchas and trapicheros charted their own middle path.

I cannot conclude this brief description of colonial silver production of silver in Potosí without underscoring the dramatic environmental impacts caused by three hundred years of mining. First, the land was denuded by intensive consumption of native fuels: forests of polyepis or *queñual*, *icchu* or high-altitude bushy grass with leaves, and yareta or *azorella compacta*. Second came the consequences of daily mercury use, particularly after 1575. This poisonous refining solvent affected the whole population.[21] Third came changes in human settlement caused by mobility over vast regions. People migrated over vast distances to other communities or regions to escape the mita. Finally, the k'ajchas emerged in the late colonial period and continue their "informal" mine work today. In terms of public health, they had the disadvantage of being part of a more informal and therefore precarious economic circuit involving dangerous labor conditions. The number of k'ajchas varied over time, according to the rhythm and conditions of production, but they did not disappear and were present across the nineteenth and twentieth centuries.

AN ECONOMIC SUPERSTATE WITHIN A NATION-STATE: TRANSNATIONAL TO NATIONALIZED TIN MINING (1900–1952)

At the end of the colonial period and with the wars of independence that started in the first decades of the nineteenth century, mines throughout the newly created department of Potosí experienced a severe decline. The mining economy in post-independence Bolivia only regained momentum in the last decades of the nineteenth century. To seize the benefits of a new mining boom, local entrepreneurs struggled to shrink the role of the state in the economy, to lower taxes, and to implement a liberal policy.[22] In this context, the new commodity of tin became crucial for "warfare and welfare"[23] worldwide and made the "tinned" food industry possible. Sergio Almaraz famously wrote in 1967 that the twentieth century arrived riding on the shoulders of tin mining.[24] Well situated to support the emerging order, Bolivia became one of the world's main tin producers between 1895 and 1945.

To understand Bolivia's twentieth-century tin industry, one must bear in mind the following: (1) the geographical expansion of the industry, (2) the division between national extraction and international refining, and (3) the emergence of a waged labor force that coexisted with other types of laborers (k'ajchas, sharecroppers,

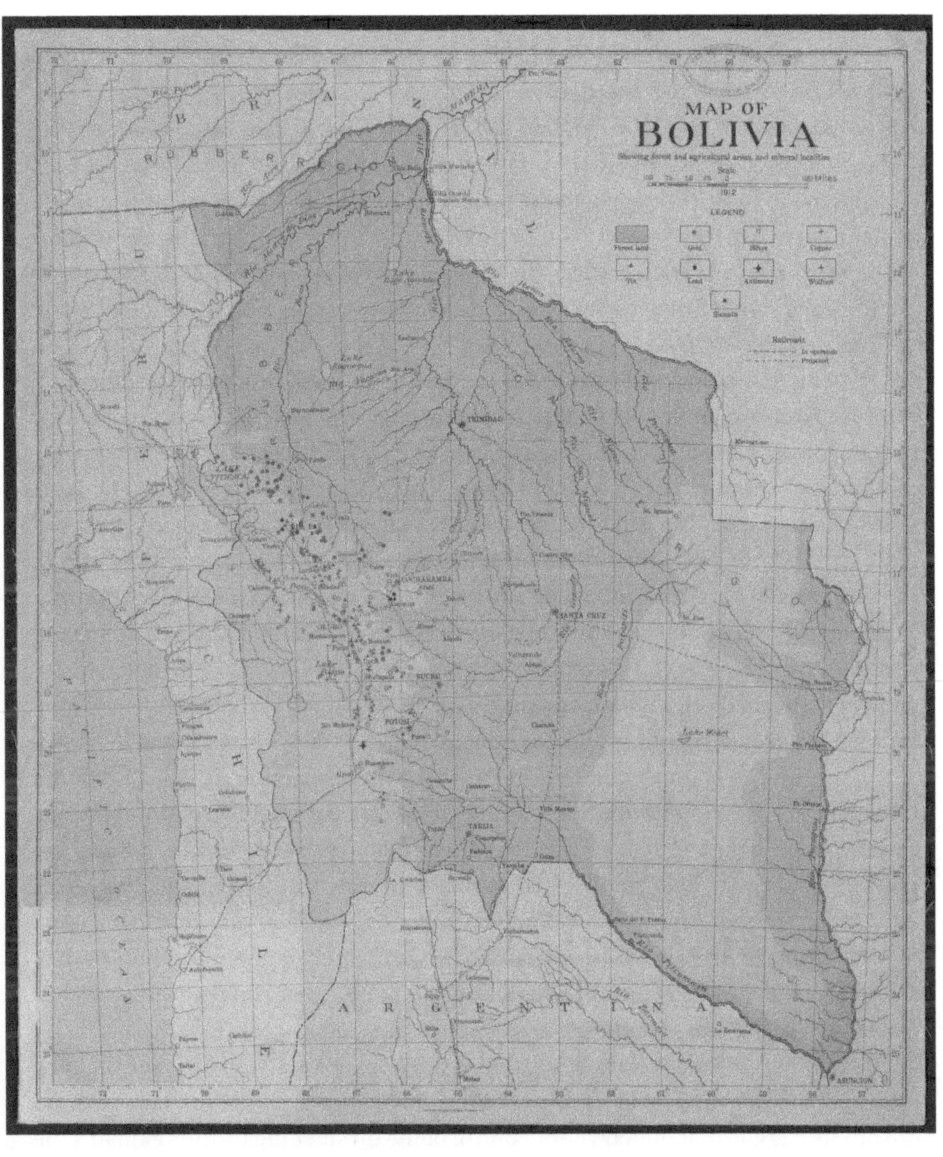

Map 2.1. Mining sites in Bolivia in 1912. Library of Congress.

and *contratistas*). One must also consider Bolivia's complex economic, social, and political situation in the two decades after 1930, a period marked by global economic depression and the Bolivian Paraguayan Chaco War (1932–1935) and its consequences. Depression-era and post-war uncertainties influenced the National Convention of 1938, during which the k'ajchas were finally recognized as legitimate actors rather than "ore thieves." All of these factors help to explain the importance of the few but important fortunes, the emergence of new entrepreneurs, and, above all, the tense dynamics between state and private actors that led to nationalization of Bolivia's mines in 1952.

The first point to emphasize is the proliferation of mining sites across the Bolivian Andes plus the sheer number of people involved. Tin vastly expanded greater Potosí's and neighboring departments' mineral frontiers (map 2.1). The iconic mountain of Potosí still had an important role to play in national production, yet it was only one among hundreds of Bolivia's newly booming mining centers. Between 1900 and 1910, tin production doubled from 9,740 to 22,885 fine metric tons, and in the next decade output increased by a further 30 percent. In terms of global supply, Bolivian tin production rose from 12 percent of the total in 1900 to 20 percent in 1910, and to 29 percent in 1929. In some years, tin constituted between sixty and seventy percent of the total value of Bolivia's exports. The number of workers employed quadrupled between 1900 and 1907, from 3,000 to 12,700. It then rose to 17,000 in 1925.[25]

Second, it is important to highlight that tin production in Bolivia differed from that of silver. In short, there was a clear segmentation and division between extraction and refining. Tin ore was crushed locally to produce metal-rich "concentrates," which were then transported from the mining camps by carts, llamas, or mules to the nearest railway track. Raw concentrates were then exported to the ports of Antofagasta or Arica in Chile, to be taken by sea to smelters, mainly in Europe. Key smelting centers were located in Britain, Germany, Belgium, and the Netherlands.[26] A technology gap was therefore already present and new access to railroads facilitated the export of tin concentrates. Bolivia's top mining entrepreneurs consolidated their control over the global supply chain by buying up overseas smelters with tin ore profits. I argue that mineowners' control of the tin smelting process explains the success of the two major "tin barons" of the early twentieth century: Simón Patiño in the northern region of Potosí Department and Moritz Hochschild in the city of Potosí.

Patiño and Hochschild were among Bolivia's top tin producers, together with the Compagnie Aramayo de Mines en Bolivie (funded with Bolivian capital), the Caracoles Tin Company of Bolivia (owned by the Guggenheims), the Compañía Minera y Agrícola Oploca de Bolivia (financed with Chilean capital), and the Empresa de Estaño Araca (financed by Bolivian, Chilean, and US capital) (table 2.2).[27]

TABLE 2.2. LARGE, MEDIUM, AND SMALL ENTERPRISES IN 1909, BY PRODUCTION IN TONS

ENTERPRISES	NUMBER	TONS PRODUCED	PERCENTAGE
Big (more than 1,000 tons)	8	22,779	74%
Medium (between 100 to 1,000 tons)	28	6,901	22%
Small (less than 100 tons	29	1,273	4%
Total	65	30,953	100%

Source: Mitre, *El enigma de los hornos*, 104.

Simón Patiño, a man of humble origins, built up a transnational company and eventually dominated the global tin industry. In doing so he became one of the few successful entrepreneurs in the world who came from a small, marginal, and nonindustrialized country like Bolivia. In fact, as a "cholo" (mestizo) of Indian origin, Patiño was considered a social climber and before he became a multimillionaire Bolivian local elites treated him with disdain. His extraordinary history echoes that of the American dream, for he sat behind a clerk's desk until 1895, when both Patiño's life and Bolivian history were changed by his extraordinary Salvadora Mine, which lay in the Llallagua Mountains in the northern region of Potosí.[28] By 1906, Patiño was able to establish his own bank (the Banco Mercantil) and acquire other mines.[29] He set up Patiño Mines Enterprises registered in Delaware, and by 1924 he controlled the William Harvey firm in Liverpool, Europe's largest tin smelter. Patiño later succeeded in acquiring a share in the National Lead Company of the United States, the world's second largest consumer of tin. His company became virtually global with interests in five countries spread over four continents.[30] Patiño became one of the world's wealthiest individuals.[31] In 1927, the *New York Times* identified Patiño, whose fortune was greater than those of the Rothschild and Guggenheim families combined, as one of the ten richest men in the world, alongside such noted figures as John David Rockefeller.[32]

Hochschild's trajectory was impressive too. He was from the rural middle class near Frankfurt, Germany, and his uncle, Zacharias Hochschild, was one of the founders of the important metal trading firm, Metallgesellschaft. Hochschild studied in Freiberg's well-known School of Mines in Saxony, earning a doctorate in mining engineering.[33] In South America, he took advantage of his role as middleman (between sellers in South America and buyers in Europe), beginning by buying copper in Chile. After World War I, Hochschild visited Bolivia. As tin prices were rising steadily between 1922 and 1927, he relocated to the traditional mining city of Potosí.

Potosí, legendary since colonial times, had no rail station until 1914. Until 1907, 60 percent of tin production came from one hundred small mines, all lacking capital and with "pre-industrial customs and habits." As described by one Irish missionary, all the mines made up a system something like a rabbit warren, and the smelters at the time worked with "stolen" minerals.[34] Although taxes were low at first,[35] access to scarce and expensive fuels was difficult; twenty-two thousand hundredweight of Andean woods, grasses, and matted plants were used per month, making up 70 percent of total mining costs.[36] This was just to prepare concentrates. The final smelting phase required reverberatory furnaces to be fed with fuels that did not then exist in Bolivia. It was easier and more convenient to export tin-rich concentrates produced by well-organized companies, small miners, and k'ajchas. Potosí's Cerro Rico ores had low tin content and high levels of impurities. They were easy to reach, but hard to sell.[37] In 1923, Hochschild succeeded in convincing a German tin smelter, the Berzelius Company, to take low-grade ore for volatilization. The same year, with capital of £25,000, Hochschild formed a company in Valparaíso, Chile's main port.[38]

Hochschild's next step was to assume the role of *rescatiri* (ore buyer) to acquire ore and concentrates, as the colonial Banco de Rescates/Banco de San Carlos and the Banco Minero had done in Potosí in the nineteenth century. These institutions provided valuable support not only as suppliers of money but also in sampling and weighing the mineral.[39] Hochschild became involved in production and expanded his business geographically. In 1929, just after the world economic crisis, he created the Compañía Unificada de Potosí by merging several enterprises.[40] He then invested over a million dollars in the Colquiri Mine, soon sporting a modern mill with its own hydroelectric plant.[41]

Meanwhile, Simón Patiño's tin mines, particularly the Siglo XX complex (Llallagua, Catavi, Uncía), created a permanent, proletarianized labor force that predominantly came from the region of Cochabamba, flush with cheap labor due to an agrarian crisis.[42] But the tin mines had difficulty attracting workers due to the availability of agricultural land plus demand for wageworkers both to build railroads and to exploit saltpeter in northern Chile.[43] Temporary and seasonal workers, child laborers (*chivatos*), and women acting as *palliris* selecting the ore were still very important. A kind of sharecropping system called *pirquiñeo* was also present, relying on informal agreements between mineowners and certain workers.[44] Finally, people known as contratistas (*obreros a destajo* or pieceworkers) proved essential. They represented 80 percent of workers running Patiño's Llallagua complex.[45]

It was in Llallagua that tin miners first struck in 1918, demanding wage increases and the reduction of work hours.[46] It was only a beginning, and the years from 1923 to 1927 proved particularly unsettled. For the first time in the twentieth century, there were public allegations of a "massacre" of workers. In the town of Uncía in 1923, four were killed and fourteen wounded when more than six thousand workers stood up to army troops.[47]

As the mining industry boomed, the Bolivian state searched for new rent streams. In the 1920s, Bolivian President Bautista Saavedra doubled taxes on exports and on profits.[48] He also introduced a new mine code and adopted a number of social measures for the benefit of the workers.[49] In this context, the big producers organized a united front in 1925 called the Association of Mining Industries (Asociación de Industriales Mineros), but their power against the state was waning.[50] The economic crisis of 1929–1930, the Chaco War of 1932–1935 between Bolivia and Paraguay, and the regimes that took power after the war all led to more state control of the mining industry.[51]

In the international realm, the crash of the New York Stock Exchange in 1929 led to the constitution of the International Tin Committee (ITC) which established quotas for the world's tin producers. The Chaco War limited the availability of workers because the Bolivian government obliged the male population to enlist as soldiers. Despite difficult conditions between 1930 and 1939, and due to investment in new machinery and tapping new sources of water, Hochschild's Empresa Minera Unificada de Potosí doubled its annual production of fine tin to 3,288 metric tons.[52] As a result, in 1938, 70 percent of the Cerro Rico belonged to Hochschild's Unificada, which now owned the lower part of the hill, considered its best part. The public fear, as noted in the socialist-leaning newspaper *La Calle*, was that the whole mountain and even the city itself would become La Unificada's mining camp.[53]

In the late 1930s, constant references in nationalist and leftists newspapers to the state as the ultimate sovereign authority over mines[54] were wielded as threats to the mining companies, reminding them that they could be "socialized."[55] Hochschild countered these claims, asserting that Bolivia had some of the highest production costs in the world, employing around twenty-five thousand to thirty thousand workers who earned more than four shillings a day. He argued he had also granted workers housing facilities, schools, free hospitals, and cheap grocery stores while the vast majority of the Bolivian population had no such things. Finally, he denounced government hostility against the biggest mineowners.[56]

It was also in this period of the tin industry that Bolivian legislators debated the legal situation of the k'ajchas. In 1937, authorities of the Ministry of Labor redefined the role of the k'ajchas of Potosí. Rather than as thieves, the head of the Labor Department categorized them as workers because they were doing jobs for the mining companies and for the benefit of their owners. However, the government noted that the k'ajchas were not wageworkers,[57] nor were they owners or concessionaires of the mines. In fact, k'ajchas' situations varied. There were some who worked alone, at their own risk with their own tools, while others worked in association with two or more people under the supervision of the mine steward, selling recovered ore to the owner. There were even some, termed "contractors," who employed other workers.

This explains why legislators considered k'ajchas as both pieceworkers and contractors when the labor code was hammered out.[58] The k'ajchas of this period thus occupied different positions in comparison to the k'ajchas of the eighteenth century. In any case, the minister of mines and the minister of commerce and industryy were both willing to support the k'ajchas. For them it was "a duty of social assistance," a plank of the official policy to take care of mine workers because, they argued, "the wealth of Potosí should not be subordinated to personal benefits but to social needs," and the state should have control over resources.[59]

It was against this background that the National Convention of 1938 announced various measures, most significantly, new economic and political plans for the future of the mines. One proposal was to lease the state's mines to the k'ajchas for fifty years.[60] For the first time, formal legal recognition of the k'ajchas' situation might put an end to their status as "thieves" in the eyes of the law. However, the project raised questions. For instance, Congressman Ayala Gamboa asked: "Was the state about to give the mines to 'a socialist cell of workers' with probable negative results for the economy?"[61] For some observers, the exploitation of Bolivia's mineral wealth had to be done "scientifically," not as part of the k'ajchas' famously informal or "artisanal" operations.[62]

The k'ajchas appeared to work in primitive and nonindustrial conditions and were treated worse than the lowest laborers (*peones*). They received less than two-and-a-half Bolivianos ($b2.40) a day when working for hire, while peones earned between eight and ten Bolivianos. Lacking both tools and capital, the k'ajchas were deemed outside the "spirit of large-scale industrial organization." They could not therefore have formed any enterprise able to decrease the costs of tin production, for that would have required significant capital investment.[63] Other participants at the convention emphasized the nature of the k'ajchas' independent and dependent relationships. They were considered petty bosses (something like today's independent contractors) because they had neither fixed working days nor working hours and were often dependent on other laborers who had no social insurance. At the same time, they had to sell their ore to mineowners.

Between 1939 and 1944, the k'ajchas organized into unions and into mining cooperatives, marking a new era for them.[64] In 1940, they published their union bylaws of the *Sindicato of Ckacchas Libres y Palliras de Potosí*, based on their 1939 agreement with the state.[65]

The 1938 convention also led to laws strengthening the role of the state over Bolivia's big tin companies through the Central Bank and the Banco Minero. The Central Bank would receive (Law of June 7, 1939) income from all exports of commodities, instituting a sliding scale for the payment of taxes on the mining companies' utilities (Arts. 14 and 16). The Banco Minero had control over purchases and sales of all ore produced by the mines, replacing Philipp brothers, Duncan and Fox, and Hochschild as intermediaries.[66] Any opposition to the new rules was considered treason, to the extent that Moritz Hochschild was sentenced to death for opposing them, although he was eventually released.[67]

Along with often tense relations between the companies and the executive branch, Bolivia's mineowners had to contend with increasing unionization. Potosí's conservative articles in newspaper *Alas* claimed that these organizations "emerged overnight by decree," converting them into "dissolving political centers." Reproving the strikers, the newspaper asserted that if it was unjust that "the employer coerces with the force of capital," then it was also unjust that the workforce, "with the force of numbers, coerces and crushes the employer."[68]

In 1939, the First Mining Congress took place in Oruro, promoted by the Confederation of Bolivian Workers (CTB). A few years later, in 1942, and as a result of an escalating conflict, the army took part in what is known as the Catavi Massacre. Unofficial estimates suggest one hundred deaths, among them that of María Barzola, the mother of one of the workers, who after her death became an enduring symbol of mine workers' rights.[69] In 1944, in part spurred by the massacre, the Syndicated Federation of Bolivian Mineworkers or Federación Sindical de Trabajadores Mineros de Bolivia (FSTMB) was founded.

World War II further altered both local and global landscapes with regard to tin and other strategic minerals. With European markets closed, the US-based American Smelting and Refining Company (ASARCO) was now the destination for tin exports from Bolivia.[70] However, in one year alone, production costs rose by 20 percent while prices fell.[71] After World War II, sponsored social measures and worker demands resurged.

The startling personal histories of Simón Patiño and Moritz Hochschild, which contrasted so sharply with the poverty of the majority of Bolivians, contributed to the idea that the mining oligarchy was the cause of the nation's misery, degradation, and backwardness.[72] Politicians painted the wealthy and powerful tin barons as the enemies. Enemies or not, the Bolivian government was so dependent fiscally on tin that it could barely assert itself against this small group of ultra-rich and powerful men. The tin barons—Patiño, Hoschshild, along with Carlos Víctor Aramayo—were seen by the press, by Bolivia's outspoken intellectuals, and by large part of the population as a mining "superstate," while the republican "substate" was obliged to serve their mining overlords from "the domesticated positions of the state bureaucracy."[73] Talk of revolution was in the air, soon to be realized.

After the National Revolution of April 9, 1952, President Víctor Paz Estenssoro nationalized the three largest mining companies. As of October 31, 1952, mines, refineries, and other company capital belonging to Patiño, Aramayo, and Hochschild were state property. In his speech, Paz Estenssoro claimed that despite being a mining country, most Bolivians had been unable to take advantage of the wealth extracted from its subsoil. Paz Estenssoro stated that Bolivia after the colonial period was subject to semicolonial exploitation at the hands of the three tin barons, whom he accused of making all Bolivia their "mining town." By this logic, the decision to nationalize all mineral resources was a "reversion to the state" of all private mining concessions. It would include all machinery and equipment, electrical installations, mills, technological studies, archives, and so on. The decree appraised the value of each company. Burke, who has studied nationalization most closely, claims that the 163 confiscated mining properties with all their equipment were worth 34.5 million USD.[74] In fact, the amounts established in the decree (fig. 2.9) were nominal and the numbers were not precise.[75] Hochschild found the situation outrageous and the government deceptive. His 1952 administrative council report claimed that the Bolivian government had frozen company accounts some months before October 1952.[76]

Be that as it may, nationalizing Bolivia's mines was not an overnight decision. Since the 1920s, the national government sought to strengthen its position vis-à-vis the industry by raising and imposing new taxes.[77] Tensions rose, and the state's attempt to control big mining enterprise created an adverse atmosphere, particularly after the Chaco War in 1935.

Burke asserted that, for various reasons, nationalization was not the panacea envisioned by its staunchest supporters. For once, ore grades deteriorated while the ore itself became more and more inaccessible, driving up production costs after World War II. From 1932 to 1951, there was no significant investment in Bolivian mining and by around 1940, several mines were greatly depleted or had been exhausted. Most were decapitalized and struggling with labor conflict.[78]

After the nationalization of the mines, tin production decreased and the numbers of employees working for the Bolivian Mining Company (COMIBOL) rose. In 1953, Bolivia produced 25,034 metric tons of tin, declining to 14,829 tons in 1961.[79] By contrast, the number of COMIBOL employees grew from 28,973 in 1952 to 32,558 in 1956,[80] with higher wages, greater social benefits, and the subsequent decapitalization of the company.[81] Other similar estimates show mine worker numbers rising from about 24,000 in 1951 to 36,500 in 1955, suggesting an early, postrevolution expansion.[82]

An important but much less well-known fact is that the mines run by the Trade Union of Ckacchas (that appeared under the name of Libres y Palliris de la ciudad de Potosí in 1945) did well[83] and the possibility for similar concessions to other k'ajchas opened. In 1952, the Ckacchas received two abandoned mines for ten years. The government concession to this union was significant because it implied that, for the first time since the eighteenth century, these independent workers were recognized by the state as actors worthy of mining concessions.[84]

LARGE-SCALE REDUNDANCY, THE PEAK OF COOPERATIVES, AND THEIR COEXISTENCE WITH TRANSNATIONAL COMPANIES (1985–2019)

The Bolivian state of 1952 divided concessions inside Potosí's Cerro Rico between the national enterprise (Corporación Minera Boliviana, COMIBOL) and groups of independent workers organized into cooperatives.[85] After this, the Cerro Rico and Bolivia produced significant amounts of tin until the international crash of 1985, when prices dropped from £10,000 to £3,400 per ton.[86] A pound of tin, previously worth 10 USD, was now selling for 2.50 USD.[87] President Paz Estenssoro, now in his fourth period of rule (1985–1989), declared more than twenty-three thousand COMIBOL workers "redundant" as part of his neoliberal restructuring. Fired miners weighed their options, but many remained in the extractive sector. For a long period after the crash, Bolivian mining companies shrank while cooperatives and their members ballooned. Some old mine workers stayed in Potosí, exploiting the former COMIBOL mines on their own account. When mineral prices were low, they "scratched the rocks" of state concessions that had been left dismantled. At that time, a member of a cooperative would be lucky to earn a monthly income of 233 Bolivianos, while the official minimum monthly wage was 400 Bolivianos.[88]

How then did the state company (COMIBOL), the cooperatives, and other new players learn to coexist in an era of fluctuating but often low commodity prices? I will refer first to the cooperatives, their evolution particularly after the 1980s, and their main features in terms of work organization and production. Second, I will analyze how the Coeur d'Alene Mines Corporation (in its day the largest US-based silver producer) with its subsidiary companies in Potosí (Manquiri-San Bartolomé Project) received concessions from the state company, COMIBOL, and how it worked in the city and mountain of Potosí. Hard times made for strange bedfellows, and it was in this setting that the cooperatives became one of the transnational corporation's main suppliers of raw minerals.

Mining cooperatives are part of Bolivia's ample artisanal and small-scale mining sector. All are characterized as informal, labor intensive, minimally mechanized, and low technology.[89] After 1973, the number of people working in the Bolivian cooperatives grew from just 20,000 to 50,000 by the early 1990s,[90] and to something like 130,000 in 2018.[91] In 2007, 81 percent (46,700 workers) of the total labor force in the mining sector was registered with the cooperatives.[92] This was a tremendous turnaround from the glory days of COMIBOL.

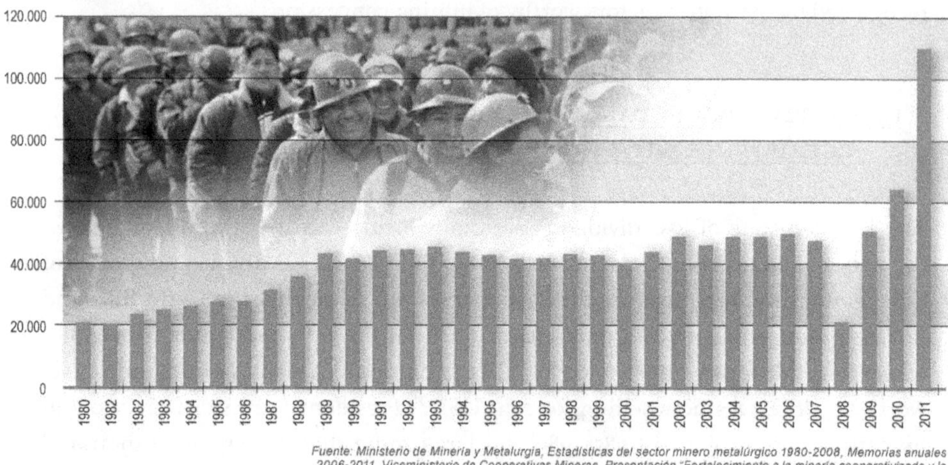

Figure 2.6. Number of workers in the mining cooperatives, 1980–2011. Francescone and Diez, "Entre socios, patrones y peones," published and authorized by CEDIB.

The number of registered mining cooperatives increased from 707 in 2000 to 2,388 in 2021 and the trend is expected to continue.[93]

Until 1991, cooperativists sold their minerals to the state-owned monopoly holder, Banco Minero (Banmin), but after it closed, several private companies took over this purchasing function. Every work-gang within the cooperatives was free to sell ore to any trader that offered the minerals to the global market. Tin had faded, so production became more diversified, forcing mine workers to look for zinc, lead, and silver ores.

In the decades since their formation in the mid-1980s, marked hierarchies within the cooperatives have become visible. Full members or associates (*socios*) and ordinary workers have different statuses within each cooperative. This means not all members have full rights. Some are recognized as bosses (*patrones*) and others as laborers (peones). In 2001, of the more than one hundred mining cooperatives in Bolivia with over 60,000 members, about 7,500 of those members were women. Scholars estimate that around 120,000 children under the age of eighteen work in small-scale mining activities, earning less than the minimum wage. Women's work consists mainly of selecting and gathering material discarded from the mines or concentration plants, then washing the material to extract small quantities of metal, principally tin. They also select and salvage material from dredge tailings. Many palliris, past and present, have been miners' widows.[94]

In Potosí in recent decades, approximately 80 percent of the workforce has served as laborers (peones) of the cooperatives. On average, these eighteen thousand–odd workers earn around 1,500 Bolivianos per month (about 200 USD).[95] In 2008, one of the most important cooperatives in Potosí, the Cooperative Unificada, formerly owned by Moritz Hochschild, counted five thousand full members or partners (socios) who contributed a percentage of their production to the cooperative, and fifteen thousand laborers (peones and *segundas manos*). Partners income ranged from 4,000 to 20,000 Bolivianos. Some laborers with a contract and fixed remuneration earned 240 Bolivianos (around 34 USD) for two "mitas" of four hours each (for a total of eight hours), while other laborers earned 50 to 80 Bolivianos (roughly 7 to 11 USD) per mita, as day-rate work. There were also women guards ("*serenas*") living in huts outside the mines earning less than 400 Bolivianos (about 57 USD) per month. Yet another group of workers were the "second hands" (segundas manos), with a status in between dayworkers and members. Sharecropping arrangements were also present, allowing laborers to work by themselves in the mine concessions of the cooperatives in exchange for sharing output. A typical agreement allotted 60 percent for the laborers and 40 percent for the partners or legal concessionaries of the mines under the cooperative system.[96] Each of these arrangements placed more of the many burdens of mining, its risks and uncertainties, on the shoulders of uncapitalized, uninsured, freelance workers, be they women, children, or men.

The work of extraction was almost always done by hand, using simple hammers and chisels. Next up were power drills that cost between 700 and 1,000 USD each. Only cooperatives could afford these. Diesel or electrically powered compressors for air drills raised those costs to around 50,000 USD, far out of any ordinary miner's price range. COMIBOL often owns these compressors, along with water pumps, winches, and mining cages, which are then leased to the cooperatives. As noted in the epigraph to this chapter, to move the ore, each worker carried forty to sixty kilograms on his back, walking for approximately forty-five minutes through narrow tunnels and treacherous galleries. Sometimes, workers rent small mining trolleys to carry the ore.[97] Some still crush the ore using the traditional crescent-shaped *quimbalete* or rocker mill. This was done immediately after the concentration process which separated the valuable minerals from other raw materials through gravity concentration, done in an artisanal manner, or with the use of flotation chemicals. These crushing and preliminary refining processes take place in plants or ingenios, many of which are owned by COMIBOL and again, like the tools, are leased to the cooperative.[98]

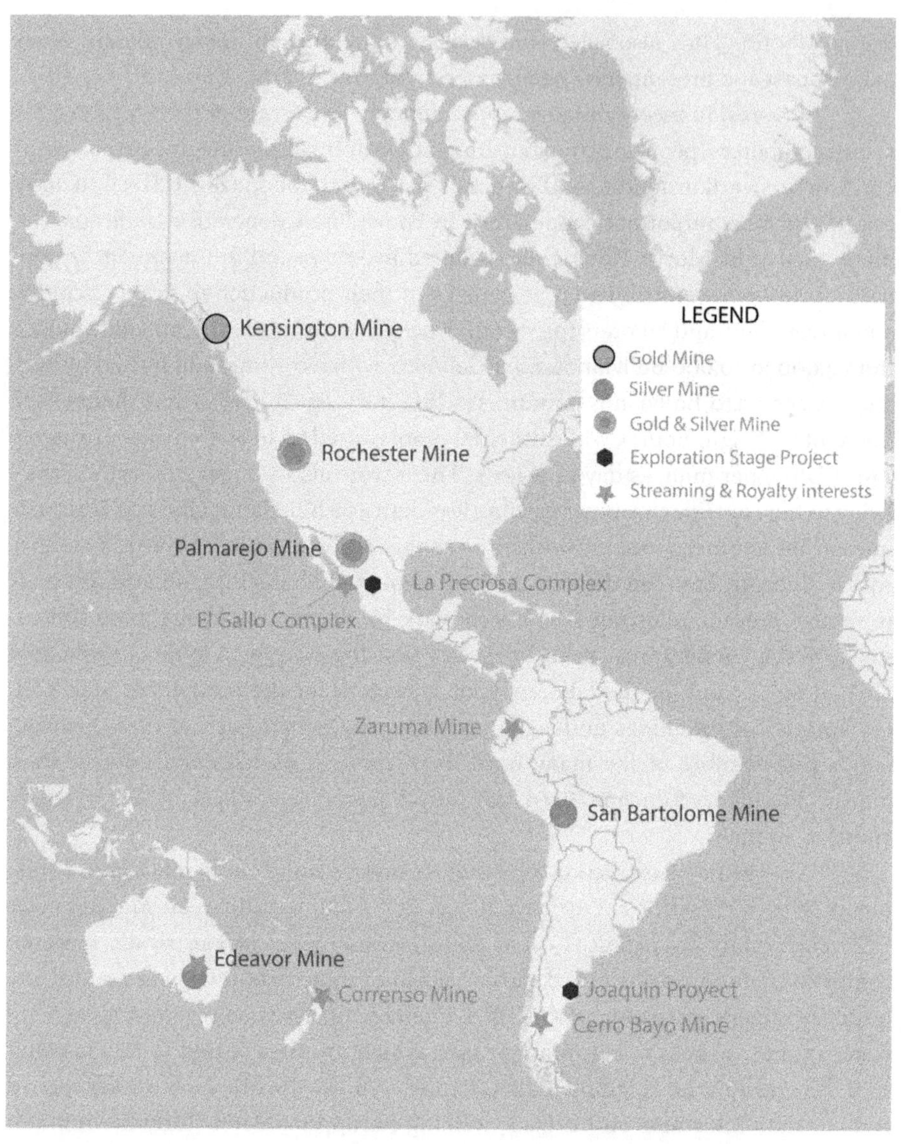

Figure 2.7. The Coeur d'Alene Mines Corporation. Scheme drawn by Giovana N. Rodríguez, Coeur Mining, *2014 Annual Report*, 21.

This type of mining, based primarily on labor-intensive practices and limited access to technology, explains the low productivity of the cooperatives. The most productive cooperative could only produce three hundred tons of ore a month, whereas well-equipped plants with modern machinery can produce more than eight thousand tons a day.[99] One may be surprised to find, then, that these cooperatives have coexisted for decades side by side and in close association with a transnational mining company. Founded in 2005, the Manquiri-San Bartolomé Enterprise was part of the Coeur d'Alene Mines Corporation,[100] active throughout the first Evo Morales government (2006–2009). Many cooperativists have sold the minerals they extracted to Manquiri (fig. 2.7).

The Manquiri-San Bartolomé concession has its own history. It initially covered 4,792 hectares, of which 3,450 hectares were leased directly from the Bolivian government and another 1,263 hectares were obtained via subleases from the cooperatives under the rubric of "joint ventures with cooperatives" (table 2.3 and fig. 2.8).[101] The company purchased another 830 hectares belonging to local families.[102]

Table 2.3. Mining rights in hectares of the Coeur d'Alene Company in 2013

MINING RIGHTS	HECTARES
Joint venture contracts with cooperatives	1,263.1
Pallaco (gravels with silver) extensions leased from COMIBOL	79.5
Concessions held directly by Manquiri at San Bartolomé: Eduardo Avaroa, Eduardo Avaroa I, II y III; Simon Bolivar, Simon Bolivar I, Promesa, Puchay, Momotani mayu, Atlántida y II y III.	3,450.0
Total	4,792.6
Surface rights from local ayllus or communities for plant and tailings site	400.0
Other surface rights	430.0
Total	830.0

Source: Coeur d'Alene Mines, San Bartolomé Technical Report, January 1, 2013, 16.

Additionally, and very importantly, the company succeeded in gaining possession of lands belonging to the local Indigenous community (ayllu) under a special provision known as "negotiated expropriation." The idea was that the land would be returned to the local community at the conclusion of the project.[103] Some of the community's surface rights were deemed "extraordinary," creating arrangements that were technically outside national rules. Similar situations occurred after UNESCO's declaration of Potosí as a world heritage site on October 14, 2009.

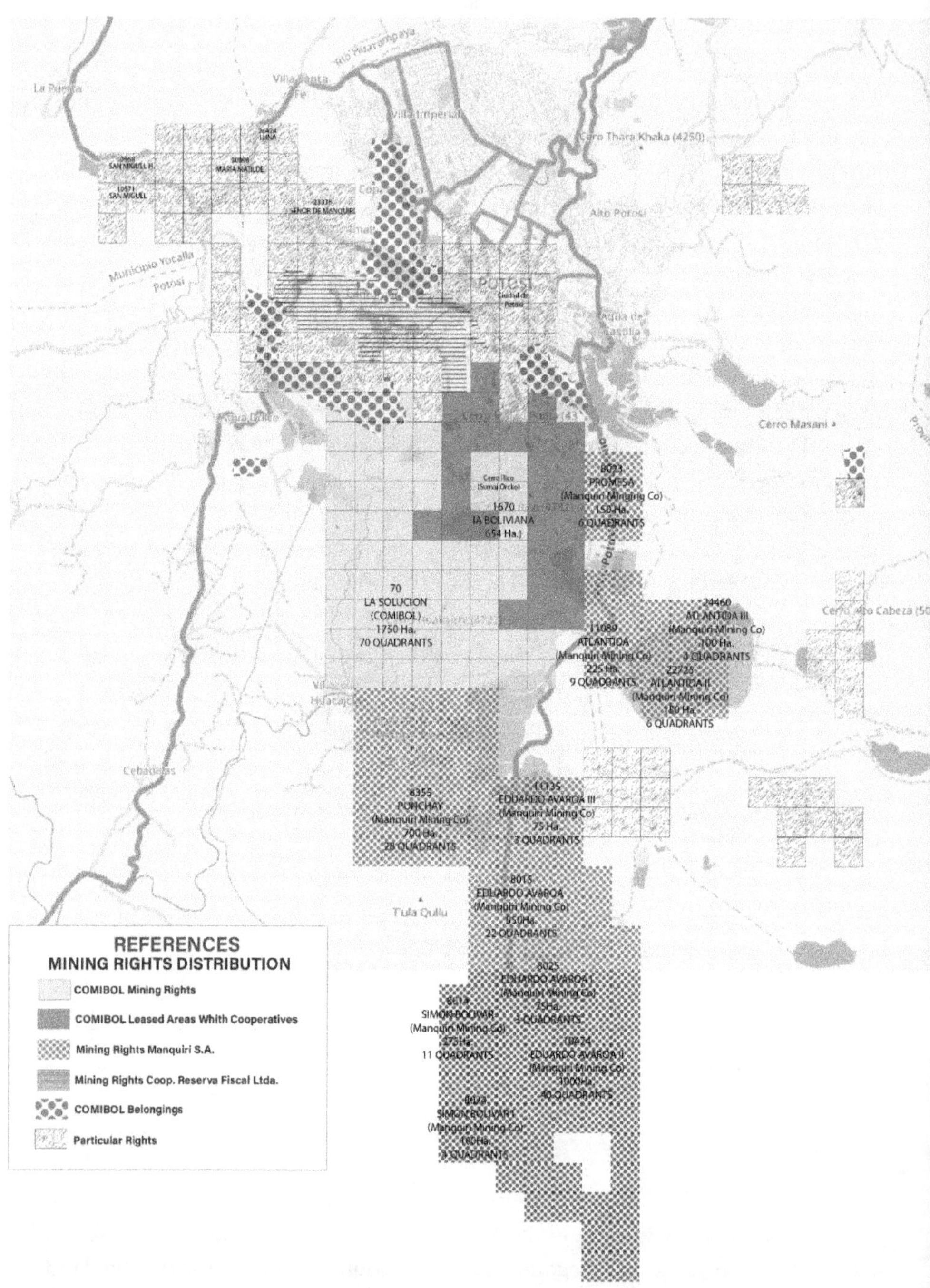

Figure 2.8. The mining rights of Manquiri-San Bartolomé Enterprises. Scheme drawn by Giovana N. Rodríguez, Coeur d'Alene Mines, *San Bartolomé Technical Report*, 2013, 18.

COMIBOL consequently announced the suspension of mining activities on the Cerro Rico above 4,400 meters (the mountain tops out at 4,782 m). Coeur d'Alene Mines contested this decree, stating that it held mining rights above that elevation under valid contracts backed by a contract with COMIBOL as well as contracts with local mining cooperatives holding rights through COMIBOL. Coeur d'Alene "temporarily adjusted its mining plan," but notified COMIBOL of "the need to lift the restriction." Accordingly, in March 2010, the San Bartolomé mine began working again above 4,400 meters.[104]

Clearly, a modus vivendi was established between COMIBOL, the state company with the legal lease on the mines, the Manquiri Firm (San Bartolomé Project), and the cooperatives of small-scale and artisanal miners (ASM) who are in a sense the offspring of the k'ajchas, or the contemporary version of them (fig. 2.9).

Mining by multiple forms of subcontracting within the Cerro Rico were not the only story, of course. Manquiri-San Bartolomé also used multiple opencast mining methods and hydraulic excavators. The company's mines yielded an average of 2.6 million metric tons of ore per year, of which its mills processed an average of 1.5 million metric tons. Silver was leached using a solution of sodium cyanide (NaCN), and the main plant was designed to recover approximately 78 percent of the ore's silver content.[105]

The company also bought ore from the cooperatives. The 2014 report to shareholders asserted that the company milled 1,749,423 tons of ore at a price of 2.00 USD per ton (table 2.4) for a total of 3,498,846 USD. The cost of milling thus represented only 4 percent of the total of 89,413,639 USD obtained from the sale of silver (table 2.5).

Table 2.4. The ore milled and the silver produced by San Bartolomé, 2012–2014

	2004	2013	2012
Ore tons milled	1,749,423	1,679,839	1,477,271
Ore grade silver (oz./ton)	3.80	3.93	4.49
Recovery/Ag oz. (%)	88.1	90.0	89.5
Silver produced (oz.)	5,851,678	5,940,538	5,930,394
Costs applicable to sales/oz. (1)	$14.29	$14.28	$12.40

Source: Coeur Mining, 2014 Annual Report, 27.

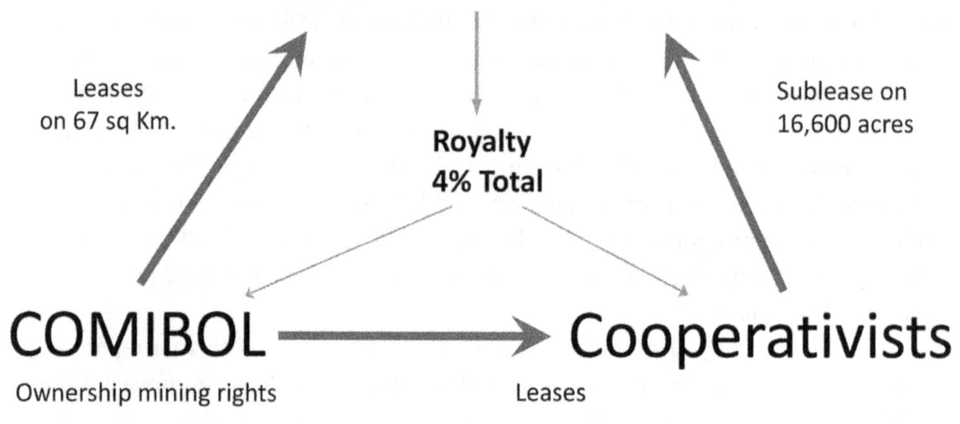

Figure 2.9. Potosí accords between private firms, the Bolivian state company, and cooperatives. Scheme drawn by Giovana N. Rodríguez, Coeur d'Alene Mines, *San Bartolomé Update and Overview*.

Table 2.5. Value of the total milled, produced, and paid to the cooperatives

1 ton	35,274 ounces = 2 USD given to the coop. per ton
1,749,423 tons of ore milled	61,709,146,902 ounces
Amount paid to the cooperatives: 2 USD per ton x 1,749,423 tons	3,498,846 USD
Silver produced	5,851,678 ounces of silver produced (or 165 tons) * 15.28 USD/ounce (lower price) =
	89,413,639.84 USD

Source: Author's calculations based on Coeur Mining, 2014 Annual Report, 27.

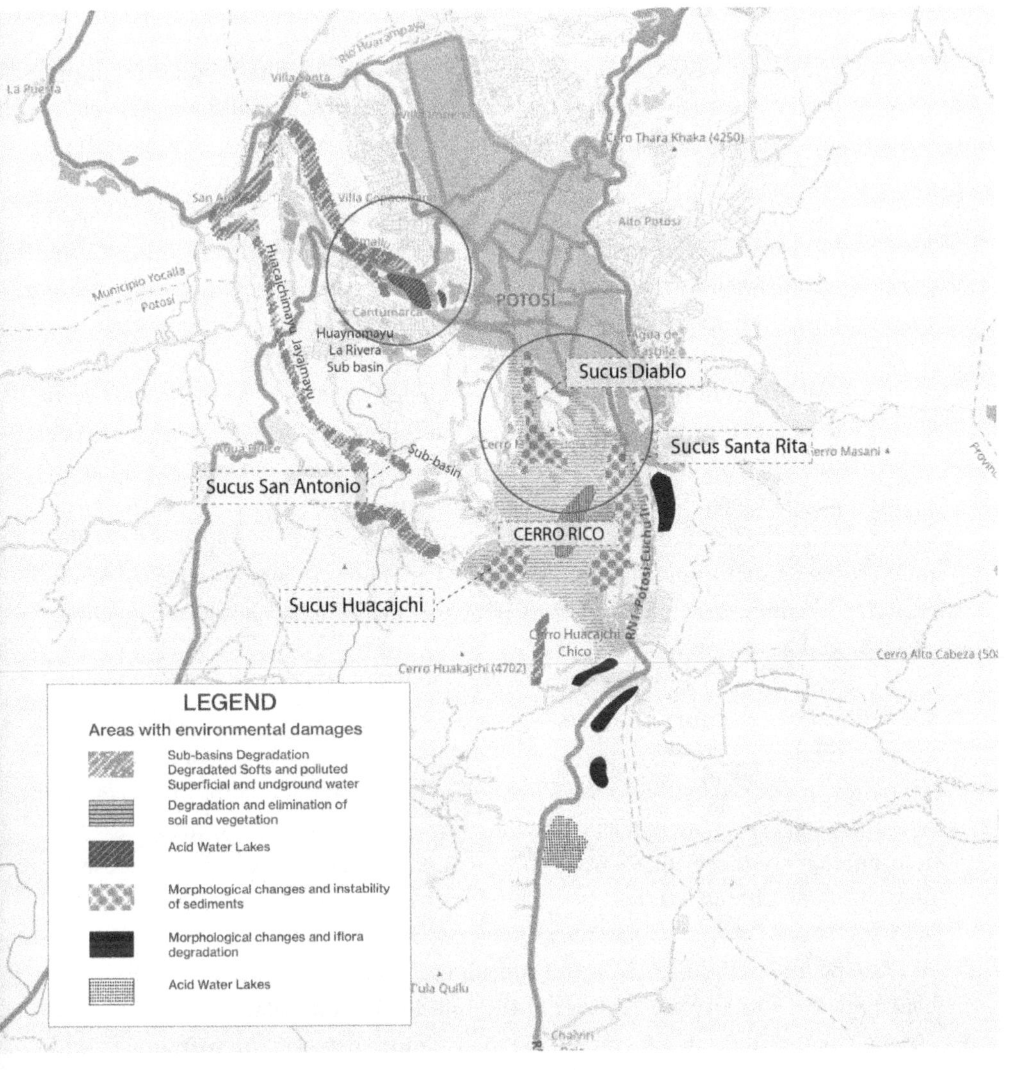

Figure 2.10. Environmental damage in Potosí. Scheme drawn by Giovana N. Rodríguez, *Technical Report for the San Bartolomé Mine, Potosí, Bolivia*, 2015, 139.

It is important to mention that of the 61,709,146,902 ounces milled, only 5,851,678 ounces of silver (amounting to 165 tons) were obtained, indicating more than 99 percent wastage. There is therefore great environmental damage, even in years of lower output and higher costs. The company's own reports (fig. 2.10) show the areas of degradation and elimination of soil and vegetation and polluted water.

In 2014, Coeur d'Alene Mines recognized that environmental impacts could lead to the suspension of operations.[106] In fact, the top of the world-famous Cerro Rico collapsed several times during the last few decades.[107] In any case, after more than ten years in Potosí, the firm was sold to an outfit called Argentum Investments in January 2018.

Evaluations of the "small-scale and cooperative miners" working the Cerro Rico asserted that they extracted around a thousand tons of lead-silver-zinc ore per day, of which nearly 200 tons of usable metal were recovered in thirty-five flotation plants around the city. The remaining 800 tons were discarded as tailings. The waste material from the flotation plants contained not only sulfur-rich solids, but also flotation reagents such as cyanide, and significant quantities of dissolved heavy metals (zinc, lead, cadmium, copper, and iron) that have been contaminating the Pilcomayo River Basin for many years.[108]

Beyond Potosí, mining cooperatives in Bolivia had a tense relationship with the national government regarding concessions and taxes. This was particularly acute in 2015, when some Potosí cooperatives complained that the benefits of the "process of change" promised by the ruling party had not reached the region, which continued to be "looted" as "an exporting region of raw materials with low incomes."[109] In 2016, another conflict erupted, with violent consequences. Cooperativists opposed a new law that included the right to form unions within cooperatives. After the police arrested 113 miners, their comrades seized forty-six policemen and more than twenty-seven people were injured. One of the miners, Rubén Aparaya Pillco, died in the confrontation and Deputy Minister of the Interior Rodolfo Illanes was murdered. His violent and tragic death marked the final rupture between the government and the cooperatives. Evo Morales, and later, Luis Arce, who won the presidency in 2020, frequently heard the cooperatives' demands, backed by their impressive numbers across the whole country. Indeed, Bolivia's cooperativist miners have remained capable of paralyzing the political capital as a demonstration of their strength, forcing all governments to compromise. In some periods the miners have moved closer to state positions and executive figures and in others further away, but neither side can disregard the other.

A NEW MINING FRONTIER FOR CLEANER ENERGY WITH DEVASTATING LOCAL CONSEQUENCES: A LITHIUM "EL DORADO"

The search for alternative sources of energy has made lithium the "white gold" of the future. The new rise of electrically powered vehicles and the requirement for batteries for mobile phones, laptops, and digital cameras is an expanding market.[110] Global demand for EVs (all-electric vehicles) is especially important and growing, likely to suck up all the lithium compounds miners can produce. The price per ton of lithium carbonate rose from 350 USD in 2003 to 3,000 USD by 2009, and it was thought that by 2050 it could rise to as much as 7,000 USD.[111] However, the price hit an all-time high of 74,475 USD per ton in 2022 when it was just 6,000 USD in 2020.[112]

Together with Chile and Argentina, Bolivia forms part of South America's "lithium triangle," a desert region said to hold more than 75 percent of the world's supply beneath high-altitude salt flats. Bolivia's vast *salar* in the department of Potosí lies at an average 3,653 meters above sea level and covers 10,000 square kilometers. The Salar de Uyuni is not only one of the most striking such landscapes but it also covers the most important lithium reserves, estimated at some twenty-one million tons.[113]

Evo Morales's long presidency (2006–2019) coincided with the growing urgency of the world economy to find alternative energy sources to offset fossil fuels and the auspicious role that lithium could play in this economy. This seemed to place Bolivia, and the department of Potosí, in an advantageous position. For the first time, after almost five hundred years of mining, Potosí could consolidate an industrialized economy instead of continuing with the policy of plunder and extractivism that had characterized its history. A promising new era and Pachakuti seemed to emerge. This section examines the national policy of industrialization, the resort to foreign companies, and the global lithium chain. I contend that Bolivian policy did not address a complex problem: the magnitude of multiple technological gaps and the speed of changes and decisions in the global world of lithium production and marketing. I argue also that there are scarce results after ten years on the road to industrialization.

Evo Morales promised to make lithium an "industrial project" owned and handled 100 percent by the state and funded with Bolivian capital.[114] In 2008, the government created the Gerencia Nacional de Recursos Evaporíticos (GNRE). In 2017, this public enterprise took the name Yacimientos Litíferos Bolivianos (YLB). According to the Morales administration, detailed in the National Development Plan 2006–2011 (Plan Nacional de Desarrollo, PND, Bolivia Digna, Soberana, Productiva y Democrática para Vivir Bien), the goal was to change the pattern of primary exports

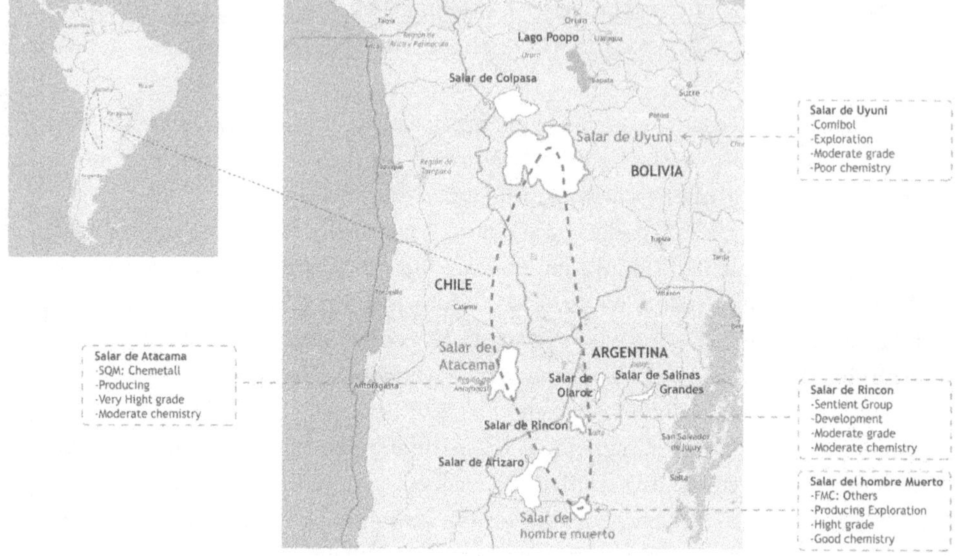

Figure 2.11. South America's lithium triangle. Scheme drawn by Giovana N. Rodríguez.

and to dismantle colonialism through industrialization by increasing added value to Bolivia's exports.[115] Vice President García Linera stated that the government was going to lift the natural resource curse by converting lithium into a blessing. President Morales, even more enthusiastic, asserted that Bolivia's role in the lithium economy was going to be so crucial that the country would end up setting the world price for batteries.[116]

The government developed a "three-phase strategy." According to this plan, international companies would only participate during the final phases. The government anticipated that the first pilot phase would take place between 2012 and 2015. The second phase, consisting of the production of lithium carbonate and potassium chloride, would culminate between 2016 and 2018. Finally, production of lithium batteries would emerge in the third phase (2019–2020).[117]

How, then, is lithium mined from salt flats? Traditional processing involves pumping brine deposits from deep saline groundwater into an extensive array of evaporation ponds where the lithium compounds (and often potassium as a byproduct) are concentrated by evaporation. In the Bolivian salares, there is a high concentration of magnesium and other minerals that must be precipitated out with lime, leaving tons of waste.[118] There remain a complex series of impurity removal steps to produce a lithium salt (e.g., hydroxide, carbonate) that is not of battery-grade purity—because this requires additional purification steps. Building and operating the ponds is a capital-intensive process, and solar evaporation can take up to two years, depending on precipitation, sunlight hours, humidity, and other factors, with high lithium losses of up to fifty per cent.

In recent years, professionals from a variety of fields have raised concerns about the environmental impact of lithium mining. Hollender and Shultz denounce "escape of . . . chemicals via leaching, spills, or air emissions" as a "danger that threatens the communities and the ecosystem as a whole;"[119] ecological problems in the poor and ecologically vulnerable region where the deposits lie;[120] and intensive use of water and chemicals that could be devastating for the whole region. In Chile, around 2.2 million liters of water is needed for one ton of lithium salt and 21 million liters are evaporated per day in the current ponds.[121] This is why the exploitation of lithium is considered a water mining.

The Bolivian government built some pilot plants in 2010. Yet, despite initial government efforts, the administration recognized the need to import a wide range of materials, machinery, and equipment to build those plants. In 2014, the government changed tactics and issued an international call for the construction of a potassium chloride plant. The government selected CAMC Engineering, a Chinese company, to run the pilot and the Chinese Maison Machinery Engineering Company to build the lithium carbonate plant. Although construction was supposed to take place between 2013 and 2018, the project did not get off the ground until 2021.[122]

In this context, various international enterprises backed by their governments have been involved in talks and some have signed agreements with the Bolivian government. This was the case of two Japanese companies, Mitsubishi and Sumitomo. Bolloré, the French manufacturer of electric cars that made an agreement with Argentina,[123] was interested in the business, while the governments of South Korea, Brazil, and Iran signed "memorandums of understanding" with the Bolivian government. An agreement was signed with the Korea Resources Corp. and Posco for a joint venture to manufacture lithium-ion battery parts. Posco is a powerful multinational steel company (Pohang Iron and Steel Company) named in 2012 as the world's 146th largest corporation. Bolivia has a contract also with the Chinese company, Linyi Dake Trade Co. Ltd, to build a battery plant in Potosí (La Palca).[124]

In April 2018, the Bolivian government selected a German company, ACY Systems GMbH, as a strategic partner of YLB. The aim was to install a plant to produce cathode materials and lithium-ion batteries. The agreement sparked short- and long-term regional and national debates. Political opponents questioned the fact that Decree 3738 signed by President Morales to regulate the Bolivian-German accord (Yacimientos de Litio Bolivianos, YLB, with a 51 percent share and ACI Systems with 49 percent) resembled the kind of "neoliberal" agreements that were signed in 1990s by President Gonzalo Sánchez de Lozada. This type of agreement seemed even more baffling when one recalls how critical Morales was of the neoliberal policies of the past that gave foreign companies the power to exploit and market Bolivian resources. Opponents also considered the decree inappropriate due to the excessively long, seventy-year contract, under which the country was obliged to produce forty thousand tons of lithium hydroxide. They qualified the move as "a neoliberal surrender of Bolivia's natural resources." In response to Morales's policy, citizens of Potosí organized a general strike. After a month of protests, Morales eventually rescinded the decree. As part of the agreement, Bolivia would have been obligated to sell around 1.8 metric tons at cost to the German company without paying royalties to the regional government of Potosí.[125]

After fifteen years, the results of this industrialization plan proved meager. As of this writing, some plants are working at less than 20 percent capacity.[126] Until 2019, production was still considered in pilot phase and not yet "industrialized."[127] But more important, lithium extraction technology has changed, and the pond system may soon be obsolete. In 2020, Bill Gates invested in an "ion exchange" technology capable of processing lithium from brine resources that is faster, cheaper, and less environmentally impactful. The Company EnergyX plans important changes to cheaper lithium supply developed by Benny Freeman of the University of Texas at Austin.[128]

Changes in the lithium market are also worrying. Olivera points to an oligopoly of three enterprises that by 2015 controlled over the 55 percent of industrial-grade lithium minerals.[129] Although the situation is more diverse now, several companies are relevant: SQM Sociedad Química Minera de Chile; the global Chemetall Foote (United States), dating back to the nineteenth century as part of the German Metallgesellschaft; FMC Corporation (United States); Talison Lithium (Australia); and Chengdu Tianqi Industry Group (China).

There are also moves toward a closer intersection between battery production and original equipment manufacturing (OEM) for automotive and power sectors. "Gigafactories" producing cells and batteries grew from three in 2015 to 150 in 2021. All are located in Japan, Korea, and China but there are relations and cross investments. Six firms (LG, CATL, Panasonic, Samsung, BYD, and SKY) supply almost 90 percent of all battery capacity. These factories require advanced manufactured products (anodes, cathodes, separators, and electrolytes) and there is a geography of electrode production focused on lithium derivatives. Below this level, the geography of material refining sits close to the raw material supply.[130]Lithium carbonate, lithium hydroxide, and lithium chloride, main targets of the Bolivian

CONVOCATORIA INTERNACIONAL
EXTRACCION DIRECTA DEL LITIO
(EDL)

Objetivo	Establecer las bases para evaluar las empresas que cuenten con experiencia y teconología capaces de adaptarse a las características de los sales de Uyuni, Coipasa y Pastos Grandes, mediante la aplicación de nuevas tecnologías enfocadas en la extracción directa del litio (EDL) y proponer alternativas de procesamiento de otros elementos de valor comercial contenidos en las salmueras de estos salares.
Presentación	Hasta el día Lunes 31 de Mayo de 2021
Consultas	Podrán remitirse al correo convocatoria@ylb.gob.bo

Las empresas legalmente establecidas e interesadas por participar podrán solicitar el DOCUMENTO DE CONCESIONES MINIMAS Y REQUISITOS al correo:

convocatoria@ylb.gob.bo

La presentación de la propuesta podrá efectuarse en documento físico o via counter en Ventanilla Unica de la institución para su registro en acta de presentación. Dirección Av. Mariscal Santa Cruz, Edificio Hansa, o via e-mail a la dirección convocatoria@ylb.gob.bo

Todas las propuestas que se recibian por los medios comunicados serán registradas en acta, siendo la fecha límite de presentación hasta el día lunes 31/05/21 horas 15:00 horario Bolivia.

La Paz-Bolivia

Figure 2.12. The 2021 international call to exploit Lithium by the MAS government of Luis Arce. Source: Yacimientos de Litio Bolivianos, https://www.ylb.gob.bo/resources/img/1convocatoria.pdf.

plan of industrialization, are considered semiprocessed lithium or basic chemicals. In synthesis, the extraction of raw material and semitransformation (into basic chemicals) is taking place in Latin America and Australasia. Production of lithium derivatives (particularly lithium cathodes) is predominantly centered in East Asia, and secondarily in South America and North America, and the manufacturing of batteries takes place in East Asia, the United States, and the European Union. By 2014, the global flows of raw and semiprocessed lithium demonstrated the persistent international division of labor between zones of production and zones of manufacturing and consumption, with the East Asian countries competing with Europe and North America.[131]

Unsurprisingly, diverse fields of conflict surrounding the exploitation and processing of lithium have surfaced as global, national, regional, and local levels interact.[132] One such conflict has to do with the allotment of tax revenues. For example, the authorities and citizens of Potosí Department asked the Bolivian national government for a greater share of lithium income.[133] They argued that this is fair because royalties from hydrocarbons provide the departments of Santa Cruz, Chuquisaca, and Tarija with an extra 15 percent or more of income. Similar conflicts have arisen within Potosí's several provinces and municipalities.

In the end, Bolivia continues to be trapped in the same historical conundrum, stuck between its desire to control, industrialize, and manage its mineral resources and the limited access to the advanced knowledge and technology required to do so. After more than a decade of limited results, and very little transparency, the MAS government again issued an international call for investment in lithium extraction (fig. 1.12).

As of this writing (2023), the Arze government's rhetoric remains quite positive, although the initial goal of "one hundred percent Bolivian" lithium industrialization has been abandoned. Legislative proposals hint at a move toward denationalization.[134]

CONCLUSION

The first two and a half centuries of silver production in Potosí contributed to global economic integration and to mining's future in the region and in the territory that would later become Bolivia. Silver from Potosí spurred the commodities trade across continents. The Spanish Crown and then the Bolivian nation-state claimed sovereignty over both mining concessions and agricultural land. During the colonial period, although there was no clear interdiction against licenses for Indigenous mine claimants, they were not the main concessionaries of Potosí's mines. In contrast, Indigenous communities held legitimate titles to their lands. This allowed the Crown to establish a labor pool of peasants in hundreds of villages who were drafted every year for the mines. The mita system meant that mitayo workers were distributed among Spanish owners and refiners. This created a world divided between owners and workers. Workers' strength lay in their sheer numbers in the silver industry, but also through involvement in Indian community management of the mita in its whole complexity. Many workers deserted in the seventeenth century, escaping their various obligations and settling elsewhere. Others paid money to avoid having to work as mitayos, instead going to work as mingas with higher wages.

Although silver production peaked between 1575 and 1610, Potosí's Cerro Rico continued to be exploited thereafter. Silver production rebounded in the eighteenth century thanks to several measures taken by the Crown. In this period, the concerted efforts of workers to avoid dependence on mine and mill owners gave rise to the k'ajchas, who learned how to obtain silver by their own efforts and for their own benefit, albeit in competition with the privileged circuits of the large industrial refiners.

In the twentieth century, when tin displaced silver, the process of ore extraction and the initial steps of refining were done locally. The smelting process was completed mainly in Europe. In the first decades of the century, state intervention was minimal. In this context, a conjunction of circumstances explains the astonishing trajectory achieved by Simón Patiño in the northern region of Potosí. Patiño was able to vertically integrate the production process in Bolivia with the refining process in other parts of the world. Moritz Hochschild also thrived in the mining industry by refining low-quality ore in Germany. Hochschild's success was clearly linked to his ability to move between local and global spheres of production and refining. For both men, however, the global tin cycle proved short.

The twentieth century brought, for the first time, a labor force that was primarily proletarian. Bolivian mine workers' organization and struggles were recognized all over the world, particularly before and after the nationalization of Bolivian mining in 1952. Gustavo Rodríguez has argued that it would be wrong to explain the workers' trajectory in terms of any revolutionary party, since that would downplay their own class experience. I consider it equally important to challenge those divisions between a preindustrial period characterized by thievery, drunkenness, and "undisciplined" workers, and an industrial period characterized by a "disciplined" labor force.[135]

This chapter also demonstrated that it was in the nineteenth and twentieth centuries when more pure forms of extractivism took place. "Modern industry" was probably at its peak during the colonial period because metallurgical processes were entirely done locally. In all periods, workers sustained production, but they were not always wageworkers. In the colonial period and after, mine workers were still closely connected to their communities and to farming, avoiding total proletarianization or total transference of their labor to the mines. Notably, local and transnational companies took advantage of these labor conditions, since they allowed the companies to avoid assuming the full cost of wages; across the highlands, women's work subsidized the work of men, as had been true in colonial times. The arrival of modern mining corporations thus did not necessarily imply the disappearance of nonproletarian forms of labor. In fact, the old k'ajchas transformed into cooperatives and trade unions which received legal recognition after 1938 and whose economic role strengthened, particularly after 1952. Subsequently, the state granted k'ajchas mining concessions, allowing them a more significant and effective presence in the production of ores. At the same time, the entire mining industry became more extractive than ever before, scaling up and branching out. The new k'ajchas (in the form of the cooperatives) were no longer in charge of refining minerals in the trapiches. They now had to sell their ores or concentrates to private firms.

Short economic booms followed by long busts and entrepreneurs' disinterest in sustaining a stable, salaried labor force with social benefits help explain the importance and magnitude of a mobile and precarious "seasonal" mining labor force from rural areas. It is also important to note that amid a worldwide intensification of mineral resource exploitation marked by highly volatile commodity prices, investments are calculated coldly, according to revenue potential. By this logic, mining sites have finite "lives," and mining firms plan accordingly. There is an inevitable logic of unsustainability in the exploitation of nonrenewable mineral resources, laser-focused on large-scale production with low labor costs. The long-established inequality between producing and consuming countries also seems to be growing as the technological gap widens.

Lithium constitutes a good example of a nonrenewable mineral whose large-scale extraction has devasting consequences at the site of production, even as it paradoxically gets sold to the world as a miracle of renewable energy. Bolivia's experience with lithium mining also illustrates the yawning gap between political rhetoric and actual policy. Before the political crisis of 2019 and before the Covid-19 pandemic, Bolivia's Ministry of Mining reported that state-owned mines accounted for just 8 percent of total production, with large private mines accounting for 61 percent and cooperativists contributing 31 percent.[136]

Bolivia has been a hub of mining production for centuries, yet high world consumption of the country's mineral resources has not resulted in a better quality of life for mine workers or their families. Generations of workers since colonial times have experienced economic cycles characterized by short booms and long periods of economic crisis and instability. This was true for the silver economy, then for the tin economy, and this seems likely to happen now with the lithium economy.

In this context, the presumed features of modernity and capitalism associated with large-scale mines—electrical infrastructure, mechanized modes of extraction, and a waged labor force—were never distributed evenly in all places. Profit-seeking firms were often dependent on a mobile and precarious labor force. In this sense, the quote with which I started this chapter describing the cooperative labor that resembles that of the mitayos in the sixteenth century is not the remnant of a precapitalist age; it is an integral part of the contemporary capitalist system. In the end, today's labor conditions are so similar to those of the past because of the long processes of reconstitution of unequal relations between countries and regions and between different actors engaged in the world of mining. These old burdens, like sacks of ore, seem difficult to shake.

ACKNOWLEDGMENTS

I deeply thank Kris Lane for his comments, suggestions, and encouragement and Sinclair Thomson for his insightful comments. I also want to thank Manuel Contreras, Manuel Olivera, and Jose Carlos Solón.

NOTES

1. Flynn and Giráldez, "Cycles of silver" and Frank, *ReOrient*. Lane, *Potosí* is an important recent book that gives information on the city of Potosí.
2. Frank, *ReOrient*, 55, 30.
3. Giraldez, "Born with a 'Silver Spoon'", 201–21, 31–32, 40; Barrett, "World Bullion flows," 225.
4. Bentancor, *The Matter of Empire*, 42.
5. Bartels, "The Administration of mining," 117. For Spanish America Molina M., "Legislación minera," 1014–15; Ramos, "Ordenación de la minería," 386.
6. Ley j. Tit. XIX, *Recopilación de leyes, vol.* 2, 68. Indians could hold and exploit gold and silver mines in the same way as the Spaniards. Ley XIII, 1551, 1563, 1575, in *Recopilación*, vol. 2, 71. "De los Descubridores, registros y estacas, Ordenanza 1" de las Ordenanzas de Minas, Francisco de Toledo, *Relaciones de los Virreyes y Audiencias T. I. Memorial y Ordenanzas de F. de Toledo*. See also Molina M., 1014–15.
7. Capoche, *Relación general de la villa imperial de Potosí* (1585). See Barragán, "K'ajchas, trapiches," 273–320. Vara = linear measurement of 0.838 meters, Bakewell, *Miners of the Red Mountain*, 198. Título I, Ordenanza V, Ordenanzas para las minas de plata de Potosí y Porco, 1574, in Francisco de Toledo, *Disposiciones gubernativas, 1569–1574* (Sevilla, 1986), 307.
8. Sempat Assadourian, *El Sistema de la economía colonial.*
9. For Garner Potosí has a growth (1549–1605), decline (1606–1723), revival (1724–1783) and finally decline (1784–1810). See "Long-Term Silver Mining," 908. For Tandeter, the revival goes from 1731 until 1800. The source for Tandeter is J. J. TePaske. Tandeter, "Forced and Free Labor," 100.
10. Bakewell, *Miners of the Red Mountain*, 20–21.
11. See Barragan, "Extractive economy and institutions?" 207–37.
12. See Velasco Murillo "Laboring above ground," 3–32.
13. Garavaglia speaks of five stages. Garavaglia, "Plata para el Rey," 129.
14. The term *minga* is a Hispanicization of an Aymara and Quechua word still in use today to describe an agricultural wage laborer or a person who works for payment in kind rather than in money. In 2017, I proposed that the system of work combined unfree (mita) and free (minga) labor, rather than separate groups of labourers (mitayos and mingas). See Barragán, "Extractive economy and institutions?"
15. Arzáns, *Historia de la Villa.*
16. Cole, *The Potosí Mita*, 36–38.
17. In 1735, the Spanish Crown decreased the mining tax from 20 to 10 percent.
18. See Barragán, "A Silver Bank."

19. They were called "mineral thieves" because they entered the mines on weekends to take ore for themselves. See Arzans, *Historia de la Villa*; Abercrombie, "Q'aqchas and La Plebe"; and Rodríguez, "Kajchas." For an overview of this historiography see Barragán, "K'ajchas, trapiches y plata," 273–320 and "Working Silver for the World," 193–222. See also Buechler, *Gobierno*; Zulawski, *They Eat from Their Labour*; and Platt "Producción."
20. Barragán, "Working Silver for the World."
21. Robins, *Mercury, Mining and Empire*.
22. See Mitre, *Los Patriarcas de la plata*.
23. Ingulstad, Perchard and Storli, *Tin and Global Capitalism*.
24. Quoted by Contreras, *The Bolivian Tin Mining Industry*, 1. Sergio Almaraz, founder of the Communist Party who later joined the left wing of the Revolutionary Nationalist Movement (Movimiento Nacionalista Revolucionario or MNR), offered acute critical observations about the history of tin mining. See Almaraz, *El Poder y la caída*, 365. Tin was already being exploited in the nineteenth century. See Hillman, "The Emergence of the Tin Industry in Bolivia," 403–37.
25. Contreras, *The Bolivian Tin Mining*, 2–3.
26. For an analysis of the competition among Great Britain, China, and Malaysia, with the triumph of the first, see Hillman, "The Emergence of the Tin Industry in Bolivia," 35–37, and the following pages for the Netherlands and other important centers in Asia. See also Ingulstad et al., *Tin and Global Capitalism*, 3–6.
27. Ayub and Hashimoto, *The Economics of Tin Mining*, 11.
28. Geddes, *Patiño*, 101; Klein, "La formación del Imperio," 237–52; Carrasco, *Simón I. Patiño*; Contreras has an important forthcoming article on him. "Simón I. Patiño Empresario."
29. Llallagua, Huanuni, Oruro, and Oploca, which was in Chilean hands. Hillman, "The Emergence of the Tin Industry," 43–44; Contreras, *The Bolivian Tin Mining*, 10.
30. Contreras, *The Bolivian Tin Mining*, 10.
31. Ayub and Hashimoto, *The Economics of Tin Mining*, 12.
32. Querejazu, *Llallagua: Historia de una montaña*, 145.
33. Waszkis, *Dr. Moritz*, 3–4, 51.
34. Rodríguez, *Capitalismo*, 96, 197. The smelting was done locally by companies like Ingenio Velarde. The most important was the Enterprise Soux, Hernádez and Velarde, which included the mills of Huaylla-Huasi, Quintanilla, and Pampa Ingenio. Mitre, *Bajo un cielo de estaño*, 111–13.
35. Contreras, *The Bolivian Tin Mining*, 4; Mitre, *El enigma de los hornos*, 36. The taxes were around 4 percent of the total value of exports during the first two decades of the twentieth century, and about 10 percent during most of the next two decades. Ali and Hashimoto, *The Economics of Tin Mining*, 12–13.
36. The keñua tree (*Polylepis tarapacana*); the paja brava or ichu (*Festuca orthophylla*) grass;

and the yareta (*Azorella compacta*) or the tola (*Parastrephia quadrangularis*) plants. See also Mitre, *Bajo un cielo de estaño*, 35.

37. The opposite was the case with ore from Patiño's mines, which contained no less than 47 percent tin content, although that figure decreased through time to 12 to 15 percent and even as low as 6.65 percent. The metal content around 1980 was below 0.3 percent.

38. Waszkis, *Dr. Moritz Hochschild*, 72.

39. Waszkis, *Dr. Moritz Hochschild*, 68. In the colonial period, the Banco paid high prices, while in the nineteenth century, the main entrepreneurs complained of the low prices paid to them. The Bolivian state ended the monopoly in the purchase of minerals in 1872. For the "rescate" and "habilitación" of Hochschild, see Tenorio, *Mauricio Hochschild*, 47–58.

40. Based on the Compañía Minera Potosí of the Soux, Bebín Hermanos and the Compagnie Aramayo. See Tenorio, *Mauricio Hochschild*, 138–42. On Huanchaca see the same author, 82–86.

41. Contreras, *Tecnología moderna*, 3. A brief report of the Hochschild interests in South America reminds us of some milestones: the purchase of twenty thousand tons of copper per year from Chile and thirty thousand tons of sulfur; the constitution of M. Hochschild SAMI (Sociedad Anónima Minera e Industrial) in 1921, the expansion of its operations in 1927 and the shipping around one hundred thousand tons of ore and concentrates annually; the creation of the South American Mining Company—a holding company—in Buenos Aires in 1928 (mainly for trade with Chile and Argentina); the opening of a new office in Rio de Janeiro and São Paulo for the purchase of manganese and iron ore; the acquisition of the Huanchaca Company in Bolivia, rich in silver and zinc, the Cia. Minera de Oruro of silver and tin, the Colquiri, Morococala, Machacamarca and Matilde, the Atocha Villazón railway, the largest hydro-electric power plant, and the Vinto Company that owned the old tin tailings. See Folder III/I, Periodicals, Ar. 25349, 694–95, in Moritz Hochschild Collection 1881–2002.

42. Rodríguez, *Capitalismo*, 106. The saltpeter camps in northern Chile received up to four thousand workers from Cochabamba around 1919, see 129–31.

43. Contreras, "Mano de obra," 97–134.

44. Mitre, *Bajo un cielo de estaño*, 132.

45. Rodríguez, *Capitalismo*, 118.

46. The first noted strike was in 1908 and the first request for the reduction of work hours came in 1914. See Contreras, "Mano de obra," 119.

47. Rodríguez, *Capitalismo*, 119–21, 147. See also Lora, *Historia del Movimento Obrero*; Smale, *I Sweat the Flavor of Tin*.

48. Contreras, *The Bolivian Tin Mining Industry*, 9; Contreras, *Tecnología moderna en los Andes*, 24.

49. Mainly work accidents and hours. See Barragán, "Inclusions and Exclusions."

50. Contreras, *The Bolivian Tin Mining*, 12.
51. See for an analysis of debt, Contreras, "Debt, Taxes, and War."
52. Contreras, *The Bolivian Tin Mining*, 16.
53. *La Calle,* June 11, 1938. The newspaper initially supported the Socialist Party and among its contributors were intellectuals such as Carlos Montenegro, Augusto Céspedes, Armando Arce, José Cuadros Quiroga, and Nazario Pardo Valle. This part is based in Barragán, "Los k'ajchas y los proyectos," 25–48.
54. *La Calle*, March 21, 1937.
55. *Alas*, October 11, 1938.
56. *Alas*, February 14, 1937, 3.
57. *Alas*, July 4, 1937, 2.
58. "Comentarios al Código de Trabajo," *Alas,* October 18, 1938.
59. An example of a contractor is Renato Barrón, who employed seventeen workers to whom he paid wages varying from $b7.50 per day to $b2.60. He also paid $b1.00 per kg of 40 percent grade minerals, $b0.70 for 30 percent, and $b0.50 for 20 percent. *La Calle*, June 14, 1938, 5.
60. Arratia, República de Bolivia, *Redactor de la Convención de 1938*, T.I. 268.
61. Ayala Gamboa, *Redactor de la Convención de 1938*, T.I. 318.
62. Romero Loza, *Redactor de la Convención de 1938*, T.I. 317.
63. Lanza Solares, *Redactor de la Convención de 1938*, T.I. 538.
64. The cooperatives reunited under the Federación Departamental de Cooperativas Mineras (known also as the Consejo Central de Cooperativas) on May 1, 1955, Alurralde, *Cooperativas Mineras*. See also Absi, "Q'aqchas y obreros."
65. *Estatutos del sindicato de Ckacchas.*
66. Mitre, *Bajo un cielo de estaño*, 161.
67. Waskis, *Dr. Moritz*, 107–9.
68. *Alas*, Septermber 28, 1938, 3.
69. Rodríguez, *Capitalismo*, 189, 207.
70. Contreras, *The Bolivian Tin Mining*, 6.
71. Mitre, *Bajo un cielo de estaño*, 165.
72. Almaraz, *El Poder y la caída*, 365.
73. Albarracín, *El poder financiero*. Contreras thinks that greater taxes on mining would not necessarily have fostered greater nor more equitable development, referring to the inadequate use made of all revenues. Contreras, *The Bolivian Tin Mining*, 9. See also *Tecnología moderna*, 22. The book by León Bieber, *Dr. Mauricio Hochschild*, recalled his assistance of more than eight thousand Jewish refugees from the Holocaust. The Bolivian press called him the "Bolivian Schindler."
74. Burke, *The Corporación Minera*, 5.

75. Reports from the US Congress established that up to September 1959 the Bolivian government had paid Patiño and Hochschild around 16,825,591 USD. "Foreign Aide to Bolivia," 109 Cong. Rec. 20457–63 (1967), https://www.govinfo.gov/content/pkg/GPO-CRECB-1967-pt15/pdf/GPO-CRECB-1967-pt15-6-1.pdf. Zondag asserted that they received 20 million USD. Zondag, *The Bolivian Economy*, 3.
76. Memoria del consejo de Administración y Balance General al 31 de Diciembre 1952, Cia. Huanchaca de Bolivia, S.A. 81 (Valparaíso: Imprenta Valparaíso), in Moritz Hochschild Collection 1881–2002.
77. Although there are frequent references to the low taxes, the Bohan Report of 1941–1942 mentioned thirty separate taxes. See "Foreign Aide to Bolivia," 20461. Ali Ayub and Hashimoto asserted that the level of taxation on Bolivian mining was one of the highest among the main tin producing countries. Ayub and Hashimoto, *The Economics of Tin Mining*, 7
78. Burke, "The Corporación Minera de Bolivia," 2–3.
79. Zondag, *The Bolivian Economy, 1952–1964*, 64.
80. Burke, *The Corporación Minera*, 7.
81. James Malloy used the Report of Ford, Bacon and Davis that explained COMIBOL decapitalization, dilapidation of the plants and equipment, exhaustion of ore deposits, and the failure to develop new mines. See *The Uncompleted Revolution*, 298.
82. Ayub and Hashimoto, *The Economics of Tin Mining*, 6; Zondag, *The Bolivian Economy*, 90.
83. In 1945, the law of 29 September apportioned all abandoned mines to the Banco Minero that could then lease them preferentially to Bolivians, particularly to the "Kacchas Unions."
84. Law 2926, 14-01-1952.
85. The surface below the 4,375 meter elevation was apportioned to COMIBOL and that above 4,375 meters could be worked by artisanal miners and local cooperatives.
86. "Financial Markets: London Metal Exchange Will Resume Tin Trading," L.A. Times Archives, April 13, 1989. See also Crabtree, Duffy, and Pearce, *The Great Tin Crash*.
87. "El Colapso del Estaño y la Marcha por la Vida," EDUCA, accessed April 1, 2023, http://www.educa.com.bo/caminos-de-democracia/el-colapso-del-estano-y-la-marcha-por-la-vida#sthash.hBoQZYWg.dpuf.
88. Statistics provided by Cerro Rico Cooperatives in June 2001. Bocangel, *Small Scale Mining*, 11.
89. Robb, Moran, Thom, and Coburn, *Indigenous Governance and Mining*, 8.
90. Bocangel, *Small Scale Mining*, 4.
91. Ministerio de Minería, "Empresas e instituciones mineras se someterán a rendición de cuentas."

92. Anderson, "The Mineral Industry of Bolivia," US Department of the Interior, US Geological Survey, August 2010, Bolivia; *2008 Minerals Yearbook* (2010), 3.1. In 2011, there were more than 110,000 workers and the ILO estimated that the cooperatives created indirect employment for between 175,000 and 300,000 people by 2011. Francescone and Diaz, "Entre socios, patrones y peones," 38; Bocangel shows that in the 1980s, 3 percent were in cooperatives. See *Small Scale Mining*, 4–5.
93. Ministerio de Minería y Metalurgia, *Boletín Informativo*, 10.
94. Bocangel, *Small Scale Mining*, 12.
95. Francescone and Diaz, "Entre socios, patrones y peones," 38.
96. Michard, *Cooperativas mineras*, 14, 16, 22, 25.
97. Michard, *Cooperativas mineras*, 26–28.
98. Michard, *Cooperativas mineras*, 28, 30.
99. Michard, *Cooperativas mineras*, 34.
100. "Overview," Coeur Mining, accessed April 1, 2023, http://www.coeur.com.
101. These contracts were held with seven Potosí mining cooperatives. The contracts' name is "*Contrato de Riesgo Compartido*" in Spanish. See Coeur d'Alene Mines, *San Bartolomé Technical Report*, January 1, 2013, 20.
102. Coeur d'Alene Mines, *San Bartolomé Technical Report*, January 1, 2013, 19.
103. Coeur d'Alene Mines, *San Bartolomé Technical Report*, January 1, 2013, 15.
104. Coeur d'Alene Mines, *San Bartolomé Technical Report*, January 1, 2013, 12.
105. Coeur d'Alene Mines, *San Bartolomé Technical Report*, January 1, 2015, 14.
106. Coeur Mining, 2014 *Annual Report*, 16.
107. See Mata P., Zamora E., Serrano B., "Riesgos de estabilidad."
108. Bocangel, *Small Scale Mining*.
109. Comité Cívico de Potosí (COMCIPO), Facebook, July 14, 2015. The demands of COMICPO were basic: build an airport, build hospitals, build roads, and build factories. See also "Bolivia: Crece la tensión por el conflicto en Potosí," *La Izquierda Diario*, July 23, 2015.
110. Nowadays, the total world production is 12.7 billion mobile phones (Ramirez-Salgado & Dominguez-Aguilar 2009), 94.4 million laptop computers, and 768.9 million digital cameras (UNdata 2010). See Cherico Wanger, "The Lithium."
111. Ribera, "Análisis general del caso Uyuni-litio (minería)," 4.
112. Olivera, "Salares altoandinos," 55. See also Alec, "Lithium Market Update."
113. Solón, *Espejismos de abundancia*, 20, 94; Fawthrop, "Top six countries with the largest lithium reserves in the world."
114. Olivera, *La industrialización del litio en Bolivia*, 42; Montenegro, "El modelo de industrialización del litio." See also Decree 29496. Law No. 3720 gave the Mining Corporation of Bolivia (COMIBOL) the possibility to participate in the entire production chain of lithium. For earlier proposals on lithium see Flores, "Regionalismo nacionalista."

115. Solón, *Espejismos de abundancia*, 50–51.
116. Solón, *Espejismos de abundancia*, 102.
117. Olivera, *La industrialización del litio en Bolivia*, 62–63.
118. Calla, "Impactos de la producción"; Guzmán, "Introducción," 14, 17.
119. Hollender and Shultz, *Bolivia and Its Lithium*, 41.
120. Ströbele-Gregor, *Litio en Bolivia*, 55–56.
121. Campbell, "In Pictures."
122. Solón, *Espejismos de abundancia*, 142.
123. Hollender and Shultz, *Bolivia and Its Lithium*, 22–23.
124. Guzmán, "Introducción," 7.
125. Deutsche Welle, "El acuerdo del litio con Alemania era desventajoso para Bolivia." For a detailed analysis of YLB-ACI, see Solón, 2022.
126. Solon, *Espejismos de abundancia*, 134–37.
127. Bos and Forget, "Global Production Networks and the Lithium Industry," 173.
128. Fawthrop, "Lilac Solutions Attracts Major Backers for Lithium Extraction Technology"; Wood and Zhang, "Getting More Value from Brines"; "Two new ways of extracting lithium from brine."
129. Olivera, *La industrialización del litio en Bolivia*, 103–7.
130. Bridge and Faigen, "Towards the Lithium-Ion Battery Production Network," 2, 5.
131. Bos and Forget, "Global Production Networks and the Lithium Industry," 172.
132. Ströbele-Gregor, *Litio en Bolivia*, 17.
133. Olivera, *La industrialización del litio en Bolivia*, 200–202.
134. Redacción de El Pueblo, "Litio: el gran salto boliviano"; Solón, "Desnacionalización del litio."
135. Rodríguez, "Los mineros de Bolivia," 276; *Capitalismo*, 23, 35, 37, 274, 276, 280.
136. Ministerio de Minería y Metalurgia, *Anuario Estadístico y Coyuntura del sector minero metalúrgico*.

DISPOSSESSION AND REDISTRIBUTION

Social Struggle Over Water

Sarah T. Hines

Contests and compromises over water for human consumption, irrigation, and later hydropower and industry have shaped the history of the Central Andes since at least the time of the Incas. Water access has been especially important in semiarid Andean valleys that have served as the breadbaskets for distant highland communities, the Inca and Spanish Empires, and postcolonial nations. Water shortages, competition among different groups of people, and hydraulic innovation have thus been particularly intense in regions like Bolivia's Cochabamba Valley. Water flows connect different regions and groups, but water dispossession under the Inca and Spanish Empires and after independence empowered and enriched colonizers and elites at the expense of Indigenous communities, smallholders, and urban residents. Dispossession was never total, but by the late nineteenth century large landholders held a near monopoly on regional water sources that they rented and sold to their smallholder neighbors and residents of growing nearby cities. In the century that followed, however, smallholders, estate workers, and urban residents dismantled the water monopoly and democratized water access through their labor, protest, and revolutionary mobilization. This shift from cycles of dispossession to cycles of redistribution starting around the turn of the twentieth century came about due to the organization of a broad array of water-using groups who drew on their expertise to build, capture, and manage water sources and infrastructure.

This chapter chronicles a five hundred–year cycle of dispossession and democratization of water property and access rights in the Central Andean region that became Bolivia after independence. It focuses on the Cochabamba region where water scarcity, dispossession, and protest were most intense and where a "water war" in the year 2000 resonated internationally. It tells interrelated stories of Cochabamba's agrarian countryside where water irrigates fields and sustains livestock and the urban world of the department capital where demand for drinking water grew as the city's population began to increase more rapidly starting in the late nineteenth century. Urban water needs put increasing pressure on surrounding rural agricultural areas where agriculturalists already competed for relatively scarce—and unevenly distributed—water sources.

The chapter begins in the late fourteenth century with the arrival of the Incas to the Cochabamba Valley, where imperial officials leveraged water to make Cochabamba a major agricultural center for the empire. After defeating the Incas, the Spanish Empire built imperial control over Upper Peru, the territory that became Bolivia after independence, by appropriating land, water, and irrigation infrastructure through a combination of purchase, theft, and royal grants. After Bolivia won its independence from Spain in 1825, a newly wealthy group of creole landowners took advantage of a severe drought, a new national water regulation, and the national government's dissolution of Indigenous communities to consolidate a near monopoly on the region's water sources. The urban population and its demand for drinking water began to grow more rapidly in the final decades of the nineteenth century—precisely when large landowners began to dominate the region's water supply more than ever before. But in the decades that followed, Indigenous communities, smallholders, hacienda tenants, city residents, and state institutions wrested control of hoarded water sources away from hacendados who monopolized water. The high moment of this struggle was after the 1952 Bolivian Revolution when hacienda workers won water sources and infrastructure through agrarian reform. In the decades after the revolution, peasant communities defended their water rights against urban encroachment, neighborhoods on the urban periphery built independent water systems, and city residents battled the municipal water company over supply and rates.

In the early 2000s, Bolivians stunned observers around the world when they successfully overturned contracts signed with transnational corporations to privatize water—in Cochabamba in 2000 and in La Paz-El Alto in 2005. In Cochabamba, protesters included not only municipal customers but also independent neighborhood residents and rural cultivators who had been dispossessed of their water sources and infrastructure through privatization. This chapter argues that protesters' success in overturning water privatization owed to the power they had won over water sources, systems, and management over a century of social struggle over water. Cochabamba's 2000 Water War opened a five-year revolutionary cycle that discredited the country's ruling elite and their political parties and paved the way for the 2005 election of Evo Morales, Bolivia's first Indigenous president. Morales and his Movimiento al Socialismo (MAS) party joined Latin America's "Pink Tide," a wave of left-leaning, vaguely socialist governments elected in various Latin American countries in the late 1990s and early 2000s after surges of popular mobilization. The history of water struggle in Bolivia, particularly in Cochabamba, is therefore crucial to understanding Bolivian history and contemporary politics. It can also offer lessons for communities across the world working to broaden access to life-sustaining resources like water.

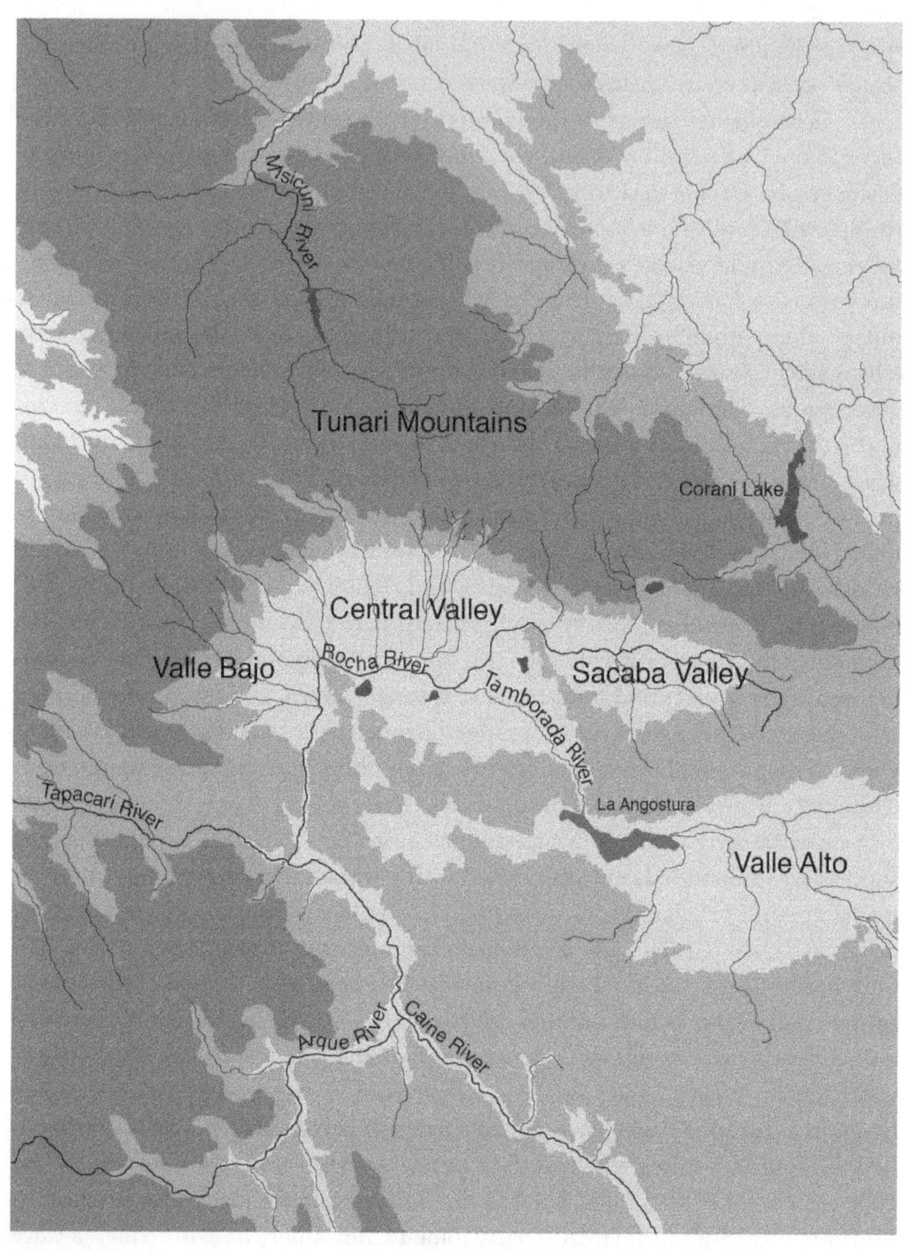

Map 3.1. The Cochabamba region. Map by Jorge Camacho Saavedra.

WATER AND EMPIRE

Water has long linked dispersed settlements in the Central Andes. Precolonial Aymara extended kin groups, or ayllus, were centered in altiplano punas where they grazed llamas and alpacas and cultivated potatoes and other tubers. Ayllus sent groups of settlers, or mitimaes, to sites scattered along what came to resemble "vertical archipelagos," as anthropologist John Murra found, establishing "vertical control" over an extended area. Water linked these locales, connecting ayllus' different "ecological niches."[1] Abundant rainfall at high elevations formed mountain glaciers, lakes, and rivers that supplied water to fields and families in the highlands, valleys, and lowlands below.[2] But rainfall is concentrated in the wet summer months, making management of water supply important for irrigation and drinking water provision during dry winter months.

Cochabamba's large semiarid valleys, set in the heart of the tropical Southern Andes, possess fertile lands that have attracted cultivators despite near desert-level rainfall levels. In Cochabamba's four principal valleys, the Valle Bajo, Valle Central, Valle de Sacaba, and the Valle Alto, average annual rainfall is just 485 millimeters per year.[3] For most of the year, mountains to the north block rain clouds from crossing into the valley. But when the long dry season gives way to summer rains, intense winds sweep heavy rainclouds over the mountains into the valleys. During the rainy season from November to March, rainwater collects in lakes in the Tunari Mountains north of the valleys, in mountainside springs that continue to flow after the yearly rains have ceased, and in the soil and deep reaches of the fractured rock layers below the valley floor. In order to capture and store this water, and channel it to agricultural fields, early cultivators built one of the earliest integrated systems of floodwater and canal irrigation in the Americas.[4]

Harnessing water sources for agriculture in large inter-Andean valleys was crucial to building the Inca and Spanish Empires. Drawn by its potential to feed the imperial army, the Incas colonized Cochabamba's valleys in the late fifteenth century under Emperor Yupanqui (1471–1493). Yupanqui's successor, Huayna Cápac (1493–1527), oversaw a major state-directed agricultural project in Cochabamba that transformed the region into the empire's premier southern food supplier.[5] Integrating ancient irrigation techniques, Inca officials drafted roughly fourteen thousand laborers from an array of highland nations to build a vast irrigation system to direct water to state-operated farms.[6] They established a rotational distribution system that granted particular land parcels a share or "turn" of water (mita) from a specific water source according to a schedule. In the rainy season, teeming rivers swelled and cut down the mountainside, providing mitas to long, narrow strips of agricultural land the Incas called *suyus*. In the dry season, irrigation canals supplied water to the suyus whose borders were defined by deep mountain ravines.[7] From this time forward, water rights became attached to land ownership as well as to collective labor necessary to capture and channel irrigation and drinking water. Land dispossession in subsequent centuries thus entailed the less visible appropriation of water sources, infrastructure, and the labor invested to engineer water infrastructure.

After defeating the Incas, Spanish settlers built imperial control by appropriating valley land, water sources, and irrigation infrastructure through a combination of purchase, theft, and royal grants. In the first few decades of Spanish rule, colonial officials granted Spanish settlers called encomenderos authority over Indian communities. In the 1570s, Viceroy Francisco de Toledo's forced resettlement program concentrated the Andes's multiethnic Indigenous population into Spanish-style towns called *pueblos reales de indios*, or more generically, *reducciones*. As Silvia Rivera Cusicanqui explains, this "forced unification . . . homogenized and degraded a diversity of peoples and identities into an anonymous collective expressed in the condition of *indio*, that is to say, of the colonized."[8] The Crown required community members called *originarios* to pay tribute and to work as draft laborers every seventh year in the Potosí mines. Nevertheless, reducciones built on and preserved the vertical archipelago and existing communal land and irrigation water allocation.[9]

Spanish and creole hacendados used various tactics, including purchase, force, and fraud, to appropriate community land and water rights.[10] One way that communities acquired cash to pay tribute to the Spanish was by leasing or selling community land, along with these parcels' irrigation rights, to neighboring hacienda owners. As they lost members to haciendas, communities sold or rented even more land and water to cover lost tributary dues. In Cochabamba, hacendados gained still greater water access by forcibly inserting themselves into the irrigation rotation system.[11] As a result, community plots received water less frequently and hacienda landholdings came to possess disproportionate water rights. While hacendados' dispossession of communities' water sources was less visible than land appropriation, it was more extreme. As historians Robert Jackson and José Gordillo write, haciendas "obtained rights to all of the important water sources."[12]

Water dispossession was offset somewhat by protections that Spanish water law and rule offered Indigenous communities, small farmers, and townspeople. When the Spanish Crown proclaimed ownership over all land and water in "the Indies," it empowered colonial officials to grant colonists land, water, woodlands, and pastures. All remaining Crown resources were supposed to be available for common use by settlers and Natives alike. But while the public could freely use Crown water sources for drinking, bathing, recreation, and watering animals, using water for irrigation required specific allocation to a Native community or privately owned land parcel. While, at first, officials gave generous land and water grants to Spaniards, in the late sixteenth century, the Crown ordered officials to protect Native communities from abuse by colonists, specifically requiring colonial officials to ensure that concessions occur "*sin agravio de los indios*."[13] If there was a dispute, a colonial water judge or other official might conduct a "*repartimiento de agua*," dividing available water among Spanish and Indian users or simply ordering them to share it.

Spanish law required officials to consider not only who could claim prior use and who held legal title, but also need, equity, and the common good. This tenure regime did not grant water to owners of the land the water was found on, as riparian or riverside systems do, unless the water source originated on the landowners' land (such as in the case of a well or a spring). Even then "the owner could not maliciously deny it to others."[14] Therefore, while private landowners and Native communities possessed water rights, these allocations were subject to change. There was no guarantee that officials would carry out a redistribution to make access more just, however, and Spaniards and creoles were able to acquire disproportionate water rights. Spanish law allowed landowners to pass water rights down to children, sell land with corresponding water rights to their neighbors, and rent excess irrigation water to them, practices that locked unequal access into place over time.

In Upper Peru, as the region that became Bolivia was known in the colonial period, Spanish officials often allowed Spanish and creole hacendados to usurp significant land and water resources.[15] When Cochabamba pueblos reales sued hacienda owners in colonial courts for illegal land and water appropriation, colonial authorities seem to have offered little remedy.[16] Geographer Karl Zimmerer has found that when faced with legal challenges to water appropriation by Native communities claiming to have been granted suyu units by the Incas, Spaniards successfully countered that their property "descended directly from holdings of the vanquished Inca state rather than . . . through usurpation of other Indian holdings."[17] But they also generally recognized pueblos reales' remaining land and water holdings in exchange for tribute and labor payment, which anthropologist Tristan Platt has called the colonial "pact of reciprocity," though more so in the highlands than in the valleys.[18] And colonial officials could reallocate available water sources according to need. After independence, these protections and commitments, feeble as they were, disappeared.

The regional hacienda economy grew in the early colonial period by exporting grain to the booming Potosí silver mines. But by the late colonial era, Cochabamba haciendas had begun to lose out to highland grain producers, a problem that became a crisis after independence. Their predicament opened space for the growth of an independent smallholding peasantry that gained control over local markets and purchased parcels of hacienda land. One way that landlords tried to mitigate these difficulties in the colonial and early national periods was to accumulate excess irrigation rights (*sobras*) through forced sales, fraud, and theft.[19] This allowed them to exploit periodic droughts by using their still vast landholdings and disproportionate irrigation water rights to produce surplus grain for storage during plentiful harvest years to sell dear when drought hit and prices soared.[20] Smallholders and pueblo members with less favorable irrigation water rights or nonirrigated holdings could lose entire crops during a drought and thus be forced to purchase grain from landlords. Meanwhile, city residents were completely at their mercy.

DROUGHT AND DISPOSSESSION IN THE LIBERAL ERA

In the decades after Bolivia became an independent nation-state in 1825, liberals and conservatives battled over whether to maintain the colonial pact and economic protectionism or abandon it in favor of free trade and privatization of communal property. For the first five decades, conservatives mostly won out. In the late 1870s, however, a severe drought gave liberals the opportunity to implement disentailment laws and privatize water. The perfect storm of drought, famine, land dispossession, water privatization, and international war reconfigured property relations and social life in Bolivia, particularly in its agricultural valleys.

The 1877–1878 famine killed an estimated twenty to thirty million people across Asia, Africa, and South America during the most intense El Niño event of the nineteenth century.[21] While floods ravaged coastal Ecuador and Northern Peru, drought swept the Central Andes of Peru and Bolivia, hitting hardest in Bolivia's inter-Andean valleys. From Cochabamba to Chuquisaca, drought gave rise to devastating famine, epidemic disease, and social unrest. But famine was not inevitable. As historian Mike Davis writes, "although crop failures and water shortages were of epic proportion" during late nineteenth-century drought waves, "absolute scarcity was never the issue."[22] In Bolivia's agricultural heartland in Cochabamba and Sucre, famine owed to land and water accumulation in the hands of a privileged few who consciously took advantage of the drought to profit off of the misery of their neighbors. More than three hundred years of land and water dispossession had left Indigenous and peasant communities vulnerable to the vicissitudes of the region's volatile climate—and to landlords who used their disproportionate control over land and irrigation water to speculate on grain during the drought.

In Cochabamba, the drought destroyed half of the corn and wheat crops and left pools of stagnant water in riverbeds where disease-carrying mosquitos multiplied, causing outbreaks of typhoid, malaria, and dysentery.[23] Sick and starving independent smallholders (*piqueros*), hacienda tenant laborers (*colonos*), and pueblo members fled the countryside where hacienda owners (and provincial authorities) failed to offer assistance to their starving and disease-stricken workers and neighbors, instead selling hoarded grain at exorbitant prices.[24] In the department capital, local hospitals overflowed, dead bodies littered the streets, and the sick and starving "swarmed the streets," begging for assistance. President Hilarión Daza's administration, which had come to power in an 1876 coup, offered no aid, leaving the municipal government, affluent citizens, and local ecclesiastical institutions to organize relief efforts.[25] As speculators took advantage of scarcity and demand to jack up grain prices, local authorities ignored calls to impose price controls and requisition grain.[26] Protests broke out across Cochabamba and Sucre denouncing hoarding and speculation and demanding price caps on basic foodstuffs. In Arani, in Cochabamba's Valle Alto, protestors threatened to kill grain-hoarding landowners. In Sucre, a crowd demanding price caps lynched hoarders.[27] As historians Michela Pentimalli and Gustavo Rodríguez Ostria argue, these protests were rooted in popular groups' belief that basic needs and survival, what anthropologist James Scott calls the "subsistence ethic," trumped rights to private property and market freedom.[28] Many Cochabambino drought survivors fled the region for Chile, just as war broke out between the two nations.

The drought-induced crisis may have helped to ignite the War of the Pacific (1879–1884) and almost certainly influenced its course and outcome. The war over Bolivia and Peru's nitrate- and guano-rich coastal provinces, one of the Americas' longest and most deadly wars, was fought between an alliance of those nations and Chile.[29] The war broke out after Bolivia imposed a new minimum tax on the British-Chilean Nitrates and Railroad Company that, according to historian and former Bolivian president Carlos Mesa (2003–2005), owed to the economic crisis wrought by the drought.[30] As historian Jorge Basadre writes, "Bolivia intervened in the war . . . under terrible conditions." Drought and disease killed thousands across Cochabamba, Sucre, and Potosí, crippling Bolivia's war machine.[31] Chile won the war and, with it, Bolivia's Litoral Province and Peru's Tarapacá.[32] Bolivia's loss sparked uprisings in La Paz and among troops on the Peruvian coast that drove President Hilarión Daza from the presidency in 1879. His fall ended an era of rule by military strongmen, opening a new period of modern parliamentary-style government. Elections became contests among civilian leaders of contending political parties committed to economic liberalism and to serving the country's mine- and estate-owning aristocracy.[33]

The drought gave national officials an opportunity to wage war on collective Indigenous community land and water holdings. The 1874 Ley de Exvinculación had abolished Indigenous communities as legally sanctioned collectivities and instructed the national state to distribute individual titles to land, forests, water sources, and animals held in common and sell off additional lands considered vacant or unused.[34] Liberal intellectuals and politicians from Cochabamba such as Nataniel Aguirre and José María Santiváñez supported this effort in hope of demonstrating the superiority of a smallholding model over that of the corporate Indian community and the hacienda, which they considered backward and inefficient. But, as Gustavo Rodriguez Ostria writes, they were "timid liberals," eager to apply their logic to community lands but unwilling to challenge hacienda owners' private property rights. Liberals' particular distain for Indigenous collective property owed not only to economic liberalism's opposition to corporate property but also to positivist anti-Indian racism. Bolivian positivist Daniel Sánchez Bustamante, for instance, believed that economic modernization would naturally entail the disappearance of "the uncivilized races."[35] While at first the state could rarely enforce disentailment laws, the drought provided an opportunity to implement them.

At a moment when the perils of private land and water ownership should have been appallingly clear, the national government launched a sustained attack on pueblos' communal land and water holdings. In 1878, at the height of the drought and famine, state commissioners circulated in Cochabamba's valleys, distributing land titles to community members who could document their usufruct rights and "returning" "excess" land to the state for sale. As historian Laura Gotkowitz explains, late nineteenth-century inspections or *revisitas* "authorized an army of bureaucrats—whose earnings were tied to the number of land titles sold—to penetrate, interrogate, and literally divide up the land of Indian communities."[36] In the highlands Indigenous communities rebelled violently against these laws and prevented their full implementation.[37] In Cochabamba, in contrast, the transition was swift and thorough due to an already advanced process of population loss and individualization of land ownership—and irrigation water access—within communities.[38] More prosperous members of Cochabamba's pueblos who acquired titles to their large holdings may have welcomed the reform as they could now sell or purchase even more land. But land-poor and water-starved community members reeling from drought, disease, and famine who would have likely opposed it were unable to stop the state from titling pre-existing inequalities. By 1900, the national state had carried out one of the most aggressive efforts to dismantle Indigenous communities in Latin America.[39]

As authorities dismantled the region's Indigenous communities, the executive introduced a new water regulation that granted water rights to landowners.[40] The 1879 water regulation, elevated to law in 1906, established a riparian water property regime that considered water an accessory to land. In contrast to colonial water law that proscribed allocation of water according to a combination of prior use and need, the new riparian system granted ownership over water sources that were found within, were located under, or flowed through a property to the land's owner, including non-navigable rivers and streams, ponds and lakes, aquifer sources, and even rainwater. The regulation allowed state institutions to carry out compensated expropriations of private water sources to supply the public during droughts, but the overwhelming thrust of the law was to establish and protect private water ownership.[41] While water had long been in private hands across the country, establishing a riparian system that granted formal property rights to water sources found within landowners' properties gave them new power in drought-prone, semiarid valley regions where smallholders, industrialists, and residents of growing cities all craved greater water access.

The new water regulation, the natural counterpart of the Ley de Exvinculación, allowed a new group of large landowners to consolidate a near monopoly over Cochabamba's water sources. After Bolivia's loss to Chile in the War of the Pacific, new free trade policies and railroads gave altiplano markets access to cheap Chilean grain imports that undercut Cochabamba estates. As a result, according to Jackson and Gordillo, community closure did not lead to expansion of haciendas in Cochabamba, as it did in the Altiplano.[42] Instead, piqueros, landless peasants, hacienda colonos, and artisans purchased much of the community land that the state put up for sale in Cochabamba's valleys.[43] Newly wealthy elites also bought community and hacienda property, displacing those traditional elites who lost all or most of their land. The most important of these new landholders was the Salamanca family. José Domingo Salamanca, who previously owned little land, began buying up large holdings in the Valle Bajo in the 1860s.[44] By his death in the 1890s, Salamanca's estates included a series of haciendas along the Tunari Mountain's foothills with territory extending up into the mountains where large lakes were located. Among Salamanca's heirs was his son Daniel, who would go on to found the Republican Party in 1914 and to serve as the nation's president from 1931 until he was ousted in 1934 during the Chaco War.[45]

While smallholders increased their ownership of land in these last decades of the century, the new large estate owners controlled the region's most important sources of water, including mountain lakes in the upper reaches of their properties. These hacendados compelled colonos and *arrendatarios* (farmers without usufruct plots who rented hacienda land) to maintain existing irrigation infrastructure and build new dams and canals to tap mountain lakes and rivers. While the customary mita rights regime still mostly reigned in practice, landlords began to peel water rights away from land by selling land parcels without all of their customary water rights by reducing the duration and frequency of the turns that corresponded to the plots they sold and adding the extra water turn portions to those corresponding to their remaining land.[46] As a result, water owners like the Salamancas, now the region's biggest, possessed more water than they needed to irrigate their own land, a surplus that they rented to their water-poor piquero neighbors and sold to the growing city. While Spanish water law had discouraged such a state of affairs, the new water regulation encouraged and facilitated it.

The drought, water privatization, and hacendados' control over regional water sources had significant implications for efforts to increase water supply in Bolivia's expanding cities. In Cochabamba, urban officials concluded that the spread of disease could have been averted with improved water distribution and hygienic practices and so set about modernizing the city's drinking water system. Before the drought, Cochabamba's urban drinking water system had consisted of a series of natural springs whose water flowed through open canals to a central water tank in the city's northeast corner that supplied public taps in half a dozen plazas. By the 1870s, many pumps were dry or provided only intermittent supply due to insufficient sources and structural problems. After the drought the central plaza's tap was the city's only functioning water source.[47] The municipal water service was technically the responsibility of the prefecture (state government), and would remain so until 1950, but the municipal council spearheaded its administration and overhaul. To increase supply, officials looked to water sources outside the city's immediate environs, now mostly owned by large estate owners.

Officials were able to expand urban water supply by purchasing hacienda water sources in the Tunari foothills in the 1890s and early 1900s. The most significant of these was the negotiated expropriation of the Arocagua Springs northeast of the city center from the owner of the Pacata estate, Ana María Terrazas, who was willing to sell.[48] Because of the 1879 water regulation, property owners like Terrazas legally owned water and could sell it away from the land it had traditionally served. Despite this purchase, water access in the city (and even more so in the surrounding region) remained inadequate and unequal. Under pressure from urban residents in the 1920s, a period of radical ferment across the Andes and Latin America, local officials began to challenge landlords' water monopoly in order to expand urban water supply. The most important instance of this challenge was a 1924 conflict over the Arocagua Springs between the municipal water service and new owner of the Pacata estate, Ramón Rivero, who offered to sell water to the city that critics believed the municipal water service already owned. Reflecting a broad cross-class sentiment in the city, the editors of the Conservative Party–allied daily newspaper *El Heraldo* argued that "private interests should be sacrificed" and private water property should be abolished to make water access a universal right.[49] The devastating Chaco War (1932–1935) temporarily halted efforts to expand water access but fueled demands for more radical change. After the war, popular groups began to take a more active role in protesting water scarcity and pushing for hydraulic development.

THE REACH AND LIMITS OF WATER REFORM

After the Chaco War, miners, urban workers, peasants, and Indigenous communities mobilized, left-leaning political parties grew and exerted influence, and junior military officers known as "military socialists" assumed the presidency. Among the demands of peasants, Indigenous communities, and residents of growing cities was improved water access. When Indigenous Quechua communities convened for a regional Indigenous congress in Sucre in 1942, for instance, they implored the government to construct "irrigation works that reach all communities."[50] Protests were loudest in Cochabamba where drought and urban migration after the war made an already difficult situation desperate.[51]

The "military-socialist" governments of Colonel David Toro (1936–1937) and Lieutenant Colonel Germán Busch (1937–1939) were committed to state-led economic and infrastructural development, which they believed could reconcile conflicting class interests. While unwilling to challenge the unequal land tenure regime, they worked to make water more accessible to urban residents and especially rural producers to foment agricultural production and national economic development. In fact, the military socialists pursued hydraulic infrastructure to develop new water sources in order to avoid redistributing land or water. Like the contemporaneous technocratic projects meant to alleviate drought in the Brazilian sertão studied by Eve Buckley, hydraulic infrastructure seemed to promise "an apolitical means to end poverty" that would "reduce elites' monopoly over natural resources and wealth without provoking violent confrontation."[52]

Military socialist governments looked to Mexico as a model for building and leveraging state power to diversify the economy and uplift the rural Indigenous peasantry. Bolivia took Mexico's lead on water tenure reform and hydraulic development by nationalizing a range of water sources and launching a national irrigation program. President Busch oversaw the drafting of a new constitution in 1938 that federalized rivers, marshes, and medicinal waters as well as "all of the physical forces able to be used for economic purposes."[53] The "physical forces" in question were not specified and it was therefore unclear if privately owned water sources that could be used for irrigation, hydroelectric production, industry, or human consumption qualified. But the constitution's declaration of state ownership of at least some water sources upset the 1906 water law (based on the 1879 regulation) that had privatized water ownership. Whereas the riparian system established in 1879 granted water property rights to landowners, the 1938 constitution's partial nationalization of water together with the assertion of the state's right and obligation to infringe on private property and industry in the interest of "public security and needs" quietly established the state's right to expropriate privately owned water sources and redirect them to needy farmers and consumers.[54]

Bolivia's military socialists modeled their national irrigation program on Mexico's and invited Mexican state engineers to Bolivia to design and build a major irrigation project. Mexico's Comisión Nacional de Irrigación (CNI) director Francisco Vázquez del Mercado and his team arrived in December 1938.[55] President Busch and Vásquez del Mercado settled on building an irrigation dam and reservoir in Cochabamba, the country's historic breadbasket, for Bolivia's inaugural state-led irrigation initiative. It was called the Angostura project. As Cochabambino Carlos Saavedra Antezana, one of the project's lead engineers and later a prominent national irrigation department official, wrote, while Cochabamba enjoyed "all of the favorable essentials for large-scale development: land, water, and climate," just forty thousand of the Central Valley's approximately one hundred thousand hectares of agricultural land were irrigated.[56] The CNI engineers proposed a twenty-two-meter-high dam to detain and store water from the Sulti River (now the Tamborada) in Cochabamba's Valle Alto to irrigate ten thousand hectares of underused land in Cochabamba's Central Valley.[57] The dam was to sit at a narrow opening in the mountains where the Tamborada flows from the Valle Alto down into the Central Valley. The appeal of this plan was that it would not require expropriating water already in use but would instead utilize water that would have otherwise followed its natural course into the Central Valley's Río Rocha and then out of the region. And both hacendados and piqueros stood to benefit. The Angostura project and others like it across Bolivia were executed in the 1940s under both military-socialist and conservative regimes that saw irrigation works as necessary to increase agricultural production in order to overcome overdependence on the mining sector.[58] The Angostura dam and canal system were completed in the 1950s under the MNR.

The CNI mission to Cochabamba inaugurated and became a model for a broader Mexican effort to spearhead irrigation projects and water tenure reform across Latin America in the final years of Lázaro Cardenás's presidency.[59] The First Inter-American Indigenista Congress, held in Pátzcuaro, Mexico, in 1940, recommended that countries with significant Indigenous populations and extreme land concentration "correct any abuse in this situation" "in accordance with equity and justice" and help Indigenous populations "improv[e] their economy" by providing them with "land, water, credit and technical services."[60] The congress's calls for governments to provide land to Indigenous peasants, protect Indigenous peasants' communal land holdings, and extend water access, credit, and technology to native peasants had radical implications, especially for the countries that had not experienced social revolution and land reform to date—all except Mexico. Bolivia's hydraulic reform was distinctive for coming so early in this regional process and for preceding land reform.

State-led engineering to make water more accessible extended to cities as well. The Chaco War as well as *minifundio*—the predominance of landholdings barely large enough for subsistence—and water scarcity in the countryside led large numbers of veterans and peasants to migrate to department capitals after the war. The city of Cochabamba, known for its agreeable climate and economic opportunities, was a popular destination.[61] The urban population almost quadrupled from an official population of 21,866 in 1900 to approximately 80,000 in 1950.[62] As the city grew, already overstretched urban water systems failed to meet increasing demand or reach the growing urban periphery, leading to intense protest and significant state action.

To increase urban water supply to the department capital, in 1940 the Cochabamba prefecture expropriated mountain lake water that flowed down into the valley by way of the Chocaya, Montesillo, and Taquiña ravines in the Tunari foothills northwest of the city. The expropriated sources irrigated around a dozen haciendas along with hundreds of small farms. In response, affected hacendados and small farmers (piqueros) protested. But while the hacendados offered no concrete alternative, the piqueros proposed expropriating the Chapisirca Lakes, owned by the children of the late president Daniel Salamanca who had led Bolivia to war in the Chaco. The piqueros emphasized the extremely unequal distribution of water rights between the region's large landowners and themselves. Water "was so unequally distributed," they wrote, that "some of us do not even have enough to irrigate our small plots while others have such an abundance that . . . after irrigating their lands they have a surplus to sell—the infamous 'waters for sale' ('aguas de venta')."[63] Remarkably, the prefecture heeded the piqueros' advice. As with the purchase of the Arocagua Springs, in the end the city purchased a hacendado family's surplus "aguas de venta" rather than smallholders' irrigation water. This entailed a rural sacrifice for the city but this time on piqueros' terms.

This episode demonstrates both the advances and the limits of water reform in the late 1930s and early 1940s. National, state, and municipal governments were united in their willingness to more aggressively confront powerful rural water monopolists in order to increase urban water supply and respected piquero water rights. But authorities still needed to purchase water from hacendados to increase supply to the growing city. The continued power of rural water monopolists like the Salamancas showed that a more radical challenge would be required to make hacienda water available to smallholders and urban residents. While the military socialists' hydraulic projects aimed to avoid land and water distribution, they set a precedent and established an expectation for state institutions to allocate water according to human need and national economic priorities. Reform-era hydraulic engineering meant to avoid land and water distribution thus helped pave the way for land and water redistribution in the revolutionary period.

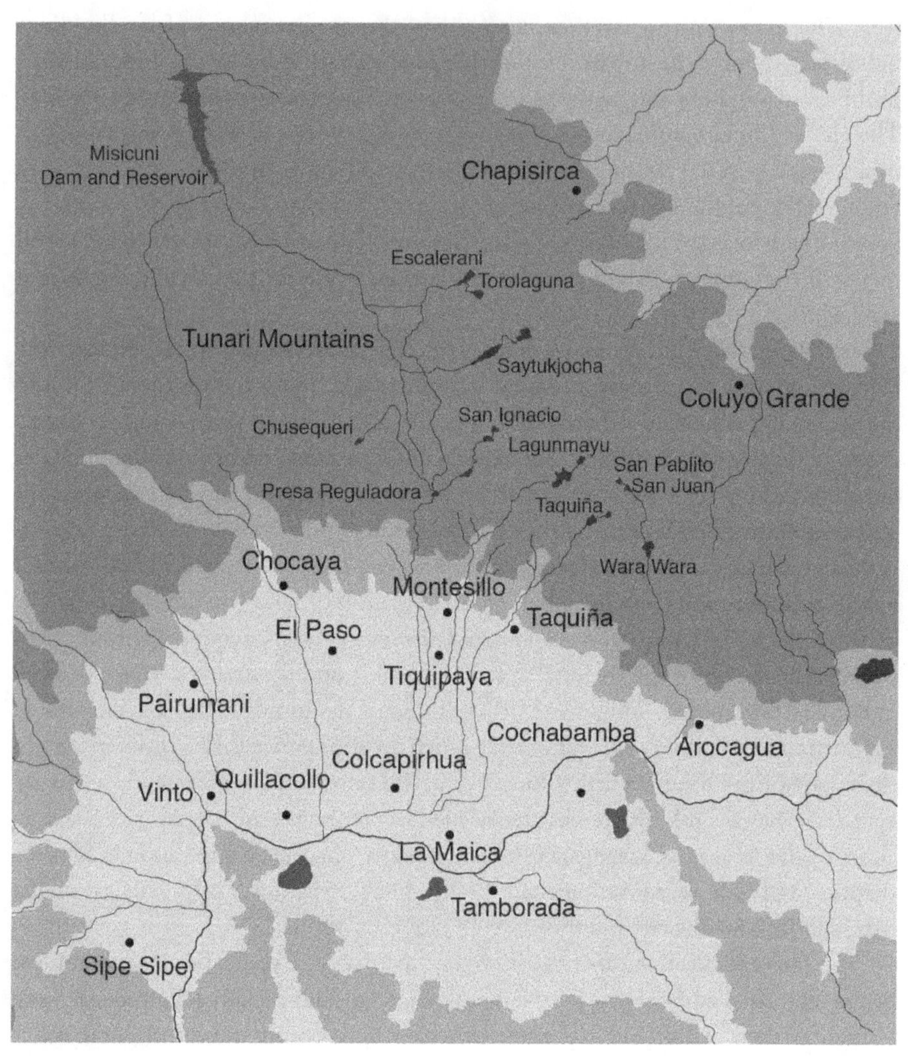

Map 3.2. Central Valley and Tunari Mountains in Cochabamba. Map by Jorge Camacho Saavedra.

HYDRAULIC REVOLUTION

The 1952 Bolivian Revolution's signature reforms involved the confiscation of substantial wealth from landed elites, mineowners, and urban landlords and its redistribution to the Bolivian state and the country's popular classes. In addition to land, tin mines, and housing, this wealth included hoarded water sources. After the Movimiento Nacionalista Revolucionario (MNR) party came to power, colonos, piqueros, Indigenous communities, and city dwellers demanded greater water access, pushing state officials to take more decisive action than in the past. Efforts to expand water access in the 1940s had mostly shied away from challenging private water ownership. After the 1952 insurrection, in contrast, the MNR oversaw a sweeping agrarian reform that redistributed land and transformed the water tenure regime by granting water sources to former estate workers.

While MNR leaders had been divided on the question of agrarian reform in the prerevolutionary period, Indigenous communities and hacienda colonos' militant demands and actions after the insurrection forced their hand. Cochabamba's valleys were among the most militant areas of peasant mobilization. As Julio Butrón Mendoza recounts, many Cochabamba colono unions invaded hacienda land to increase the size of their plots and thereby "establish precedents that would serve them" in the agrarian process.[64] Such unilateral action led Peasant Affairs Minister Ñuflo Chávez to urge "*orden en el agro*" in Cochabamba's Valle Alto.[65] While some colonos waited for the revolutionary state to fulfill leaders' promises to redistribute land and water, it was *dis*order that pushed the MNR to carry out agrarian reform.

Along with land, colonos, smallholders, and Indigenous communities demanded irrigation water to make effective use of their land. Rural land claims sometimes included explicit discussion of water, as in Indigenous petitions preparing for the August 1952 Indigenous Congress just a few months after the insurrection. A Tarija peasant delegation requested that the government carry out a study of the Zola River's potential to irrigate the Guerrahuaico and Tolomosa Cantons and a letter from the Sindicato Agropecuario de Sora representing a former Indigenous community in Oruro's Dalence Province asked the president for "a water pump for irrigation of the property . . . in order to have a larger area to plant."[66] The evolution of the MNR's water policy flowed from attention to such demands as well as officials' recognition of the importance of water access to increasing agricultural production and fostering urban and industrial development. Like their military-socialist predecessors, MNR leaders sought to spur economic diversification by increasing agricultural production, which required providing greater irrigation water access to small farmers.

The MNR's strategy for increasing water access combined large-scale hydraulic infrastructure development with hacienda water redistribution. Like their military-socialist predecessors, the MNR engineered new water sources by building dams across the country. The MNR inaugurated the inherited Angostura dam, which it renamed the Presa México, in April 1952, just days after seizing power, and completed Angostura's canal system in 1955.[67] Expanding irrigation infrastructure was a continuation of an earlier program of water reform through hydraulic infrastructural development. What was revolutionary was that the MNR also committed itself to redistributing existing water sources and infrastructure, especially in the agricultural heartland of Cochabamba. President Paz Estenssoro thus tasked the agrarian reform commission with studying and reforming the country's "water tenure regime" ("*régimen de aguas*").[68]

The 1953 Agrarian Reform Decree-Law set out a revolutionary water policy.[69] Unlike the vague nationalization in the 1938 constitution, the Agrarian Reform Decree-Law fully and clearly nationalized the country's water sources, abolished the rural water market, and mandated water redistribution to give farmers, ranchers, and consumers greater access. In the law's words, "agricultural and animal-raising properties shall use the *necessary flow* with *equal right* for production, irrigation, or watering holes" and "populations have the right to use drinking water sources for domestic purposes."[70] These terms, especially guarantees of "equal rights" to "necessary flows," upended the riparian regime established by the 1879 water code, promising, alongside the MNR's famous promise of "land for those who work it," water for those who need it. These terms made water for all the law of the land. It would take agrarian reform cases, however, to make this law reality.

Agrarian reform cases, which sometimes took more than a decade to wind their way through agrarian courts, were contests over both land and water. To keep their properties, estate owners had to prove that they had made productive use of them. Colonos demanding redistribution often contended that an owner had not done enough to use or expand the property's irrigation water access. In response, landowners routinely argued that they lacked enough irrigation water to make their land productive, used what irrigation rights they had, or had purchased additional sources. Agrarian judges based their decisions in part on who they determined was correct, frequently pointing to a property's water sources as evidence that it should have been more productive than it was.[71]

Agrarian reform reordered the nation's water tenure regime by granting water sources to former estate workers and other beneficiaries. By 1967, 7.2 percent of Bolivian land along with corresponding irrigation water rights had been redistributed, the most extensive land reform in South America by that time.[72] Through agrarian reform, former hacienda colonos and other beneficiaries won significant hacienda land and water sources away from landlords who had built their properties by usurping the land, water, labor, and hydraulic expertise of Indigenous communities, smallholders, and colonos over centuries.[73] As one former Cochabambino colono recounted, "Before the customs were different than now: [we] did not have water to irrigate [our] farms, . . . the *patrón* sold water in turns, by the hour. Ever since the agrarian reform water is free and for all."[74] Through agrarian reform cases, Cochabamba colonos won rights to some of the region's most important irrigation water sources.

But land and water redistribution also reinscribed inequalities between estate owners and ex-colonos and excluded many rural and urban groups. Courts often allowed landowners to keep the best hacienda land and corresponding irrigation rights, awarding colonos only their usufruct plots and irrigation rights. The process also created new inequalities. In the countryside, water redistribution excluded independent peasants (piqueros) and mostly left out poor farmers who rented land or sold their labor. And water redistribution almost entirely ignored residents of the growing city. This led municipal water officials to strike deals to increase supply with the region's newest group of water owners: ex-colono peasant unions.

Despite the unevenness of agrarian reform's benefits, piqueros and ex-colonos worked together in peasant union federations and developed a common mestizo campesino identity in the process of claiming and defending land and water after the revolution. As José Gordillo has argued, mestizaje was a long-term subaltern process of resistance to colonial exploitation. After the revolution, Gordillo writes, "atomized valley peasants . . . experimented for the first time with . . . a collective identity as campesinos."[75] Identifying as mestizo campesinos did not require disavowing Indigenous ancestry or culture. Rather, it allowed smallholders to unite, claim equality and a degree of political autonomy, and connect with urban and peri-urban workers, artisans, and market vendors.

Continued water shortages fueled renewed popular protest and new forms of popular action in Cochabamba's department capital in these years. In 1950, administration of the municipal water service had passed from the prefecture to the municipal government. The system, which consisted of home connections and neighborhood standpipes, covered a quarter of the city's territory and half of its population of 106,000 by 1960.[76] In the decade after municipalization, the water service added 350 to 400 new connections to the distribution system each year without significantly increasing water sources. As a result, residents received poor quality water in scarce quantities from a deteriorated distribution network.[77] In 1960, the water network served less than a quarter of the city's territory and only around half its population.[78] Some neighborhoods built their own supply and distribution systems, but this required significant funds and was not possible in areas where water sources were contaminated or unavailable. After it became clear that agrarian reform would not deliver hacienda lake water to the city, neighborhood groups, unionized workers, and the press demanded increased water supply and foreign funding for hydraulic development.

During Víctor Paz Estenssoro's second term (1960–1964), the MNR negotiated an Inter-American Development Bank (IDB) loan to fund urban drinking water expansion projects in La Paz, Oruro, and Cochabamba.[79] While loan negotiations were underway, Cochabamba residents took matters into their own hands. To protest delays on the overdue Chapisirca project, in December 1962 a two-hundred-worker "brigade" climbed the mountainside to take over work on the project.[80] Seemingly in response, Paz Estenssoro announced that he had signed a loan agreement with the IDB and West Germany.[81] Bank officials opted for wells to increase supply to the department capital. But in the years and decades that followed, a majority of Cochabambinos became convinced that a major dam project in the mountains, which could supply water to both the city and the countryside, would be the best way to fulfill the revolutionary promise of water for all.

DICTATORSHIP AND NEOLIBERALISM

General René Barrientos's 1964 coup ushered in nearly two decades of military rule with just brief moments of relief. Like in many other Latin American countries in the 1960s, Bolivia's dictatorships violently repressed labor, cracked down on students and leftists, and tried to control peasant organizations. But unlike in other countries that experienced counterrevolutionary coups in this period, most notably Guatemala (1954) and Chile (1973), Bolivia's military regimes sustained revolutionary-era reforms. The dictatorships continued land and water redistribution, upheld state ownership of mines, and fortified a developmentalist state committed to urban and rural infrastructural development. Bolivia's military regimes meted out increasingly brutal repression, especially during the regimes of Hugo Banzer (1971–1978) and Luis García Meza (1980–1981). But Barrientos (1964–1969) and Banzer proved receptive to pressure from mobilized water users to expand water access and democratize water governance.

Rather than scuttle the IDB loan for urban water supply expansion in La Paz, Oruro, and Cochabamba negotiated by the MNR, the Barrientos administration and the German contractor Global Engineering submitted the loan proposal in May 1965 and signed the $11 million loan agreement with the IDB in January 1968. The agreement required that the Cochabamba municipality found a new autonomous water company, that the new company raise rates, and that additional supply for the city come from new deep wells outside the city. The efforts of the new water company, the Servicio Municipal de Agua Potable y Alcantarillado (SEMAPA), to adhere to these terms provoked fierce opposition.

In order to meet IDB requirements, SEMAPA's architects reimagined water users as customers and investors and tried to shift financial responsibility away from the state and lenders onto them. Water service fees had until then been low and often went unpaid without consequences. In 1967, rates rose from $1.25 a year to $1.50 a month, sparking the first of a series of rate fights that occurred from the late 1960s to the 1990s. Urban residents vehemently opposed rate increases out of a strong conviction that the state should provide low-cost water service to all urban residents. Residents accepted charges for services like electricity and road paving, if begrudgingly, as they considered them modern luxuries. Water, however, was a basic necessity vital for life. Starting in 1975, civic and neighborhood associations organized collective payment strikes that often succeeded in keeping rates low.[82] At stake in these fights over water rates was whether urban water users would become customers and investors who paid for services, repairs, improvements, and loan obligations but were otherwise passive recipients of water service or whether they would directly participate in water company management and hydraulic development and collectively own and manage independent and municipal water sources and systems.

Water users also opposed the IDB's mandate that SEMAPA drill deep wells in the countryside to supply the city and rallied behind the Misicuni Dam project as an alternative. The Misicuni project, first proposed by water service engineer Luis Calvo Soux in the 1940s, involved damming the waters of the Misicuni, Viscachas, and Putucuni Rivers to produce hydroelectricity and supply irrigation water and drinking water.[83] Bank officials reasoned that wells would be cheaper than a dam project and that aquifer water would be more secure from "theft" by peasants than surface water sources.[84] But many urban residents saw mountain lakes as more abundant, renewable, and reliable sources than aquifer water.

By the early 1970s, the coalition demanding realization of the Misicuni project had grown from a nucleus of urban engineers and civic leaders into a broad cross-class alliance of city elites and professionals, urban popular groups, and rural smallholders. In 1973, peasant union leaders visited the Misicuni Valley and expressed "alarm" at the "hurdles" that authorities put in the project's way.[85] The proposal was appealing to smallholders because it promised to provide irrigation water for eleven thousand peasant households and drinking water to the city without threatening their water sources.[86]

In September 1975, the Cochabamba civic group Junta de la Comunidad (JUNCO) and other groups organized a caravan to the Misicuni River in the mountains above Cochabamba to pressure national authorities to execute the Misicuni

Dam project. More than one thousand Cochabambinos made the journey. Within a month, the Banzer administration secured a $2 million loan for feasibility studies from the Andean Development Corporation. *Los Tiempos* reported that the loan was a direct result of the JUNCO-organized caravan, which the newspaper called "a resounding success due to the 'multitudinous' participation of Cochabamba's people."[87] A year later, the national government founded the Asociación Misicuni (reorganized as the Empresa Misicuni in the 1990s) to oversee feasibility studies, which a Canadian firm conducted from 1977 to 1979.[88] By refusing to pay their bills and caravanning to the proposed project site, Cochabambino water users had won a stalemate on rate increases and advances on the Misicuni project.[89]

Two years later, peasant cultivators from Vinto, an agricultural community west of the city, protested SEMAPA's plan to drill deep wells for the city there in what became known as the first "War of the Wells." State engineers assured peasants there that the new wells would not interfere with existing irrigation wells. But when Vinto peasants discovered that their wells' production had decreased by 75 percent, they formed the Pro-Vinto Committee and attempted to stop the project.[90] In open mass meetings and petitions, Vinto peasants called on state authorities to guarantee consistent water supply, drill additional wells for community use, connect them to the new water main, and immediately begin work on the Misicuni project.[91] Drawing on long-term experience and recent observations, Vinteño peasants maintained that the aquifer's layers were interconnected so that pumping water from deeper layers would deplete upper layers' water as well. In a letter to SEMAPA, the Pro-Vinto Committee reported that "after the [new] wells were drilled, it became clear that there is filtration and communication among the layers, such that the population's wells are completely dry." A military commander overseeing the project criticized the peasants' position as lacking a "solid basis" and scolded them for "emitting opinions without understanding the causes [of the problem]."[92] But the allegedly unsophisticated peasants' position aligned with the private assessment of emergency committee engineers (that were kept secret from Vinteños) and every other study of the Central Valley's underground water resources before and since.[93] Vinto peasants did not stop the drilling, but they won significant concessions from SEMAPA.

Not only were the rates strike, caravan, and wells war effective, but they also occurred during the most repressive years of the Banzer dictatorship. Through these fights, water users gained greater control over water sources and infrastructure and developed a participatory model of water governance rooted in a collective and redistributive idea of social citizenship at odds with the embryonic neoliberal model advanced by the Banzer government and the IDB.

Bolivia's "return to democracy" between 1982 and 1985 occurred during trying economic times. Like other Latin American countries, Bolivia's exports slumped

Figure 3.1. March from Vinto and Sipe Sipe to Cochabamba, October 1994. Source: *Los Tiempos*, October 8, 1994.

while foreign debt ballooned. By 1983, debt service required an outlay equivalent to more than a third of total exports while inflation skyrocketed.[94] Soon after reelection to the presidency in 1985, the MNR's Víctor Paz Estenssoro dismantled the remnants of the social welfare state that he had helped to build and restructured the economy along strict neoliberal lines, making Bolivia the first Latin American country to pursue neoliberal reform under democracy. Bolivia's "New Economic Plan" successfully reined in inflation and reduced the deficit. But it also threw the economy into recession and tens of thousands of public employees out of work, leaving Bolivia's workers and poor to bear the colossal burden of these policies.[95]

Among neoliberal reformers' many targets was Bolivia's water sector. The architects of neoliberal water policy, including the national government and powerful new international partners, aimed to privatize municipal water utilities, as is well known. But this was just one component of a broader effort to dispossess the population of water sources and systems as well as the social right to steer water management and hydraulic engineering. In 1990, the Paz Zamora administration took out a $35 million loan from the World Bank for urban drinking water system improvement in La Paz, Santa Cruz, and Cochabamba. Twenty million dollars were designated for new deep wells, renovations, and network expansion in Cochabamba.[96] The bank moved away from funding large infrastructure projects in these years, focusing instead on institutional restructuring to ensure efficiency and cost recovery to make water utilities attractive to investors.[97] As it did elsewhere, the World Bank conditioned loans to Bolivia on water sector reforms that would enable the government and lenders to exert greater control over water sources, infrastructure, rates, and governance.[98] These reforms aimed to facilitate privatization, private sector management of water provision, and commercialization and treated water as a commodity with an economic value rather than as a social good or right.[99]

The campaign to "rationalize" the national water sector was most aggressive in Cochabamba, where water access was most contentious and water users were especially powerful. Through extensive hydraulic studies, new rate increases, and new deep wells, officials attempted to bring water governance under state and lending-institution control, igniting new rounds of popular organization and protest in the 1990s. SEMAPA customers challenged new rate hikes, peripheral neighborhoods protested exclusion from SEMAPA service and constructed additional independent water systems, and smallholders opposed new well-drilling plans. In 1992, SEMAPA water users staged the decade's first "March for Water and Life" opposing rates hikes and demanding improved and expanded service through realization of the Misicuni project. In the decade's second March for Water and Life in 1994, peasant union members marched to the city center, demanding the authorities execute the Misicuni project instead of drilling deep wells. Well wars in the Valle Bajo had been ongoing since the late 1980s. The third March for Water and Life in 1997 opposed the national government's effort to privatize SEMAPA without local consent or participation. Through these and many other mobilizations, water users halted rate hikes, well-drilling, and the first effort to privatize SEMAPA and won execution of the Misicuni project—construction began in 1996.[100] These actions expressed and strengthened Cochabambinos' belief that, due to their longstanding contributions to expanding water access, the region's water sources and infrastructure belonged to them. These fronts in the fight over neoliberalization of the water sector, which most accounts overlook, are crucial to understanding why a "war" broke out over water privatization in Cochabamba in 1999–2000.

WATER WARS

Cochabamba's 2000 Water War was the culmination of a long history of social struggle over water access, management, and property rights. The anti-privatization movement's slogan, "*¡El agua es nuestra, carajo!*" ("The water is ours, damn it!"), embodied this history, which has not received much scholarly attention in the rich literature on Cochabamba's 2000 Water War but is crucial to understanding the population's claims to the region's water sources and systems—and the source of their power. The Water War was not only a struggle over the municipal water company SEMAPA, nor was it primarily about water rates, though those were important issues. At its heart, Cochabamba's 2000 Water War was a struggle over collective hydraulic property and rights to manage water sources, infrastructure, and development. While they had vied over water access in the past, during the Water War peasants, irrigators, provincial and peripheral neighborhoods, and SEMAPA customers united to protect water systems they considered collective property. Their power rested on their collective control over water sources, infrastructure, engineering, and governance established over decades of social struggle, organization, labor, and investment.

When the government reopened bidding on Cochabamba's water concession in 1999, an international consortium registered in the Cayman Islands called Aguas del Tunari made the only bid. The consortium was comprised of International Waters, a subsidiary of the construction firms Bechtel (US) and Edison (Italy) that held 55 percent of shares, the Spanish construction company Abengoa that held 25 percent, and four Bolivian contractors that held five percent each. Fearful of losing this lone bidder, government representatives sweetened the deal's terms. The contract guaranteed the company a 15 to 17 percent return and gave the company exclusive rights to provide and charge for drinking water and sewerage services, set water rates, sell irrigation and "bulk" water, and use the region's water sources. The agreement also cut the Misicuni project down to what the Society of Engineers called a "bonsai" version.[101] In theory, the contract even prohibited rainwater collection, as immortalized in William Finnegan's *New Yorker* article "Leasing the Rain," one of the first reports on the Water War in the US, and the Spanish film *También la lluvia*.[102]

In September 1999, the Bolivian government signed the contract with Aguas del Tunari, awarding the consortium a forty-year concession for water provision in Cochabamba.[103] The following month, Congress passed Ley 2029 de Agua Potable y Alcantarillado Sanitario that gave the contract legal backing and a legal framework. The law established that "private entities could participate in water and sanitation service provision" and gave concessionaries exclusive rights to provide water in concession areas, thereby prohibiting the collection of water without permission from the new national water authority. The law also gave concessionaries the right to use public goods free of charge and threatened service cuts and legal sanction for failure to pay bills.[104] Like the 1879 water regulation and the 1906 water law that the 1938 constitution had partially nullified and the 1953 Agrarian Reform Decree-Law had in effect overturned, Ley 2029 privatized water. This time however, instead of conferring property rights to landholders, it bestowed them on private companies.

Figure 3.2. "El agua es nuestra" banner, COD office, April 2000. Photo by Tom Kruse.

State authorities argued that private sector involvement and national oversight were needed because municipalities had not provided good service. But Aguas del Tunari planned to improve service—and make a profit—by raising rates, something SEMAPA had tried and mostly failed to do for three decades. By threatening to raise rates and dispossess independent neighborhoods and irrigators of their water sources and systems, the new water regime threatened the hard-won rights of all the region's water users.

As the public learned about the contract's terms, water users from across the valley began to organize. Among the Water War's key participants were peasants, provincial town residents, periphery dwellers, and SEMAPA customers, groups that had been divided on water issues in the past. When the Coordinadora de Defensa del Agua y de la Vida (Coordinating Committee for the Defense of Water and Life) called its first protest in December 1999, spokesperson Oscar Olivera recalls that organizers assumed the turnout would be small given that, as he put it, "the interests of city dwellers and country dwellers had often been opposed" since "increased supply of city water came at the expense of water for the farmers." On the day of the protest, however, ten thousand people filled the streets.[105] They united because privatization threatened increased rates for municipal customers and dispossession of municipal, independent neighborhood, and peasant and irrigator union water sources and infrastructure. For the first time since the 1952 Bolivian Revolution, urban and rural popular groups mobilized together around a common cause, this time to defend collective ownership of water sources and infrastructure.

Cocaleros, organized in the Seis Federaciones del Trópico, and their leader Evo Morales supported the Coordinadora from the beginning of the conflict. As Marcela Olivera explains, "many cocaleros live on the periphery of the city" so their "communitarian water systems were affected as well."[106] Like opponents of water privatization, cocaleros in the Chapare were fighting for their livelihoods and against what they saw as plunder of their natural resources by the national government and powerful foreign interests. The Water War offered Evo Morales and his Movement Toward Socialism Party an opportunity to increase their visibility in the department capital and across the country.

Coordinadora strategy deftly combined direct action with a willingness to negotiate and compromise.[107] Its actions creatively melded classic forms of protest, including marches, strikes, and blockades, with new kinds of spectacular direct action like the symbolic takeover of the city, burning water bills, graffiti, and a popular referendum.[108] In April 2000, after months of mass actions and deliberations, meetings with government officials, occupation of Aguas del Tunari's offices, detention of Coordinadora representatives, and violent clashes with the military and police that left seventeen-year-old Victor Hugo Daza dead and over one hundred people wounded, the government agreed to rescind the contract with Aguas de Tunari and modify Ley 2029 according to the Coordinadora's demands. Protestors tore down the Aguas del Tunari sign and replaced it with one that read Aguas del Pueblo.[109]

The Water War opened a five-year period of social mobilization that brought down two presidents and paved the way for the 2005 election of Evo Morales, the country's first Indigenous president. Social movements staged uprisings opposing privatization, foreign control over natural resources, and other policies that increased the cost of living in these years, including the 2002 Coca War, the February 2003 Tax Revolt, and the October 2003 Gas War.

Among these fights was a conflict over water privatization in El Alto, the sister city of the national capital, La Paz. In 1997, at the behest of the World Bank, the Bolivian government had granted a thirty-year concession to administer La Paz and El Alto's water service to an international consortium called Aguas de Illimani South America (AISA). The consortium's lead member was the French water company

Suez, which held 55 percent of shares. International financial institutions considered the contract to be "pro-poor" due to its focus on expanding connections. But the company only increased connections within the contracted service area where customers could afford to pay and excluded hard-to-reach areas of El Alto, home to the metropolitan area's poorest residents. Even within the "served area," high connection costs left 70,000 residents without service.[110] In total, around 200,000 of El Alto's approximately 700,000 residents lacked connections.[111] While protests against Aguas de Illimani began soon after the concession was granted, in 2004 and 2005 El Alto's neighborhood federation (FEJUVE) built on the momentum of the 2003 Gas War to organize large mobilizations demanding cancellation of the contract due to high rates, poor service, and exclusion.[112] Like in Cochabamba, El Alto water users rejected privatization in favor of local control over water provision. Strikes, blockades, and a massive protest march in January 2005 forced President Carlos Mesa to cancel the contract.

During these years of upheaval, social movements began to call for a national constituent assembly to refound the nation in the interest of Bolivia's poor, working class, and Indigenous majority on the basis of collective rights to wealth and resources. Coordinadora activists called for such an assembly soon after the 2000 Water War, echoing the demand of lowland Indigenous organizations during national marches in the 1990s. Having united and mobilized different groups across class, ethnic, and spatial lines, the Coordinadora offered a model for a grassroots representative body that could democratize access to the commons and public goods and establish just stewardship of natural resources. In Oscar Olivera's words, their goal was to "forge a new democracy" that is "neither delegated nor representative, but authentic, participatory, direct, and without intermediaries."[113] In 2004, some of the most important organizations behind the 2000–2005 left and Indigenous uprisings formed the Unity Pact (Pacto de Unidad) to push for a constituent assembly.[114] The Unity Pact called for drafting a new constitution that would "completely refound the Bolivian State" as "an inclusive and plurinational state that would allow for building a shared country."[115] Promoting collective ownership of natural resources like land and water were foremost among their goals. This vision emerged not only from the 2000 and 2005 Water Wars but also out of the long history of community control over water provision in Cochabamba and other parts of Bolivia.

WATER GOVERNANCE IN THE MORALES ERA

Evo Morales rode the tide of social upheaval to the presidency, promising to "rule by obeying" the organizations and communities that brought him to power by reversing the privatization of state industries and public services and convening a constituent assembly. At his January 2006 inauguration in Tiwanaku, a pre-Columbian ceremonial center, Morales pledged to respect and restore Indigenous and peasant communities' autonomous control over their territories and the natural resources within them. He also vowed to restore state control over extractive industries and public services like drinking water in order to provide for citizens' wellbeing. While Morales's commitment to public water provision responded to social movement demands, during Morales's presidency (2006–2019) MAS officials attempting to exert state control over the water sector often clashed with water users who had developed a bottom-up, collective, and participatory community water management model. Advocates of statist and communitarian models of water governance shared a rejection of the neoliberal model of private sector governance but differed over what should replace it.

Tensions between statist and communitarian models of water governance and efforts to resolve them were evident in deliberations over water provision at the Constituent Assembly that took place in Sucre from August 2006 to December 2007. The Unity Pact proposed that water be considered a social good and a human right and that it be administered by a combination of public, place-based, and Indigenous and peasant community organizations. Its first proposal required the state to consult with Indigenous and peasant communities around water use and to guarantee sustainable water use and equitable distribution, "prioritizing women, the elderly, Indigenous people, and the poor."[116] The 2007 "consensus version" afforded more power and responsibility to the state. But it still insisted that "water resources and watersheds within the territories of Indigenous, originary, peasant, and Afro-descended nations and peoples be managed according to their own rules, procedures, practices, uses, and customs." It also stipulated that public drinking water utilities "incorporate participation, co-management, and social control of users according to their own norms and procedures."[117]

The new constitution, ratified in a January 2009 popular referendum, refounded the nation as the Plurinational State of Bolivia, recognizing the rights of Bolivia's Indigenous peoples and nations. The preamble credits the Cochabamba and El Alto Water Wars with inspiring the creation of a new state based on "collective coexistence with access to water, work, education, health, and housing for all."[118] The new charter affirms that "all people have the right to water" and to "universal and equitable access to basic services," including drinking water provision, and that "access to water and sanitation is a human right." Water and sanitation services therefore can neither be offered in concession nor privatized but rather are subject to a system of licenses and registries according to law.[119] But, like the Unity Pact proposal, the constitution embodies friction between statist and communitarian paradigms: The text declares that water sources fall under the "exclusive jurisdiction of the central state" and that "Indigenous, originary, peasant autonomies have control over irrigation systems, hydraulic resources, and water sources within their jurisdictions." While the charter requires the national state to "recognize, respect, and protect uses and customs of communities, their local authorities, and Indigenous, and peasant organizations over water rights, management, and sustainable administration," the power and responsibility to provide and oversee water access and management lies with the state.[120] While some Cochabambino activists advocated a communitarian model and maintained their independence from the MAS and MAS-led state, others supported a statist approach and accepted positions in national and local state offices.[121]

The 2012 Law for the Rights of Mother Earth took the constitution's mandates further, tasking the state with ensuring equitable distribution of natural resources in order to establish a just society. The text established that the state should "reduce differences in Bolivian people's access to land, water, forests, biodiversity, and other components of Mother Earth" and to guarantee the "right of water for life" in order to build "a just, equitable, and solidarity-based society without material, social, or spiritual poverty." The commitments to eliminate "concentrations of landed property in the hands of private property owners or businesses" and establish "equitable conditions of access to water for consumption, irrigation, and industrial use" reflected the ambition and optimism of the times.[122] But the issue of what bodies should oversee water provision remained contentious.

At the urging of the Morales administration and water activists, the United Nations General Assembly declared water access a human right in July 2010. After campaigning for adoption of a constitutional right to water in Bolivia, Bolivia's ambassador to the United Nations, Pablo Solón, pushed for the United Nations to adopt it as well.[123] The UN resolution recognized "the right to safe and clean drinking water and sanitation" as a human right and called on governments and international organizations to finance efforts to "provide safe, clean, accessible, and affordable drinking water and sanitation for all."[124] At global water forums in Kyoto, Istanbul, and Mexico, some Bolivian activists had helped pressure the UN to declare water access a human right in order to give citizens a legal basis for demanding that states supply water and opposing initiatives like privatization that curtailed water access.

Yet many water activists, in Bolivia and elsewhere, worried that the human right to water might prioritize human use to the detriment of ecosystems, could conflict with existing water rights regimes, and would not necessarily prevent privatization. Indeed, at the Fourth World Water Forum in Mexico City in 2006, a group of private water companies declared their support for the right to water. Soon after, Nestlé's CEO disavowed his earlier opposition and began to call himself a devoted supporter of the human right to water. As a result, as anthropologist Andrea Ballestero writes, "the boundary between a human right and a commodity" became "blurrier than ever" and many water activists came to see "human rights as weak anticapitalist tools."[125] Critics also argue that rights-based approaches elevate the state rather than communities as the rightful guardians of natural resources like water.[126]

In Bolivia, debates over the merits of a human right to water pitted MAS officials intent on increasing state authority over the water sector in order to expand irrigation and drinking water access against water rights holders and their advocates defending hard-won historic rights and a communitarian water governance model. The "Agua Para Todos" program, part of the 2006–2010 National Development Plan, promised to extend drinking water service to 1.9 million of the 2.3 million Bolivians lacking it and to provide water to small farmers lacking rights while respecting customary usage (*usos y costumbres*).[127] The "Mi Agua" program provided $300,000 to municipalities for improvement of community water systems. In 2019, the Ministry of the Environment and Water reported that since 2006, the government had invested $292 million in drinking water and sanitation projects and another $141 million in irrigation and hydraulic resources projects, increasing drinking water access from 71 to 86 percent (95 percent in urban areas, 67 percent in rural areas) of households and putting 258,145 hectares of land under irrigation, benefitting 234,708 families.[128] These numbers did not reflect quality, quantity, or reports of poor project execution, however.[129] Furthermore, government projects at times threatened the historic rights of smallholders and peri-urban water cooperatives that Morales had vowed to protect. Provision of Mi Agua funds, for instance, was contingent on municipalization of community water systems.[130]

Numerous conflicts between state officials and water rights holders erupted in Cochabamba during the Morales presidency. While MAS officials argued that it was sometimes necessary to challenge existing systems of rights allocation to extend water access to those who lacked it, Cochabamba water activists and rights holders defended community management and existing rights regimes. For instance, in Sacaba, the municipality just east of Cochabamba, the MAS-run municipal government tried to appropriate the independent water sources and distribution systems of neighborhood water cooperatives for the new municipal water company. For opponents of such efforts, in the words of sociologist and water activist Carlos Crespo, the MAS was using "the principle of a human right to water to legitimate, in a new context, the long history of the destruction of water commons by the Bolivian state."[131] But not all conflicts were between public institutions and community-run systems, however. Some involved competition between public water utilities and others pitted different groups of water users against each other.

Conflicts over water access in Bolivia in recent years raise a difficult question: Is it possible to expand water access while also respecting community-administered water systems and rights? They also point to a deep and debilitating contradiction at the heart of the MAS project between statist developmentalism and communitarianism. The MAS under Morales increasingly pursued a state-led developmentalist vision dependent on state direction, foreign capital investment, fossil fuel extraction, and commercial agriculture.[132] Many MAS supporters, in contrast, envisioned a bottom-up democracy rooted in the self-activity and organization of the country's poor and working peoples. For them, refounding the country meant strengthening grassroots community control rather than establishing state power over natural resources like water.[133]

The vision that won out nationally was Evo's. But his administration's hegemonic agenda was always aspirational, especially in the water sector. In practice, public and community systems coexisted, and their managers clashed, negotiated, and collaborated. At times, state efforts gave peasants, irrigators, peri-urban residents, and municipal customers opportunities to strengthen social control over water sources and systems. Water users who stood to lose water rights generally opposed state intervention, while those who lacked rights often welcomed it. Yet contending groups of water users agreed that state involvement should occur on local water users' own terms, and that secure access to plentiful and clean water was necessary to live and to improve their lives.

CONCLUSION

The history of social struggle over water traced here suggests that the Bolivian state has not been weak in the water sector due to incompetence or lack of trying. Nor have water users rejected a relationship with state institutions.[134] Rather, water users have often dictated where, when, and how the state has intervened. For Bolivians and especially for Cochabambinos, water is different than electricity, roads, transportation, and other services. It is not a luxury but rather a basic necessity for survival and a decent life that the state should either guarantee or allow communities to provide for themselves.

Starting under dictatorship, international financial institutions and municipal water companies tried to offload financial responsibility for improving water access onto urban water users through raising rates; they also attempted to appropriate rural cultivators' water sources for the city. In the neoliberal period, neoliberal governments and international financial institutions continued and intensified these efforts, this time through privatization, transferring administration of municipal water utilities—and independent water systems—to transnational corporations. Water wars in Cochabamba and El Alto in the early 2000s defeated privatization and dispossession and returned municipal and independent water systems to municipal and community control. The Morales administration attempted to expand water access by subordinating community systems to state control, often attempting to transfer community water sources and infrastructure to public water utilities. Members of the water collectives opposed these moves, defending a communitarian water governance model where water users own, plan, build, and manage water sources and systems—and state involvement—themselves.

Despite restitution of municipal and community control over water after Aguas del Tunari departed, water access in Cochabamba remains highly unequal. Increasing and improving water access will require confronting the tensions between statist and communitarian models. While the statist (public) model tends to ignore the concerns of water users with hard-won historic rights, the communitarian model risks excluding those who lack them. To deal with these complexities, some Cochabamba water activists have proposed creating a new body modeled on the Coordinadora de Defensa del Agua y de la Vida with representatives of all water-using groups, institutions, and communities.[135]

Global justice activists have hailed the Cochabamba Water War for its victory against neoliberal privatization. A long-term historical perspective shows that Cochabamba's experience also has lessons to offer about what should replace it and who should decide.

NOTES

This chapter draws from my book *Water for All: Community, Property, and Revolution in Modern Bolivia* (Oakland: University of California Press, 2022), which develops the story told and analysis given here in greater depth.

1. Murra, *Formaciones económicas*, 59–116.
2. Borsdorf and Stadel, *The Andes*, 62.
3. The pools, ponds, and lakes that once formed in the Valley's shallow depressions gave Cochabamba its name, derived from the Quechua *q'ocha pampa*, meaning "lake plateau" or the "valley of lakes." Navarro and Maldonado, *Geografía ecológica de Bolivia*.
4. Zimmerer, "The Origins of Andean Irrigation," 481–83. Cultivators in the Tarata area of Cochabamba used an "extensive and integrated system of floodwater and canal irrigation" in the eighth century BCE that "functioned as early as 3,500 years before present (BP)."
5. Zimmerer, "Rescaling Irrigation in Latin America," 150–75.

6. Wachtel, "The Mitimas of the Cochabamba Valley," 202.
7. Zimmerer, "Rescaling Irrigation," 156; Larson, *Cochabamba, 1550–1900*, 10, 20–21.
8. Rivera Cusicanqui, *Violencias (re)encubiertas en Bolivia*, 42.
9. Mumford, *Vertical Empire*, 113.
10. Jackson and Gordillo Claure, "Formación, crisis y transformación," 734.
11. Larson, *Cochabamba, 1550–1900*, 88; Zimmer, "Rescaling Irrigation," 164–67; Fernández Quiroga, "La Relación Tierra-Agua," 20–21.
12. Jackson and Gordillo Claure, "Formación, crisis, y transformación," 759.
13. Spain and Consejo de Indias, *Recopilación de leyes de los reynos de las Indias*, 407.
14. Meyer, *Water in the Hispanic Southwest*, 120.
15. Larson, *Cochabamba, 1550–1900*, 145; Zimmerer, "Rescaling Irrigation," 165–66.
16. Larson, *Cochabamba, 1550–1900*, 145.
17. Zimmerer, "Rescaling Irrigation in Latin America," 165–66.
18. Platt, *Estado boliviano y ayllu andino*.
19. Fernández Quiroga, "La Relación Tierra-Agua," 20–21.
20. Larson, *Cochabamba, 1550–1900*, 218–19; Jackson, *Regional Markets and Agrarian Transformation*, 17.
21. Davis, *Late Victorian Holocausts*, 7, 108–15; Aceituno et al., "The 1877–1878 El Niño Episode," 389–416.
22. Davis, *Late Victorian Holocausts*, 11.
23. Pentimalli de Navarro and Rodríguez Ostria, "Las razones de la multitud," 17.
24. Concejo Municipal de Cochabamba, "Memoria de 1878" (Cochabamba: Imprenta del Siglo), Archivo Histórico Municipal de Cochabamba (AHMC).
25. Querejazu Calvo, *Guano, salitre, sangre*, 255–58; Jackson, *Regional Markets and Agrarian Transformation*, 17–19.
26. Concejo Municipal, "Memoria de 1878"; Concejo Municipal de Cochabamba, "Memoria de 1879" (Cochabamba: Imprenta del Siglo), Biblioteca Arturo Costa de la Torre (La Paz, Bolivia); "Miseria pública" and "Beneficencia," *El Heraldo*, January 3, 1879, 2; "Plan de Subsistencias," *El Heraldo*, April 22, 1878, 1.
27. Pentimalli and Rodríguez, "Las razones," 19–20.
28. Pentimalli and Rodríguez, "Las razones," 20–22; Scott, *Moral Economy of the Peasant*.
29. Cushman, *Guano and the Opening of the Pacific World*, 73; Sater, *Andean Tragedy*, 2.
30. Sater, *Andean Tragedy*, 19.
31. Basadre, *Historia de la República del Perú*, Vol. 8, 117.
32. Sater, *Andean Tragedy*, 1.
33. Klein, *Parties and Political Change in Bolivia*, 18–21; Klein, *A Concise History of Bolivia*, 142–43; Langer, *Economic Change and Rural Resistance*, 36–51.
34. Rodriguez Ostria, "Entre reformas y contrareformas," 307; Larson, *Trials of Nation Making*, 219.

35. Quoted in Francovich, *El pensamiento boliviano*, 20.
36. Gotkowitz, *A Revolution for Our Rights*, 30.
37. Rivera Cusicanqui, *Oprimidos pero no vencidos*; Choque Canqui, *Sublevación y masacre de Jesús de Machaqa de 1921*; Cárdenas, "'La lucha de un pueblo'"; Larson, *Trials of Nation Making*; Hylton, "Reverberations of Insurgency"; Ari Chachaki, *Earth Politics*.
38. Larson, *Cochabamba, 1550–1900*, 311; Rodriguez Ostria, "Entre reformas y contrareformas," 288, 322.
39. Gotkowitz, *A Revolution for Our Rights*, 18; Larson, *Trials of Nation Making*, 218–29. On a similar process of land dispossession in Mexico, see Mallon, *Peasant and Nation*. On Peru, see Mallon, *Peasant and Nation*; Mallon, *Defense of Community*; Larson, *Trials of Nation Making*, 141–201. On Guatemala, see Grandin, *The Last Colonial Massacre*, chap. 1; Grandin, *The Blood of Guatemala*.
40. Bolivia, *Reglamento de aguas*, 8 September 1879.
41. Bolivia, *Reglamento de aguas*, 8 September 1879, Articles 41, 205, 212.
42. Gordillo and Jackson, "Mestizaje y proceso de parcelización," 20; Jackson and Gordillo Claure, "Formación, crisis y transformación," 736–39.
43. Larson, *Cochabamba, 1550–1900*, 202–9; Jackson, *Regional Markets and Agrarian Transformation*, 75–77.
44. According to Robert Jackson, whereas most elite families relied on hacienda income and were therefore vulnerable to fluctuations in agricultural prices, the Salamancas were among the few who invested in bank and mining stock and interest-bearing bonds. Jackson, "The Decline of the Hacienda," 737–38.
45. Jackson, *Regional Markets and Agrarian Transformation*, 159–61.
46. "Juicio civil seguido por José Caraballo contra Francisco Guillen sobre entrega de aguas," 26 August 1878, Expedientes Republicanos Cochabamba, vol. 131, no. 7, fs. 676–723, AHMC.
47. "Sesión ordinaria de 7 noviembre 1930," *Gaceta Municipal*, AHMC; "Aguas Potables," *El Heraldo*, May 10, 1878, 1.
48. "Escritura de compra-venta de las aguas de Arocagua," 3 November 1891, published in "Aguas de Arocagua," *El Comercio*, December 14, 1894.
49. "Los derechos del Estado sobre las vertientes de Arocagua," *El Heraldo*, August 27, 1924, 2.
50. *Tierra*, August 11, 1942. Quoted in Soliz, *Fields of Revolution*, 58.
51. See daily press coverage in *El Imparcial* and *El País*, 1939–1940, for instance, "Carestía de agua," *El Imparcial*, July 11, 1939, 2; "¡Cochabamba se morirá de sed!," *El País*, April 27, 1940, 5.
52. Buckley, *Technocrats and the Politics of Drought*, 4, 9.
53. Bolivia, 1938 Constitution, Article 107.
54. Bolivia, 1938 Constitution, Article 17.
55. Sanjinés, *La reforma agraria en Bolivia*, 2nd ed., 148–64; Kiddle, *Mexico's Relations with Latin America*, 143–49.

56. Saavedra Antezana, “Ideas generales sobre obras de irrigación en Bolivia,” *Irrigación en México* 27, no. 1 (1946): 16.
57. Sanjinés, *La reforma agraria en Bolivia*, 166.
58. Saavedra, “Ideas generales,” 11.
59. Thornton, “‘Mexico Has the Theories’”; Sanjinés, *La reforma agraria en Bolivia*, 159, 163; Kiddle, *Mexico's Relations*, 145.
60. First Inter-American Conference on Indian Life, “Final Act,” Pátzcuaro, Mexico, 14–24 April 1940 (Washington, DC: Bureau of Indian Affairs, 1941), 13–14.
61. Solares Serrano, *Historia, espacio y sociedad*, 309.
62. Goldstein, *The Spectacular City*, 61.
63. “Respuesta de piqueros,” 22 July 1940, “Expropiación Chocaya, Montesillo y Taquiña,” Archivo Histórico de la Prefectura de Cochabamba, Exp. Rep. 1940, vol. 286.
64. Butrón Mendoza, *Eran solo unos indios*, 65–66.
65. Ñuflo Chávez Ortiz, “Discurso prenunciado en la ‘Semana de la Siembra,’” *Gaceta Campesina*, April 1953, 30.
66. Petition dated 3 July 1952, Archivo y Biblioteca Nacional de Bolivia (ABNB), Exp. Pres. Rep. 765; Petition dated 30 June 1952, ABNB, Exp. Pres. Rep. 759.
67. Dec. Sup. 3185, 15 April 1952; Jorge Muller Barragán, “Transformación de la Socio-Economía del Altiplano de La Paz,” *Gaceta Campesina*, August 1954.
68. “Plan General para el Estudio de la Reforma Agraria,” April 7, 1953, *Gaceta Campesina*, August 1953, 83–118.
69. A *decreto ley*, or decree-law, has the power of a law but has not been passed by Congress. As Carmen Soliz explains, they are usually “signed by a de facto president or in a revolutionary context.” Soliz, *Fields of Revolution*, 183–84. Because Congress dissolved after the April 1952 insurrection, MNR President Victor Paz Estenssoro implemented revolutionary reform through a series of decree-laws. The August 2, 1953 Agrarian Reform Decree-Law 3464 was passed into law by the new congress on October 29, 1956. Bolivia, Ley de 29 October 1956, *Gaceta Oficial*.
70. Bolivia, Agrarian Reform Law, 2 August 1953, Articles 151, 102. My emphasis.
71. Hines, *Water for All: Community*, 81–120.
72. Heath, Buechler, and Erasmus, *Land Reform and Social Revolution*, 373–74.
73. In 1954, the MNR specifically recognized highland Indigenous communities' land claims with Decree-Law no. 3732, 19 May 1954. On Indigenous community mobilization leading to this decree, see Soliz, “‘Land to the Original Owners’,” 259–96; and Soliz, *Fields of Revolution*.
74. Quoted in Gordillo Claure, *Arando en la historia*, 111.
75. Gordillo Claure, *Peasant Wars in Bolivia*, 261. See also Silvia Rivera's discussion of mestizo culture, what she calls *ch'ixi*. Rivera Cusicanqui, *Ch'ixinakax Utxiwa*, 105. On campesino identity formation in Mexico, see Boyer, *Becoming Campesinos*.

76. "Periferia urbana," *El Pueblo*, 16 October 1960, 5; "Perforaciones de pozos," *El Pueblo*, June 15, 1960, 5.
77. "Agua potable," *Prensa Libre*, 20 October 1961, 5; "Servicios públicos," *Prensa Libre*, January 13, 1962, 4; "Desarrollo," *Prensa Libre*, February 23, 1962, 4.
78. "Periferia urbana," *El Pueblo*, October 16, 1960, 5; "Perforaciones de pozos," *El Pueblo*, June 15, 1960, 5.
79. República de Bolivia, Ministerio de Economía, and Nacional Deutsche Projekt Unión GMBH Ingeniería Global, "Solicitud de préstamo para el abastecimiento de agua potable para la ciudad de Cochabamba–Bolivia, Primera etapa de la solución definitiva plan maestro, Volumen I de III tomos: Informe, Contrato del 11.12.1962, HC-294 v. 1, Archivo del Departamento de Planificación de la Gobernación de Cochabamba ("Ex-CORDECO").
80. "Chapisirca," *Prensa Libre*, December 5, 1962, 4.
81. "Inversiones," *Prensa Libre*, December 25, 1962, 5.
82. "JUNCO pedirá informe," *Prensa Libre*, June 27, 1974, 4.
83. "Estudios preliminares" *El Pueblo*, February 23, 1960, 1.
84. Global Engineering, "Solicitud de Préstamo para el abastecimiento de agua potable para la ciudad de Cochabamba," vol. 2 (Cochabamba, 15 May 1965), art. 324, SEMAPA Archive.
85. *Los Tiempos*, July 9, 1973.
86. SOFRELEC síntesis.
87. "CAF acordó crédito," *Los Tiempos*, November 10, 1975.
88. Bolivia, Decreto Supremo 13212, 18 December 1975, *Gaceta Oficial*. See daily coverage in *Los Tiempos* and *Prensa Libre* October 1975–January 1976.
89. For more on the fight to win execution of the Misicuni project, see Hines, "The Power and Ethics of Vernacular Modernism," 223–56; Hines, *Water for All*, 121–50.
90. See daily coverage in *Prensa Libre* in August 1977 and correspondence and agreements between SEMAPA and Vinto communities in SEMAPA's Legal Department files.
91. Agenda of the cabildo abierto en Vinto, 17 September 1977, SEMAPA Legal Department files; Carta Comité Pro-Vinto; "Construcción del acueducto Vinto – Cala Cala," *Los Tiempos*, September 3, 1977.
92. "Denuncias," *Prensa Libre*, August 26, 1977, 4.
93. Comité Técnico Inter-Institucional Cochabamba, "Abastecimiento de agua potable de la ciudad de Cochabamba: Estudio de alternativas de emergencia," February 1977, SEMAPA. A 1978 United Nations Development Program (UNDP) and GEOBOL study of hydraulic resources in Cochabamba's four valleys, for instance, determined that "future exploitation will affect the hydrodynamic situation and interfere with existing wells, and this interference will need to be compensated." GEOBOL and UNDP, "Proyecto integrado de recursos hídricos Cochabamba, investigaciones de aguas subterráneas," 1978, SEMAPA Archive, 224.

94. Klein, *A Concise History*, 241.
95. Kohl and Farthing, *Impasse in Bolivia*, 111–15.
96. International Development Association and Republic of Bolivia, "Development Credit Agreement (Major Cities Water Supply and Sewerage Rehabilitation Project)" (17 December 1990), 23–24.
97. Marvin and Laurie, "An Emerging Logic," 346.
98. Goldman, *Imperial Nature*, 232.
99. García Orellana, García Yapur, and Quitón Herbas, "La crisis política," 24–25; Assies, "David versus Goliath," 16.
100. Hines, *Water for All*, 151–94; Hines, "The Power and Ethics of Vernacular Modernism."
101. Assies, "David Versus Goliath," 22; García Orellana, García Yapur, and Quitón Herbas, "La crisis política," 40.
102. Finnegan, "Leasing the Rain"; Bollaín, *También la lluvia*.
103. Kruse, "La Guerra del Agua," 99.
104. Law 2029, 29 October 1999, Article 70.
105. Olivera and Lewis, *¡Cochabamba!*, 30.
106. Marcela Olivera, personal communication with author, 20 October 2020.
107. García Orellana et al, "La crisis política," 103.
108. Crespo Flores, Fernández, and Peredo, *Los regantes de Cochabamba*, 192; García Orellana et al., "La crisis política," 551; Orellana Aillón, "El proceso insurrecional de abril," 520.
109. Bjork-James, *The Sovereign Street*, 77.
110. Spronk, "Roots of Resistance," 18–20; Komives, "Designing Pro-Poor Water and Sewer Concessions," 29–30.
111. Hailu, Guerreiro Osorio, and Tsukada, "Privatization and Renationalization," 2565.
112. Botton, Hardy, and Poupeau, "Water from the Heights," 5.
113. Olivera, *¡Cochabamba!*, 129–39.
114. These organizations included the Confederación Sindical Unica de Trabajadores Campesinos de Bolivia (CSUTCB), the Confederación Sindical de Comunidades Interculturales de Bolivia (CSCIB), the Confederación Nacional de Mujeres Campesina Indígena Originarias de Bolivia "Bartolina Sisa" (CNMCIOB-BS), the Confederación de Pueblos Indígenas del Oriente Boliviano (CIDOB), and the Consejo Nacional de Ayllus y Markas del Qullasuyu (CONAMAQ).
115. Arts. 2 and 15, quoted in Garcés, *El Pacto de Unidad*, 37.
116. "Propuesta del Pacto de Unidad hacia la Asamblea Constituyente (primera version)," Sucre, 5 August 2006, chaps. 3, 4.
117. "Propuesta consensuada del Pacto de Unidad, Constitución Política del Estado," Sucre, 23 May 2007, Arts. 32, 166–72.
118. Bolivia, Constitución Política del Estado, 2009, Preamble.
119. Bolivia, Constitución Política del Estado, 2009, Arts. 16, 20.

120. Bolivia, Constitución Política del Estado, 2009, Arts. 304, 373, 374.

121. Hines, *Water for All*, 206–11.

122. Bolivia, Ley de la Madre Tierra, 2012, Arts. 4, 13, 14, 19, 27.

123. Baer, "From Water Wars to Water Rights," 358; Fredy Omar Fernández Quiroga, personal communication with author, October 2020.

124. United Nations General Assembly, Resolution 64/292, 28 July 2010, Arts. 2–3.

125. Ballestero, *A Future History of Water*, 18.

126. Bakker, *Privatizing Water*, 147–52.

127. Bolivia, Plan Nacional de Desarrollo, 2006, 30, 74–80, 123–27.

128. Ministerio de Medio Ambiente y Agua, "Rendición pública de cuentas, Audiencia Inicial 2019," accessed 23 October 2019, https://www.mmaya.gob.bo/transparencia/rendicion-de-cuentas/; Baer, "From Water Wars to Water Rights," 359.

129. Razavi, "'Social Control' and the Politics of Public Participation," 14; Orellana Halkyer, "Agua, saneamiento y riego."

130. Baer, "From Water Wars to Water Rights," 367.

131. Crespo Flores, "El derecho humano al agua en la práctica," 2.

132. Webber, "From Left-Indigenous Insurrection," 171; Gustafson, *Bolivia in the Age of Gas.*

133. Postero, *The Indigenous State*, 57–58, 114; Escobar, "Latin America at a Crossroads," 4.

134. Scott, *The Art of Not Being Governed*, 330.

135. "Todos somos Coordinadora del agua y la vida," Somos Sur, accessed April 29, 2022, https://www.somossur.net/index.php/sociedad/1837-todos-somos-coordinadora-del-agua-y-la-vida.

THE RUBBER BOOM AND INDIGENOUS TERRITORIES

Export Economy, Colonization, and the Bolivian Nation-State

José Octavio Orsag Molina

Historians have described the South American rubber boom as the perfect example of a dependent enclave economy that failed to develop the Amazon. The narrative follows, typically, a dramatic history of the rising price of rubber during the late nineteenth century, the history of labor exploitation and debt peonage, the quick fortunes made by a few adventurers and merchants through extreme violence, the cities that flourished in the middle of the rainforest, and the almost impossible infrastructure built to encourage the export-import economy that collapsed after rubber prices dropped. But the history of Amazonian rubber is much more than just a boom-and-bust cycle of an export commodity. Rubber production was the result of the conquest and colonization of Indigenous territories in the name of nation-states and "civilization." The export economy intensified narratives of civilization against savagery as a justification for the expansion of export economies and nation-states' sovereignty in the nineteenth century. This process also transformed Indigenous people into a pool of labor and Indigenous landscapes into geographies of capitalism. The rubber boom was the continuation of colonization on the continent, yet it was propelled, paradoxically, not by European empires but by recently independent nation-states.

As colonization allowed for the consolidation of geographies of capitalism in the Amazon, productivity and increasing volumes of commodity exports and imports became the center of life for most institutions, businesses, and people in the region. Rubber tappers supported themselves by bleeding latex from Hevea[1] trees; steamboat captains made a living from the exchange of rubber for various imported commodities; export houses collected the rubber to send it off to industrial markets in Liverpool or New York; and a few government representatives in the Amazon earned their salaries by collecting taxes from this export-import economy. In fact, the rubber boom created a massive network of commerce and governance, all sustained by the high price of rubber and the appropriation and colonization of Indigenous territories.

In this chapter I analyze the entanglement of the nation-state, export economies, and capital expansion into Indigenous territories in the Amazon during Bolivia's rubber boom. The chapter engages two critical historiographical questions: First, it notes how previous scholarship has taken for granted Bolivia's territorial claims in the Amazon without considering how colonization made it possible to build what was, in fact, a precarious administrative infrastructure in regions with no history of European control. The historiographical normalization of national claims to territory minimizes the role of colonization and appropriation of sovereign Indigenous land as a condition for the emergence and consolidation of nation-states in the nineteenth century. Second, the chapter challenges narrow economic approaches to the history of the rubber boom as a failed attempt at development and as an example of commodity dependence, following the conventional narrative about boom-and-bust cycles. It is crucial to understand the transformation of Indigenous territories into export landscapes articulated through commercial networks between local and international markets as a process of colonization driven by the rubber boom.

The chapter begins by rethinking debates around the Bolivian rubber boom from a pan-Amazonian perspective. In contrast to the notion of the nation-state as implicit backdrop for the rubber boom—which has made the process of colonization of Indigenous territories invisible—I show in the first section how scholars have overestimated the penetration and even existence of the state without considering the prior history of colonization. It is not a question of whether there was a weak state or a strong state—the chapter argues for the effective nonexistence of the state. The second section shows that the Bolivian Amazon was part of a broader continental territory shaped by Indigenous knowledge and exchanges that colonizers turned to their advantage. The Amazon had been primarily Indigenous but through the expansion of Bolivia's rubber economy, it was possible for colonizers to build the legal and administrative structures we call a state. Finally, the third section examines the exponential growth of the rubber economy after 1880, reminding us that the appearance of state infrastructure like customhouses on different rivers and private roads was only possible after the colonization of Indigenous territories.

NATURALIZING THE STATE

The history of the rubber boom has almost always been told from the perspective of the relevant South American nation-states: Brazil, Peru, Colombia, Bolivia, and Ecuador. Traditionally, the rubber boom marks the moment in which the Amazon basin enters the modern history of these nations. Yet this obscures a long, prior history in which most of the Amazon was not controlled by any nation and was, in fact, effectively Indigenous territory. How did the rubber economy emerge in the first place in Indigenous territories where states did not have any real presence? In this section I explore two main moments in the rubber-boom historiography to show how scholars have assumed that the Amazon already and naturally belonged to the states and that Indigenous resistance was subsumed within a nation-state logic. This tendency appeared in the 1980s, part of an economic approach to the history of the rubber boom. In the late 1990s, a new narrative emerged, adopting a new subaltern paradigm.

The economic approach of the 1980s focused on questions of development, the success or failure in incorporating the Amazon and its population into the nation-state and export markets.[2] To measure development, historians have tended to emphasize the links between the Amazon and the world market, the absence of wage labor, the central government's disinterest in developing peripheral areas, or the specific geographical and social characteristics of the Amazon.

It is possible to identify two main approaches to the problem of interaction between the Amazonian economy and the world market. José Flores Marín described the rubber economy as an appendix of the global capitalist structure, reliant upon a semi-slave workforce and simply unable to compete with more industrialized plantations that later emerged in Southeast Asia.[3] By contrast, Barbara Weinstein recognized the role of the world market but emphasized the internal "relations of production and exchange that defined the regional economy" in the Brazilian Amazon.[4] By focusing on the internal dynamics of the region, Weinstein drew a much more complex picture that acknowledged the role of local actors, internal power struggles, and physical geography in determining the conditions of Amazonian development.[5] Most historians who address the economic aspect of the rubber boom move between these two perspectives on external and internal conditions. However, neither approach explores how nation-states gained sovereignty over territories they had not controlled in the first place, how they built and enforced state administration in the region, and what this meant for the Native territories and people who lived in territories claimed as national space.

By writing the history of the rubber boom from the perspective of each nation-state, the idea that the state was the self-evident form of social and geographical organization in the region was rarely challenged. I call this the "naturalization of the state." Paraphrasing anthropologist Eduardo Viveiros de Castro, we can say that the state is taken as a given, understood as the backdrop for economic progress but not as an object of historical analysis in its own right.[6] In the historiography of the 1980s, analysis of economic development did not pay sufficient attention to the profound social and territorial transformation caused by "internal" colonization. More specifically it skimmed over the decades before the rubber boom when state claims began to be projected over Amazonian Indigenous territories.

The economic approach to the history of the rubber boom in the 1980s also gave rise to a regional as opposed to a national frame of analysis. Though this could appear to be an alternative to the national perspective, it can also be seen as a form of atomization based on the same principles; that is, focusing only on a region represented by its elites or entrepreneurs with an assumed right to a territory. The organization of the region is analogous to that of the nation-state, insofar as it was based on formal political jurisdictions, government office holders, and an official ideology of civilization or development. Nor does the regional framework recognize that colonization was the precondition for state formation and the discourse of "civilizing the Amazon" that denied Indigenous sovereignty.

A good example of the regional approach comes from Bolivia's rubber boom historiography. María del Pilar Gamarra asks: "What economic, political, and social factors prevented the exporting-importing trading groups and producers of elastic rubber from having a positive impact on human development, based on the most significant extractive-productive economy in the region?"[7] Her question presupposes that export-import trading groups could have had a positive impact and that something or someone blocked them. Gamarra answers her own question by arguing that the possibilities for socioeconomic transformation were left to the export and import houses instead of being supported by the state.[8] She contends that the national government's only interest and role in the region was that of tax collector, and that this was insufficient to encourage development.[9]

Criticism of the central government for not giving enough support to the regional export economies is common in the rubber-boom historiography. However, in the region-versus-nation perspective, the idea that the state should have given more support to various export economies implies that the state was already built, and it was a matter of the will of national authorities. This leads to a sort of national self-condemnation, while elites in charge of the local economies are portrayed as isolated and neglected entrepreneurs. But in fact, all circum-Amazon nation-states were facing the same problem, which is that there was no state presence almost anywhere in the basin and it would have to be built. In contrast to standard national and regional approaches to Amazonian incursion, we could argue that local elites representing regional export economies demanded more support for pushing colonization into Indigenous territories, thus simultaneously guaranteeing national sovereignty and their own interests. This approach makes visible the eventual alliance between national and regional elites that made possible the creation of nation-states at the cost of Indigenous territories.

Most circum-Amazon nation-states were in similar or worse situations than Bolivia in establishing sovereignty and building infrastructure and control over basin territories right up to the beginning of the twentieth century. Only Peru and Brazil built some administrative infrastructure upon previous European colonial foundations (including missions), pushing colonization further and claiming possession of Indigenous territories as part of national territory. But even Peru and Brazil did not build roads in the area until the mid-twentieth century, and even those governments faced attempts at secession by local Amazonian elites who felt disconnected from the national elites in the capital.[10] Carlos Zárate suggests that Colombia basically did not have an Amazonian region in the nineteenth century and that the few attempts to claim sovereignty over the Putumayo, Caquetá, and Vaupés Rivers came from the Colombian consulate in Manaus (Brazil) and not from the central government in Bogotá. Central state claims on "Colombian Amazonia" occurred only after the collapse of the rubber boom and the war with Peru in the 1930s.[11]

In Bolivia, historians claiming a lack of state interest towards the Amazon (and thus that the state was responsible for lack of development and loss of territories to other nations) aligns with the view that local elites were the only bearers of progress, development, or civilization. Elites from eastern Bolivia, especially from the departments of Beni and Santa Cruz, saw a reemergence of agricultural production by the end of the nineteenth century, a market that emerged separate from Andean commercial circuits thanks to an increased demand for supplies from rubber settlements. They saw this as their own accomplishment even as they complained about the central government's scant political support for infrastructure and commercial connections with the Andean region, which was still the most stable market.[12] An emphasis on clashes between regional elites and the central government has marked historical writing on the Amazon and the lowlands. Intellectuals from Santa Cruz have portrayed people from this city as bearers of civilization for other Bolivian lowland areas, such as the Amazon and the Chaco, in opposition to "weak" efforts from the central government. In doing so, they effectively erased processes of colonization.[13] The regional perspective, like the national one, remains centered around who or what brought development to the Bolivian Amazon while overlooking the varied experiences of Indigenous inhabitants. This can also be considered a naturalization of the state, not in a national form, but as a regional expression of land and development claims built on the same principles as the nation-state and opposed to Indigenous geographies.

Stephen Nugent recognizes that since the rubber boom, the history of the Amazon has been "generally fairly brusquely rendered as a series of brutal encounters and successive failures to exploit the region to its full colonial potential: Conquest, desultory colonization, the *Directorate*,[14] the rubber boom, economic stagnation, the Transamazon Highway, etc."[15] Like Nugent, I believe that historical interpretations of the rubber boom, both from a regional or national approach, follow such narratives. Each is framed in terms of failure to exploit a rich and promising region. Ultimately, writers of such histories bury the significance of colonization of the Amazon's many Indigenous territories as a precondition for the emergence of the rubber economy as well as local or national administration.

Starting in the 1990s, a new generation of scholars began to analyze the history of Bolivia's many Indigenous peoples. Lorena Córdoba, Frederic Vallvé, and Gary Van Valen studied the effects of labor demands on Indigenous Amazonians during the rubber boom.[16] Pilar García Jordán and Anna Guiteras Mombiola studied state formation and the expansion of the Amazon frontier led by the Catholic Franciscan missions in Beni Department.[17] Authors moved away from studies focused on economic growth and development to include discussions of other themes, including state formation, hegemony, citizenship, subaltern groups, and representation.

New perspectives emerging in the 1990s were closely related to views proposed by Florencia Mallon, Gilbert Joseph, and Daniel Nugent in other Latin American contexts. By using Antonio Gramsci's notion of hegemony and inputs from subaltern studies, this scholarship helped us understand the role of Indigenous peoples and subaltern groups in shaping the state.[18] García and Guiteras, for example, described the formation of the Bolivian nation-state as waves of slow assertion of bureaucracy in the Amazon during the nineteenth and twentieth centuries, and contend that Indigenous peoples defined their own roles and rules of engagement with the state.[19] The subaltern approach was crucial to understanding struggles within the state and in local government but especially Indigenous learning about and use of colonizing structures. However, by focusing solely on the assertion of bureaucracy and Indigenous relations with the state, we can lose sight of Indigenous relations with the territory itself, including the transformation of land-use patterns that colonization itself brought about. Bureaucracy was the result of colonization, the result of the reorganization of the territory, the result of the appearance of administrative infrastructure, the result of the state attempting to create population and resource legibility for its own purposes.

The subaltern approach mostly focused on missionized Moxos Plains Indigenous groups who were able to exert some degree of citizenship. All but unnoticed were the experiences of those whom local elites called "savages," living outside the citizenship regime.[20] Indigenous history centered almost invariably on missionized Indigenous groups such as the Tacanas and Lecos in northern La Paz, the Moxos and Guarayos in Beni, or the Chiquitanos in Santa Cruz. Independent Indigenous groups like the Araonas and Pano-speakers were typically left out of the history of nation-state formation and appear only tangentially in the history of the Bolivian Amazon as people who used to live in the rubber territories. The history of colonization and relations with the state were different for these and other groups and it is crucial to acknowledge the rubber boom as part of the colonization process. They must be written back into the script.

With the rise of rubber, Bolivia's Amazonian Indigenous territories—barely delineated on colonial and republican maps—were transformed into public lands open to private colonization. Local, independent Indigenous peoples were routinely forced to work or expelled from productive land. In contrast to the missionized Indigenous people of the Moxos Plains, the Bolivian state did not consider independent forest or desert groups suitable for citizenship until later in the twentieth century.[21] Land privatization, the transformation of community members into individual dependent workers, and their incorporation into the citizenship regime were quintessential elements of the process of state formation. In the late nineteenth century, colonization of Indigenous territories coupled with the rubber boom created conditions for the "legibility" of the Amazon for the Bolivian state. Based on James Scott's concept of legibility, giving attention to the ways in which the state seeks to organize territories and people as the basis of state functioning, I think about how local and national elites' links to the world market created the basis for modern, national territorial administration.[22] In this sense, by framing Indigenous history within the history of the state without fully highlighting the process of colonization continues to naturalize the state. Bureaucracy appears as a given and not as the result of colonization or the transformation of territories and social relations on the ground.

This quick review of the historiography builds on previous approaches to the history of the Amazon and of the rubber boom. Specifically, it seeks to make the history of Indigenous populations more visible by shifting economic, political, social, and cultural analysis away from the narrow framework of the nation-state to instead see the nation-state as a product of the historical process itself. The story of rubber extraction in Amazonia is about states in the making, emphasizing the enduring significance of Indigenous action. Given the power of the economic approach and the standard account of the rubber boom as a narrative of Amazonian modernization, it is crucial to link the history of the commodity to the colonization of Indigenous territories. As Fernando Coronil wrote: "If narratives of modernity are constructed on the basis of exclusions and denials, we should pay attention to the hidden operations that select and naturalize historical memory, to the filter that creates national and global memories and their respective forms of amnesia."[23]

INDIGENOUS LANDS BEFORE THE NATION-STATE

What today is considered the Bolivian Amazon was the territory of many independent Indigenous groups during the nineteenth century.[24] The rubber boom was built on relations Indigenous peoples had developed with colonizers long before the "rubber barons"—as they are known—had the capital to bring workers to the region from Moxos, Santa Cruz, or northern La Paz. This section explores Indigenous-colonizer relations in the decades before rubber extraction took off in the 1880s, and how they were transformed during the boom. By describing the colonization process in Indigenous territories, this section also highlights the dependence of colonizers on Indigenous social structures and knowledge for starting up their extractive projects.

Cohabitation between traders and independent Indigenous groups was the norm in the western continental Amazon basin, and merchants depended on and profited from Indigenous economies. On the Marañón River, in what is today the Peruvian Amazon, the merchant Manuel Ijurra described in 1845 how the local economy of the colonial city of Moyobamba was dependent on trade in salted fish and other forest products exchanged by independent Indigenous groups of the Ucayali, Marañón, and Huallaga Rivers. Ijurra described his trip to visit the Ticuna people, from whom he bought hammocks, poisons, and other forest products which he sold in Manaus.[25] Examining these small traders around the continental Amazon basin allows us to understand the history of the region before the rubber boom, as well as the importance and power of Indigenous groups in generating the colonizers' economy. At the same time, trading relations in these early years, before the introduction of steam navigation which occurred in 1852, reveals a world in which the Indigenous population had considerable control over trading dynamics.

Early Indigenous participation in trading circuits ought not be surprising since they had engaged in trade since pre-European times. After the invasion of America, European colonizers inserted themselves into Indigenous trading networks to obtain and export forest products. Portuguese and the local population of the lower Amazon basin had traded with Indigenous communities for "backlands commodities" or *drogas do sertão*[26]since the seventeenth century.[27] In the nineteenth century, all around the Amazon basin, towns and villages at the boundaries of Indigenous territories were sites of constant trade.[28] Some Indigenous groups also established relations with Catholic missionaries to access resources, gain protection from other colonizers, or change the interethnic balance of power.[29] In the Bolivian Amazon, the Pacaguaras, for example, were in contact with Franciscan missions as far as Reyes, and other Pano groups were constantly seen in Exaltación on the Mamoré River.[30] When José Agustín Palacios explored the Mamoré River up to the

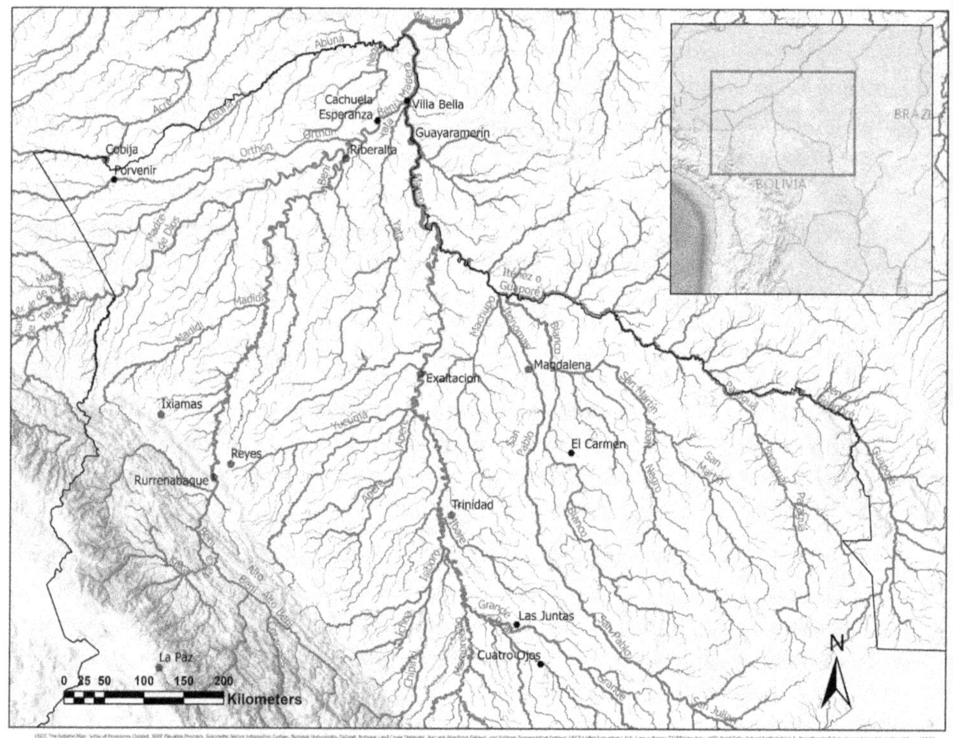

Map 4.1. Bolivia's Amazon, Beni-Mamoré Basin. The Beni and Mamoré Rivers form the Madeira, establishing the historic commercial route that connected Bolivia to Manaos and Para in Brazil. Rubber commerce in Bolivia was organized around these rivers through the main cities and ports of Riberalta, Cachuela Esperanza, Villa Bella, and Guayaramerín. The only exception was the city of Cobija, known in the nineteenth century as Bahía, which connected the rubber trade to the Purus River. Map by the author.

dangerous Madeira Falls in 1846, he was found by the Caripunas. Palacios described how his crew, mainly Trinitario people from the Moxos Plains, exchanged their provisions with the Caripunas for birds and other animals. This behavior offended Palacios because he feared his crew was going to abandon him.[31]

Fray Jesualdo Maccheti also described in 1869 how north of Exaltación—at the time the northernmost colonial town in Bolivia—many Indigenous groups lived on both sides of the Mamoré's riverbanks. Maccheti mentioned an encounter with seven or eight people navigating the Mamoré River in a small boat; none wished to talk with Maccheti, and they continued their trip undisrupted. The travelers were the Mayosa or "friends of the Cayubaba," according to Maccheti, which probably meant they engaged in trading relations with the missionized Cayubaba who lived in Exaltación.[32] Palacios's and Maccheti's accounts show that riverine trade was not limited to relations between white colonists[33] and Indigenous peoples but also encompassed missionized populations and independent Indigenous groups.

It is important to clarify that the Mamoré River economy in what is today Bolivia before the rubber boom looked different from the more general pattern of interethnic commerce in the western Amazon, where trade relations with white outsiders were standard. Relations between the Moyosa and Cuyubaba that Maccheti noted, and exchanges between Trinitarios and Caripunas mentioned by Palacios, show that an Indigenous economy existed without the intervention of white traders. White colonizers in the Mamoré area were probably focused on economic activities they could control, like cattle ranching, and depended less on Indigenous economies compared to colonizers in the rest of the western continental Amazon.

The rubber boom is set in Bolivian historiography as beginning after Edwin Heath's 1880 expedition to the Manutata––today's Madre de Dios River, which runs into Bolivia from its upper tributaries in Peru. When Antenor Vásquez founded the rubber settlement (*barraca gomera*) of Concepción near the Biata River's mouth, people were bringing rubber from as far away as the Geneshuaya River near Madre de Dios but still far away from where the Beni River joined the Mamoré.[34] Most people who extracted rubber for these pioneer trading entrepreneurs were local inhabitants, such as the Pacaguara and the Araona, who had not been reduced to rubber settlements. In Santa Ana, the last rubber settlement downriver at the time, Heath recalls how Endara worked with the Pacaguaras and even learned their language. Something similar happened in San Antonio, where Araona families were living around Antonio Vaca Díez's barraca, extracting rubber in exchange for iron tools.

In the early years of the rubber economy, just before and after Heath's expeditions, colonizers depended on Indigenous groups for different reasons. For his trip, Heath exchanged information with the Araonas through an interpreter who lived with Vaca Díez in San Antonio. The Araonas gave Heath precise geographical information for the journey. They described landmarks that he would see paddling downriver, especially adjoining rivers, mentioning two on the left margin: first the broad Manutata and, a few miles away, the Dati-Manu. The Araonas told Heath that they crossed the Tahuamanu, Manuripi, and Manutata Rivers going south to San Antonio, revealing their extensive mobility through today's Bolivian Amazon. Also, they were able to inform Vaca Díez about places rich in rubber trees.[35]

The Araonas were not the only Indigenous group on the scene. In these early years of the rubber boom, various Pacaguara communities, who belong ethnolinguistically to the Pano people, lived on the Beni River's opposite bank. Heath described the Pacaguaras working with Fidel Endara. Nicolás Armentia, a Franciscan missionary who wished to establish a new mission during the early years of the rubber trade, also visited them and made censuses of the tribes near the Biata River and the regions surrounding the Geneshuaya, Ivón, and Madre de Dios Rivers.[36] Either as informants, guides, or workers, Indigenous groups like the Araona and Pacaguara provided the basis for the early rubber economy.

Before the expansion of import networks in the Amazon, colonizers also sometimes required supplies from Indigenous communities. Víctor Mercier and Coronel Antonio Rodrígues Pereira Labre's binational, Bolivian-Brazilian expedition to the region between the Madre de Dios and the Acre Rivers in 1887 produced many sources detailing relations with the local population. Mercier was the business partner of Timoteo Mariaca, a pioneer rubber baron of the Madre de Dios. The two men founded their settlement (barraca) at Maravillas on the Madre de Dios River's left bank in 1883 in a territory frequented by the Araonas.[37] From there, they departed together with Labre toward the Aquiry River, known today as the Acre. The purpose behind their trip is not entirely clear, but we may speculate on two possibilities. First, the men may have wanted to connect their extractive network to steam navigation, which was quickly growing upriver through the Purus and Acre Rivers. And simultaneously, as the expedition's own accounts show, Mercier was interested in establishing contact with Indigenous villagers and exchanging merchandise with them while portraying himself as benefactor.[38] Establishing trade seems crucial since colonizers were not only looking for labor or information but also for resources, which were scarce during the first years of the expanding rubber frontier. Indeed, Mercier describes shortages suffered plus lack of supplies when he and Mariaca first founded Maravillas, a typical "hardship phase" experienced by new rubber settlements. During an especially difficult year, Mercier, Mariaca, and their workers had only locally abundant Brazil nuts (*Bertholletia excelsa*) to eat. But as they tell the story of their expedition, their good relationship with the "barbarians" (*bárbaros*) provided them with supplies of manioc and maize, which eventually saved them.[39]

As the rubber economy grew in the 1880s and 1890s, the nature of Indigenous-colonizer relations began to change. In short, colonizers wanted labor. As pressure for more rubber production rose, the trade mechanism that Indigenous groups used to acquire tools from foreign merchants in the Amazon quickly turned against them. When Vaca Díez founded his rubber settlement in San Antonio at the end of the 1870s, he started receiving visits from Araonas looking for iron tools in exchange for different objects. He claimed that with time their demands became "an avalanche" that caused him to quickly run out of supplies. To set limits, he asked them to work in exchange for the tools provided, an agreement which, according to Díez, they accepted happily. However, Díez made clear that the deal only lasted a month, since Indigenous people, if they did work, never stayed in one place for long, a sign of their high degree of bargaining power.[40] Most rubber barons made the same sort of piecemeal, short-term arrangements. Endara sought to recruit the Pacaguaras on the eastern bank of the Beni River. Armentia described an expedition to the Ivón River to contact and recruit groups of Pacaguaras. Vásquez paid for Armentia's journey on the promise that he would reduce the Indigenous population into a new mission that would guarantee their labor.[41]

The 1880s marked a turning point in the Amazon. A new geography of capitalism concurred with increasing violence against Indigenous peoples, sparking a veritable war for their labor and territories. By the time Mercier and Labre crossed the forest between the Madre de Dios and the Acre Rivers, change was evident throughout Araona, Pacaguara, and Caripuna villages. Indigenous groups with decades of trading experience began to reject contact with merchants and colonizers since they recognized the chances of being forced into bonded labor were high. Indeed, Mercier and Labre were almost killed when they arrived at an Hipurina village near the Acre River where it seems the population was avoiding contact with white colonizers. The night the travelers stayed in the village, Pacaguara Chief Tata Canupáru convinced the Hipurina chiefs during an official assembly—in which neither Mercier nor Labre participated—not to attack the two interlopers. The next day, as they recalled, the usual trade rituals were reestablished, and they continued on their journey.[42]

Indigenous groups were displaced from their original territories during this first decade of rubber production in Bolivia. Epidemics brought by the colonizers were a significant driver of this displacement, intensified by the decomposition of communities. Armentia describes the catastrophic effects of epidemics among the Araona in 1885, near the Beni River. He states that mortality exceeded 50 percent among the Araonas' extended families.[43] This was why families started migrating north to the Orthon and Abuná Rivers by the end of the 1880s, to escape contact with colonizers.[44] The same was probably true among the Hipurinas with whom

Mercier and Labre made contact near the Acre River, although presumably they were fleeing south away from the commercial expansion that began in 1868 with steam navigation on the Purus River.

Violent demands for labor in the rubber settlements also drove migration and the displacement of Indigenous people, and local newspapers and travelers denounced the rubber barons' harsh treatment of Indigenous groups during these years. Armentia reported that Pacaguaras feared Fidel Endara because he began shooting at them when he got drunk. Nevertheless, he went farther up the Biata River looking for more workers, partly to replace those who had escaped.[45] In *La Gaceta del Norte*, Antonio Vaca Díez's newspaper, a note denounced Timoteo Mariaca for shooting two Araona workers who had escaped from his settlements.[46] Luigi Balzan described how demand for workers slowly led to their enslavement. During his 1885 to 1893 trips into the forest along the Madre de Dios and Beni Rivers, Balzan saw Araona and Toromona people sold for 150 to 190 dollars. He described how, at first, the Araonas and Toromonas came to work in the rubber settlements on their own terms, and even sent their children freely and in good faith to rubber barons. Such voluntary work proved insufficient, and soon the rubber barons began sending out *correrías* or expeditions to catch and enslave people.[47] There is no reason to deny that Bolivian rubber barons were involved in slave raids; colonizers openly embraced slavery to deal with their labor shortages.[48] In fact, it is known that the Casa Suárez firm, the largest rubber export house in Bolivia, sent correrías into the Madre de Dios region and up to the Manu River (in present-day Peru), when this territory was not yet colonized.[49]

By 1900, most local Indigenous groups had been displaced from the core rubber-producing regions of Madre de Dios, Beni, and Orthon. Indigenous peoples withdrew into unexplored rivers and forests or those with no rubber, and they defended their territories from further encroachment. They did not take incursion lightly. José Santos Mercado, for example, was killed while trying to open new rubber settlements in the Abuná River in the territory of the Caripunas.[50] In 1905, the famous British explorer Percy Fawcett, while marking the borders between Brazil and Bolivia and between Peru and Bolivia, had violent encounters with the Caripunas on the Abuná River, and the Ese'ejjas or Guarayos on the Heath River.[51]

Some encounters outside the central rubber-producing regions were more peaceable, but this only occurred when Indigenous groups were in control of the situation. The administrator of the Almendros settlement on the Geneshuaya River, Ernst Leutenegger, described how the Chácobos, who had taken refuge in Lake Rogoaguado, returned his favor of saving the life of a child with malaria. They worked on his rubber claim to clear the forest, but just for a short period of time.[52]

In sum, the rapidly expanding rubber economy of the late nineteenth century displaced several Amazonian Indigenous groups, and those that survived did so outside rubber-producing regions. The degree of this displacement cannot be fully comprehended unless we see Amazon colonization in a continental perspective. Many Indigenous territories affected by rubber expansion remain outside modern Bolivian national borders.

While local Indigenous groups were displaced or enslaved by the rubber barons, migration from former Franciscan and Jesuit missions peaked and remained the primary labor source during the last decades of the rubber boom.[53] Frederic Vallvé analyzed the census of the Ingavi rubber settlement, which shows only one individual registered as native to the Madidi region. He probably belonged to a Guarayo, Araona, or Cavina group. The rest of the 118 workers were from Santa Cruz de la Sierra and towns north of La Paz, including Ixiamas and Tumupasa.[54]

The fact that local Indigenous people do not appear to have been working in rubber after 1890 does not mean they were never there or, more critically, not still struggling against colonization. Even in one of the most conflictive regions of the Bolivian Amazon, the Madidi River, Ese'ejjas families were still struggling against colonization in 1910. They suffered at least two openly genocidal wars waged against them by traders who wanted to gain access to rubber tree groves in the Madidi area. First, Albert Mouton sent a punitive expedition to exterminate the Ese'ejjas or Guarayos on the pretext that they had killed two members of José Manuel Pando's expedition in 1893. Mouton proudly claimed to have killed fifty or sixty men and women.[55]

In 1899, a local Riberalta newspaper described how after Mouton's punitive expedition, colonizers thought the Ese'ejjas were exterminated, but they were wrong. Local rubber barons sent another punitive expedition, this time led by Fernando Goguet. He assassinated more than a hundred people and took women and children to his rubber enclave "to be civilized."[56] Sources indicate that after this last expedition, the Ese'ejjas were forced to work on the rubber claim of someone named Pareja,[57] yet documents from the 1910s continue to report Esse'ejja sightings and encounters. Traveler Erland Nordenskiöld described how settlers of the Madidi River still complained about them, claiming that despite having bought the land from the Bolivian government, the "savages" did not allow the colonizers to exploit their properties.[58] The Ese'ejjas' troubled history offers just one example of how Indigenous groups were still struggling with the advancing rubber frontier decades after initial colonization. Labor and land became increasingly important for the greater Amazon basin's colonizers, which sent shockwaves of violence into Indigenous communities.

As the rubber boom expanded across the South American interior, producers coveted still more Indigenous territory. After 1900, a series of events propelled

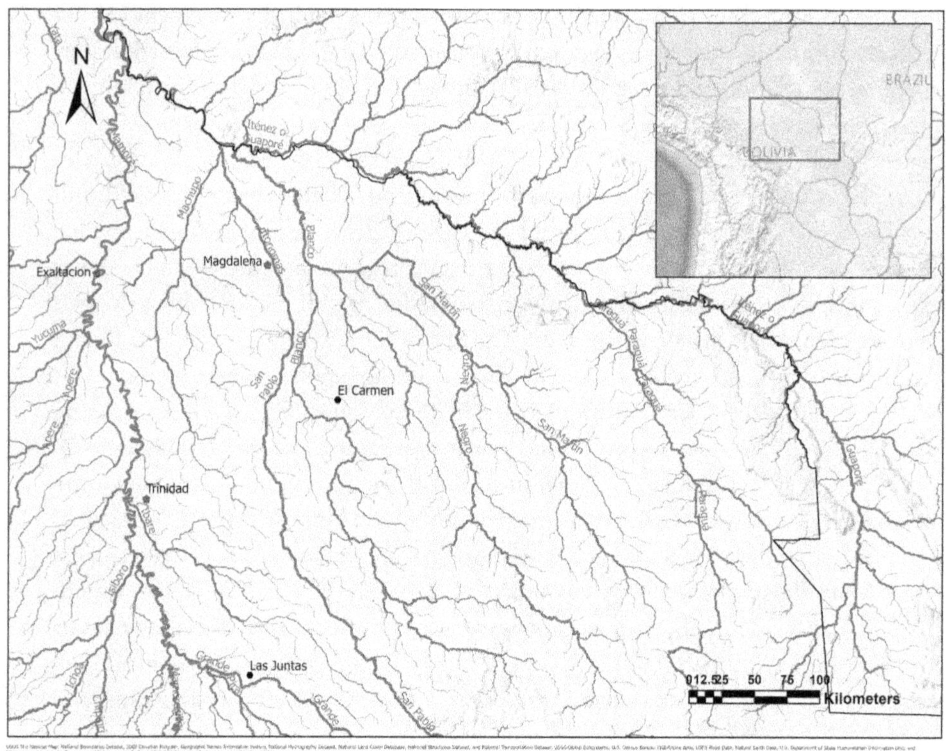

Map 4.2. The Iténez River. The Iténez River basin is a forgotten territory in the Bolivian rubber boom historiography. Shared today between the departments of Beni and Santa Cruz, it was slowly colonized at the beginning of the twentieth century. It has a historical link with Mato Grosso and the cities of Villa Bella and Descalvado in Brazil. Map by the author.

colonization into the Iténez or Guaporé River basin. As sources indicate, expansion toward Iténez began after the disastrous Acre War (1899–1903), when many Bolivian rubber extractors were expelled from the Acre River and moved to the Iténez basin and its tributaries.[59] At the end of 1880, local authorities from Trinidad complained that navigating the Mamoré was dangerous due to the number of Indigenous groups on the Mamoré and Madeira Rivers near the mouth of the Iténez.[60] The density of the Indigenous population along the Mamoré was so high that even in 1911 Fray Francisco Pierini, who was in charge of the Guarayos missions, complained that there were small Indigenous villages near civilized towns that were exploited for labor on rubber settlements in the north.[61] Period documents indicate the region was still densely inhabited by a population that was not yet brought under national auspices.

After the Acre War in 1903, colonizers pushed Indigenous populations toward the east of the Mamoré River into Iténez Province, and from the south towards the forests of the northern region of the department of Santa Cruz. In 1900, a newspaper in Magdalena reported that most of the territory was occupied by "savages" who did not allow any exploitation of the region's resources. It mentioned that the province only had 8,750 inhabitants according to the census of 1900—this in a region measuring more than 497,222 square kilometers. Most of the territory was controlled by independent Indigenous groups: the Sirionós, Sansimonianos, Paucernas, and Paunacas. The article called on the government to create a military colony to reduce and "civilize" the population.[62] Indigenous people in this area did not allow easy expansion of rubber colonizers into their territories. A 1901 newspaper article described how a group of "savages" attacked a rubber settlement close to the town of Magdalena. Men from the surrounding rubber settlements gathered and pursued the attackers and even killed one of them.[63] North of the famous Franciscan missions of Guarayos, Pierini reported in 1911 that there were "savage" Guarayos, not reduced to the mission, near the recently opened road to Carmen, a project pushed by rubber interests.[64]

After the first decade of the twentieth century, most of northern Santa Cruz and Iténez Provinces were producing and exporting rubber into Brazil. The expansion of the rubber economy, commercial expeditions, new roads, and the intensification of commerce in general had a devastating effect on the local population. This destructive process is scarcely mentioned in Bolivian historiography. The expansion of the rubber economy and the geographies of capitalism were not just felt in the northern forest. Records show that genocidal campaigns took place also around the roads surrounding the city of Santa Cruz.[65]

In sum, Bolivia's rubber boom economy, like that of its neighbors, involved heavy colonization of Amazonian Indigenous territories. Indigenous peoples had lived with, adapted to, and learned from commercial circuits since the earliest European presence in the region. However, South American independence brought a new wave of colonization with the expansion of export economies and the state into territories that had remained largely Indigenous until the nineteenth century. Colonizers converted older commercial relations with Indigenous communities into a source of labor supply as demand for rubber exploded after 1880. The Bolivian state also introduced new ways of organizing the territory, including a land market that it regulated. With time, colonizers' perception of Indigenous peoples shifted radically: from crucial resource to obstacle to civilization and progress. Private and state colonizing interests aligned to build a "civilized world" in territories purported to be "savage." Colonization generated the need for state legibility of territory, resources, and population, and that legibility, in turn, boosted export economies for the world market. Nevertheless, Indigenous peoples remained and resisted colonization, especially in regions where rubber was not profitable, like the Heath River, Lake Rogaguado, and smaller tributaries that lay farther from commercial circuits.

NATIONAL CLAIMS AND GEOGRAPHIES OF CAPITALISM

This section analyzes the emergence of the Bolivian state in the Amazon through the expansion of colonization and rubber tapping. It shows how the export economy, which was made possible through colonization, also created the legibility that the state required to function. Colonization and extraction enabled the appearance of the state, deepening the effect of colonization by pushing a standard citizenship/labor regime and transforming Indigenous lands into the national territory, labeled *tierras baldías*. It is important to see that the displacement of Indigenous groups, appropriation of land, and construction of new roads and commercial networks provided the conditions for the emergence of the nation-state. They gave the vast Amazon region legibility and allowed for the reorganization of space and people in a way that could be centrally administrated.[66] At the same time, nation-states provided the legal framework to legitimize colonization under the rhetoric of occupying "public lands." Indigenous landscapes were available for state organization, and colonization transformed them and rendered them manageable.

Before rubber extraction spurred colonization, the state's assertion over the Amazon forests in the Beni, Mamoré, and Iténez basins were at most symbolic. According to the department of Beni's prefect reports, until 1880 the Bolivian government had only one small customhouse in the town of Exaltación that controlled trading navigation along the Mamoré.[67] Exaltación was a former mission located

250 miles from the northernmost border of what is today Bolivia and more than 600 miles from the Javary River, which Bolivia claimed as its frontier during the nineteenth century. The arbitrary claim over a vast region that the central government and local elites were utterly unfamiliar with was quite common in Bolivia and all nation-states in the nineteenth century. Newly independent state governments projected their claims onto maps based on the rule of *uti possidetis juris*, a recognition of sovereignty according to preexisting territorial boundaries that derives from Roman law. The legal system upon which the national state claimed territory did not recognize any claims by the Indigenous populations that inhabited those regions. Geographical claims drawn onto maps by national governments were not so different from the legal documents (known as *requerimientos*) that the Spanish proclaimed to Indigenous people during initial colonization, asserting the Crown's possession of the American continent.[68]

However, these were no more than illusory claims until the rubber boom, since the territories were de facto Indigenous lands. It was only in 1882, at the beginning of the rubber boom, that the Bolivian government founded the port of Villa Bella with a customs office placed strategically at the confluence of the Beni and Mamoré Rivers.[69] However, the customhouse's distance from both government centers in Sucre and La Paz created problems of communication. Orders, letters, provisions, or help of any type just took too long to reach the outpost. It took almost a decade until migration yielded a modicum of national administration. Initial tapper incursions allowed the government to establish a special administration and a new political division directly under control of the executive branch. The government created the Delegaciones Nacionales de los Ríos Madre de Dios y Purús by law on October 28, 1890. In 1893, Manuel Vicente Ballivián and Lisímaco Gutiérrez, two important members of the Liberal Party, reached the Beni River to put the customhouse in order and administer the region.[70]

The Bolivian government's main interest was collecting profits from rubber exports flowing down the river; it was also the first assertion of sovereignty by any nation-state in the Amazon. In the 1890s, the Bolivian objective was to extend central administration into the Acre region, which was known to be rich in rubber but hitherto entirely out of reach given Bolivia's administrative capabilities. In 1891, the Bolivian government initiated conversations with the Brazilian government to build a customhouse on the Acre River.[71] By 1895, the outpost continued to be a project rather than a concrete reality, yet that did not deter Bolivia from calculating that around 300,000 Bolivianos ($b) could be levied from the import and export commerce on the river.[72] Acre rubber production was the richest in all the Amazon basin. At the time, those $b300,000 were a third more than Villa Bella's total rent for the same year, including revenue from imports. Villa Bella supported all the administrative costs of the new Delegaciones unit and 90 percent of the department of Beni's administrative expenses in 1895.[73] Rubber extraction clearly sustained Bolivian state administration and was an important condition for the state's emergence.

Puerto Alonso was finally founded in 1899 at the start of José Manuel Pando's presidency (1899–1904).[74] By this time, frontier expansion of rubber capitalism had entirely changed the geography of the Amazon, with provisional international boundaries delimited by customhouses. However, most of the population in the Acre River rubber settlements came from the Brazilian northeast as laborers. A month and a half after the foundation of the Bolivian customhouse in Acre, Luis Galvéz Rodríguez de Arias, along with the rubber entrepreneurs Domingo Carneiro and Joaquín Víctor Da Silva, declared Acre an independent nation, starting the Acre War (1899–1903).[75] Galvéz was a journalist who complained vociferously about the US gunboat *Wilmington* approaching Bolivian territory, violating the sovereignty of the Amazonian territories and putting their future at risk. The boat was carrying orders to sign a pact of formal collaboration between the National Delegation of Acre led by José Paravicini, US president William McKinley, US consul K. Kennedy in Brazil, and the Bolivian vice-consul, Luiz Truco. The pact guaranteed US assistance to the Bolivian army in a war against Brazil by providing the Acrean territories with weapons. It also promoted a commission to establish the borders of the Juruá and Javary Rivers as well as other arrangements that would benefit Bolivian commerce with the United States.[76]

Bolivia's government understood that both the colonization of the Acre region and sovereignty over it was out of its hands. Today, Bolivia's international borders in the Amazon coincide more or less with the limits of Bolivian colonizers' activities at that time. While the Beni, Mamoré, and even the Madre de Dios regions were easily accessed by colonizers in Santa Cruz or La Paz, the complicated communications between the Purús and the Madeira basins worked as a barrier. Communication and access to Acre were much more straightforward from the Amazon River than from Bolivia, giving Brazil's Manaus elites an advantage, which goes to show the close relationship between international borders and the geographies of capitalism. It is possible that this commercial border and the knowledge that Brazilian *nordestinos* or impoverished northeasterners were populating the region was the motivation for the Bolivian government to sign international treaties for the colonization of these areas. In 1895, the government was already talking about the necessity of foreign capital to boost colonization of Acre.[77]

After a complicated military campaign, Galvéz's attempt to "liberate" Acre was thwarted in 1901.[78] Nevertheless, the Bolivian government continued to seek foreign support for colonization. Félix Avelino Aramayo, already one of the most important mineowners in Bolivia and at the time a Bolivian diplomat in London, was searching for charter companies as partners. After several failed attempts with Belgian companies, Aramayo signed a contract with Frederick Wallingford Whitridge, an agent of the Vanderbilt family, for a lease of the Acre territory for thirty years. The beneficiary was a charter company that had been set up for that purpose, usually known as the Bolivian Syndicate, with the participation of Wall Street speculators.[79] The contract raised alarm in the Brazilian government, which decided to support another revolution in the Acre region. This second campaign in Acre was less successful for Bolivia, which finally lost its claims to the region after signing the Treaty of Petrópolis in 1903.[80] The Acre rebels narrowly missed penetrating the core rubber regions in Beni and Madre de Dios.[81]

Susanna Hecht describes this moment of international border formation as the "scramble for the Amazon," referencing the appropriation of African territories by European elites in the nineteenth century. It is worth paying attention to how export circuits, hubs of commerce, and the settlements for rubber production during the colonization of Indigenous territories allowed for this "scramble." Bolivia stands out for its choice of pursuing global capital to colonize the Acre region, a notable contrast to expeditions sent by the Brazilian and Peruvian governments to their borders.[82]

Trade routes were the basis for expanding national claims. For example, the *varaderos* in Peru, small roads that latex collectors used to travel between rivers, were seen as proof of Peruvian sovereignty by the state. Thus, the state used previous expansion of colonizers to claim sovereignty.[83] In Brazil, migration to the Juruá and Purús Rivers began early in the 1870s; by 1900, the river basins were settled and producing rubber. For Brazilian merchants, rivers were the main roads for commerce, as for most elites in the Amazon. The rubber economy and the expansion of capitalist geographies boosted steam navigation, migration, commodity export, capital import, and the foundation of cities. This also provided the platform for state administration in the region. As Scott argues, to control and administer a region, a state must produce the legibility of the territory and its population. We could add to Scott's formulation that in the Amazon legibility was produced by private interests aligned with the interests of the national government. The only way to ensure legibility of the Amazon was by breaking the illegibility of local practices and thus transforming Indigenous territories into public or private land and its inhabitants into citizen-workers. In the Amazon, that first step toward legibility was provided by rubber extraction, incorporating Indigenous territories into the geography of capitalism.

It was colonization and the rubber economy that ultimately enabled a degree of legibility. It is important to note that the logic of incorporating territories into the nation had been attempted with many failed projects before rubber. One must indeed compare the rubber boom to previous attempts at sovereign expansion by way of various eye-catching but failed projects. One of the most impressive projects was that of Asahel Dana Piper, a traveler and speculator, who tried to colonize the Purús River based on an agreement signed in Lima in 1869 by Bolivia's minister plenipotentiary, Juan de la Cruz Benavente. The project promised Amazonian immigration and development and stated that all rights and privileges should be conferred to the settlers. The aim of the project was agriculture, in expectation of good markets in the United States and Europe. Piper promised commodity markets for:

> ... oranges, lemons, limes, citrons, figs, pomegranates, chirimoyas, pineapples, melons, grapes, tamarinds, apples, pears, peaches, papaya, sweet potatoes, cassava, yucca, plantains, potatoes, tapioca, arrow-root, maize, quinua, peas, rice, wheat, barley, beans, nuts of all kind, cotton, hemp, coffee, cocoa, cacao, sugar cane, tobacco, indigo, Peruvian bark, sarsaparilla, vegetable wax, tonka-beans, isinglass, gum copal, nutmeg, cinnamon, ginger, pepper, vanilla, guarajura, guarana, rocou, jalap, copaiba, copal, ipecacuanha, cascarilla, annatto, and Indian rubber, and cabinet woods.[84]

That description immediately exposes the ignorance that national and foreign colonizers had of the region. First, it promised to produce a range of products that were not suited for the Amazon and second, for this to happen, a major migration of colonizers that could work as laborers and farmers would be required. State officials and private contractors were imagining the Amazon as a hub for commercial agriculture without considering the actual ecology of the tropical forest. Piper's project also seems entirely tailored to what the government must have wanted to hear, especially foreign immigration for plantation agriculture, paired symbols of civilization. The project was accompanied by a map in which one can see the word "gold" near the Andes and close to the colonization area. It is possible that Piper concocted the project for purely speculative purposes, but his dreams died hard. Fourteen years after the Bolivian government signed the Piper contract in 1873, two engineers, Charles Barrington Brown and William Lidstone, traveled to the area to expand the steam navigation routes of the Companhia Fluvial do Alto Amazonas. They found Piper alone and ill in a small boat in the port of Lábrea, the ruins of his project all around him.[85]

The dreams of a civilized agricultural Amazon before rubber were a common preoccupation of national elites around the region. Elites in the Brazilian province of Amazonas were eager to boost cacao, coffee, and sugar cane production. The same was true in Peru, although there they succeeded in creating foreign agricultural colonies in the valleys of Chanchamayo and Pozuzo.[86] However, before rubber it was impossible to achieve a successful economic project since national elites lacked the knowledge, labor, or capital inputs needed to sustain agricultural colonies. Only Indigenous communities had the know-how and organization to produce in the forest. Yet their methods of territorial management were not suited to the legibility of the nation-states or to the demands of export markets.

Colonel George E. Church attempted a comparable Amazonian colonization project at almost the same time as Piper, singing a contract with the Bolivian government in 1868. Seeking to improve navigation through the Madeira rapids, he had hit upon the idea of constructing a section of a canal or perhaps building a railway. His venture was christened the National Bolivian Navigation Company and, after Brazil consented to building the railroad, Church created a second corporation called the Madeira-Mamoré Railway Company, which he incorporated into the first. Church gathered a substantial amount of money and even brought laborers and some materials to San Antonio. However, foreshadowing Piper's later failure, Church proved himself unable to make his dream come true after he lost his creditors due to speculation and political instability.[87] Hecht has argued that the real lure for Piper and Church were the gold mines of La Paz's northern province of Caupolicán.[88] Yet we need to stress how impossible these projects were without the support of a network of settlements and commercial routes and the migrant population that a few years later the rubber boom would bring to the Amazon.

These examples demonstrate that even with state support, lack of infrastructure in Amazonia meant that speculation and desire for wealth via commercial agriculture or gold mining were not enough to set in motion successful capitalist development and state formation. Only the rubber boom created these networks and infrastructure through colonization, allowing the slow but consistent geographical expansion into the Amazon's fluvial networks. The basis for development of both private and state economies was the opening of trade routes, connecting producer regions to foreign markets, and labor from migrants rather than the local Indigenous population; this was the result of colonization pushed by export economies. Again, all of this was possible only after displacing or subsuming the local Indigenous population and transforming Indigenous territories into public and private lands. Thus, colonization made possible the rubber boom, the reorganization of Amazonian Indigenous territories, and the emergence of a tangible state that at the same time could support and legalize the export economy.

CONCLUSION

The two sections presented in this chapter show that the emergence of both the rubber export economy and the Bolivian nation-state were only possible through the colonization of Indigenous territories. Indigenous territories had a long history of trade and commerce before the rubber boom and of adaptation to colonizers. As I have illustrated, it is a mistake to conceive of the Amazonian forests in the nineteenth century as national territories because public lands or *tierras fiscales* only resulted from their colonization at the end of the century. International borders drawn on maps meant little to most inhabitants of the region before the rubber economy and even after the rubber boom. The political and economic history of Bolivia's fabled rubber boom needs to be understood not only as the beginning of modern national history in the Amazon but also as the result of systematic colonization, a twin process of penetration and extraction.

It is also essential to note the blurred lines between state and private interests once colonization reorganized lands, waterways, and peoples, especially from the perspective of independent Indigenous peoples. Export and import houses, trading networks, migrant populations, local municipal councils, associations of exporters, and local elites created the foundations upon which national-level administration was established, and at the same time, these institutions needed the legitimacy of a nation-state in the world market. While colonizers from different countries started to fight over rubber, especially after 1890, it was clear that some type of agreement was needed, and this came in form of international borders and land markets. The existence of independent Indigenous groups became a threat to property and the supply of labor for colonizers as the rubber boom pushed forward. Here again, private interest relied on the state to protect private property, as demonstrated by the case of the attempted genocide of the Ese'ejjas.

Neglecting the history of colonization in the formation of the Bolivian nation-state is pernicious in that it perpetuates nationalist narratives of progress and civilization. The formation of nation-states in the nineteenth century was accompanied by a discourse of civilization that carried Enlightenment and positivist perspectives about how to profit from nature, especially in the Amazon. Western scientists and travelers classified Indigenous populations as part and parcel of Amazonian ecologies, comparing them to indomitable nature and positioning them at the bottom of the scale of human evolution. As a result, scientific travelers who engaged in the colonization process conceived of the Amazon as virgin nature and of its inhabitants as archaic cultures. National elites elaborated civilizational discourses, using them as an excuse to colonize and conquer independent Indigenous lands. But these scientific discourses, which in one way or another still prevail in views of the Amazon, have concrete and material effects. As Jason Moore argues, we should consider them productive factors, especially at the frontiers of export economy markets where violence became a tool for appropriation of value.[89] That is, these narratives conditioned development projects across the geographical frontiers of capitalism. The contemporary history of the Amazon seems to repeat the pattern of colonization and development solidified during the creation of nation-states in the nineteenth century.

Brazilian authors have described how, after the rubber boom and its suffocating system of coerced labor, people in the Amazon, especially migrant workers, finally formed more stable communities. After the Amazon lost its economic importance, rubber tappers moved into what liberal economists dismissively see as subsistence economy. However, this new situation allowed them to create networks of sociability. Amazon communities were born in those spaces from which coerced labor disappeared as the rubber boom declined.[90] We find a similar tendency in Bolivia. Gamarra, for example, explains how after the global collapse of rubber prices, Casa Suárez, the biggest export house in Bolivia, leased much of its land to small, local contractors.[91] By shifting the cost of production to local communities, Casa Suárez avoided the cost of labor coercion and maintenance, which in turn allowed people in the rubber settlements to dedicate more of their time to agricultural activities for community subsistence, following precisely the process that Cristina Scheibe Wolff describes for rubber settlements in the Juruá River basin in Brazil.

The extractive communities in Bolivia, made up of people who once were rubber tappers housed in "rubber barracks" (*barracas caucheras*) but who remained in the region after the collapse of the rubber boom, engaged in a subsistence economy, trading sporadically in latex and Brazil nuts (*Bertholletia excelsa*) until the 1980s.[92] However, that was not the case in most parts of the continent. The southern Amazon shared between Bolivia and Brazil saw a new wave of colonization when national governments expanded the frontier for industrial agriculture under the premise of the green revolution. Since the 1950s, Bolivian governments of different political tendencies (progressives, nationalists, and conservatives) have continued to expand the agricultural frontier.[93] It becomes evident how the discourses of civilization—transformed into discourses of national development—have influenced private and public policies arguing for allegedly more efficient and productive ways to use land when, in reality, the development model still privileges profit over local necessities, like food sovereignty.

The policies of expansion of the agricultural frontier in southern Brazil are a good example. From Pará through Mato Grosso, Rondônia, and Acre, ranchers and colonizers from southern Brazil have devastated millions of kilometers of forests to make space for cattle and monoculture, appropriating communal lands that belong to Indigenous groups and communities that practice local sustainable resource extraction.[94] In Bolivia, satellite images demonstrate that most of the northern Amazon forests are still in a relatively good state of preservation. The expansion of the agrarian frontier and agribusiness are centered to the south in Santa Cruz. However, in 2019, national and local authorities approved a new Plan for Land Use (Plan de Uso de Suelos or PLUS) for Beni Department. The plan will open more than ten million hectares of forests to agribusiness, cattle, and so-called flex crops (soy, oil palm, sugar, maize), following the Brazilian model. This is creating an even more precarious situation for Indigenous populations in the Bolivian lowlands, whose voices and opinions were not considered in the elaboration of this plan.

Agribusiness and gold mining are today the economic activities pushing a new wave of colonization in the Bolivian Amazon. From the Andean mountains of La Paz, miners descend through the Beni River tributaries, causing distress among Indigenous populations, especially in the Madidi National Park. The situation has become more dramatic since gold prices skyrocketed in 2022. In Santa Cruz, the geographies of soy and cattle are slowly expanding into the Beni forests and are beginning to affect communities that practice local sustainable resource extraction in the forests of Pando, which had remained until now secluded from these new geographies of capitalism. The history of the Amazon shows us how national discourses of development are still tied to capitalist projects that deeply affect local societies. Left-wing nationalist governments have not proved to be much different from liberal and neoliberal governments since all follow the same Western paradigm of civilization and developmental ideologies in which nature and local populations alike are to be subjected to the logics of profitability—a heritage of the colonization and creation of nation-states in the Amazon in the nineteenth century. The long history of the Amazon shows how important it is to recognize that modern states like Bolivia are built out of the colonization of Indigenous territories and their transformation as part of geographies of capitalism, an unrecognized process that still conditions national projects in the Amazon.

ACKNOWLEDGMENTS

I deeply appreciate and thank Sinclair Thomson for his thoughtful comments and observations that helped me sharpen the ideas and arguments of this chapter.

NOTES

1. *Hevea brasiliensia* and *Castilla ulei* were the two main types of trees that rubber extractors searched for in the continental Amazon. *Castilla ulei* could be found closer to the Andean mountain range and *Hevea brasilinesis* south of the Amazon River, close to flooded river banks, in the territories of what today is Brazil and Bolivia. Domínguez and Gómez López, *La economía extractiva*, 82; Ballivián and Pinilla, *Monografía de la industria de la goma*.
2. See for example: Bonilla, "El Caucho," 69–80; Weinstein, *The Amazon Rubber Boom*; Flores Marín, *La Explotación del caucho en el Perú*; Dominguez and Gómez López, *La economía extractiva en la Amazonia colombiana*; Gamarra Téllez, "La frontera nómada," 39–78; Gamarra Téllez, *Amazonía norte de Bolivia: Economía gomera*.
3. Flores Marín, *La Explotación del caucho en el Perú*, 170.
4. Weinstein, *The Amazon Rubber Boom*, 2.
5. From this perspective, see also Barham and Coomes, who adopted what they called a microeconomic perspective, which sees the main characteristics of the industry as being derived from the essential characteristics of wild rubber and its extraction technology. Barham and Oliver Coomes, "Wild Rubber," 37. The authors challenge previous literature by arguing that the microeconomic conditions allowed a significant appropriation of surplus capital in the Amazon, and that the debt peonage system was the most efficient system given the geographical conditions of the Amazon. Coomes and Barham, "The Amazon Rubber Boom," 231–57.
6. Viveiros de Castro, *The Relative Native*, 100.
7. Gamarra Téllez, *Amazonía norte de Bolivia*, 67.
8. Gamarra Téllez, 141.
9. Gamarra Téllez, 143.
10. Barclay, *El estado federal de Loreto*.
11. Zárate Botía, *Amazonia 1900–1940*, 41.
12. Rodriguez Ostria, *Poder central y proyecto regional*; Orsag Molina, *Circuitos económicos*. A letter from the Chamber of Deputies of Santa Cruz in 1910 describes how the department's economy survived after the imposition of liberal policies thanks to the rubber economy in the north. It also complains about the national budget distribution and stresses the unfinished projects like the telegraph lines or the lack of stable roads to the west. This letter encapsulates the local elites' perception of the lack of interest of the central government to develop the region. "Carta de Ángel Sandoval, Benigno Lara, Plácido Sánchez y Julio A. Gutiérrez," *El Beni*, March 10, 1910.
13. Roca states for example: "The occupation of the Northwest was a kind of culmination of the 'manifest destiny' of Santa Cruz, as were California and the Wild West for the

United States." Roca, *Economía y sociedad en el Oriente boliviano*, 40. See also Sanabria Fernández, *En busca del Dorado*; Tonelli, *El caucho ignorado*.

14. The Directorate was the Portuguese colonial organization of Indigenous towns in the Amazon. It was revived again in the nineteenth century to try to colonize independent Indigenous groups in the western Amazon. Roller, *Amazonian Routes*; Isidio Cardoso, *O Eldorado dos Deserdados*.
15. Nugent, *The Rise and Fall of the Amazon Rubber Industry*, 5.
16. Vallve, "The Impact of the Rubber Boom"; Córdoba, "El boom cauchero"; Van Valen, *Indigenous Agency in the Amazon*; Córdoba, "Barbarie en plural," 173–202.
17. García Jordán, *Fronteras, colonización y mano de obra indígena*; García Jordán, *Cruz y arado, fusiles y discursos*; Guiteras Mombiola, *De los llanos de Mojos a las cachuelas del Beni*; García Jordán, *Relatos del proyecto civilizatorio en Guarayos*; García Jordán and Guiteras Mombiola, "The Construction of a Frontier Space," 691–716.
18. Mallon, "The Promise and Dilemma of Subaltern Studies" 1491–515; Joseph and Nugent, *Everyday Forms of State Formation*; Mallon, *Peasant and Nation*.
19. Guiteras Mombiola, *De los llanos de Mojos a las cachuelas*, 8–9; García Jordán and Guiteras Mombiola, "The Construction of a Frontier Space," 692–93.
20. García Jordán and Guiteras Mombiola, "The Construction of a Frontier Space," 700.
21. Guiteras Mombiola, *De los llanos de Mojos*, 29.
22. Scott, *Seeing Like a State*, 24.
23. Coronil, *The Magical State*, 17.
24. The Bolivian Amazon today occupies the totality of the Beni and Pando departments, and the northern provinces of La Paz, Cochabamba, and Santa Cruz.
25. Ijurra, "Resumen", vol. 6, 276–410.
26. Forest products, such as sarsaparilla, copaiba, turtle oil, precious woods, and salted fish, were traded by Indigenous communities with merchants traveling along Amazon tributaries as early as the second half of the seventeenth century. Roller, *Amazonian Routes*, 59.
27. Santos, *História econômica da Amazônia*, 159.
28. In Peru for example, the expeditions of Miller and Nystrom describe how in the contested valleys of Paucartambo—a region in which, according to the voices of the period, the *chunchos* or "savages" constantly attacked the haciendas—people from Indigenous groups of the upper Madre de Dios would arrive at the haciendas to trade. Miller, "Notice of a Journey to the Northward," 77; Nystrom, "Informe al Sumpremo Gobierno del Peru," 264. Authors in Colombia describe a similar situation in the Putumayo and Caquetá valleys, although due to the easy navigation on both rivers from the Amazon, Indigenous villages in these rivers were frequently subject to incursions by Brazilian merchants and slavers. Pineda Camacho, *Holocausto en el Amazonas*, 37. But the most direct example is the life of Crisóstomo Hernández, a black merchant and fugitive in

upper Caquetá who established himself among the Huitotos and began collecting rubber through the exchange of iron tools. See the memories of Tovar in Gómez López, *Putumayo: La Vorágine de Las Caucherías, Primera Parte I*, 56.

29. Ugarte, "Alvores da conqusita espiritual," 39.
30. Villar, Córdoba, and Combès, *La reducción imposible*, 45.
31. Palacios, *Exploraciones de Don José Agustín Palacios*, 31.
32. Maccheti, *Diario del viaje fluvial del padre fray Jesualdo Maccheti*, 4.
33. Taussig describes that for Indigenous groups in the Putumayo region, the idea of whiteness was not just phenotypical, but it was more related to the perception of the "civilized" culture that settlers and colonizers were trying to enforce in the Amazon. Taussig, *Shamanism, Colonialism, and the Wild Man*, 96.
34. Heath, "Exploration of the River Beni in 1880–1," 332.
35. La Gaceta del Norte, *El rio Orton y su colonizacion: Datos Tomados de la Seccion "Noticias de Ayer" de La Gaceta del Norte de Orton*, 22.
36. Armentia, *Diario de sus viages*, 129.
37. Mariaca, "Exploracíon al río Acre," 8–9.
38. "Itinerario. De la expedición al Acre presentado por los suscritos. Al Dr. A. Vaca Díez (continuación)," *La Gaceta del Norte*, November 20, 1887.
39. Mercier, "Diario de una expedición del Madre de Dios al Acre," 4.
40. Vaca Díez, "Puntos picados. Replica," *La Gaceta del Norte*, October 15, 1888.
41. Armentia, *Diario de sus viages*, 105.
42. Mercier, "Diario de una expedición," 12; Labre, "Viagem exploradora," 9–10.
43. Armentia, "Navegación del Madre de Dios," 497–98.
44. Armentia, "Navegación del Madre de Dios," 498.
45. Armentia, *Diario de sus viages*, 25.
46. "Fusilamientos," *La Gaceta del Norte*, March 25, 1889.
47. Balzan, *A carretón y canoa*, 219–20.
48. For slavery in the southwestern Amazon see Paredes Pando, *Explotación del caucho-shiringa*; Roller, *Amazonian Routes*; Espinosa, "Los asháninkas y la violencia," 137–55; Santos-Granero, *Slavery and Utopia*.
49. The accusations against Bolivian expeditions for obtaining Indigenous labor by force are common in the publications of *Junta de Vías Fluviales* from Peru. Certainly, this kind of information was used to attack the Bolivian presence on the river; however, the slave trade developed by the rubber extractors within Bolivia had been often denounced as well. *La Gaceta del Norte*, Riberalta's newspaper, denounced the correrías during early 1890s. José Manuel Pando also described the slavery expeditions into the Madre de Dios. Besides the geopolitical interests behind the publications of the *Juntas*, the slave trade in the Madre de Dios was a known activity in the region. José Manuel Pando, *Viaje á la región de la goma elástica*, 210; Junta de Vias Fluviales, *El Istmo de Fitscarrald*, 67.

50. "D. Santos Mercado," *La Gaceta del Norte*, August 1, 1899.
51. Fawcett, *Lost Trails, Lost Cities*, 225.
52. Leutenegger, "Gente en la selva: Vivencias de un suizo en Bolivia," 344.
53. Vallve, "The Impact of the Rubber Boom"; Lema, *El sentido del silencio*, 216.
54. Vallvé, "The Impact of the Rubber Boom," 405.
55. "Las Víctimas del Madidi," *La Gaceta del Norte*, October 30, 1893.
56. "Guarayos en el Madidi," *La Gaceta del Norte*, December 12, 1899.
57. Nordenskiöld, *Exploraciones y aventuras en Sudamérica*, 412.
58. Nordenskiöld, *Exploraciones y aventuras en Sudamérica*, 412.
59. Beni's prefect, Miguel Mancilla, mentioned that the first rubber extractors in the region were Emilio Peña, Agustín Landívar, Enrique Cuellar, and Augusto Toledo. All started working in 1897. *El 10 de Abril*, May 2, 1903. However, rubber was part of a global market and the road opened by Balbino Meciel in 1901 was what allowed the export of rubber through Descalvado in Brazil at better prices. After this, the region always suffered from smuggling to Brazil. *El Ytenez*, December 9, 1899; *El Ytenez*, September 24, 1901.
60. Ministerio de Hacienda Bolivia, *Anexos al Informe del Ministro de Hacienda*, 142–45.
61. Pierini, *Informe Anual que presenta al Supremo Gobierno el R.P.*, 14–15.
62. *La Voz del Ytenez*, November 16, 1906.
63. "Asalto a los bárbaros," *El Ytenez*, December 14, 1901.
64. Pierini, *Informe Anual que presenta al Supremo Gobierno el R.P.*, 6.
65. Jesús Escalante Paz and fifteen men carried out an expedition towards the Puerto de Cautro Ojos in 1897. Museo y Archivo Histório Regional de Santa Cruz (MAHRSC), Fondo Prefectura, box 137–11, 63.
66. Scott, *Seeing like a State*, 24.
67. Ministerio de Hacienda, *Informes y Documentos referentes al Departamento del Beni*, 2, 10.
68. Juan López de Palacios Rubios, *Notificación y requerimiento que se ha dado de hacer a los moradores de las islas en tierra firme del Mar Océano que aún no están sujetos a Nuestro Señor*.
69. Ballivián y Pinilla, *Monografía de la industria de la goma en Bolivia*, 64.
70. Ballivián, *Diario del Viaje de la Delegación Nacional*; Gamarra Téllez, *Amazonía norte de Bolivia*, 103.
71. Ministerio de Hacienda, *Informe del Ministro de Hacienda* (1891), 64.
72. Ministerio de Hacienda, *Informe del Ministro de Hacienda* (1895), 177–78.
73. Orsag Molina, *Circuitos económicos*, 91.
74. Gamarra Téllez, *Barraca gomera y dominio amazónico el conflicto del acre*, 125.
75. Gamarra Téllez, 134.
76. Hecht, *The Scramble for the Amazon*, 167.
77. Ministerio de Hacienda, *Informe del Ministro de Hacienda* (1895), 177–78.
78. For a direct account of the first part of the Acre War see: Achá, *De los Andes al Amazonas*; Posnansky, *Campaña Del Acre*, 1904.

79. Hecht, *The Scramble for the Amazon*, 173; Gamarra Téllez, *Barraca gomera y dominio amazónico*, 162–63.
80. Hecht, *The Scramble for the Amazon*, 181; Gamarra Téllez, *Barraca gomera y dominio amazónico*, 185.
81. For an account on the second phase of the war see: Suárez, *Anotaciones y Documentos Sobre La Campana Del Alto Acre*.
82. Junta de Vías Fluviales, *Vías del Pacífico al Madre de Dios*, 1902; Junta de Vías Fluviales, *El Istmo de Fitscarrald*; Junta de Vías Fluviales, *Nuevas Exploraciones en la Hoya del Madre de Dios*, 1904; Comisiones mixtas, *Informes de las Comisiones mixtas peruano-brasileras encargadas del reconocimiento de los ríos Alto Purús i Alto Yuruá*; Junta de Vías Fluviales, *Ultimas exploraciones ordenadas por la Junta de Vías Fluviales a los ríos Ucayali, Madre de Dios, Paucartambo y Urubamba. Informes de los señores Stiglich, Von Hassel, Olivera y Ontaneda*; Da Cunha, *Um Paraíso Perdido*.
83. Comisiones mixtas, *Informes de las Comisiones mixtas peruano-brasileras encargadas del reconocimiento de los rios Alto Purús i Alto Yuruá*.
84. Colonization and Commercial Co. of Bolivia, *Bolivian Colonization*.
85. Cardoso, "O Eldorado dos Deserdados: Indígenas, escravos, migrantes, regatões e o avanço rumo ao oeste amazônico no século XIX," 218.
86. Santos-Granero, *Selva Central: History, Economy and Land Use in Peruvian Amazonia*.
87. National Bolivian Navigation Company, *La Empresa Church en sus relaciones con Bolivia y sus complicaciones en Europa. Exposición detallada de todas la operaciones de la Compañía Nacional de Navegación Boliviana y de todas las cuestiones pendientes que embarazan su pronta realizción [sic]. Por Juan Francisco Velarde. Contiene además todos los contratos relativos a la Empresa i la correspondencia cambiada entre los Comisionados Bolivianos en Londres i el Coronel Church*, 43.
88. Hecht, *The Scramble for the Amazon*, 162.
89. Moore, *Capitalism in the Web of Life*, 195.
90. Wolff, *Mulheres da floresta: Uma história: Alto Juruá, Acre, 1890–1945*, 96, 106, 108; Avelino Leal, "Direitos e processos diferenciados de territorialização."
91. Gamarra Téllez, *Amazonía norte de Bolivia*, 253.
92. Zeitum, *Amazonía boliviana*.
93. Orsag and Guzmán Narváez, "Tecnología, modernidad, y desplazamiento del conflicto social," 170.
94. Hecht and Cockburn, *The Fate of the Forest: Developers, Destroyers, and Defenders of the Amazon*; Hoelle, *Rainforest Cowboys*; Acker, *Volkswagen in the Amazon*.

SMOOTHING THE CONTRADICTIONS

The Political History of Fossil Fuels

Kevin A. Young

"It's a matter of the very existence of Bolivia," Daniel Bedregal warned the other delegates to the 1945 constitutional convention. Bolivia's state oil company, Yacimientos Petrolíferos Fiscales Bolivianos (YPFB), had existed for almost a decade, but its production levels remained low. YPFB "signifies the last hope of economic redemption for Bolivia, because this eminently national industry is called upon to resolve in the near future all of the country's economic, industrial, and social problems." The imminent decline of the country's mining industry gave oil even greater economic importance. "The Bolivian people, who know intuitively that the mining industry will no longer be able to guarantee their wellbeing in the future, turn their anguished gaze to the petroleum of the Southeast, anxious to see it as the guarantee of their future." By developing YPFB into "the keystone" of the economy, Bolivian officials would fulfill their "sacred duty" as custodians of subsoil wealth and would ensure the right of all Bolivians "to live free of the fear of misery and hunger."[1]

Hydrocarbons have long been at the center of Bolivian hopes for economic development and social justice. Statements like Bedregal's have been a near constant in Bolivian politics for the past century. The horrific carnage of the Chaco War with Paraguay (1932–1935), which became widely understood as a war to protect Bolivia's oil resources, gave hydrocarbons a "sacred" significance for Bolivian nationalists. Millions of Bolivians began looking to oil, and later natural gas, as the primary means by which the country could achieve economic development. The dream was never simply to extract and sell the oil, but to use it as a "lever" for overcoming Bolivia's dependence on raw material exports and lack of domestic industry. As oil refinery workers argued in 1959, "oil can and should constitute one of the firmest pillars for a new type of Bolivian economy."[2]

Many, like Bedregal, also saw hydrocarbon wealth as the key to reducing inequality and the "misery and hunger" that went with it. Bolivian anti-imperialists attacked not only foreign oil companies but also the traitorous domestic elites who sat atop the country's class pyramid. As in many countries where resource nationalism took root in the early twentieth century, nationalists often tied the quest for sovereign control over natural resource wealth to the struggle for education, healthcare, housing, and other social rights.[3] This association remains common in Bolivia, and much of the world, today.

Oil and gas embody the opposing forces, or contradictions, that have driven modern Bolivian history.[4] The opposition between Bolivians and foreigners is the most obvious of these contradictions. The country's historic alternation between policies of nationalism and liberalization reflects the ever-changing balance of power in this commodity-centered conflict. The most visible nationalist policies have included the nationalization of Standard Oil in 1937, of Gulf Oil in 1969, and the quasi-nationalization of gas companies in 2005–2006. In the periods in between, the state has reopened the hydrocarbon sector to private capital on generous terms. Hydrocarbon policy cannot be understood in strictly dichotomous terms, however. Nationalizations can take various forms, differing, for instance, in the extent of compensation offered to the expropriated companies. Nationalist policies have also included lesser measures like increases in taxes and royalties, state control over marketing or refining, and diverse measures designed to regulate the activities of private enterprise. Hydrocarbon nationalism thus encompasses all "attempts to redirect the incidence of costs and benefits" of extraction in favor of the nation.[5] How that *nation* is defined—namely, who within it makes the key decisions about production, consumption, and spending—is another crucial question sometimes lost in the debate between nationalists and privatizers.

Additional problems have become more visible in the early twenty-first century. Our age of escalating climate chaos lays bare the contradiction between fossil fuel–based economic growth and ecological sustainability. This conflict was virtually absent from political discourse in Bolivia until quite recently. Political struggles of recent decades, and the new crop of scholarly studies that has accompanied them, have highlighted still more contradictions. They have demonstrated how hydrocarbon economies help fuel regional, interethnic, and gender-based conflicts due to fierce competition over resource rents and territorial control, and to the masculinist ethos and male-dominated labor system that tends to accompany hydrocarbon extraction.[6] Each of these contradictions has been thrown into relief at certain moments over the past century.

Yet at the same time, hydrocarbons have also helped to smooth over these contradictions. Hydrocarbon nationalism has united diverse classes and social groups within Bolivia, much to the satisfaction of governing officials and the domestic ruling class. Nationalist mobilization around oil and gas has often served as the grease that reduces friction among classes, communities, and regions. The revenues resulting from hydrocarbon nationalizations (1937, 1969, 2006) have funded social spending and public investments, yet they have blunted most Bolivians' concerns about the ecological and social costs of extraction. Nationalizations have redistributed wealth from foreigners to Bolivians, but they have reduced the government's incentive to target large landholders, industrialists, and other affluent Bolivians with progressive taxes or property redistribution. Hydrocarbons have thus often defused social conflict, if only temporarily and illusorily.[7]

This chapter explores the history of Bolivian hydrocarbons through the prism of these contradictions and various attempts to mitigate them. Rather than attempting a comprehensive account of hydrocarbon politics, economics, or technology, which is available elsewhere,[8] I highlight key conflicts and what they reveal about the contradictions at the heart of Bolivian history. Addressing the profound economic, social, and ecological challenges facing Bolivia today requires grappling with these complexities. Most of the same essential problems can be found in other extractive economies, especially in the Global South and to some degree even in the North.[9] As a case study, Bolivia's hydrocarbon economy may be helpful for understanding some of the central tensions animating modern politics and economic development.

OIL IS BOLIVIA'S FUTURE

Indigenous peoples had been using petroleum found on or near the earth's surface for medicine, lighting, and warfare long before the creole elite took an interest in oil exploration. Only in the 1890s did that elite begin geological studies with the intention of large-scale drilling. In 1892, the Bolivian state's war against the Chiriguano people in the southeast ended with the massacre or enslavement of several thousand people, a genocidal campaign typical of Latin American states in the late nineteenth century. Oil was not the motive, but the subjugation of the Chiriguanos did help open the door for prospecting in the hydrocarbon-rich southeast. At that same moment, the growth of oil-powered transportation around the world provided new incentives for exploration and extraction.[10]

Initial progress was slow. Early private investors from Sucre, Santa Cruz, and elsewhere failed to attract much state support. The geographic remoteness, lack of roads, and tropical climate of the southeast posed formidable obstacles. Moreover, the southeast was still "inhabited by savages," in the words of Bolivia's finance minister in the early 1920s, and they did not always welcome invaders in their territory.[11] Hopes for industrial-scale drilling were thwarted by a combination of hostile terrain and Indigenous people whom the creole elite despised as uncivilized—a trope that would resurface time and again whenever the region's inhabitants were said to be obstructing the path to progress.

Despite this delay, however, the prospect of future oil production was much discussed by the mid-1910s. Oil nationalism became an increasingly central part of urban political culture. In 1916, the Liberal government of Ismael Montes, under pressure from nationalists, asserted state control over lands with potential oil. Oil laws in 1920 and 1921 established new royalty rates and regulations on private companies, including the requirement to prioritize production for the domestic market and obligatory employment of Bolivians. These measures were early examples of hydrocarbon nationalism.[12] Events in Bolivia paralleled the rise of oil nationalism across Latin America in the first three decades of the century. From Mexico to Argentina, the consolidation of foreign control in oil and other primary export sectors galvanized new nationalist movements calling on governments to regulate, tax, or expropriate these foreign investments.[13]

World War I and the emerging interimperial competition for oil led to new conflicts between foreign capital and nationalists. In Bolivia—which the US Geological Survey identified as the world's fifth biggest oil source—nationalists began to stress both the economic and military importance of the country's oil.[14] For one prominent nationalist, Pedro Nolasco López, "Bolivia's economic future is contained in its oil." He wrote that "in military terms, petroleum is like the blood of the soldier who fights, and victory goes to the warring party that has more petroleum and reserves." Oil would enable Bolivia "to reclaim its imprescriptible rights of access to the Pacific and the Atlantic" following its loss of ocean access to Chile in the War of the Pacific (1879–1883).[15]

Oil nationalism was not just an elite phenomenon. Although most accounts date the rise of popular nationalism to the Chaco War, the country's nascent labor and student movements took up the banner of resource nationalism in the 1920s. The 1927 National Workers' Congress in Oruro called for nationalization of the mines. A national convention of university students in 1928 echoed that demand and also advocated oil nationalization. The students decried the "monstrous personal and economic privileges established in favor of foreign capitalists" and called on the Bolivian government to imitate Mexico's 1917 constitution, which embodied "the healthy values of nationalist defense."[16] In later years Mexican oil policy would remain a reference point for nationalists in Bolivia and other South American countries where nationalist movements challenged the prerogatives of foreign oil companies.

The main foreign capitalist in Bolivia in the 1920s was the giant Standard Oil Company of New Jersey, acting through its local affiliate the Standard Oil Company of Bolivia. In the previous decade, Standard had expanded its investments in Mexico,

Peru, Venezuela, Colombia, and elsewhere in response to a domestic crude shortage and global competition from its British rival Royal Dutch Shell. By 1929, Standard and other US oil companies had 444 million USD invested in South America alone, about two and a half times the amount that US companies invested in manufacturing on the continent.[17] In 1921, Standard acquired several million hectares of territory in the Bolivian southeast, in a process that violated Bolivian law but won the blessing of President Bautista Saavedra. Soon it had wells in operation at Camiri (Santa Cruz Department) and other choice locations. However, the company's main sources of oil were outside Bolivia, and it was more interested in controlling Bolivian supplies than producing. It limited its production to token amounts, particularly after it obtained concessions in the Middle East in 1928. By decade's end, Standard had produced less than one million barrels of Bolivian oil.[18] This perfidy gave Bolivian oil nationalism a somewhat different inflection than in Mexico or Colombia, where nationalists focused on the need for higher taxes or state-controlled production. In addition to those demands, Bolivians also accused Standard of "hoarding the best reserves of Bolivian oil," as Pedro López argued in 1929.[19] The Chaco War would turn this growing resentment into an explosive and widespread popular hostility.

BLOOD IN THE CHACO

Pedro López's reference to oil as "the blood of the soldier" took on more visceral meaning with the war against Paraguay, in which some fifty-six thousand Bolivians and thirty-six thousand Paraguayans were killed. The war almost immediately gave rise to rumors that it had been instigated by Standard Oil and Royal Dutch Shell, which were said to covet the potential oil of the disputed Chaco Boreal region and control over export routes through the area.[20] Despite its dubious factual basis, this narrative of the conflict as an imperialist "war for oil" has had tremendous staying power in Bolivians' collective understanding of the war.

Aside from Standard's evident disinterest in the war's outcome,[21] the biggest problem with the traditional narrative is that it obscures the Bolivian government's own motives and culpability. President Daniel Salamanca (1931–1934) had entered office amid the Great Depression, which hit Bolivia and its tin export economy especially hard. He also faced political opposition from the Liberal Party and increasingly radical agitation by the urban working class, mine workers, students, and intellectuals. Salamanca was thwarted in his effort to enact a draconian "social defense" law that would crush the left, and thus "impotently watched the growth of leftist and labour agitation," notes historian Herbert Klein. In this context, Salamanca came to see a foreign war as the cure for class conflict and political weakness. A successful campaign "to stand firm in the Chaco" against Paraguay would showcase "all the legendary virility of our people," and, of course, of their leader. In his assessment of the Chaco War's causes, Klein stresses "the humiliations of the embittered president and the obvious feeling of many leaders that foreign conflict would resolve mounting class tensions." Salamanca's subsequent actions support this interpretation. Once the war began, President Salamanca was finally able to impose his social defense law, send leftists to the front lines or into exile, and outlaw collective bargaining.[22]

Oil may have increased Salamanca's desire for war. Historian Stephen Cote suggests that the conflict was indeed a "war for oil," but on the part of the Bolivian government. Cote argues that desire to increase oil export revenues led Salamanca to instigate the conflict in order "to gain an export route to the Atlantic."[23] There is some evidence to support this hypothesis. In 1929, a treaty between Peru and Chile had foreclosed Bolivia's chance of regaining its outlet to the Pacific, while Argentina had also refused to permit construction of a pipeline through its territory. In 1931, Salamanca complained that Bolivia's "great oil wealth" was "useless" as long as Argentina and Paraguay were "denying passage" to the Atlantic. "Bolivia cannot resign itself to living miserably" as a landlocked country, he said.[24] Salamanca was echoing a common nationalist grievance. Soon after Bolivia's loss of coastal territory in the Pacific War, politicians and intellectuals had begun speaking of obtaining Atlantic access as an alternative. Salamanca had campaigned for president in part on this "Atlantic option."[25] It remains unclear just how central this economic motivation was to Salamanca, who also had political and personal reasons for favoring war. But oil may have been one factor.

Whatever the mix of causal factors behind Salamanca's decision, the Chaco War had profound political consequences. It entered Bolivians' collective memory not only as an indication of the crimes of imperialists and traitorous Bolivian elites but also as a heroic campaign to defend Bolivia's hydrocarbons. In the second half of 1934, Paraguayan forces had advanced well beyond the formerly disputed territory and threatened to seize some of the known oil fields of the southeast. At that moment oil became central to the war, and repelling the Paraguayans did in fact safeguard the region's oil and gas resources for future Bolivian use.[26] Soldiers' blood thereafter became closely associated with oil and gas wealth. War veterans' organizations, which became key political actors, often presented themselves as the "defenders of oil" in future disputes over hydrocarbon policy. Their "blood had paid for YPFB's creation" after the war. Patriots thus had a solemn obligation to the "Chaco martyrs" to defend YPFB and Bolivia's hydrocarbon wealth.[27]

What should we make of the fact that the growth of hydrocarbon nationalism was largely based on a myth about foreign oil companies' role in starting the Chaco War? The popular faith in that myth is often the basis for scholarly lamentations about the alleged irrationality of the Bolivian masses. Some have characterized resource nationalism as a collective pathology, a "deep-seated loss aversion" that "is not faithful to historical fact." Popular misunderstanding of the war's causes is wielded as proof that resource nationalism is rooted in "supernatural" thinking and "conspiracy theories." Such characterizations of mass sentiment betray pro-capitalist and antidemocratic impulses, often overlaid with anti-Indigenous racism.[28]

Most critics of the Chaco War "conspiracy theory" miss the forest for the trees. In assailing a factual error in popular memory, they obscure the fundamental truths at the heart of the misperception. Though nationalists were wrong in seeing Standard Oil and Royal Dutch Shell as the "puppet masters" of the Chaco War, their analysis of economic and political power was otherwise generally correct. Foreign oil companies like Standard did hoard oil reserves and evade taxes while contributing little to economic development in countries like Bolivia, a pattern now widely recognized by historians.[29] They did form cartels. They constantly sought, and usually received, support from the governments and banks in their imperialist home countries. Most Bolivian politicians eagerly collaborated with them.[30] Sometimes popular beliefs are wrong on particulars but right about the big picture.

The immediate postwar years saw the formation or reconstitution of many labor and leftist organizations, in which Marxists, anarchists, and social democrats competed for influence. Resource nationalism and demands for progressive redistribution of wealth were the key threads that united most of these groups. Anti-imperialism and socialism often went hand in hand. War veterans decried "the private appropriation" of Bolivia's resources and "the unequal distribution of collective wealth," thus indicting both foreign and national capitalists.[31] Calls for nationalization of the mines and oil fields spread rapidly among popular organizations in the cities.

This context is essential for understanding the reformist military governments of David Toro (1936–1937) and Germán Busch (1937–1939). Toro's ascent was made possible by a May 1936 general strike in La Paz, which precipitated the military takeover.[32] Once in power he responded to popular demands by creating YPFB, adapting the model of the state oil company that Argentina had formed in 1922.[33] In March 1937 he nationalized Standard Oil's properties, which was the first expropriation of a foreign oil company in Latin American history, a year before Mexico's more well-known nationalization. Busch's 1938 constitution embodied the "social constitutionalism" that gained popularity across Latin America after the Mexican Revolution, in which governments limited the rights of private property holders in the interest of the public good. The Bolivian version declared a state monopoly on oil exports and sought to force foreign investors to respect domestic laws rather than recurring to their home governments to intervene on their behalf.[34]

Oil nationalization remained a focal point of political contestation for the next five years as Standard sued and Bolivians mobilized to defend the policy. Many of the future leaders of the Movimiento Nacionalista Revolucionario (MNR) party gained prominence during this conflict. Carlos Montenegro's newspaper articles and 1938 pamphlet attacking Standard Oil's record in Bolivia received wide attention. In 1941, MNR leaders played a central role in forming the Unión Boliviana de Defensa del Petróleo, which published a manifesto that accused Standard of sabotaging YPFB and called for a resolute nationalist defense against the company's legal claims.[35] Such efforts were one factor in the 1942 settlement between Bolivia and Standard, wherein the government paid the relatively small sum of 1.5 million USD in exchange for the company's geological data.[36]

Between Busch's 1939 suicide and the 1952 revolution, YPFB grew slowly. For most of that time pro-business politicians ruled Bolivia and were disinclined to challenge US hostility to oil nationalism, as reflected in the Department of State's obstruction of loans to YPFB and other state oil companies and the ambassador's demand that Bolivia keep its "petroleum industry wide open to American private enterprise."[37] The exception was the regime of General Gualberto Villarroel (1943–1946), who held power in cooperation with the MNR. The Villarroel-MNR government reprised the reform-oriented nationalism of Toro and Busch. It purchased new rotary drills for YPFB, funded construction of a pipeline between Camiri and Cochabamba, and integrated into YPFB a new crop of skilled technicians who had been trained in Mexico starting in 1937.[38] Future oil nationalists would remember Toro, Busch, and Villarroel fondly.[39]

Yet the oil nationalism of these years was by no means entirely progressive. Nationalist politicians often used it as a way to divert attention from other social and economic hierarchies. Toro exemplifies this tendency. After taking power he declared communism and anarchism illegal and tried to prohibit Bolivians from publicly debating economic policy.[40] When considered alongside his other policies, his oil nationalism appears to have been intended in part to prevent a radical class upheaval. Standard Oil had few friends in Bolivia, and nationalization was a surefire way for a tenuous regime to rally the support of popular sectors and military officers. Moreover, Toro's key moves on oil came at the same moment that he was shifting rightward in other ways. Weeks after establishing YPFB in December 1936, and just before expropriating Standard in March 1937, he appointed a representative of the mining oligarchy as labor minister and purged radicals from the ministry. Klein observes that Toro "retained support of the rural landed interests and the urban middle classes by tempering his verbal radicalism with minimal changes of a drastic nature."[41]

The rise of nationalism in the postwar period came at the expense of other political imaginaries, including ideologies of class struggle and the pro-Indigenous and feminist currents that had won adherents starting in the 1920s. These radical alternatives were suppressed or subsumed as nationalism became the hegemonic framework in Bolivian politics. While many anarchists and Marxists had spoken of Indigenous liberation and built alliances with rural Indians, the nationalist regimes saw the Indian as an uncivilized "child" in need of "redemption" and tried to prohibit urban-rural political coalitions.[42] The working-class feminism of anarchist women was displaced by a chauvinistic discourse that called on "all the real men of Bolivia" to take a "virile position in defense of the nation's oil patrimony."[43]

While anti-imperialist nationalism is not inherently incompatible with antiracism or feminism, in the hands of most nationalist politicians, it was. All the MNR's founders were middle class, white or mestizo, and men, and their politics reflected it.[44] They were progressive insofar as they sought to capture more of the economic surplus for Bolivians but were wary of radically altering Bolivian society itself (and even on the first count, they proved eager to compromise with foreign capital).

REVOLUTION AND THE OIL CARD

This blend of progressive and conservative elements continued to characterize hydrocarbon nationalism in the decades following the 1952 revolution. Anti-imperialist voices denounced foreign oil companies and looked to YPFB to promote economic development and social justice. Hydrocarbons remained flashpoints of political contestation, yet they simultaneously helped reduce tension. Between the MNR period (1952–1964) and the 1969 nationalization of Gulf Oil, diverse government leaders called upon oil and natural gas to smooth over class conflict. Oil and gas performed a similarly ambiguous role in the brewing regional conflicts of the era. In the late 1950s, oil ignited a regionalist movement in Santa Cruz that demanded oil revenues for the department, and the revenues in turn helped ease tensions by the early 1960s.

The MNR promised that higher oil production would play a central role in the diversification of the economy.[45] The administration of Víctor Paz Estenssoro (1952–1956) more than tripled YPFB's funding, leading to a fivefold increase in production levels and, for the first time, the full supply of the domestic market for most petroleum products. In 1955, the state company created its own exploration office in hopes of expanding beyond established oil fields like Camiri. YPFB was by all assessments a promising state enterprise, with even the anti-statist US State Department privately conceding its "reputation for efficiency."[46]

Progress was short-lived, however. The United States conditioned its aid to the MNR on a series of policy changes favoring foreign investment. One of the new government's explicit "obligations" in return for aid was "an oil law which will afford [a] sound and attractive basis for the US companies to come into the country," as assistant secretary of state (and future oil company lawyer) Henry Holland instructed the US Embassy in La Paz.[47] Paz Estenssoro obliged, decreeing a new oil code in 1955 that was rubber-stamped by the Bolivian legislature the following year. The law offered lucrative opportunities for foreign investors, setting royalties at just eleven percent and the duration of concessions at forty years. It reserved most of the country for private production while confining YPFB to the country's southeastern corner. The Bolivian president was also empowered to lease territory in YPFB's zone to private investors. The next year a US-sponsored austerity plan dramatically reduced the budget for YPFB and other public investments.[48] The 1955 reform thus signaled the MNR's definitive retreat from oil nationalism.

Why did MNR leaders bow to US pressures and abandon a nationalist oil policy? Clearly, Washington had enormous power: by that time it was supplying about one-third of the Bolivian government's budget, and the country's economic situation was exceedingly precarious. The United States had repeatedly demonstrated its ability to punish defiant third world leaders, as recently as 1953 in Iran and 1954 in Guatemala. These demonstrations weighed on Paz Estenssoro and other leaders, who concluded that "being against the United States" was impossible.[49] Another problem was YPFB's lack of resources. In issuing his 1955 oil decree, Paz Estenssoro argued that only the private sector could supply the investment capital needed for new exploration and production. These two constraints—US imperialism and Bolivian poverty—are the factors most commonly cited by historians to explain the MNR's shift in oil policy.

Nonetheless, MNR leaders did have options. Most notably, they could have pursued loans from the Soviet bloc and European lenders. In fact, the Soviets would soon offer the MNR a 150 million USD loan, which would have included 60 to 80 million USD for YPFB by the estimate of future YPFB head engineer and president Enrique Mariaca Bilbao. Officials in YPFB and the Ministry of Mines and Petroleum elaborated detailed plans for how the loan money would be spent. Just how viable this option was is difficult to know. One recent scholar has questioned the seriousness of the Soviet loan offer and expressed skepticism about the quality of Soviet-bloc machinery.[50] Regardless, the fact remains that MNR leaders had a plausible alternative and declined to seriously explore it.

Their decision makes sense only if we also consider MNR officials' class politics alongside the external constraints under which they operated. Courting the Soviets obviously would have triggered the wrath of US government and capital.

Surviving the inevitable backlash would have necessitated a radicalization of the Bolivian Revolution, akin to what the Cuban government did in the 1960s when it nationalized virtually the entire economy and redistributed wealth on a giant scale. A socialist revolution was ideologically anathema to the MNR leadership, who had assiduously sought to keep the left at bay. Their goal was an "economic revolution, not social revolution."[51] The 1955 liberalization of the oil sector reflected, in part, MNR leaders' attempt to keep the domestic class war under control.

To their chagrin, however, the new oil code soon ignited political contestation. The first hotspot was hydrocarbon-rich Santa Cruz, where urban residents mobilized under the auspices of the Pro-Santa Cruz Committee to demand direct royalty payments to oil-producing departments. The 1955 decree and its 1956 legislative confirmation had left vague the question of departmental royalties. The ensuing struggle helped galvanize regional identity in Santa Cruz, which would be closely linked to right-wing politics in the decades that followed. In 1959, the national government succeeded in temporarily demobilizing the Santa Cruz Committee when it passed legislation that directed a portion of YPFB revenues and royalties from private companies to producing districts, provinces, and departments.[52]

The 1955 oil code soon generated nationalist resistance, as well. By the end of the decade diverse working-class sectors, peasant unions, Chaco veterans, students, intellectuals, and even some MNR congressional representatives were demanding the abrogation or revision of the law. They assailed it as excessively generous to foreign companies and prejudicial to both YPFB and Bolivia's larger goals of industrialization and economic diversification. This criticism became the focus of a series of well-documented polemics by nationalist authors, starting with Sergio Almaraz's 1958 *Petróleo en Bolivia*, which achieved enough visibility to set off alarm bells in the US embassy.[53]

Oil workers were especially vocal. In 1958, the Federación Sindical de Trabajadores Petroleros de Bolivia (FSTPB) called on the government to tighten regulations, close tax loopholes, expand YPFB's exploration efforts, and accept loan offers from the Soviet bloc. The Chaco martyrs were an important symbol. The federation exhorted Bolivians to "preserve the life of the petroleum industry of Bolivia which you have defended with your blood in the Chaco war."[54] The FSTPB and its local affiliates announced strikes at various times in the years that followed, usually citing these demands in addition to bread-and-butter grievances. Bolivian oil and gas workers are not known for their militancy, but in this moment they played an active and often confrontational political role. Future research may further illuminate the sector's labor history, which has been little studied.[55]

By the mid-1960s, the US-based Gulf Oil and its subsidiary the Bolivian Gulf Oil Company became the focal point of nationalist resistance. At the same moment that YPFB was being squeezed by austerity and the 1955 code, the government granted Gulf permission to repatriate 79 percent of profits. The company invested huge sums in exploration, resulting in new discoveries of both oil and gas in the early 1960s. As natural gas seemed poised to overtake oil as the most important hydrocarbon of Bolivia's future, the Ministry of Mines and Petroleum revealed that up to 90 percent of all known gas reserves were controlled by Gulf.[56] Nationalist protests increasingly blamed the *entreguista* (sellout) hydrocarbon policy of General René Barrientos, who had overthrown the MNR's Paz Estenssoro in 1964. Barrientos's legitimacy suffered considerably as a result, leading him to make gestures toward revision of the 1955 code soon before he died in a helicopter crash in April 1969.[57] Civilian vice president Luis Siles Salinas continued those gestures during his brief five months in the presidency.

The real change came after the head of the armed forces, Alfredo Ovando Candia, overthrew Siles Salinas in September. Ovando represented the economic nationalist current within the Bolivian military. In 1968, he had publicly called for a 50 percent tax on foreign companies and a state monopoly over downstream operations in the gas sector.[58] He assembled a joint cabinet of officers and civilians, including the fiery nationalist legislator Marcelo Quiroga Santa Cruz, whom he appointed Minister of Mines and Petroleum. After a few weeks of debate within the new regime, Ovando sided with Quiroga's call to nationalize Gulf.

The shifts in policy that culminated with the October 1969 nationalization were a response to the broad-based nationalist struggle that had spread since the late 1950s. However, they must also be understood in the context of escalating class struggle, state repression, and widespread political disenchantment. The violence of the Barrientos dictatorship had reduced but not squelched worker militancy in the mines and cities. In June 1967, the regime had murdered scores of striking mine workers at the Siglo XX tin mine. Soon there were even signs of discontent in the countryside, where Barrientos had cultivated a reliable alliance between the military and peasant unions. In this context, embracing hydrocarbon nationalism was a logical governance strategy. Ovando's planning minister, José Ortiz Mercado, later commented that Siles Salinas had tried "to appropriate nationalist sentiments by playing the oil card," in an attempt "to save his weak government." Once Ovando took power, he was "hemmed in and on the defensive with regard to the oil question." Ovando faced skepticism or hostility from labor and the left, and a divided military command. For this reason nationalization held added appeal.[59] "Playing the oil card" was partly an attempt to keep a lid on domestic tumult, just as it had been when David Toro nationalized Standard Oil in 1937.

The rest of Ovando's policy record supports this analysis. He dutifully promised compensation to Gulf, a move that failed to dissuade the US government and foreign companies from retaliating.[60] Then, with the ink barely dry on the nationalization decree, Ovando announced a wage freeze for workers. He abstained from any attempt at progressive taxation or other redistributive measures throughout the rest of his time in power. Few Bolivians were surprised by this trajectory, especially given that Ovando had directed the 1967 massacre at the Siglo XX mine as chief of the armed forces.[61]

In contrast, many nationalists since the 1920s had insisted on combining nationalization with other forms of downward redistribution. Social democrats called for progressive wage policies and more spending on public goods like education, while the radical left sought worker control in the workplace and the full abolition of capitalist property. These currents found expression in the left parties, the mine workers' unions, the urban labor movement, and university circles, and among nationalist intellectuals like Quiroga Santa Cruz. These voices were well aware of how conservative leaders tried to use nationalist coalitions to obscure "the fundamental importance of class struggle."[62] Nor were attempts to play the oil card necessarily successful in building durable conservative coalitions: witness the quick demise of the Toro and Ovando regimes.

Still, if the conservative version of hydrocarbon nationalism never became hegemonic, it did help to constrict the political space available to the Bolivian left. It also retained strong support within the military hierarchy, helping to ensure that the progressive military regime of Juan José Torres (October 1970–August 1971) would not be able to consolidate itself.

THE MOST SCANDALOUS THEFT OF OUR HISTORY

The US-backed overthrow of Torres and the installation of the right-wing dictatorship of Hugo Banzer (1971–1978) brought less change to hydrocarbon policy than might have been expected. Banzer welcomed foreign investors, but on stricter terms than the 1955 oil code had done. In 1972 he increased royalties from 11 percent to 30 percent and replaced the old concessions system with operation and service contracts that would channel more benefits to YPFB. Otherwise, Banzer's hydrocarbon policy was characterized by major corruption, politicized appointments to YPFB, and a general failure to take advantage of the propitious market environment of the 1970s.[63]

The wholesale reversal of hydrocarbon nationalism came only in the 1990s. The 1985 New Economic Policy inaugurated Bolivia's neoliberal era of austerity, trade liberalization, and deregulation. Privatization of state-owned enterprises followed with a series of laws passed in the mid-1990s. The consequences of YPFB's privatization were especially dramatic, since oil and gas accounted for about half of state revenues at the time. The company was carved up into three separate entities, and the majority of its shares were sold off to multinational firms. Other aspects of President Gonzalo Sánchez de Lozada's energy plan included the restoration of the old concessions system, the reduction of the royalty rate for new drilling to 18 percent, private control over commercialization, and plans for a new gas pipeline to Brazil. Sánchez de Lozada promised that new foreign investment would more than compensate for the revenue that YPFB would lose, creating 287,000 new jobs and nearly tripling economic growth by 1997. As part of a bid to create public support for the plan, he also created a new privatized pension system linked to the minority shares of YPFB still held by the public.[64]

The promises were fantastical. There was indeed a big influx of new foreign investment in Bolivian hydrocarbons, which led to an eightfold surge in known gas reserves. Bolivia officially became South America's second-largest holder of gas reserves after Venezuela. Gas went from 8 percent to 28 percent of Bolivia's total exports between 1995 and 2004. However, the new investment was capital-intensive and thus generated few jobs. It coincided with a drop in YPFB's own employment from 9,150 workers in 1985 to about 600 in 2002. The loss of state revenue that followed privatization predictably became the excuse for new taxes on energy consumption, which fueled strikes and protests.[65]

Nationalist critics also decried the transfer of existing hydrocarbon reserves to private hands. Former YPFB president Enrique Mariaca wrote that with the appropriation of 13 billion USD in known oil and gas reserves by private companies, "Bolivia suffered the most scandalous theft of its history."[66] The San Alberto gas "mega-field" in Tarija became a special focus of outrage. Though the field's existence had long been known by YPFB, the government classified it as new and thus subject to the lower 18-percent royalty rate and other pro-business provisions of the 1996 hydrocarbon law. The San Alberto controversy helped galvanize an emergent nationalist coalition of oil workers, urban neighborhood activists and union members, peasant unions, and intellectuals like Mariaca.[67]

The most explosive spark for that coalition came in 2003, when a newly reelected Sánchez de Lozada pursued a deal with Pacific LNG to export Bolivian gas to California via Chile and Mexico. While Pacific LNG executives predicted 1 billion USD in yearly profits from the deal, estimates projected that the Bolivian government would receive just 50 million USD a year. Moreover, the raw gas would be compressed into liquid in Chile and then converted back into gas in Mexico for export to the United States, meaning that non-Bolivians—including historic rival Chile—would reap the benefits of processing. To add to the insult, in February 2003 Sánchez de Lozada had responded to the International Monetary Fund's pressures for a tax increase by choosing the most regressive option available: rather than increasing taxes on hydrocarbon companies or affluent Bolivians, he raised taxes on formal sector workers. When protests followed, he sent the military to occupy La Paz's Plaza Murillo, resulting in thirty-four deaths.[68]

Twice as many were killed in the "Gas War" of September–October 2003, when President Sánchez de Lozada sent the military to repress road blockades and protests in La Paz Department. The popular mobilization combined opposition to the Pacific LNG scheme with a host of other demands, including an end to political repression, forced coca leaf eradication, neoliberal policies affecting land and water, and infringements on communal autonomy.[69] When the armed forces' killing of sixty-seven people failed to crush the movement, Sánchez de Lozada resigned and began a comfortable retirement in the United States.

Gas nationalization was central to the "October Agenda," the broadly shared social movement program that emerged from the Gas War.[70] In response, a citizens' referendum on gas policy was scheduled for July 2004. However, the government of Carlos Mesa, who took over after Sánchez de Lozada's ouster, crafted the referendum questions in a pro-business way. Radical policies like nationalization and control of the gas industry by popular organizations were excluded from consideration. The option of limiting gas extraction was also omitted. Consequently, the referendum results showed overwhelming support for abrogating Sánchez de Lozada's 1996 gas law, reestablishing YPFB, and increasing royalty rates, but the public was not consulted about the more ambitious options favored by many grassroots organizations.[71] Mesa justified these exclusions based on the need to produce "a viable, acceptable law for the international community"—meaning a law that would safeguard private investments and debt repayment.[72]

The hydrocarbon policy that took shape in 2005–2006 was a compromise between the "international community" (that is, foreign capitalists) and the radical movement that forced Sánchez de Lozada, and later Mesa himself, from office. The Movimiento al Socialismo (MAS) party acted essentially as a mediator in this struggle. MAS legislators put forward a proposal to increase gas royalties to fifty percent. Mesa and the international community opposed it, with foreign companies pledging to withdraw their investments and sue in foreign tribunals if their taxes were increased. In May 2005, a campaign of road blockades by working-class and peasant groups led Congress to pass the bill over Mesa's objection, leading to his resignation. This law set the foundation for Evo Morales's May 2006 quasi-nationalization of Bolivian hydrocarbons, which in reality preserved essentially the same royalty structure of the 2005 law while giving YPFB more control over commercialization, investment disputes, and other aspects of the business.[73] Together, these new laws enabled Bolivia to capture a larger share of the surplus wealth generated by hydrocarbon production, even if they failed to meet the more radical demands of Bolivian protesters.[74]

The hydrocarbon conflicts of 2003–2005 were mitigated by the laws that followed. The Bolivian gas industry settled into a new equilibrium, with foreign gas companies reluctantly adjusting themselves to the changed business environment. At the same time, the conflicts of those years reflected unresolved contradictions that would become more visible in the years to come. For most of the highland and valley Indigenous groups who spearheaded the movement for gas nationalization, the Indigenous groups in the gas-rich territories of the southeast lowlands were barely a consideration.[75] How would those groups relate to each other after 2006? The silences of the 2004 referendum concealed related tensions. How would Bolivia reconcile gas extraction with ecological concerns? Would Bolivia be able to break out of its historic cycle of primary export dependence? What would "social control" of the economy look like? These questions would become more relevant than ever once the MAS took power.

ANTI-IMPERIALISM AND CONTRADICTION IN THE MAS ERA

The presidency of Evo Morales (2006–2019) brought major improvements in economic and social indicators. Most tellingly, the poverty rate fell from 60 percent to 35 percent and extreme poverty from 38 percent to 15 percent. Although critics often attribute this progress to the good luck of the commodity price boom of the 2000s, Bolivia performed more impressively than most other commodity exporters. The main reasons for Bolivia's greater success were the 2005 and 2006 hydrocarbon laws and the decision to channel the proceeds into major new social spending and public investments. Between 2007 and October 2019, hydrocarbons contributed 37 billion USD to government coffers, including 16 billion USD from the direct hydrocarbons tax created in 2005.[76] Much of that money benefitted working-class Bolivians in the form of direct cash payments to new mothers, the elderly, and families with children, in addition to housing initiatives and other social spending programs. A significant portion went into public services like schools and health centers.[77] Hydrocarbons were finally helping Bolivians "to live free of the fear of misery and hunger," as Daniel Bedregal had envisioned at the 1945 constitutional convention. Without those reforms, the primary beneficiaries of the price boom would have been foreign corporations. Right-wing criticisms of nationalist hydrocarbon policy miss this point.[78]

Similarly, the defeat of a violent right-wing "autonomy" movement in the east in 2008 ensured the central state's access to hydrocarbon revenues. The movement echoed the regionalist struggle in Santa Cruz fifty years earlier, now animated by a more explicitly racist antipathy to the Morales government and its Indigenous supporters (and strengthened by US support). The eastern elite appropriated the discourse of autonomy associated with the Indigenous liberation movement in order to demand control over eastern departments and the subterranean hydrocarbon wealth located there.[79] Had the movement succeeded, the MAS would have been deprived of much of the hydrocarbon revenue that it used to reduce poverty.

MAS hydrocarbon policy has also generated a range of critiques from the left, however, which tend to be more thoughtful than those from the right. These arguments parallel leftist criticisms of energy policy in other "Pink Tide" countries like Ecuador, Brazil, and Venezuela. One critique faults the compromise with capital embodied in the reforms of 2005 and 2006. By eschewing true nationalization, the MAS allowed private companies to retain control over key aspects of the industry, including exploration and drilling. This choice was consequential because the companies deprioritized new exploration after 2006. Furthermore, although the companies have been forced to pay higher taxes, they have continued to appropriate a large minority of total revenues. Meanwhile, more radical visions for grassroots control over the industry were defeated or put on paper but never implemented.[80]

Leftists have also criticized the lack of deeper transformation of the economy and the class structure. Bolivia remains dependent on primary exports and thus its subordination within the global economy continues. Industrialization had been a longtime focus of nationalists, who aimed to industrialize the gas sector by producing petrochemicals and to use hydrocarbon revenues to fund manufacturing in other sectors. The Morales administration sponsored construction of new plants for ammonia, urea, propane, and other products, but progress has been slow and manufactured goods continue to be a negligible percentage of total exports.[81] Continued dependence on hydrocarbons is particularly problematic since much of Bolivia's gas will need to remain unburned in the interest of stabilizing the climate, and thus gas production will have to decline in the near future.

Moreover, in a pattern reminiscent of earlier periods in Bolivian history, the influx of gas revenues has reduced the pressure for more radical change to the domestic class structure, including measures like progressive income taxes or redistribution of private estates. As scholars Linda Farthing and Benjamin Kohl note, "Alleviating poverty through modest redistributive programs masks the structural changes needed to fundamentally revamp society."[82] Most wealthy Bolivians have been unharmed by the MAS's progressive policies. The clearest example is the agricultural elite of the Santa Cruz region. Though Morales won reelection in a landslide in 2009, he soon reached a modus vivendi with many of the same capitalists who had sponsored the violent rebellion against his government in 2008. He refrained from aggressive redistribution, most visible in his choice not to target the vast eastern estates for land reform. In exchange, the agro-capitalists relaxed their political opposition, at least until they sensed a chance to overthrow Morales in 2019. The rapprochement between the MAS and the eastern economic elite coincided with a growing distance between the MAS leadership and the rank-and-file of the social movements that had brought Morales to power.[83]

In a departure from past patterns, the left has begun to criticize the ecological impacts of hydrocarbon extraction. Recent decades have brought much greater awareness of both the local and global destruction wrought by the fossil fuel business. In January 2000, for example, the rupture of Enron and Shell's Transredes pipeline sent twenty-nine thousand barrels of oil spewing into the Desaguadero River near Lake Titicaca, causing major harm to nearby farming communities.[84] Many drew parallels between the Desaguadero spill and similar oil company crimes around the world, from Ecuador to Nigeria. The heating of the planet, meanwhile, is increasingly felt in water shortages and other impacts throughout the country.[85] Though the MAS has enshrined the "rights of Mother Earth" in legislation and has helped spearhead poor countries' demands for climate justice at the global level, its extraction-intensive domestic policy has drawn charges of hypocrisy from the ecological left. MAS rule has coincided with a significant expansion of the "petroleum frontier" to new swaths of Bolivian territory, and during his last term in office, Morales opened national parks for drilling and even signaled his openness to fracking.[86]

Usually the ecological critique is accompanied by a defense of the rights of Indigenous communities on whose lands the extraction takes place, which marks another healthy difference from the national debate of earlier eras. Many have accused the MAS of violating communal rights to prior consultation in its zeal to expand hydrocarbon extraction. Opponents of the government's highway project in the Isiboro Sécure Indigenous Territory and National Park (TIPNIS) allege that hydrocarbon extraction is part of the government's motivation for pushing the initiative so aggressively since 2011. In the gas-rich lowlands of the southeast, Indigenous activists have charged the government with impeding the formalization of their territorial claims for fear that titling would jeopardize gas extraction.[87]

These critiques highlight the unresolved contradictions in the MAS's economic development model, and by extension in the development strategies of left-leaning governments in Ecuador, Venezuela, and elsewhere. The MAS has altered the balance of power between the Bolivian government and foreign corporations in a progressive direction, a shift made possible by the disruptive social movements that have demanded an anti-imperialist resource policy. Yet the hydrocarbon economy has exacerbated or concealed other pressing problems.

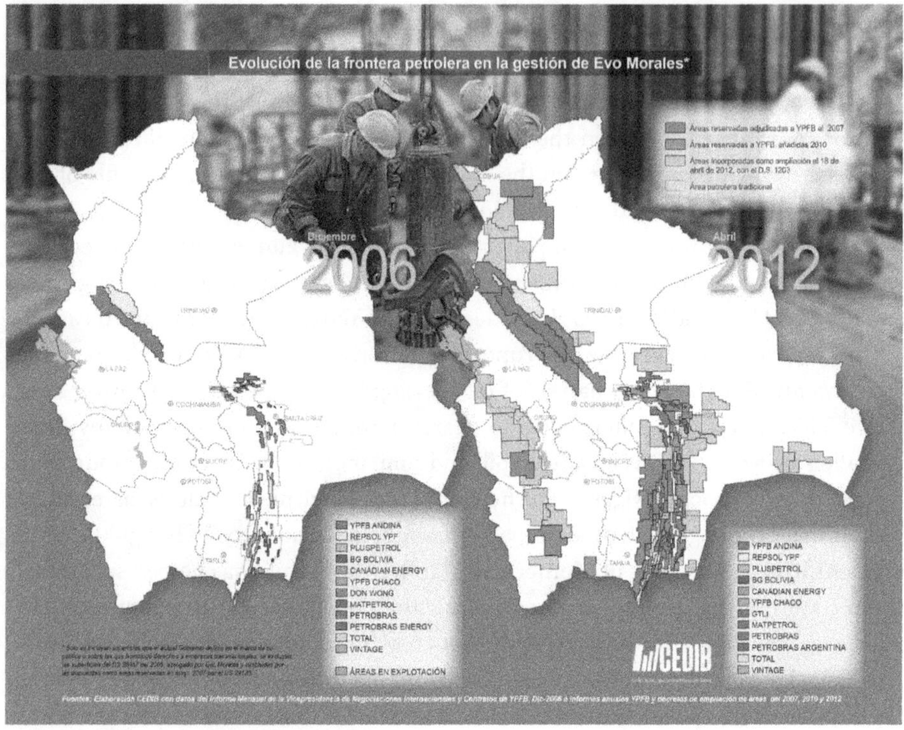

Figure 5.1. Evolution of the hydrocarbon frontier under Evo Morales. Georgina Jiménez, "Territorios indígenas y áreas protegidas en la mira: La ampliación de la frontera de industrias extractivistas," 6. Reprinted with permission of CEDIB.

Unfortunately, most progressive critics have failed to propose concrete and viable alternatives. The Vivir Bien (Living Well) paradigm in Bolivia and Ecuador powerfully criticizes the limits of economic growth as an indicator of well-being. Its proponents seek to reorient economic policy toward improving quality of life, community solidarity, and ecological sustainability rather than just increasing material consumption. However, discussions of Vivir Bien have tended to remain abstract. Advocates have not adequately grappled with the wrenching predicaments facing poor countries where economic growth and poverty reduction are, in the short-to-medium term, dependent on the continuation of extractive enterprise.[88] This dependence is especially acute given that elites of the Global North, who bear most of the responsibility for the ecological emergency, refuse to pay their debt to the Global

South by funding sustainable alternatives.[89] There is little practical discussion of how countries like Bolivia can transition to a sustainable economy that meets everyone's basic needs.

Many proponents of Vivir Bien who oppose MAS policies also tend to romanticize Indigenous culture, ignoring the fact that millions of Indigenous Bolivians support gas drilling. The logic of hydrocarbon extraction has enveloped Bolivian society as a whole. Even in the southeast lowlands, Indigenous contestation often focuses not on stopping the gas industry but on influencing how gas rents and jobs will be divvied up.[90] In Bolivia as in other poor, hydrocarbon-dependent economies, the temptations of expanding extraction are great, while the structural constraints of global capitalism compound the difficulty of forging alternatives. Glibly dismissing the MAS as just another extractivist government or demanding an immediate end to all extraction does little to overcome those constraints.

The hope for addressing these problems lies with Bolivian social movements, which have time and again demonstrated a degree of politicization and militancy that sets Bolivia apart from most other countries. If there was an inadvertent silver lining in the November 2019 coup that overthrew Evo Morales and unleashed murderous repression against MAS supporters, it was in the reinvigoration of the MAS base that took place in the months that followed. Workers and peasants actively debated the future of the party, including the economic, ecological, and social contradictions mentioned above. They mobilized to constrain the coup regime's actions and to give the MAS candidate, Luis Arce, a resounding victory in the presidential election of October 2020.[91] Unfortunately, the contradictions of hydrocarbon-based development have not lessened under Arce's administration; if anything, the economic downturn associated with Covid-19 has added further incentive for the government to maximize extraction.

It bears emphasizing that the primary responsibility for resolving these contradictions lies with those who have created the ecological emergency, starting with the capitalist firms and governments of the Global North. It is they who must be made to pay for the economic transformations that are urgently necessary if living things are to have a decent future. Foreigners, especially those of us who reside in the rich countries, have a crucial role to play in providing movements of the Global South with the space and support they need to develop sustainable and equitable alternatives to fossil fuel–based economies. This does not absolve governments of the Global South of all responsibility, for they do have some latitude to pursue alternative policies. As climate destruction increasingly imperils people's ability to "live free of the fear of misery and hunger," building those alternatives couldn't be more urgent.

ACKNOWLEDGMENTS

Thanks to Rossana Barragán, Sarah Hines, Carmen Soliz, and Sinclair Thomson for comments on this chapter, and to Juan José Anaya Giorgis and Linda Farthing for sharing sources and insights that informed my analysis.

NOTES

1. Daniel Bedregal in República de Bolivia, *Redactor de la Convención Nacional, 1945*, 278.
2. Almaraz Paz, *Petróleo en Bolivia*, 287 (first quote); Marcos Orgaz et al., "Exposición de motivos," *El Petrolero*, February 1959, 3 (second quote).
3. See for instance Grandin, "The Liberal Traditions in the Americas."
4. I understand a contradiction as a set of opposing interests that cannot be resolved without the transformation of the system itself, meaning the mutual dissolution of the opposing groups or at least the elimination of hierarchy or asymmetry between them. Contradictions need not always take the form of "open antagonism," as Mao stressed in his 1937 essay "On Contradiction," 344.
5. Rodman, *Sanctity versus Sovereignty*, 63.
6. Gustafson, *Bolivia in the Age of Gas*; Anthias, *Limits to Decolonization*; Hindery, *From Enron to Evo*.
7. There is a large literature on the paradoxical downsides of resource wealth, which typically focuses on how revenues can reduce a state's capacity and/or incentive to promote diversification, industrialization, and progressive redistribution. For example, as Timothy Mitchell writes of Iraq after Qasim's 1958 seizure of power, "Taking state ownership of the country's petroleum resources would offer a way to finance social reforms while bypassing those modes of wealth-creation that make the well-off vulnerable to egalitarian demands. Oil revenues would remove the need to create national wealth through a radical redistribution of land and large increase in manufacturing." *Carbon Democracy*, 145. See also Coronil, *The Magical State*; Tinker Salas, *The Enduring Legacy*; Watts, "Oil Worlds."
8. The most comprehensive recent treatment is Anaya Giorgis, *Estado y petróleo en Bolivia*. See also Royuela Comboni, *Cien años de hidrocarburos en Bolivia*; Cote, *Oil and Nation*.
9. See for instance Behrends, Reyna, and Schlee, *Crude Domination*.
10. Anaya Giorgis, *Estado y petróleo*, 23, 27. Land for cattle grazing was the central motive behind escalating settler and state violence against the Chiriguanos and other Indigenous peoples in the second half of the century. See Langer, *Expecting Pears from an Elm Tree*, 41–49.
11. Cote, *Oil and Nation*, 1–29, 42 (quote); Anaya Giorgis, *Estado y petróleo*, 55.
12. Klein, *Parties and Political Change in Bolivia*, 73–76.

13. Rosales, "Resource Nationalism"; Krenn, *U.S. Policy toward Economic Nationalism in Latin America.*
14. Anaya Giorgis, *Estado y petróleo*, 56, 73–82.
15. López, *Política petrolífera*, 349, 400–401. See also Nolasco López, *Bolivia y el petróleo.*
16. Comité Ejecutivo de la Universidad Boliviana, *Convenciones nacionales universitarias, 1928–1929*, 46 (quote), 48–49.
17. Krenn, *U.S. Policy toward Economic Nationalism in Latin America*, 9; O'Brien, *The Century of U.S. Capitalism in Latin America*, 30.
18. Anaya Giorgis, *Estado y petróleo*, 76–79.
19. López, *Política petrolífera*, 345 (quote).
20. Socialist intellectual Tristán Marof was influential in promoting this argument early on. See his book *La tragedia del altiplano*, 159–74. US senator Huey Long also played a major role in popularizing it; see Cote, *Oil and Nation*, 86–87.
21. As evidenced by its refusal to help supply the Bolivian military and its interest in hoarding reserves rather than exporting. See Anaya Giorgis, *Estado y petróleo*, 87–91; Cote, *Oil and Nation*, 66, 68, 80.
22. Klein, *Parties and Political Change*, 114–59, 177 (quotes on 145, 153). The call "to stand firm" comes from military chief Colonel Filiberto Osorio.
23. Cote, *Oil and Nation*, xiii, 91.
24. Quoted in Romero Loza, *Temas económicos de actualidad*, 200. See also Cote, *Oil and Nation*, 64, 79.
25. Anaya Giorgis, *Estado y petróleo*, 83–85, 95.
26. Zook Jr., *The Conduct of the Chaco War*, 192; Klein, *Parties and Political Change*, 182–86; Gustafson, *Bolivia in the Age of Gas*, 32.
27. "Ex-combatientes y Beneméritos de la Patria piden renuncia de la actual Mesa Directiva," *Prensa Libre*, February 28, 1969, 3 (first quote); Chacón, "Prólogo," 7 (second and third quotes).
28. Weyland, "The Rise of Latin America's Two Lefts," 156; Molina, *El pensamiento boliviano*, 5, 44, 46.
29. Mitchell, *Carbon Democracy*, 43–65. The quote is from Almaraz Paz, *Petróleo en Bolivia*, 74.
30. Young, *Blood of the Earth*, 175. Standard also helped finance Bolivia's prewar military buildup, via John D. Rockefeller's Equitable Trust Co.; see Gustafson, *Bolivia in the Age of Gas*, 40.
31. "De nuestro programa de acción," *El Ex-Combatiente* (Sucre), February 13, 1936, 2.
32. Álvarez España, *Los gráficos en Bolivia*, 94–100.
33. Cote, *Oil and Nation*, 98.
34. Klein, "'Social Constitutionalism' in Latin America," 270.
35. Montenegro, *Frente al derecho del estado*; Unión Boliviana de Defensa del Petróleo, *¡Defendamos el petróleo!*, 1996 [1941]).

36. Another factor was the US State Department's support for a settlement. In the run-up to World War II US officials were eager to resolve the conflict to ensure that the Bolivian regime sided with the United States, namely by supplying critical minerals. See Rodman, *Sanctity versus Sovereignty*, 104–25.
37. Irving Florman to Edward G. Miller, December 27, 1950, in US National Archives and Records Administration, College Park, MD (hereafter USNA), Record Group (RG) 59, Entry 1130, Box 2.
38. Anaya Giorgis, *Estado y petróleo*, 124–29.
39. See for instance Mariaca Bilbao, *Mito y realidad*, 103.
40. "Comunistas y anarquistas serán declarados al margen de la ley," *El Diario*, June 26, 1936, 6; "Prohíbese el debate público sobre asuntos económicos," *El Diario*, June 28, 1936, 6.
41. Klein, *Parties and Political Change*, 257, 265 (quote).
42. Young, *Blood of the Earth*, 16–34, 50, 91.
43. Unión Boliviana de Defensa del Petróleo, *¡Defendamos el petróleo!*, 7 (first quote); Montenegro, *Frente al derecho*, 96 (second quote).
44. Mitchell, *The Legacy of Populism in Bolivia*, 18; Weston Jr., "An Ideology of Modernization," 89–90.
45. For the main statement of early MNR economic doctrine see Guevara Arze, *Plan inmediato de política económica*, 67–88. Guevara Arze's plan was largely based on the 1942 report by the US Economic Mission, headed by Merwin Bohan. The Bohan Report had heralded the "brilliant prospects" for oil production in Bolivia. United States Economic Mission to Bolivia, *Plan Bohan (Bolivia)*, 9.
46. Young, *Blood of the Earth*, 62 (quote); Anaya Giorgis, *Estado y petróleo*, 297.
47. Holland to Edward Sparks et al., April 4, 1955, in USNA, RG 59, Entry 1132, Box 1; Young, *Blood of the Earth*, 209n14.
48. YPFB, *Código del petróleo*, Articles 67, 104, 161; Young, *Blood of the Earth*, 62–63, 153. Article 106 specified an additional 30 percent tax on profits, though critics estimated that actual tax payments were considerably lower due to loopholes. See Almaraz Paz, *Petróleo en Bolivia*, 188; Mariaca Bilbao, *Mito y realidad*, 160–70; Quiroga Santa Cruz, *Desarrollo con soberanía*, 26–28.
49. Paz Estenssoro, *Discursos parlamentarios*, 228. This paragraph and the next two are based on Young, "From Open Door to Nationalization," 108–11.
50. Anaya Giorgis, *Estado y petróleo*, 156.
51. Adrián Barrenechea (Minister of Public Works), quoted in "Se está logrando la revolución económica, no la revolución social," *El Diario*, January 11, 1953, 6.
52. Pruden, "Las luchas 'cívicas.'"
53. Almaraz Paz, *Petróleo en Bolivia*. See also Mariaca Bilbao, *Mito y realidad*; Canelas O., *Petróleo: Imperialismo y nacionalismo*. On this resistance movement, including

the oil workers mentioned in the next paragraph, see Young, "From Open Door to Nationalization," 111–21.

54. Quoted in English in Dispatch 288, October 15, 1958, in USNA, RG 59, Central Decimal File 824.2553/10–1558.

55. YPFB's reticence to open its archives to researchers may force us to rely mostly on oral history. Bret Gustafson has conducted oral histories with retired YPFB workers. He stresses the conservatism of their class, racial, and gender politics, as demonstrated by their lack of militant class rhetoric, the habit of distancing themselves from (or ignoring) the Indigenous residents of the oil/gas regions, and the chauvinism evident in men's extramarital affairs. *Bolivia in the Age of Gas*, 77–93.

56. Dunkerley, *Rebellion in the Veins*, 128; Anaya Giorgis, *Estado y petróleo*, 147, 165; Quiroga Santa Cruz, *Desarrollo con soberanía*, 36.

57. Royuela Comboni, *Cien años de hidrocarburos*, 137–38; Young, "From Open Door to Nationalization," 121.

58. Philip, *Oil and Politics in Latin America*, 265.

59. Ortiz Mercado, "La histórica 'Estrategia socio-económica,'" 39. Philip argues that "the most important reason" in Ovando's decision to nationalize "was perhaps his concern to carve out a political base which up until then had been lacking." *Oil and Politics*, 270.

60. US aid to Bolivia fell by 63 percent and foreign companies boycotted the country's oil, leading to a compensation agreement of 78 million USD. This amount far outstripped the compensation to Standard after the 1937 nationalization. The disparity reflected several factors, including production levels and the differing international contexts: Standard had produced little oil, and the approach of World War II and the need for Latin American allies had made the US government eager to settle the earlier conflict. See Mitchell, *Legacy of Populism*, 112–13, 119n21; Royuela Comboni, *Cien años de hidrocarburos*, 142–46; Rodman, *Sanctity versus Sovereignty*, 104–25.

61. Young, *Blood of the Earth*, 168–69.

62. Zavaleta Mercado, "El proletariado minero en Bolivia," 116.

63. Anaya Giorgis, *Estado y petróleo*, 176–88.

64. Kohl and Farthing, *Impasse in Bolivia*, 108–9, 118; Anaya Giorgis, *Estado y petróleo*, 235–54. See also Orgáz García, *La guerra del gas*; Villegas Quiroga, *Privatización de la industria petrolera en Bolivia*.

65. Kohl and Farthing, *Impasse in Bolivia*, 112, 115, 118; Anaya Giorgis, *Estado y petróleo*, 248; Comisión Económica para América Latina y el Caribe, *Anuario estadístico* (2006), 200.

66. Quoted in Anaya Giorgis, *Estado y petróleo*, 252.

67. Anaya Giorgis, *Estado y petróleo*, 240–42, 263.

68. Anaya Giorgis, *Estado y petróleo*, 258–59 (Marco Gandarilla estimate), 270–71.

69. Webber, *Red October*, 184–238.

70. The other two core demands were for a new Constituent Assembly and the prosecution of officials from the Sánchez de Lozada regime. Various organizations added land redistribution, Indigenous autonomy, and other demands.

71. Gustafson, *Bolivia in the Age of Gas*, 113–20. On popular demands for nationalization under "social control," see Gutiérrez Aguilar, *Rhythms of the Pachakuti*, 108–28, 217.

72. Speaking in March 2005, quoted in Gutiérrez Aguilar, *Rhythms of the Pachakuti*, 155. Mesa's speech made clear what he meant by the "international community": he noted the resistance of "the oil companies" plus the World Bank, International Monetary Fund, United States, Great Britain, the European Union, Spain, and Brazil.

73. Anaya Giorgis, *Estado y petróleo*, 278–84, 300.

74. Protests continued following the May 2005 law, for instance. See Webber, *Red October*, 249–51.

75. Perreault, "Extracting Justice."

76. Arauz et al., *Bolivia's Economic Transformation*, 12–15; YPFB, "Información financiera: Contratos de servicios petroleros," accessed January 19, 2021, https://landmatrix.org/media/uploads/publicacin-pagina-web-ypfb-a-oct-2019-final.pdf. See also Zelada Aprili, "Resource Rents, Public Investment and Economic Development."

77. Ministerio de Economía y Finanzas Públicas, *Memoria de la economía boliviana 2017*, 205–34. Between 2005 and 2017, education and health spending increased by 200 percent and 302 percent, respectively (212).

78. For instance, some have painted the changes of 2005–2006 as the latest swing in the tragic "pendulum" of resource policy, whereby Bolivia has historically swerved back and forth between extremes of liberalization and statism. The image is superficially accurate, but by attributing nationalistic policy to a collective pathology it obscures the material interests at the center of the power struggle. See for instance Candia and Pacheco, *El péndulo del gas*. Before the reforms of 2005–2006, foreign oil and gas companies "anticipated making ten dollars for every dollar invested, some of the world's highest returns"; Farthing and Kohl, *Evo's Bolivia*, 84–85.

79. Weisbrot and Sandoval, "The Distribution of Bolivia's Most Important Natural Resources." For historical background see Pruden, "Las luchas 'cívicas'"; Soruco, Plata, and Medeiros, *Los barones del oriente*.

80. See for instance Orgáz García, *El poder de la nacionalización*; Kaup, *Market Justice*, 127–49; Anaya Giorgis, *Estado y petróleo*, 288, 291, 303–4; Tahbub, *Las transnacionales no son socias*, 243–81.

81. In 2021 natural gas comprised 27 percent of exports. Minerals were another 36 percent, and agricultural products most of the rest. Data from the UN Economic Commission for Latin America and the Caribbean, CEPALSTAT database, accessed April 16, 2023, https://estadisticas.cepal.org.

82. Farthing and Kohl, *Evo's Bolivia*, 112. Furthermore, most of the poverty reduction under Morales came between 2006 and 2013 (Arauz et al., *Bolivia's Economic Transformation*, 15).
83. Wolff, "Business Power and the Politics of Postneoliberalism"; Farthing, "An Opportunity Squandered?"
84. Haglund, "A River Turns Black."
85. Andersen and Mamani Paco, eds., *La economía del cambio climático*.
86. Jiménez, "Territorios indígenas y áreas protegidas en la mira," 4–18 (quote); Gustafson, *Bolivia in the Age of Gas*, 242; Achtenberg, "Morales Greenlights TIPNIS Road"; Campanini, "El Decreto 2366 dicta la sentencia a las Áreas Protegidas en Bolivia," Centro de Documentación e Información Bolivia, May 25, 2015, https://cedib.org/post_type_documentos/el-decreto-2366-dicta-sentencia-a-las-areas-protegidas-en-bolivia/.
87. Anthias, *Limits to Decolonization*, 196–99.
88. See for instance Gudynas, "Beyond Varieties of Development"; Solón, *¿Es posible el Vivir Bien?* Solón's analysis of Bolivia oscillates between simplistically blaming the MAS government and a thoughtful consideration of the structural obstacles to Vivir Bien, including capitalist power and social movements' own shortcomings. Most studies critique extractivist logic and articulate general alternative principles but remain vague on practical policy matters. Farah and Vasapollo allude to this problem in the introduction to their edited volume, *Vivir bien: ¿Paradigma no capitalista?*, noting that, even in their wide-ranging collection, "sufficient exploration and reflection about the structure of the economy for [Vivir Bien] is still lacking" (30).
89. The role of the Global North in undermining the movement to "keep it in the ground" is apparent in the outcome of the 2007 Ecuadorian proposal to forego drilling in the Yasuní National Park if global donors would compensate the government for half the expected value of the reserves, or 3.5 billion USD. The proposal garnered only a small fraction of that amount and was soon abandoned. See Dennis, "Keep It in the Ground," 83–88.
90. Gustafson, *Bolivia in the Age of Gas*, esp. 205–22.
91. The 2019 coup was the expression of a reactionary opposition though it was facilitated by the contradictions of MAS rule. See Farthing and Becker, *Coup*.

Figure 6.1. A village in the Yungas of La Paz. Photo by the author.

Chapter Six

A BRIEF HISTORY OF COCA

From Pre-Columbian Trade to the Cocaine Economy

Thomas Grisaffi

The production, distribution, and consumption of coca and its derivative, cocaine, have had immense social, political, and economic impacts that reverberate not just in Bolivia but across the globe. To tell the story of coca is to examine colonialism, the country's unequal insertion into global markets, and the battles of ordinary people to claim citizenship.

Coca is an alkaloid-rich bush, *Erythroxylon coca*, which is native to the Andean region. Growing like a weed at elevations between 200 and 1,500 meters above sea level, the Andean crop covers (as of this writing) close to 250,000 hectares,[1] farmed by up to a quarter of a million households.[2] Colombia produces the lion's share, accounting for 70 percent of world output; Peru grows 20 percent, and Bolivia places a distant third.[3] In 2020, Bolivia counted 30,500 hectares in production, with an annual harvest valued at between 352 million and 431 million USD.[4]

Coca's rich social, cultural, and medicinal significance in Indigenous Andean cultures dates to pre-Columbian times.[5] However, since the 1970s coca has been largely grown for one explicit purpose, as the raw material to process cocaine.[6] Andean cocaine manufacture reached a peak in 2020 of just over 1,982 metric tons,[7] valued at around 169.2 billion USD,[8] a turnover roughly equivalent to Ford Motor Company sales.[9] Unlike Colombia, Bolivia remains at the very lowest rungs of the international drug trade, producing low-value cocaine paste, a first step in refining pure cocaine.[10]

This chapter traces coca's history from the pre-Columbian trade to the contemporary illicit cocaine economy while considering the commodity chain's broader impacts on the social, political, and economic life of Bolivia and further afield. In what follows, we will see how coca underwrote the silver boom of the 1600s, enriched hacienda owners in the colonial period, sustained soldiers in the Chaco War, justified US imperial adventures in the second half of the twentieth century, and reshaped the contemporary political landscape—propelling an

Indigenous peasant to the office of president. More broadly, this chapter shows how in their defense of coca, Bolivia's Indigenous-peasant movements have advanced a vision of development that values the experiences, cultures, and ideas of grassroots organizations and in so doing, have challenged status-quo views of what modernity is and what it can be.[11] The chapter draws together secondary literature and the author's first-hand ethnographic observations and interviews in Bolivia's coca-growing regions.[12]

COCA: FROM THE INCAS TO THE 1952 REVOLUTION

Coca is one of the oldest known cultivated plants in the Americas. It has been consumed for thousands of years by Indigenous Andeans.[13] The leaf's mild stimulants dull hunger and fatigue, aid digestion, combat altitude sickness, and offer vitamins and minerals often lacking in local staples.[14] Consumed widely as tea, it is also chewed by taking dried leaf mixed with an alkaline ash known as *lejía* and slowly sucking it into a wad buried in the cheek. In Bolivia, this practice is known as *pijchear*, *bolear*, or *akullikar*. The most regular users are adult men, often long-distance drivers, workers (particularly miners), and farmers, who value coca's power to suppress hunger, thirst, and fatigue.[15]

Bolivia has two main coca growing regions, the Yungas and the Chapare. The Yungas district, which sits to the east and northeast of La Paz, produces approximately 65 percent of Bolivia's coca crop.[16] Here coca is cultivated on steep, terraced slopes alongside tropical fruit and coffee (see fig 6.1). Most of the thirty-thousand-odd Yungas coca growers claim Indigenous Aymara descent, but there is also a significant Afro-Bolivian population.[17] Coca has been cultivated in the Yungas valleys for at least 1,500 years, supplying the Tiwanaku Empire, then the Inca Empire, and later, during the colonial period, the silver mines of Potosí.[18] Yungas coca leaf is highly valued, as the small, green, sweet leaves are widely considered the best to chew.

By contrast, the Cochabamba lowlands, more often known as the Chapare, has only been settled since the 1950s. This massive region, equivalent in size to the US state of New Hampshire, produces a third of Bolivia's coca.[19] The Chapare's population is well over 200,000 people, the majority of whom self-identify as Quechua, and most people are bilingual, speaking a mixture of Quechua and Spanish.[20]

The archaeological record confirms that coca use in the Andes dates back at least 8,000 years. Researchers have found trace amounts of cocaine in the hair of ancient mummies[21] and discovered coca leaves in tombs alongside figurines of people with bulging cheeks, indicating a wad of coca.[22] The varied locations of these findings, stretching from the dry desert coast of northern Chile up into the highlands of northernmost Colombia, indicate that an expansive pre-Inca coca trade existed.[23]

The Incas considered coca sacred, and scholars believe that coca was a form of tribute payment throughout the Inca Empire with only nobles, priests, and state messengers possessing the right to chew the leaf.[24] Andeanist John Murra[25] challenged this idea that coca was reserved for the elites, however. He argued that its limited circulation was not because it was a sumptuary good, but rather because it was in short supply, coming as it did from a lower altitude. Murra explained that in addition to barter or trade, Indigenous Andean communities obtained lowland crops like maize, hot peppers, and coca through what he called the "vertical archipelago."[26] Indigenous communities owned land at different ecological tiers (altitudes) where they could harvest products that then flowed to other members of their same group.[27]

The Spanish conquest of the Inca Empire, beginning in 1532, initially led to the suppression of coca. Spanish authorities saw it as an addictive substance and vilified chewing as a disgusting habit that corrupted colonial society. They denounced coca as "ungodly" and associated its use with the devil because of the role it played in native rituals.[28] What is more, colonial authorities feared coca's symbolism and links to the Incas might pose a threat to European authority, and prominent church leaders campaigned to fully prohibit coca use.[29]

And yet the coca trade endured, in part because powerful economic interests were at stake. By the late 1500s, the lucrative trade involved around two thousand Spaniards and generated over one million pesos annually.[30] Most of this income came from the booming silver mines of Potosí, where coca was so highly valued that it was often used instead of money.[31] In 1573, Viceroy Toledo, representative of the king of Spain, gave up trying to suppress coca and taxed it instead.[32] From that point on, coca became "commoditized" and consumption expanded socially and geographically.[33]

As seen in chapter two, each year the Spanish Crown forced up to 14,000 Indigenous males[34] to pay tribute in the form of labor (known as mita) in the silver mines of Potosí. The Spaniards quickly recognized that the miners could work longer and harder when they consumed coca.[35] Much like sugar in eighteenth-century Britain, which fed the working classes and powered the industrial revolution,[36] coca can be credited with an equally revolutionary role. Gootenberg[37] writes: "The silver boom of Potosí (1570–1640), facilitated by Andean coca labor, drove the global commercial expansion that jump-started the European world capitalist system."

Coca became "the most highly commercialized Indian product in the colonial Andean world."[38] For the first two hundred years of colonization, Yungas production remained in the hands of Indigenous Andean communities who paid tribute, usually in kind or labor, to Spanish overlords or encomenderos, part of the so-called encomienda system.[39] This began to change in the late 1600s, when entrepreneurial Spaniards established large-scale haciendas (estates) in the Yungas to produce coca for sale in the mining districts. Given the high price coca commanded, these coca-growing haciendas proved to be some of the wealthiest in the Andean region.[40] But while hacienda expansion displaced Indigenous communities, it did not eliminate them entirely.[41, 42] Independent communities, particularly in the southern Yungas, always had some degree of control over the production and circulation of coca, and even on the haciendas cultivation depended on Indigenous know-how, technique, and labor.[43]

The formation of an independent Bolivian republic in 1825 transformed coca's place in the national imagination. Gootenberg[44] explains that "new national identities and politics meant revaluating coca's status," which convinced elites to embrace coca leaf as "national" and to promote its commercial expansion. The coca trade only intensified with the tin boom of the early 1900s, driving up the price of the little green leaf. Yungas hacienda owners, who represented a Europeanized commercial class, formed a trade association, the Sociedad de Propietarios de los Yungas (later known as the SPY) to ensure their lucrative business continued.[45] They aligned with the mineowners (known as "La Rosca,") to form the Liberal Party that ruled Bolivia from 1899 to 1920.[46]

Mayer argues that until the 1952 national revolution, hacendados (large landowners), mineowners, and merchants distributed coca as a way to create dependence.[47] Fausto Reinaga,[48] the founder of the Bolivian Indian Party (PIB), went further, arguing that the coca leaf has been a historic instrument of colonial oppression and subjugation. Reinaga characterized coca as an "opium of the masses" and as a "vice" (equivalent to alcohol) that "subdues the revolutionary spirit of Indigenous peasants." But others have pushed back against the idea that elites saw coca as an instrument of social control or that they determined the meanings and practices of Andean consumption.[49] According to historian Andrew Ehrinpreis, in Alcides Arguedas's 1919 *indigenista* novel *Raza de bronce*, landlords conceived of and accepted Indigenous coca use as part of the seigneurial caste order they presided over.[50]

And yet, while Bolivian elites valued the leaf for its profitability and its perceived utility as a stimulant for Indigenous labor, they never considered consuming it themselves.[51] In the early 1900s, coca chewing, which marked Indigenous identity, was rejected by those aspiring to leave these roots behind. This began to change when Bolivia went to war with Paraguay in the 1932–1935 Chaco War. Poorly provisioned soldiers relied on coca as a substitute for food, and for the first time, non-Indigenous working-class soldiers (the urban poor who identified as mestizo) chewed the leaf, breaching the traditional ethnic boundaries of coca culture. The Chaco War thus transformed coca into "a popular symbol of an emergent interethnic working class," and in so doing laid the foundations for today's coca nationalism.[52]

The 1952 national revolution and the 1953 agrarian reform that followed created another turning point for Bolivian coca. Peasant rebellions upended the Yungas hacienda class, and this allowed peasant farmers to exert greater control over the coca economy.[53] Coca cultivation was also expanding into the eastern lowlands (the Chapare) as mostly Quechua Valley peasants on overcrowded highland and valley plots took advantage of government-sponsored colonization schemes.[54] The MNR government, which pursued an assimilationist project of mestizo nationalism that aimed to turn "Indians" into "peasants," adopted an anti-coca position. "For the MNR, the disappearance of coca culture was a crucial indicator of progressive assimilation and 'modernization' in Bolivia," writes Ehrinpreis.[55] And yet this was happening just as coca culture was beginning to emerge as a counterhegemonic element of the left-wing working classes.

COCA: SACRED AND PROFANE

Coca is a commodity that circulates widely in the peasant economy and historically has functioned as a means of exchange in remote parts of the Bolivian highlands where market penetration was limited.[56] Mayer[57] saw coca functioning as a "quasi coin" because it acted as "a medium of exchange, a standard of value, a means of deferred payment and a way to accumulate wealth." In my own fieldwork, Chapare coca growers told me that up until the early 2000s, when cash was tight, they used coca in barter exchanges known as *trueque* or *cambio* to secure highland goods like potatoes that could not be grown in the lowlands. Barter is beneficial because it links up diverse regions, eliminates the need for profit-seeking intermediaries, and exchange rates tend to be favorable.[58]

It is not just the exchange of coca for comestibles that connects people, but also the quotidian act of sharing the leaf. Allen[59] describes how in Quechua-speaking communities in highland Peru, chewing coca—known locally as *hallpay*—is highly ritualized. People carefully select the best leaves to share and while chewing say prayers honoring the animate landscape. Allen argues that adherence to these practices "orients the actors spatially, socially, and religiously, and in so doing integrates them into a larger cultural framework."[60]

Figure 6.2. People celebrating a Q'owa in the Chapare region. Photo by the author.

The solidarity engendered by sharing coca is vividly illustrated in June Nash's[61] 1979 ethnography of Bolivian tin miners and their observance of preconquest rites, in which coca plays an important role. The miners chewed coca together on their breaks and engaged in elaborate rites (the Ch'alla) to honor the *supay* or lord of the underworld.[62] Nash saw involvement in these quotidian rituals as a form of building solidarity and class consciousness.

Coca is widely considered to be sacred. Origin myths link coca to Inti, the sun god, but also the Virgin Mary. Coca plays a central role in all life-cycle rituals, from initiations, marriages, and death rites to the dedication of a new building. Its distribution and communal consumption is essential for stimulating trust and community as a ritualistic element of every exchange.[63] Coca is most often used as part of a burned offering, known as the Q'owa (see fig. 6.2), alongside other valued goods such as *chicha* or maize beer, cane alcohol, and llamas that together help to sustain the balance between the human and supernatural worlds.[64] Celso Ugarte, director of Bolivia's Sacaba legal coca market, said in 2019: "We call it the sacred leaf: it was used by the Incas and was given to us by god."[65]

Coca leaf is also a key element in traditional medicine and is used for divination rituals. The *curandero* or healer uses coca to diagnose the causes of illness or misfortune. The taste of the coca, "sweet," "bitter," or "boring," provides positive, negative, or noncommittal oracular answers. The leaves can also be "read": a curandero tosses the leaves onto a cloth and interprets the pattern in which they fall.[66] More prosaically, coca is used as a medicine to treat digestive problems, altitude sickness, and mouth ulcers, among other ailments.[67]

Coca use is widespread throughout Bolivia, in both rural and urban settings. A 2013 study calculated that about 30 percent of the Bolivian population regularly chewed the leaf, and the majority used coca-based products like coca tea.[68] Coca chewing extends over Bolivia's frontier into northern Argentina[69] and Chile, and it is equally common to the north, in Peru.[70] Gootenberg[71] argues that the widespread acceptance of coca in Bolivia has fed into sentiments of what he refers to as coca nationalism, which, "like most strands of national identity, is a protean, invented tradition."[72]

However, while views on coca have changed, there is still a racist stigma attached to chewing it.[73] Postero[74] records how during Bolivia's 2006–2007 Constituent Assembly, Indigenous delegates in the city of Sucre endured racism daily, including "being insulted in the streets for carrying bags of coca." While undertaking fieldwork, I observed that while most adult males chewed coca in the Chapare, they would not do so when in the city. People affirmed that it would be considered "vulgar" or "inappropriate" to chew coca in an urban setting. They feared being insulted as a *pico-verde* or "green mouth."

The symbolism of coca and its derivatives has not only changed over time but across space too. This is evident if we consider value shifts along the commodity chain from production to consumption. In many parts of Bolivia, coca is something that is morally loaded, imbued with power, used as a vehicle to connect human and supernatural worlds and as a sign of Indigenous identity. But while coca leaf is widely considered to be sacred by Indigenous Andeans, cocaine is neutral, a banal substance the production and trafficking of which is simply a way to make a living. On the contrary, for the predominantly Western consumers of its derivative, coca leaf is nothing more than a weed, whereas cocaine is exciting and dangerous. It too can connect users on the street who trade drugs in exchange for respect, love, and money.[75]

THE INTERNATIONAL CONTEXT

In Europe, during the colonial period, people had heard of coca leaf and wanted to try it, but it was difficult to acquire as the quality of the leaf degraded on the long voyage, leaving very little cocaine alkaloid present. The first person to preserve coca leaf and market its benefits was Angelo Mariani, a French chemist who soaked the leaf in red wine in the mid-1800s. The resulting "tonic" was sold for its health benefits and was widely popular, enjoyed by the czars of Russia, various pontiffs, and US presidents.[76] Given its commercial success, imitations soon arose, including Coca-Cola.[77]

In 1859, German chemist Dr. Albert Nieman discovered how to extract cocaine from the leaf, and it soon became a popular and widely available stimulant in Europe and the United States. Sigmund Freud[78] was an avid user who between 1884 and 1887 penned five essays extolling cocaine's virtues. The drug was also lionized in literature: Sherlock Holmes consumed it and Robert Louis Stevenson's *Dr. Jekyll and Mr. Hyde* is alleged to be a book about cocaine use.[79]

The validation of coca and cocaine abroad led to a reappraisal of the leaf in the Andes. Urban elites in Lima, Peru, came to view it less as a backward Indigenous vice, but rather as a modern resource to be capitalized.[80] But this tolerance toward coca and cocaine was short-lived.[81] By 1914, cocaine was illegal, fast becoming a "pariah drug" in the United States. As Gootenberg explains: "abolitionist zeal . . . became the driving force . . . behind the unfolding global prohibition regime," a process that eventually led to the criminalization of coca leaf.[82]

In 1949, when a UN commission visited Peru to study coca leaf, the lead researcher immediately said in an interview with the national daily *El Comercio* that he hoped to bring about the abolition of coca chewing, which he classified as a "pernicious habit."[83] The final UN study concluded that chewing coca "induces in the individual undesirable changes of an intellectual and moral character," "hinders the chewer's chances of obtaining a higher social standard," and "reduces the economic yield of productive work."[84] The 1950 report has since been discredited as inaccurate and racist, but it was instrumental in shaping subsequent legislation that outlawed the leaf.[85]

In 1961, the status of coca leaf as a dangerous drug was enshrined in law when it was listed on the UN Single Convention on Narcotic Drugs (the most important international drug control framework). The convention called on signatory governments to eradicate all coca bushes, even those that grow wild, and to abolish the traditional practice of coca leaf chewing within twenty-five years of ratification. Subsequent conventions maintained these hardline positions.[86] Bolivia signed the document in 1976 but has long since missed the twenty-five-year target to eradicate the bush.[87]

Zoe Pearson[88] argues that the history of listing coca leaf as a controlled substance reflects colonial, ethnocentric, and racist attitudes towards the Andean region and traditional users of so-called drug plants. Going further, Reiss explores the interlocking powers of industrial firms, regulatory agencies, and the United States in the profitable licit/illicit regime built around coca and cocaine in the mid-twentieth century. In this analysis, drug prohibition regimes, including the formulation of the UN 1961 Single Convention on Narcotic Drugs, were enacted to further the economic agendas of the expanding global US pharmaceutical industry.[89]

Studies have established that in leaf form, coca does not generate toxicity or dependence.[90] Instead, coca leaf contains untapped resources for the benefit of humankind in the form of foods, pharmaceuticals, and other high-value, plant-derived products.[91] A 1995 World Health Organization (WHO) study stressed coca's positive therapeutic uses, but because of US threats to withdraw funding, the WHO never officially published the research.[92] In addition, the Single Convention contradicts the UN's own 2007 Declaration on Indigenous Rights, which promises to uphold and protect Indigenous cultural practices.

Andean countries have made numerous attempts to negotiate an exceptional status for coca and its traditional use. In the 1920s, Bolivian diplomats, representing the SPY, attended the League of Nations' drug conventions in Geneva and put up a "spirited defense" of coca, but they deployed racist language to do so—including how coca was the only thing that would motivate "their Indians" to work.[93] In the early 1990s, Bolivian President Jaime Paz Zamora (1989–1993) embarked on "coca diplomacy" when he visited Europe to promote the export of coca leaves in the form of herbal tea, toothpaste, and wine. However, Paz Zamora's efforts were undermined when two of his ministers (Guillermo Capobianco and Oscar Eid) were linked to drug traffickers. These charges were generated by the United States, which did not appreciate the administration's coca advocacy.[94] It was not until Evo Morales came to power in 2006 that a Bolivian president again dared to argue that coca in its natural state is not a drug.

Morales immediately led the fight to decriminalize the leaf. Under the slogan "Coca yes, cocaine no," his government committed to aggressive interdiction of illicit cocaine and announced plans for "development with coca" to industrialize legal coca leaf products. Bolivia's 2009 constitution grants coca leaf legal protection for the first time, declaring that it is part of the nation's cultural heritage, its biodiversity, and a factor in social cohesion.[95] In 2012, Morales stood before the UN Commission on Narcotic Drugs in Vienna, held a leaf aloft and declared: "The coca leaf is not cocaine. We must get rid of this misconception . . . this is a millennia-old tradition in Bolivia."[96] Bolivia petitioned the UN to remove coca from the list of globally banned substances in the face of strong opposition from the US and its allies. By 2013, Bolivia won an exception, allowing for traditional uses of the leaf (see fig 6.3). The amendment was an important

Figure 6.3. A march in support of Evo Morales and the MAS in the Chapare in 2013. The sign reads: "Coca Merchants: Thank you, President, for the legalization of chewing coca leaf." Photo by the author.

symbolic victory, but as the reservation only applies to its national territory, the international export of coca or coca-based products remains proscribed.[97]

Morales's defense of coca, not to mention his pushback against US drug war policies, which included expelling the US ambassador, the Drug Enforcement Administration (DEA), and the Agency for International Development (USAID), put his government on a collision course with Washington. In 2008, the United States ended all financial assistance; suspended trade preferences, which the country had received in the framework of the Andean Trade Promotion and Drug Eradication Act (ATPDEA); and vetoed Bolivian applications for loans from the World Bank and Inter-American Development Bank.[98]

COCA'S HOME: YUNGAS OF LA PAZ

Fifty-five percent of land cultivated in the Yungas is dedicated to coca, contributing eighty percent of agricultural income in the region.[99] Spedding[100] describes coca as a "total social fact" in the Yungas, central to the social, political, symbolic, and economic fabric of Aymara communities. Yungas slopes are steep, which means families are limited to employing manual labor in agriculture. Rival products like coffee and oranges grow better at lower altitudes and in richer soil, making coca the only consistently reliable and profitable crop.[101]

Peasant union organizations are universal[102] and were set up under government control after the 1953 Agrarian Reform released Indigenous peoples from haciendas and granted them their own plots of land. These *sindicatos* were structured to ensure the equitable distribution of land, water, and other public resources, address internal conflicts, and represent community interests.[103] They eventually gained their independence from the government and evolved to often serve as local government as well as growers' representatives.[104]

By the late 1980s, many of the soils in what Law 1008 demarcated as "traditional areas" were degraded and too small to be subdivided among the next generation.[105] This "*minifundio* dilemma" led to young farmers heading to the east, south, and north in search of new terrain. Coca is almost the ideal crop for the small peasant farmer: it grows like a weed, it is light and easy to transport, it provides between three to four harvests per year, and it generates higher returns than any other crop (see fig 6.4).

A marketing arm (ADEPCOCA) focused on legal coca sales began operating in 1989 in reaction to exploitation by La Paz–based intermediaries. Then in 1994, the six agrarian federations in the Yungas united into one (under the acronym COFECAY), which included growers both within and outside Yungas areas that had traditionally grown coca. These differing memberships have led to fierce rivalries erupting within and between COFECAY and ADEPCOCA.

Throughout Bolivia, peasant unions represent the domestic unit with the oldest male serving as representative, or "head of the family." Only in his absence is he replaced by a woman, usually his wife or widow, oldest son, or on occasion, oldest daughter. Single mothers are also generally recognized as family heads.[106] Similar to peasant unions in the rest of the country, coca-growing unions gradually developed male and female chapters, giving coca advocacy a more gender-balanced, if still divided voice.

Figure 6.4. Preparing coca seedlings to plant. Photo by the author.

THE EASTERN FRONTIER: COLONIZATION AND THE CHAPARE UNIONS

The Chapare region east of Cochabamba was first populated by lowland Indigenous groups, the Yucararés and Yuquis, and then in the 1800s by scattered groups of highland peoples. But after the 1952 revolution, migration to the region really picked up.[107] It was driven by overcrowding in highland valleys, leading the National Revolutionary Movement (MNR) government to promote rural-rural migrations to "colonize" the eastern lowlands.[108] The Chapare was designated as a "priority settlement area" with the National Institute of Colonization charged with facilitating this process.[109] Most settlers were unhappy about the limited freedom implied by directed colonization programs, such as technicians deciding what crops should be grown (they did not permit coca) and dictating where people could live.[110] Consequently, most migrants took advantage of the new roads and spontaneously settled the land.[111]

Figure 6.5. Clearing land for coca cultivation in the Chapare. Photo by the author.

As colonization advanced, the Indigenous Yuracarés and Yuquis were forced to the margins.[112] One coca farmer told me: "They didn't want to give up their lands . . . but we conquered them with alcohol, cigarettes, and salt."[113] Today, the Indigenous Territory and National Park Isiboró-Securé (more often known by its Spanish acronym, TIPNIS), located in what is commonly known as the Tropics of Cochabamba, is home to forty-seven Amazonian Indigenous communities totaling over 4,500 people.[114] The Yuquis, now one of Bolivia's smallest Indigenous groups, live in the designated Yuki Indigenous Territory along the Ichilo River. These groups have a strikingly different relationship to land and territory to the highland migrants. Highlanders "often aspire to individual ownership, whereas lowland Indigenous groups usually seek communally controlled territories."[115]

An imaginary red line (defined in 1992 by Indigenous and peasant authorities) demarcates the agricultural colonization area of the Chapare (known as Polígono 7) from TIPNIS, but this border is seldom respected. Farmers regularly enter Indigenous territory to plant coca, fish, hunt, and engage in illegal logging.[116] Land invasions have on occasion provoked violent conflicts—including over the future of a proposed road.[117] But the sense of ethno-racial difference is by no means absolute, as Yuracaré people have settled in coca-grower communities and vice versa.[118]

Given the almost total absence of the Bolivian state, highland settlers began to organize themselves into sindicatos, first to distribute and control land, but very soon they became a form of self-government that addressed everything from resolving boundary disputes to building schools and disciplining antisocial behavior.[119] By the mid-2000s, the Chapare's base level unions numbered close to one thousand and were grouped into ninety-three "centrals," which in turn were organized into six federations that together formed a coordinating body—encompassing around 45,500 families.[120]

The first settlers to reach the Chapare in the 1950s, the so-called pioneers, chopped down trees and burned off the scrub (see fig. 6.5). They began by planting rice and manioc (known locally as yuca) to eat, and then coca. From the very beginning, coca was a cash crop produced for the market, mostly to be sold in the mines of Potosí.[121] With a regular cash flow from coca, the colonists were able to improve their economic situation and support family members still resident in the highlands.[122] Roberto Laserna[123] argues that because of the economic security coca provided, not to mention its symbolic value, "coca is for the 'colonist' farmer what land is to the peasant."

ECONOMIC CRISIS, THE COCA ECONOMY, AND RURAL SOCIAL CHANGE

Beginning in the early 1980s, Bolivia responded to burgeoning demand for cocaine in the United States and other industrialized nations to become a major supplier of the drug. Cocaine paste was already being produced in Bolivia in the 1950s,[124] but the trade really took off in the 1970s when Colombian criminal organizations came searching for cheap raw materials, initially coca leaf, but eventually cocaine paste too, which they transported to Colombia to refine into pure cocaine and from there exported to the United States and Europe.[125] Bolivian coca was in high demand because, as one top police official (of the anti-drugs squad) explained to me in 2019, "Bolivian leaf has a far higher cocaine alkaloid content and makes for better quality drugs. It's the best, unfortunately."

The cocaine trade proliferated against a background of severe economic crisis. In the early 1980s, the oil-driven bonanza in foreign credit had dried up, tin mining had collapsed, and Bolivia was in the throes of a severe drought.[126] The country experienced one of the highest rates of inflation in world history, an eyewatering 60,000 percent in 1985.[127] This rapidly eroded purchasing power and led to a decline in living standards exacerbated by the 1986 New Economic Policy, a "shock treatment" that called for privatization of state-owned enterprises, froze all public sector wages, relaxed labor laws, cut welfare expenditure, allowed the currency to float against the US dollar, and abolished import substitution policies and protective tariffs.[128]

The policy achieved economic stabilization but at great social cost.[129] Immediate effects included the mass sacking (euphemistically referred to as "relocation") of twenty-three thousand miners and tens of thousands of factory workers.[130] Peasants also came under attack as the government dismantled all trade barriers, which allowed cheap agricultural imports to flood the country, undermining the market for domestically grown products.[131] This hammered the peasantry so badly that many suffered from a rise in malnutrition and infectious diseases.[132]

At the same time, United States and European demand for cocaine drove up the price of coca. In 1985, one hectare of Chapare coca generated 9,000 USD annually. The next most profitable crop was citrus, which earned only 500 USD per hectare.[133] The sharp rise in the value of coca leaves, combined with deteriorating economic conditions in the rest of the country, led to a mass movement of unemployed workers, ex-miners and hard-pressed farmers to the Chapare.[134] The district's population, which was no more than 25,000 in 1967, soared to over 350,000 by 1989.[135] Land dedicated to coca cultivation went from 15,900 hectares in 1978 to 50,000 by the mid-1980s.[136] Mass migration to the Chapare was so substantial and rapid that it created labor shortages in the highlands and contributed to socioeconomic differentiation within peasant communities.[137]

There was plenty of work for the new migrants planting, harvesting, and drying coca leaf or processing cocaine paste in the small workshops (known as kitchens) located close to the coca fields. The first step in processing cocaine is relatively simple. Workers soak shredded coca leaves in a mixture of gasoline, sulfuric acid, and caustic soda to extract the cocaine alkaloid. These days most drug processers use weed whackers (strimmer), adapted cement mixers, and large tanks of up to a thousand liters of solvent to turn over the mulch. But in the 1980s, everything was done by hand. Most workshops relied on young men, known as *pisa-cocas*, to stomp on the coca leaf in shallow, plastic-lined ditches to mix up the solution. This was a tough job. The coca stompers spent hours wading in a toxic stew, suffering intense headaches and ulcerated sores on their feet. But a worker could earn up to ten times the average daily wage by processing coca in this way.[138]

By the mid-1980s, Bolivia was earning an estimated 1 to 1.6 billion USD annually from coca and cocaine, a revenue equivalent to or greater than legal export revenue.[139] Even though substantial sums never entered the country, passing directly into bank accounts in Switzerland, Panama, and Miami,[140] the drug trade revitalized the Bolivian economy and prompted an urban construction boom. Drug dollars trickled down to support a large informal economy,[141] generating high levels of employment in the Chapare,[142] but also in the urban peripheries where coca farmers most often invested their cash.[143]

James Painter[144] estimates that at its height in 1989, Bolivia's coca-cocaine economy provided direct employment to more than 10 percent of the population, and even more jobs in support and service roles, such as restaurant work, transport, and commerce. By generating employment and much-needed foreign revenue, the illicit cocaine trade provided a bulwark against the ravages of neoliberal structural adjustment.[145] In 1992, anthropologist June Nash[146] wrote: "without drug traffic . . . the Bolivian people could not survive."

While the cocaine trade generated wealth for farmers, coca growers and paste processors were not the main beneficiaries of the trade. Rather, just as in any other sector of the Bolivian economy, it was the white-elite groups who controlled the business.[147] It is estimated that of the 60 billion to 80 billion USD street value of cocaine sold in the early 1980s, only about 100 million USD found its way back into peasant hands.[148] Wealthy and well-connected cattle ranchers and businessmen in Beni and Santa Cruz, many of them friends and family of Bolivia's military dictators from 1964 to 1982 who had been granted large swaths of land, smuggled large volumes of cocaine paste to Colombia. These agro-industrial capitalists were ideally positioned for this role, as they owned extensive land holdings and had aircraft and airstrips on their properties.[149]

Ironically, this powerful new group emerged as a direct result of US government advisors' promoting the formation of an export-oriented, agro-industrial sector in the eastern lowlands during the 1950s.[150] A sharp decline in the price of key export crops like cotton and sugar prompted these new elites to turn to the illegal cocaine industry.[151] Gootenberg[152] argues that it was not a lack of economic development but rather state-led, postwar modernization projects, like those promoted by the MNR, that led to the expansion of illicit economies in the Amazonian lowlands.

From the 1960s to 1980s, successive military governments maintained strong links to the illicit drug trade.[153] In July 1980, a group of military officers headed by Luis García Meza seized control of Bolivia in what came to be known as the "Cocaine Coup." The military was directly involved in trafficking drugs, and officers pocketed large sums of money.[154] Chapare coca growers whom I spoke with recalled soldiers in uniform processing cocaine paste by the side of the road. They also saw officers buying up drugs, which they loaded into trucks for export. Meza was forced out after only a year, but this did not stop the cocaine industry, which only grew as demand soared. There was also the so-called balloon effect, as eradication efforts elsewhere increased. After 1990, US drug war pressure in Colombia pushed production south into Peru and Bolivia.[155]

To this day, coca and cocaine paste production represent an important pillar of the Bolivian economy. As of this writing (2023), coca cultivation represents up to 8 percent of the value of Bolivia's GDP in the agricultural sector.[156] In the Chapare, participation in the illicit trade is widespread, with many people either processing paste or smuggling precursor chemicals and coca. These actions carry no negative stigma, nor are they seen as being socially disruptive. The drug trade supports many people in low-skilled positions, stabilizes families' livelihoods, enables them to stay in rural areas rather than migrating to cities (as vast numbers of rural Bolivians have done), and supports small businesses. While Chapare farmers do not become rich, engagement in the cocaine trade represents an avenue for unparalleled social mobility.[157]

DRUG WAR IMPERIALISM

Cocaine production and trafficking is driven by demand, mostly from the United States, which despite a recent decline in consumption, remains the single largest national market.[158]As an example, North Americans consumed an estimated 145 metric tons of cocaine valued at 24 billion USD in 2016, a decrease from 384 tons worth 58 billion USD only ten years previously.[159] Other nations have taken up the slack. There are growing markets in Latin America (particularly Brazil), as well as in Africa, Asia, and Oceania. Some analysts speak of cocaine's "shift south."[160]

In the mid-1980s, in the face of a crack epidemic at home that brought pressure on the government, the United States launched an offensive against drug producers and traffickers south of the border. The argument behind the War on Drugs was straightforward: disrupting the supply at source equates to less drugs available on the street, a message that resonated with voters. But militarized interventions with names like Operation Blast Furnace, the Andean Initiative, and the Triennial Plan sowed chaos in the Andes, while doing little to stem the drugs flowing northward.[161]

Washington-based policy makers identified coca farmers as the first link of the drug commodity chain and cast them as criminals,[162] turning them into the "enemy" in the War on Drugs.[163] In 1988, the Bolivian Congress passed the Law to Regulate Coca and Controlled Substances, commonly known as Law 1008 (in force until 2017), under significant US pressure.[164] At that time, Bolivia was still suffering the fallout from a deep economic crisis and was almost completely dependent on financial support from the United States and international lending institutions, like the International Monetary Fund (IMF) and World Bank. The United States made aid and loans contingent on Bolivia's adherence to unilaterally determined eradication and interdiction targets through a process known as "certification."[165]

Given the historic use of coca in Bolivia, it was impossible to outlaw the crop outright. This would have generated overwhelming social and political conflict. Instead, Law 1008 made a distinction between three cultivation zones. The Yungas of La Paz was identified as a "traditional production area, where 12,000 hectares of coca plantings were permitted to supply the traditional market. By contrast, the Tropics of Cochabamba or Chapare were demarcated as a "transitional production area," subject to gradual eradication combined with alternative development programs. Coca production anywhere outside of these regions was outlawed and slated for eradication.[166] In making these distinctions the law created tensions between Chapare and Yungas growers, and between Yungas growers in traditional zones (aligned with ADEPCOCA) and those in newer expansion zones (members of COFECAY).

Observers have described Law 1008 as "draconian," as it ensured that those charged with drug-related offences were imprisoned indefinitely without the possibility of bail and set heavy minimum sentences.[167] Conzelman[168] explains: "One of the most notorious and insidious prescriptions of the law is that people arrested under suspicion of participating in the illegal cultivation of coca leaf, the transport of precursor chemicals, or the elaboration of cocaine are considered guilty until proven innocent and are placed in the custody of the judicial system." To this day, Bolivia has one of the highest rates of preventive detention anywhere in Latin America.[169]

Initially, eradication efforts were slow to get off the ground. The administrations of Paz Estenssoro (1985–1989), Paz Zamora (1989–1993), and Sánchez de Lozada (1993–1997) preferred voluntary reductions to forced eradication. They recognized the crucial role coca played in absorbing labor and they wanted to avoid a showdown with the powerful Chapare coca unions.[170] Chapare farmers were incentivized to allow the state to destroy their crops in return for cash payments of up to 2,500 USD, but overall, this policy failed, as no viable alternatives were on offer. Coca farmers simply allowed the military to pull up their old and unproductive plants, and then used the cash payments to invest in land to plant yet more coca. For every hectare eradicated under voluntary programs, another was planted.[171]

Beginning in 1994, the United States took a harder line. In March of that year, Ambassador Richard Bowers publicly stated that "the people of Bolivia, specifically the coca growers, have to accept responsibility for the deaths of thousands of US citizens. As a result, the bush must disappear." This statement only stoked anti-US sentiment throughout the country.[172] The following year (1995), the United States "decertified" Bolivia for failing to meet its eradication targets, ending all economic assistance.[173]

President Hugo Banzer (1997–2001) and his National Democratic Action (ADN by its Spanish acronym) party came to power in 1997 with a promise to restore Bolivia's "dignity" by destroying all coca above the limit mandated by Law 1008. Banzer unleashed the Leopards, special commandos from the Mobile Rural Patrol Unit (Unidad Móvil de Patrullaje–Rural; UMOPAR). This US-funded and trained anti-drug police unit led missions to destroy cocaine-paste labs and staffed checkpoints along the main roads. The Joint Task Force (Fuerza de Tarea Conjunta; FTC), a combined military-police force created in 1988 and directly funded by the United States, was charged with uprooting coca plants across the Chapare and elsewhere.

Banzer's government also orchestrated the only attempt to forcefully eradicate coca in the Yungas. Troops from the FTC entered the Yungas to destroy 1,700 hectares of "excess" coca. Unannounced, the soldiers set to hacking the plants out of steep hillsides in La Asunta, an expansion zone. The action struck a nerve. Hundreds of cocaleros, merchants, students, and truck drivers gathered to protest this violent affront to their livelihoods, forcing the Banzer government to back down.[174]

US involvement in Bolivia's drug war weakened Bolivian institutions, destabilized the political system, and severely undermined national sovereignty.[175] As part of a 900 million USD package, the US government donated equipment, including transport aircraft, helicopters, and assault rifles,[176] and arranged for officers to undertake training courses at the School of the Americas.[177] This infamous military institute was where Latin American officers were encouraged to identify with US values and interests.[178] The Narcotic Affairs Section of the US embassy paid members of the Bolivian security forces and public prosecutors involved in the War on Drugs a bonus, and until 2002 the embassy operated its own paramilitary group, the Expeditionary Task Force.[179]

By the year 2000, Bolivian security forces had destroyed around 28,000 hectares of coca, approaching Plan Dignidad's goal of zero coca in the Cochabamba Tropics. The US embassy considered the Dignity Plan a "success story," but success came at a high price.[180] Coca eradication decimated Cochabamba's regional economy, and by 2001 the Chapare had some of the highest rates of extreme poverty in the country.[181] Security forces killed, abused, sexually assaulted, and seriously wounded scores of coca farmers, torched homesteads, and incarcerated thousands of people.[182] Journalist Alex Contreras states that since 1988 "more than 115 people died, the majority coca growers and a minority uniformed. No one responsible for the murders was arrested, nor were those responsible sentenced. There was total impunity."[183]

Following the 9/11 attacks in the United States in 2001, the War on Drugs shifted gear.[184] Sociologist Silvia Rivera Cusicanqui[185] states: "Evo Morales (the leader of the coca growers) and the coca growers were no longer political adversaries in the democratic arena: they were now drug terrorists, defenders of armed struggle with links to guerrillas in Colombia or Peru." The Chapare was declared a "red zone" subject to special policing measures. Over 20,000 troops were deployed in the region, where they enacted what Raquel Gutierrez Aguilar[186] has described as a "systematic terror policy." A male coca grower in his late fifties explained to me: "Back then there was no peace here. If the police found just ten dollars in your pocket, they denounced you as a drug trafficker. It was enough that if they found a bit of wire close to your house or some batteries then they [the police] would denounce you for being a terrorist. They said they were for use to make a *cazabobo* [explosive device]. Back then it was dangerous to be a union leader—you were hunted down."

When President Hugo Banzer became ill with cancer, he stepped down and was replaced by his vice president, Jorge Quiroga, in August 2001. Quiroga immediately approved Decree 26415, which prohibited the drying, transport, and sale of Chapare coca leaf, an activity which until that point had been legal. The penalty was eight to twelve years in prison.[187] In January 2002, the coca growers mobilized to demand the reopening of markets where they could sell their coca. The resulting "Coca War," which lasted for one month and involved roadblocks and violent clashes with security forces, left four *cocaleros* and two soldiers dead, and more than seventy people injured. State security forces destroyed the coca growers' station, "Radio Sovereignty," in a bid to undermine the union's ability to mobilize.[188]

In January 2002, the Bolivian Congress expelled Evo Morales from the parliamentary position he had been elected to in 1997 for allegedly inciting the Coca War. Working class and Indigenous people across the country mobilized to reinstate him.[189] When Morales ran for president later that year, US ambassador Manuel Rocha threatened voters that his country would cut all funding if they voted for him. Contrary to Rocha's intention, such attacks only bolstered Morales's popularity and his Movimiento Al Socialismo (MAS) party came in a close second place.[190]

While US policy makers lauded their alternative development and payment-for-eradication initiatives in the Chapare, these programs generally failed to benefit coca growers and their families.[191] The problems have been attributed to poor sequencing of assistance, the types of programs on offer, and the fact that USAID did little to open new markets for the alternative crops they promoted.[192] Alternative development was always an afterthought to the main goal of eradicating coca. Also, alternative development crops could never compete with coca because of its high price, buoyed in large part by its criminalization.[193]

One USAID staffer recalled:[194] "The irony was that if eradication efforts experienced a period of success, the price of available coca would increase substantially," and "the increased price usually was sufficient incentive for many farmers to accept the risk and return to growing coca." In 2008, the unions banned USAID from operating in the Chapare and erected a sign on the main road that read: "territory free of USAID."[195] In 2013, President Morales called an end to all USAID programs nationwide.[196]

After forty years of militarized drug war polices—and billions of dollars—the flow of drugs northward continues apace.[197] Against the background of consistent failure, critical scholars have suggested that the so-called War on Drugs has less to do with cutting cocaine (or any other drug) supply than with giving the US military a role in the post–Cold War world and securing US corporate interests in Latin America.[198] It is certainly the case that as a result of interventions ostensibly aimed at tackling drugs, the US gained significant leverage over successive Bolivian governments, even if Bolivians pushed back.[199] That pushback included the creation of potent, new political parties.

PEASANT RESISTANCE AND THE FOUNDING OF THE MOVIMIENTO AL SOCIALISMO (MAS)

Before 1985, the Chapare coca unions were politically incoherent, with coca growers supporting various traditional parties.[200] Nor was the cocalero identity explicitly political; coca was thought of in much the same terms as any other crop that farmers grew, like bananas, rice, or oranges. But the criminalization of coca and by association, cocaleros, changed all of that. State-backed eradication programs radicalized and united them against their common enemies, namely the Bolivian state and the US embassy.[201] In the face of ongoing military and police repression, the cocaleros built a powerful union. In the words of one union leader: "Necessity forces us to plant coca . . . that's why we built the union—to stop the politics of zero coca."

The first wave of Chapare migrants in the 1950s and 1960s were peasants from the Cochabamba valleys, and they modelled their sindicato on the "revolutionary syndicalism" of their agricultural unions.[202] Initially, these unions were aligned with the MNR and subsequent military governments as part of the "military-peasant pact." The pact lasted until 1974, when the military under the Banzer dictatorship murdered one hundred peasant marchers outside of Cochabamba.[203]

When unemployed miners migrated to the Chapare in the mid-1980s, they brought with them their union experience and militancy.[204] One ex-miner told me: "I was a miner, I wasn't afraid, I knew how to light dynamite. I knew the union life." He went on to say that because of people like him, "more leaders were formed here in the tropics; we strengthened the unions." Coca growers adopted the miners' command structure and protest strategies, including hunger strikes, roadblocks, and national-level protests.[205] Women played important roles as union leader and later

Figure 6.6. Female coca grower in front of a mural depicting peasant resistance. Photo by the author.

member of congress Leonilda Zurita recalled, by (among other actions) shielding the men, "when the women did not participate, the men were run over, beaten, dragged off."[206]

In 1994, during Gonzalo Sánchez de Lozada's first administration (1993–1997), cocaleras and cocaleros organized a massive march on the city of La Paz, proclaiming "life, coca and dignity." The demonstrators intentionally echoed the 1986 March for Life organized by Bolivian miners.[207] The growers demanded withdrawal of the military and police from Chapare, depenalization of coca, and immediate expulsion of USAID. As repression intensified, women led a follow-up demonstration in 1995, the March for Life and National Sovereignty. Upon arriving in La Paz, they declared a hunger strike, forcing the government into negotiations (see fig 6.6).[208]

The marches of the mid-1990s marked the start of a protest cycle and the radicalization of the coca unions. The unions established self-defense committees to prevent the military from eradicating coca plantations.[209] These groups were lightly armed with rifles (mostly Mausers) dating back to the 1930s Chaco War, plus homemade explosive devices known as *cazabobos* or booby traps. Veteran mining leader and coca union advisor Filemón Escóbar writes, "everyone was trained to make caza-bobos."[210] Even so, skirmishes between coca growers and state forces were infrequent.[211]

The largest of the six coca unions, the Federación Especial de Trabajadores Campesinos del Trópico de Cochabamba (FETCTC), worked to enhance the presence of the coca unions both within the Unified Confederation of Campesino Unions of Bolivia (Confederación Sindical Única de Trabajadores Campesinos de Bolivia or CSUTCB, Bolivia's main peasant federation) and the Central Obrera Boliviana (COB), the overarching trade union federation.[212] The coca growers also lent their support to allied causes, such as the 2000 Cochabamba Water War, building strategic alliances with other sectors.[213]

There were early debates over the future of the coca growers' movement. Some, drawing inspiration from Mexico's Zapatistas, who also burst onto the scene in the early 1990s, argued for armed insurgency.[214] Among them was Evo Morales, who publicly threatened that the Chapare was close to becoming a new Chiapas.[215] Filemón Escóbar explains: "The concept of the guerrilla was very popular with the cocaleros."[216] However, after literally hundreds of workshops, in which among other issues the failure of Che Guevara's 1967 insurgency in Bolivia was analyzed, the coca farmers opted for the electoral path.[217] Early democratic victories after the introduction of the 1994 Law of Popular Participation (LPP) introduced municipal elections and funding throughout the country, which further eroded the appeal of guerrilla tactics.[218]

In contrast to the Chapare, where unions took over town halls, the introduction of the LPP in the Yungas created rivalry between unions and Yungas municipalities as many governance functions overlapped between the two. The Yungas municipalities of Chulumani and Coroico had been founded a hundred years earlier, which made it difficult for local growers' unions to exert the kind of control they enjoyed in the Chapare. This marked difference in strength between the Chapare and Yungas unions was shaped by both geography and the Yungas history of haciendas (versus rapid peasant colonization in the Chapare). This left the Yungas with a local elite that the Chapare never had, union structures split between marketing and representation, differing relationships with municipalities, and contrasting experiences with the US-financed Drug War. Not only did the Drug War bring less repression to the Yungas, but it also effectively created another fissure: the division between traditional and expansion zones codified in Law 1008. The Chapare has always been more homogenous in geography, population, and history.[219]

In 1995, the Chapare growers established their own political vehicle that would eventually become the MAS. The objective was to scale up the struggle against neoliberalism, ensure access to land, implement pro-peasant policies, and defend the right to cultivate coca. The decision to create a political instrument as opposed to a party reflected a prevailing crisis of legitimacy, as parties were widely considered corrupt and controlled by elites.[220] One male union member who attended the founding meeting explained: "We realized that through union action alone we couldn't achieve anything. So, we thought we needed another tactic to make ourselves heard."

The Movimiento Al Socialismo began in the Chapare, expanding beyond municipal victories to the national level by linking up with other grassroots organizations and allowing them to run their own candidates on the MAS ticket.[221] The organization's national profile rose after Evo Morales entered parliament as a deputy in 1997. Less than a decade later, in 2006, the MAS became the governing party of Bolivia, a role that (as of this writing, 2023) it has maintained for all but one year ever since.

THE REVALIDATION OF COCA

"Before, life was very different. Everyday there were deaths, everyday there was a conflict in the battle to defend Mother Earth and our natural resources, but more than anything, the battle was to defend our sacred coca leaf. Coca is the emblem of our identity, of all first peoples of the Aymaras, the Quechuas, and Guaranís. . . . Long Live Coca, Death to the Yankees!" These were the words of a female union leader at the opening of a coca union congress in 2019. The speech was reminiscent of many I heard while carrying out fieldwork in the Chapare. No matter if it was a low-level sindicato meeting or a national level event, union leaders would always start by emphasizing the centrality of coca to Indigenous Andean culture and stress the injustice of foreign troops attacking their "sacred" plants.

Today, coca is intimately bound to Indigenous liberation. "Popular Coca Nationalism" of the kind espoused by Evo Morales has roots that can be traced back to the inter-ethnic coca culture that emerged following the Chaco War.[222] But it was only in the 1970s and 1980s that two distinct strands of popular pro-coca politics fully emerged: that of unionized peasant cocaleros in the Chapare lowlands and pro-Indigenous Kataristas in the highlands. Both called for open, adamant revalorization of the leaf. But who were the Kataristas?

In the early 1970s, a small group of urban-based Aymara intellectuals began to blend class and ethnic discourses into what came to be known as Katarism, borrowing the name of Tupaj Katari, an eighteenth-century anticolonial rebel.[223] Katarista activists embraced coca as part of a broader effort to revalidate native Andean medical knowledge, and this contributed an explicitly Indianist element to peasant organizing and politics.[224] Though *indianismo*, the pro-Indigenous movement pioneered by Fausto Reinaga, and *katarismo* can be traced to the same 1960s root,[225] by the 1970s the movements were starting to become distinguishable from one another. Adherents of Katarism identified with the peasant/trade union movement and were open to interethnic alliances with other progressive forces. By contrast, Indianism operated mainly in the political party sphere, rejecting the mestizo-creole left.[226]

It was by no means inevitable that coca growers in either the Chapare or the Yungas would mobilize around Indigenous cultural difference to justify their oppositional politics. While outsiders label Chapare and Yungas coca growers as "Indigenous," they exhibit a stronger class identity as upwardly mobile peasants, and many reject the Indigenous label.[227] Nevertheless, given the diminishing power of the class-based left as a result of the neoliberal onslaught on labor, coca growers joined the Indigenous resurgence sweeping Bolivia and the rest of Latin America.[228] Coca growers began to present the defense of coca not only in terms of protecting the right to produce it, but also in terms of protecting its traditional uses and cultural value. They felt this approach could broaden their sector-specific demands into something that appealed to all peasants.[229]

By the late 1980s, the CSUTCB created a Coca Commission aiming to encourage consumers to back the protection and consumption of coca leaf.[230] In the words of one observer, peasant activists "successfully made coca a symbol of Indigenous ethnicity and pride."[231] From that point on, the coca unions, the CSUTCB, and later the MAS seized the initiative to generate a new common sense about coca, politics, and nation. They argued that by defending coca, they were fighting for national sovereignty and dignity.

This narrative was particularly powerful for three reasons. First, widespread coca consumption creates a basis for what Gootenberg[232] calls "coca nationalism." Second, coca (and the cocaine trade) brings in hard currency, which means that eradication programs damaged the larger regional (and national) economy and cut off coca's vital role in providing work for the unemployed.[233] Finally, the pro-coca, anti-US message was popular at a time when the Bolivian public identified externally imposed neoliberal policies as the root cause of their hardship.[234] "Sacred coca" became a perfect meta-symbol, tying together distinct demands into a powerful banner of anti-imperial resistance.[235] Evo Morales and the MAS wisely adopted the vocabulary of indigeneity wrapped around the coca leaf to build broad-based support in a heterogeneous society (see fig 6.7).[236]

Figure 6.7. (*above*) A MAS candidate with coca leaf garland at a political rally in Cochabamba. Photo by the author.

Figure 6.8. (*below*) Union leader interviewed by the media at the inauguration of a government-built paper factory in the Chapare. Photo by the author.

A COCA GROWER IN THE PRESIDENTIAL PALACE

On coming to power in 2006, Evo Morales's MAS-led government aimed to "refound" the nation by challenging colonial legacies, which were said to have permeated society, politics, and the economy.[237] The administration advanced redistributive policies built around the notion of Vivir Bien (to live well).[238] Central to this endeavor was to advance policies to protect and promote coca. The strategy, initially introduced in 2004 by the Carlos Mesa administration (2003–2005) under pressure from coca growers, legalized the cultivation of a small amount of coca leaf known as a "cato" (a 1,600-square-meter plot) in specific zones. The measure effectively ended forced eradication in the Chapare region, and protests, violence, and human rights violations subsided immediately.[239] The Morales administration expanded this strategy to encourage coca unions to self-police to ensure that growers did not exceed this limit, also frontloading development assistance to coca-growing regions. The overriding aim of MAS policy was to reduce harms to coca grower communities.[240, 241]

Beginning in 2007, coca unions collaborated with the Morales government to develop a sophisticated monitoring, control, and coca reduction system with support from the European Union.[242] Local unions drew on their long history of self-governing to ensure that farmers respected the limit. Each union organized regular inspections of coca plantations, and if commissions made up of local union members found coca plantings above one cato, they leveled fines, ordered community service, and restricted access to municipal public works projects. The inspectors could also eradicate the entire crop and prohibit replanting for one year.[243] When communities refused to comply, workers from the coca control agency, the Unidad de Desarrollo Económico y Social del Trópico (UDESTRO), negotiated with community leaders for the coca to be forcibly eradicated by government troops. In contrast to past Drug War policies, eradication under this scheme has rarely involved violence.[244]

In addition, access to assistance to diversify crops was no longer conditional on the prior eradication of coca. The sequencing of assistance is important because the guaranteed income from the coca cato, which is around 300 USD per month (equivalent to the minimum wage), has allowed farming families to experiment with alternative crops and fish farming (pisciculture). Coca farmers have said that government funding for rice-husking machines, tractors, and processing plants for fruit, honey, and fish has expanded the market for local produce (see fig. 6.8).[245] Bananas, rice, citrus fruit, and palm hearts now cover more cultivated land than coca in the Chapare, a result of sustained and integrated development efforts.[246]

Tensions between Yungas and Chapare coca growers remain, however. On the one hand, Chapare growers have long considered Law 1008's classification of the Yungas as a "traditional area" as arbitrary and deeply unfair. On the other, Yungas growers have fiercely defended their historic monopoly over the coca trade and presented Chapare coca as lower quality and only good for drug trafficking.[247] Susan Brewer-Osorio[248] argues that the new coca policy has further exacerbated these divisions by rewarding Chapare coca producers with significant investment, while undermining Yungas growers' historic privileges and protections.[249] Yungas growers have rejected participation in government-led development programs and have strongly opposed the expansion of legal coca in the Chapare.[250] ADEPCOCA, the marketing branch of the Yungas growers, withdrew its support for the MAS.[251]

These tensions came to a head in 2017 with the passage of a new coca law, ten years in the making because of negotiation difficulties with Yungas growers. The new law was designed to legitimate the twenty thousand hectares of leaf cultivation informally permitted since coca grower leader Evo Morales became the country's president in 2006. This was eight thousand hectares above the limit established under Law 1008. The amount was arrived at by multiplying the quantity of coca allowed per registered grower under a 2004 accord times the number of registered coca farmers. Subsequent compromises with Yungas growers raised the permitted amounts to twenty-two thousand hectares: fourteen thousand in the Yungas, seven thousand in the Chapare, and one thousand in the north of La Paz Department.[252]

Researchers have shown that the new approach introduced by the MAS government has been successful in reducing illicit cultivation and the violence associated with eradication, as well as in generating sustainable incomes for local communities.[253] Bolivia's program has received widespread praise as a "best practice" from the Organization of American States[254] and the United Nations Development Programme.[255] The model has served as inspiration to coca growers in Peru[256] and Colombia.[257]

And yet, while the MAS program has succeeded in reducing coca cultivation overall, it would be naive to believe it has controlled drug trafficking. In a 2019 interview, a retired Bolivian drugs official told me that with the Drugs Enforcement Administration (DEA) out of the picture, Bolivia has become a major drugs transshipment hub for cheaper Peruvian cocaine paste. It is refined in Bolivia or Brazil, supplying Brazil's domestic market, with the remainder exported to Europe and Asia. As of this writing (2023), the United Nations Office on Drugs and Crime (UNODC) reports that cocaine refineries are mushrooming in Cochabamba, La Paz, and Santa Cruz[258] and some estimates put Bolivia's annual cocaine production as high as 254 metric tons.[259] The ex-police official explained that Colombian drug traffickers consider Bolivia to represent an "acceptable level of risk," because with no DEA present and having paid off the police and judiciary, they know that if they are caught, they will spend no more than one year in prison.

When the Morales government was ousted in November 2019, a military-backed administration avowedly opposed to the MAS's *Coca Sí* or "Yes, Coca" strategy took power.[260] The interim Áñez government cracked down on the opposition and committed human rights abuses, including killing ten coca farmers when troops opened fire on a peaceful demonstration.[261] Añez's brief government swung Bolivia's antidrug approach back to hard-line measures, reinitiating forced eradication and publicly denouncing coca growers as "narco-terrorists."[262]

The US government heralded the Áñez administration, saying it had made "important strides in drug interdiction"—despite little evidence—and that cooperation between the two nations had "increased."[263] Less than a year later, in October 2020, Luis Arce of the MAS scored a landslide victory in presidential elections and promised to continue with the "social control policies" put in place by his predecessor. Even so, Arce faces a complex drug scenario with high levels of trafficking and the threat of Brazilian criminal organizations increasing their operations on Bolivian territory.[264] The 2019 coup undermined coca grower trust in the state, leaving Chapare farmers less willing to adhere to established cultivation limits.[265] In 2020, the total area under cultivation increased by fifteen percent over the previous year and in 2021 it increased by a further four percent, reaching 30,500 hectares that year.[266]

CONCLUSION

From the pre-Colombian trade to the contemporary cocaine economy, coca has been a motor of Bolivian history. Few commodities have been as controversial or pivotal in shaping Bolivia's politics, economy, or society. Coca's contested history reveals three broader lessons about the struggles over natural resources in Bolivia.

First, coca is unique among the commodities analyzed in this book. Unlike silver, tin, rubber, or lithium, coca is associated with criminality and is internationally outlawed. The public defense of coca thus has not focused on ownership of a resource or the distribution of revenues (as has been the case with gas, for example) but rather it has centered on coca itself and its status as an ancestral plant with legitimate uses. As a result of Indigenous peasant activism, coca leaf has become a potent banner of resistance tying together diverse struggles over natural resources and has been deeply implicated in Indigenous identity and nation building. To defend coca is to defend the inclusion and claims to full citizenship of the Indigenous majority.

Second, while protestors might use a language of indigeneity to defend coca cultivation, the fight is not about defending an ancestral plant or identity per se but rather about maintaining the cultivation of a resource that generates constant, stable income precisely because it is a core component of the cocaine value chain. Bolivia's continued dependence on coca and illicit cocaine production is symptomatic of the country's long history of dependence, poverty, and inequality. Coca and cocaine paste production has provided modest yet dignified livelihoods for the tens of thousands of people who have been dispossessed by the neoliberal economic model. Coca is one of the few natural resources that has value added in Bolivia through processing it into cocaine paste. This in turn generates employment, investment, and secondary markets.

Arguments for the full legalization of coca are valid, but defenders of the crop are mostly blind to the fact that the price of coca is buoyed by its very illegality. If coca were fully legal and anyone could grow it, then the price would surely crash, mirroring other tropical export crops like coffee.[267] When it comes to drug policy then, a frank conversation must take place, including consideration of the unequal insertion of marginalized urban and rural territories into the global economy that makes drug crop farming and drug trafficking the only realistic livelihood options.

Third, for some people, Bolivian social movements have been at the forefront of defining a new development paradigm in the schema of Vivir Bien to address their problems in line with their own identity and traditions. Notwithstanding the limits of this approach,[268] Bolivia has opened novel paths to manage and commercialize the country's natural resources for the benefit of its citizens. Coca is a case in point. The innovative coca control policies advanced by the MAS in conjunction with the coca growers unions since 2006 is among the world's first supply-side "harm reduction" schemes. It is a model that has not only shrunk coca acreage but has also respected human rights, shifted the Chapare's economy towards non-coca crops, and worked to revalidate coca leaf use. Drug crop producing nations from Afghanistan to Thailand are taking note of the Bolivian experience.[269] The ideas, policies, and practices pioneered by Bolivia's natural resource defenders, then, can provide inspiration, knowledge, and expertise from which the rest of the world would surely benefit.

NOTES

1. UNODC, *World Drug Report*, 11.
2. Restrepo et al., "Erythroxylum in Focus," 16.
3. UNODC, "Drug Supply," 21.
4. UNODC, *Estado Plurinacional, Monitoreo de cultivos de Coca* (2021).
5. Henman, *Mama Coca*; Carter and Mamani, *Coca en Bolivia*.

6. This is less true for Bolivia than Colombia and Peru. In Bolivia traditional domestic coca consumption is put at fourteen thousand hectares and the country has just over twenty-five thousand hectares under cultivation. García-Yi, "Social Control," 60.
7. UNODC, *World Drug Report* (2022), 15.
8. Gutierrez, "The Paradox," 1008–9.
9. "The 100 largest companies in the world ranked by revenue in 2019," Statistica, accessed February 28, 2021, https://www.statista.com/statistics/263265/top-companies-in-the-world-by-revenue/.
10. Grisaffi, "The White Factory."
11. See Yampara, "Cosmovivencia Andina."
12. This chapter is based on more than three years of ethnographic fieldwork undertaken in coca growing regions of Bolivia between 2005 and 2019.
13. Tom Dillehay et al., "Early Holocene Coca."
14. Carter, *Ensayos Cientificos*.
15. Those in need of a more serious pick-me-up consume crushed coca leaf that has been soaked in coffee and then mixed with bicarbonate of soda and sweetener. This more powerful cocktail, known as *coca machucada*, is often consumed accompanied by an energy drink.
16. UNODC, *Estado Plurinacional*.
17. Numbering about twenty-five thousand people, Afro-Bolivians are descendants of slaves who were bought to Bolivia to work in Potosí's silver mines during the colonial period.
18. Klein, "Coca Production."
19. Coca bush is also grown in extension zones in the Norte de La Paz (1.5 percent). UNODC, *Estado Plurinacional*.
20. PNUD, *Bolivia*, 302.
21. Brown, "Investigating the Use of Coca."
22. Rivera et al., "Antiquity of Coca-Leaf Chewing."
23. Gagliano, *Coca Prohibition*, 14.
24. Rowe, "Inca culture," 291; Cintron, "Coca," 26.
25. Murra, "Notes on Pre-Colombian Cultivation."
26. Murra, "Notes on Pre-Colombian Cultivation," 50.
27. Murra, *The Economic Organization*.
28. Hemming, *The Conquest*, 354; O'Phelan, *La gran rebelión*, 141.
29. "Coca and Cocaine in Latin American History," *Oxford Research Encyclopedia*, accessed February 8, 2020, https://oxfordre.com/view/10.1093/acrefore/9780199366439.001.0001/acrefore-9780199366439-e-754.
30. Gagliano, *Coca Prohibition*, 34–43.
31. Klein, "Coca Production," 53.
32. Flores and Blanes, *¿Donde va el Chapare?*, 156.

33. Gootenberg, *Andean Cocaine*, 20.
34. Personal communication with Rossana Barragán, 30 May 2022.
35. Gootenberg, "Cocaine Histories," 5; Klein, "Coca Production," 53.
36. Mintz, *Sweetness and Power*.
37. Gootenberg, "Coca and Cocaine."
38. Klein, "Coca Production," 53.
39. Encomiendas were grants awarded by the Spanish Crown conferring the right to demand tribute and forced labor from the local Indigenous inhabitants. The encomienda property did not give land title and it started to decline as an institution in the late sixteenth century, while private property held by hacendados was gradually expanding throughout the colonial period.
40. Given the high price coca commanded, these coca-growing haciendas proved to be some of the wealthiest in the Andean region. Klein, "Coca Production," 56.
41. Gootenberg, *Andean Cocaine*, 114.
42. The Yungas Ayllus played an important role in the 1780–1781 anti-colonial rebellion led by Tupaj Katari and Bartolina Sisa and supplied the Aymara warriors with coca leaf. Conzelman, "Coca Leaf," 90.
43. Lema, "Production et circulation."
44. Gootenberg, "Coca and Cocaine."
45. Lema, "The Coca Debate."
46. Soux, *La coca liberal*.
47. Mayer, "Coca Use," 11.
48. Reinaga, *La Revolucion India*, 27, 100.
49. The idea of coca as a vice fomented by landlords was an indigenista trope in the early twentieth century. Reinaga's view is less a sociological perspective on Indigenous life than it is a polemic against his mestizo/criollo enemies.
50. Ehrinpreis, "Coca Nation."
51. Ehrinpreis, "Coca Nation," 68.
52. Ehrinpreis, "Green Gold," 220.
53. Leons, "Land Reform."
54. Blanes and Flores, *Campesino*.
55. Ehrinpreis, "Coca Nation," 262.
56. Spedding, *Wachu wachu*, 68.
57. Mayer, "Coca Use," 5.
58. Mayer, *The Articulated Peasant*, 177.
59. Allen, *The Hold Life*.
60. Allen, "To Be Quechua," 157.
61. Nash, *We Eat the Mines*.
62. See also Absi, *Los ministros del diablo*.

63. Carter and Mamani, *Coca en Bolivia*.
64. Wiedemann, "The Folklore of Coca," 39; Bolton, "Doing Waki."
65. Grisaffi, Farthing, Ledebur, Paredes, and Pastor, "From Criminals," 1–14.
66. Mayer, "Coca Use in the Andes," 8.
67. Andrew Weil, "The therapeutic value of coca"; Biondich and Joslin, "Coca."
68. CONALTID, *Gobierno presenta*.
69. Rivera, *Las fronteras*.
70. González Miranda, "La hoja transfronteriza."
71. Gootenberg, *Andean Cocaine*, 113–15, 214–17.
72. Gootenberg, "Cocaine Histories," 5.
73. Pearson, "Bolivia," 286.
74. Postero, *The Indigenous State*, 121.
75. Arias and Grisaffi, *Cocaine*.
76. Gagliano, *Coca Prohibition*, 113.
77. Gootenberg, *Andean Cocaine*, 60.
78. Freud, "Uber Coca."
79. Andrews and Solomon, "Coca and Cocaine," 197.
80. Gootenberg, *Andean Cocaine*.
81. Paoli, Greenfield, and Reuter, "Change Is Possible."
82. Gootenberg, *Andean Cocaine*, 191.
83. Warren, "Collaboration and discord," 37.
84. Pearson, "Bolivia, coca, culture and colonialism," 291.
85. Metaal et al., *Coca Yes, Cocaine, No? Legal Options*.
86. Metaal, "Coca in Debate."
87. The convention includes an important exception that allows the export of de-cocainized coca as a flavoring agent, to allow for the continued manufacturing of Coca-Cola in the United States (Gootenberg 2004, 247).
88. Pearson, "Coca Sí, Cocaína No?"
89. Reiss, *We Sell Drugs*.
90. Weil, "The Therapeutic Value of Coca."
91. Duke, Aulik, and Plowman, "Nutritional Value of Coca."
92. Metaal et al., *Coca Yes, Cocaine, No?*, 7–8.
93. Gootenberg, *Between Coca and Cocaine*, 21.
94. Menzel, *Fire in the Andes*, 89–91; Dunkerley, *Warriors and Scribes*, 54.
95. Vazualdo, "Coca y representación."
96. UNDP, *Reflections on Drug Policy and Its Impact on Human Development*.
97. Jelsma, *UNGASS, Prospects for Treaty Reform*.
98. Kohl and Farthing, "Less than Fully Satisfactory," 61; Wolff, "Negotiating Interference," 886.

99. UNODC, *Estado Plurinacional.*
100. Spedding, "The Coca Field."
101. Conzelman, "Coca Leaf," 145.
102. Arnold and Spedding, *Mujeres en los Movimientos Sociales*, 73.
103. Spedding, *En Defensa de la Hoja de Coca*, 169.
104. Conzelman, "Coca Leaf."
105. Traditional and expansion zones under Law 1008 were poorly delineated, generating boundary conflicts on the ground.
106. Arnold and Spedding, *Mujeres en Los Movimientos Sociales*, 95.
107. Flores and Blanes, *¿Donde va el Chapare?*, 76; B Larson, *Colonialism and Agrarian Transformation*, 253–58.
108. Gill, *Peasants.*
109. Sanabria, *The Coca Boom*, 43.
110. Eastwood and Pollard, "The Development of Colonisation."
111. Blanes, *De Los Valles al Chapare.*
112. Maclean Stearman, *Yuqul: Forest Nomads*; Jabin, "Nómadas en la ciudad."
113. Grisaffi, "We are *Originarios.*"
114. Yashar, *Contesting Citizenship*, 206.
115. Farthing and Kohl, *Evo's Bolivia*, 114.
116. "Bolivia: el avance de la coca."
117. Laing, "Re-producing territory," 32–34; McNeish, "Extraction, Protest and Indigeneity."
118. Sturtevant, "Some Time From Now."
119. Ramos Salazar, "Las federaciones del trópico," 19.
120. Salazar et al., *Kawsachun Coca*, 19.
121. Laserna, "Desarrollo alternativo en Bolivia."
122. Albó, *Coripata*; Blanes, *De los Valles al Chapare.*
123. Laserna, "Information and Illegality,"127.
124. Millington, "Creating coca frontiers," 100–101; Henkel, "The Bolivian Cocaine," 55.
125. Gootenberg, *Andean Cocaine*, 274.
126. Crabtree, *The Great Tin Crash*; Dunkerley and Morales, "Crisis in Bolivia."
127. Sachs, "The Bolivian Hyperinflation," 279.
128. Sanabria, "Coca, Migration and Social Diferentiation," 91; Dunkerley, *Political Transition and Economic*, 32–39.
129. Kohl and Farthing, *Impasse in Bolivia.*
130. Crabtree, *The Great Tin Crash.*
131. Urioste, *Resistencia campesina.*
132. Grandin, *Empire's Workshop*, 202.
133. Healy, "The Cocaine Industry."

134. Sanabria, "Coca, Migration and Social Diferentiation," 92; Cortes, *Partir para quedarse*, 125–62.
135. Perez-Crespo, *Why Do People Migrate?*, 1.
136. Sanabria, "Coca, Migration and Social Diferentiation," 95.
137. Sanabria, *The Coca Boom*.
138. Dunkerley, "Bolivia at the Crossroads," 144.
139. De Franco and Godoy, "The Economic Consequences," 387; Dunkerley, "Bolivia at the Crossroads," 144.
140. Gill, *Peasants, Entrepreneurs, and Social Change*, 187.
141. Blanes, "Cocaine, Informality, and the Urban Economy."
142. Healy, "The Boom Within the Crisis."
143. Shakow, *Along the Bolivian Highway*, 69–71.
144. Painter, *Bolivia and Coca*, 41.
145. Leons and Sanabria, "Coca and Cocaine," 54.
146. Nash, "Interpreting Social Movements," 290.
147. Leons and Sanabria, "Coca and Cocaine."
148. Doria Medina, *La Economia Informal*.
149. Dunkerley, *Rebellion in the Veins*, 318–19.
150. Mesa, Gisbert, and C. Mesa, *Historia de Bolivia*, 664.
151. Gill, *Peasants, Entrepreneurs, and Social Change*, 173–94.
152. Gootenberg, "Introduction."
153. Laserna, *Las Drogas*, 4.
154. Healy, "The Boom Within the Crisis," 106–7; Gillies, "Theorising State–Narco Relations."
155. Clawson and Lee, *The Andean Cocaine Industry*.
156. In 2021 coca represented between 7 to 8 percent of gross domestic product in the agricultural sector. UNODC, *Estado Plurinacional de Bolivia: Monitoreo de cultivos de coca, 2021*.
157. In contrast to other sites along cocaine's commodity chain, this stage is not marked by serious interpersonal violence linked to the drug trade. See Grisaffi, "Why Is the Drug Trade Not Violent?," 576–99.
158. One threat to the coca economy is that drug consumption patterns are changing. In the US consumers are shifting to pot, meth, or legal opiates and demand for cocaine is declining. If this trend continues, and other countries follow suit, it could potentially spell disaster for Bolivia's coca farmers because the price of coca would drop.
159. Midgette et al., *What America's Users Spend*, xiv.
160. Gootenberg, "Shifting South."
161. Youngers and Rosin, *Drugs and Democracy*.
162. Csete et al., "Public health," 1458.
163. Albó, *Pueblos Indios en la política*, 75.

164. Conzelman, "Coca," 190; Ledebur, "Bolivia: Clear Consequences," 151.
165. Painter, *Bolivia and Coca*, 85.
166. Durand Ochoa, "Coca," 56.
167. Farthing, "Social Impacts."
168. Conzelman, "Coca Leaf," 152–53.
169. Giacoman, "Drug policy," i.
170. Brewer-Osorio, "Uniting the Opposition," 269.
171. Kohl and Farthing, "The Price of Success," 36.
172. Contreras, *La marcha histórica*, 18.
173. Ochoa, "Coca, Contention and Identity," 150.
174. Spedding, *En Defensa de la Hoja de Coca*.
175. Stippel and Serrano-Moreno, "The Coca Diplomacy."
176. Farthing and Ledebur, "The Beat Goes On."
177. The School of the Americas is now known as the Western Hemisphere Institute for Security Cooperation.
178. Gill, *School of the Americas*.
179. "Bolivian Police Arrest."
180. Kohl and Farthing, "The Price of Success," 36.
181. Grisaffi, Farthing, and Ledebur, "Integrated Development," 148.
182. Ledebur, "Bolivia: Clear Consequences"; Salazar Ortuño, *De la coca al poder*, 137–238; Spedding and Fernandez, "Testimonios."
183. Stippel and Serrano-Moreno, "The coca diplomacy," 372.
184. "The U.S. and Latin America After 9–11 and Iraq."
185. Rivera, "Coca," 24.
186. Gutierrez, *Rhythm's of Pachakuti*, 86.
187. In December of that year, an UMOPAR officer executed Casimiro Huanca—a leader of one of the Six Chapare Federations—a crime for which he was not punished. Gill, *School of the Americas*, 187.
188. Grisaffi, *Coca Yes, Cocaine No*, 43.
189. Oikonomakis, *Political Strategies*, 159.
190. Van Cott, "From Exclusion to Inclusion," 772.
191. Bradly and Millington (2008) have shown that the shift to alternative development crops led to elevated levels of deforestation
192. Marconi, *El drama de Chapare*; Quiroga, "El desarrollo alternativo"; Farthing and Kohl, "Conflicting Agendas."
193. Buxton, "Drug Control."
194. Pielemeier, *Interview with David Cohen*.
195. "Bolivian Coca."
196. "Bolivia: USAID Out."

197. UNODC, "Drug Supply."
198. Paley, *Drug War Capitalism*.
199. Gillies, "Contesting the 'War on Drugs.'"
200. Grisaffi, "From the Grassroots," 51–52.
201. García Linera, Chávez, and Costas, *Sociología de los movimientos sociales*, 396.
202. Gordillo, *Campesinos revolucionarios en Bolivia*.
203. Hylton and Thomson, *Revolutionary Horizons*, 83.
204. Brewer-Osorio, "Uniting the Opposition," 267.
205. García Linera, Chávez, and Costas, *Sociología de los movimientos sociales*, 414–37; Laserna, ed., *Empujando la Concertación*.
206. Zurita, "La organización," 89.
207. Contreras, *La marcha historica*.
208. Agreda, Rodriguez, and Conteras, *Mujeres Cocaleras*; Camacho Balderrama, "La marcha."
209. Oikonomakis, *Political Strategies*, 155; García Linera, Chávez, and Costas, *Sociología de los movimientos sociales*, 421.
210. Escóbar, *De la Revolución al Pachakuti*, 179.
211. Ledebur, "Bolivian Police Arrest."
212. Historically the COB had always been dominated by workers' interests, specifically those of miners—but the decline of the mining sector weakened their position within the organization at the same time as the massive migration of miners to the Chapare blurred traditional distinctions between peasant and worker. See Blanes and Mansilla, *La percepción social*. Thus, the COB began to take interest in the Chapare peasants and incorporated their demands. See Healy, "Political Ascent," 101–2.
213. Gutierrez Aguilar, *Rhythms of Pachakuti*, 3–27.
214. Prest, "Rough Peace," 189.
215. Oikonomakis, *Political Strategies*, 170.
216. Escóbar, *De la Revolución al Pachakuti*, 179.
217. Oikonomakis, *Political Strategies*, 182.
218. Stefanoni, *Qué hacer con los indios*, 147.
219. See Conzelman, "Coca Leaf," 159.
220. Zuazo, *¿Cómo nació el MAS?*, 38.
221. Anria, *When Movements Become Parties*, 61–97.
222. Ehrinpreis, "Green Gold, Green Hell," 219.
223. Escárzaga, "Comunidad indígena y revolución en Bolivia."
224. Ehrinpreis, "Coca Nation," 270; Ticona, Rojas, and Albó, *Votos y Wiphalas*, 42.
225. In Bolivia *indigenismo* is distinguished from *katarismo* and *indianismo* insofar as the former was a mestizo-creole movement to represent Indians while the latter were movements in which Indigenous intellectuals and activists represented themselves.

226. Albó, "From MNRistas to Kataristas to Katari."
227. Pellegrini, *Beyond Indigeneity*; Alderman, "Unpacking disavowals."
228. Yashar, *Contesting Citizenship*, 189–90.
229. Contreras, *La marcha historica*, 3.
230. Healy, "Political Ascent," 93–94.
231. Pearson, "Coca Sí," 103.
232. Gootenberg, "Cocaine Histories," 5. See also Ehrinpreis, "Coca Nation."
233. Sanabria, "Consolidating States."
234. Albó, *Movimientos y poder indígena*, 60; Ochoa, "Coca," 109.
235. Grisaffi, "We are *Originarios*. . ."; Canessa, "Todos Somos Indígenas."
236. Komadina and Geffroy, *El poder del movimiento político*, 127; Madrid, *The Rise of Ethnic Politics*.
237. Political participation increased through enshrining elements of direct democracy, indigenizing the political sphere, rewriting the constitution, nationalizing strategic economic sectors, and investing in public services. Postero, *The Indigenous State*.
238. The extent to which the MAS government's vision for development marks a break with the previous neoliberal model has been contested. See Anthias, *Limits to Decolonization*; Hope, "Losing Ground?"
239. Ledebur and Youngers, "From Conflict to Collaboration."
240. Ledebur and Youngers, "From Conflict to Collaboration."
241. The developments in Bolivia are part of a broader shift toward more progressive drug policy across Latin America—including recommendations for the creation of regulated markets for narcotic substances, amnesties, transitional justice, and greater investment in harm-reduction practices. But progress has been slow as the United States has maintained its hardline position abroad, even while relaxing drug laws at home—particularly in relation to marijuana "regulation."
242. Farthing and Ledebur, *Habeas Coca*.
243. Grisaffi, "Social Control in Bolivia."
244. Grisaffi, Farthing, and Ledebur, "Integrated Development," 143.
245. Grisaffi, "Social Control."
246. Grisaffi, Farthing, and Ledebur, "Integrated Development," 145.
247. Grisaffi, *Coca Yes, Cocaine No*, 124–25.
248. Brewer-Osorio, "Turning Over a New Leaf."
249. See also Ramos Salazar, "Nueva Ley."
250. Pellegrini, *Beyond Indigeneity*, 112–16.
251. Pellegrini, *Beyond Indigeneity*, 47–48.
252. Farthing, "Bolivia Sees Coca."
253. Farthing and Ledebur, *Habeas Coca*.
254. OAS, *Scenarios for the Drug Problem*.

255. UNDP, *Development Dimensions*, 9.
256. Grisaffi et al., "From Criminals to Citizens."
257. Mortensen and Gutierrez, "Mitigating Crime"; Ramos, Benavides, Vélez, Jauregui, and Restrepo, *Control Social de la Coca*.
258. "Principales hallazgos."
259. "Peru and Bolivia."
260. For a comprehensive account of the coup see Farthing and Becker, *Coup*.
261. Bjork-James, *Mass Protest*.
262. "Bolivia: El avance de la coca más allá del polígono 7 del Tipnis," Mongabay/El Deber, 2018, accessed March 3, 2021, https://es.mongabay.com/2018/08/bolivia-coca-poligono-7-tipnis-deforestacion/.
263. "Trump Bets on Closer Ties with Bolivia," NACLA, 2020, https://nacla.org/bolivia-trump-anez.
264. "Business as Usual? Cocaine Seizures on the Rise at Bolivia-Brazil Border," Insight Crime, 2020, accessed March 4, 2021, https://insightcrime.org/news/brief/cocaine-seizures-rise-boliviabrazil/.
265. Grisaffi, "Enacting Democracy," 1273–94.
266. Coca covered 25,500 hectares in 2019 and went up to 29,400 hectares in 2020. UNODC, *Estado Plurinacional*.
267. "Cocaine: Falling Coffee Prices Force Peru's Farmers to Cultivate Coca," The Conversation, 2021, accessed November 18, 2021, https://theconversation.com/cocaine-falling-coffee-prices-force-perus-farmers-to-cultivate-coca-154754.
268. Marston and Kennemore, "Extraction, Revolution, Plurinationalism."
269. See Buxton, "Drug Control."

THE SPECTER OF EL DORADO AND EXTRACTIVISM IN BOLIVIAN HISTORY

Myrna Santiago

Father Francisco López de Gómara, private secretary and confessor of Hernán Cortés from 1541 to 1547, recounted that when the conquistador met the emissaries Moctezuma sent to meet him in 1519, he asked them if the emperor had any gold. Upon receiving a positive reply, Cortés allegedly said: "Send me some of it, because I and my companions suffer from a disease of the heart which can be cured only with gold."[1] According to historian Roger Schlesinger, the attraction to the shiny object was instantaneous for the first Europeans who gazed upon the Arawak people of the Caribbean: "The gold ornaments that some of the natives wore around their necks attracted Columbus and his crew to the point of obsession."[2] We know that the cost of the sickness that afflicted the Spanish became "the greatest human catastrophe in history" when the European arrivals spread all sorts of real diseases among the peoples of the continent over the next 150 years.[3]

Soon enough, the metaphor of illness and cure turned into true quests for the land where gold was so abundant that the local king dusted himself with it as part of his morning toilette. Gonzalo de la Peña was the first to write about El Dorado, in 1539, when he noted that Sebastián de Benalcázar headed to the Colombian highlands looking for the fabled city.[4] Descriptions of the elusive El Dorado became commonplace in the literatures of the discovery and the conquest for the rest of the sixteenth century, inflaming the imaginations of English and Dutch explorers too.[5] Europeans scoured the continent looking for El Dorado for the next two centuries, until reality prevailed and scientifically minded writers declared it apocryphal in the mid-1700s.[6] Yet El Dorado did not die. If we see El Dorado as extractivism by another name, as the obsession with finding riches and taking them without hesitation, the legend remains as subtext for the history of Latin America as a whole.[7] As this volume attests, the specter of El Dorado haunts Bolivia. Sometimes, even, as Kevin Young tells us in the case of fossil fuels, the enthusiasm among the ruling elite at the prospect of immense riches is as palpable as it was during the Spanish colony. At other times the myth seems to linger in the background, as a cautionary tale about the perils of seeing the nation and the earth as a cash-retrieving machine.

As an outsider to Bolivian history, I found the idea of writing the history of Bolivia from the histories of six commodities and the social movements instigated by them profoundly illuminating. Land, minerals, water, rubber, fossil fuels, and coca in the expert pens of this collection of scholars decisively break the view of Bolivian history from the vantage of its great men, as the interactions between the different social groups and the country's natural resources take center stage. The traditional periodization of Bolivian history becomes inadequate while the richness of Bolivia's social movements emerges as a hallmark. The approach is truly fruitful in many ways, but I will focus on three aspects that stood out to me, coming from the northern part of the continent: (1) coverage of national geography, (2) the historical continuities highlighted by extractivism, and (3) the possibilities of alternative futures—imaginaries, if you will—implied in social movements.

The six natural resources the editors selected make the book read like a historical tour through the regions of Bolivia. Although that was not the idea the editors were pursuing, that is one result of their work. It means that for the past five hundred years, decision makers in Madrid, Lima, La Paz, and Washington, conquistadores reenacting the search for El Dorado, have subjected Bolivia's diverse ecosystems and ecologies to the minimal rewards and substantial ravages of extractive activity and attitudes. Those who inhabited such environments as well as those who migrated there in search for opportunities became actors in the expanding "geographies of capitalism," in José Orsag Molina's words, experiencing the structural and sometimes physical violence embedded in a process of territorial exploration, social dislocation, and environmental degradation that they did not choose in the first place. Thus in the first chapter Carmen Soliz traces the fundamental basis, the genesis, of extractivism in Bolivia: colonial attempts to take Indigenous land in the highlands, in the western side of the country, for the straightforward reason that this is where the silver and the population to extract it were concentrated. Conquering Europeans did not despoil Indigenous communities from their land, primarily in the highland regions of La Paz, Oruro, and Potosí, however, focusing instead on their labor force both to mine metal and grow the foodstuffs necessary to sustain the labor force, including coca. Soliz shows that appropriation of the temperate valleys of the highlands took off in the independent period and continued into the 1950s, when the plunder shifted to the vast eastern lowlands as part of a plan to push the agricultural frontier.

Rosanna Barragán demonstrates next how the mining that began during early colonial times in Potosí in the southern end of the highlands eventually expanded along the entire central cordillera. By the 1930s, hundreds of mining sites dotted the mountain range like a pox, from the eastern flank of Lake Titicaca in the north, through La Paz and into Oruro, both on the west and the east sides, moving south along the eastern side of Lake Poopó to locations to the west of historic Potosí, and meandering farther south to Uyuni and a few areas beyond. All those agglutinations constituted a geography of contamination, where heavy metals concentrated and littered the land, the water, the air, and, of course, the bodies of workers pulled from every community into the mines and the outposts of urbanization they generated. Today, lithium promises and threatens to spread the geography of extractivism into Bolivia's unique *salar* and its southernmost border with Chile and Argentina, an unhappy prospect for Bolivians who worry about their environment.

Our three other authors home in on smaller portions of territory, but together they cover the country. José Orsag Molina examines Bolivia's northernmost Amazonia and the social and economic ties that the intensity of the exploitation of rubber created to Acre and Pará in northwestern Brazil. Orsag Molina argues, in fact, that it was that extractive activity that shaped the state in Beni at the end of the nineteenth century, as the ruling elites realized that they needed to exercise effective control over the territory. While the incorporation of the northernmost rainforests into the capitalist orbit through the extraction of rubber was short-lived and gave way to cattle ranching, Bolivia's Amazonia is under scrutiny again. Orsag Molina tells us that gold companies and agribusiness have shown an interest in exploiting the region. Needless to say, both would change land and peoples in even deeper ways than rubber. Sarah T. Hines, meanwhile, looks at water struggles in the Central Andes, where the most populated valleys are located, the center of Bolivia's domestic food production. Hines focuses on Cochabamba and also La Paz-El Alto, the places where the most intense conflicts over water took place for the past five hundred years, reminding us that struggles over land have been battles over access to water even if the literature does not go there. These clashes continued into the twentieth century until they became "water wars" in the twenty-first, catching the attention of the world and, as Hines points out, contributing to the election of Bolivia's first Indigenous president, Evo Morales, in 2006.

Kevin Young brings attention to the lowlands of Santa Cruz, the southeastern borderlands of Bolivia, where fossil fuels were first found. Oil and gas raised the profile of a region already infused with major emotional significance due to the Chaco War of the 1930s. The riches of hydrocarbons in what seemed like faraway lands engendered multiple social and political contradictions that have not been resolved, even though the "Gas War" of 2006 played a crucial role in bringing the Movimiento al Socialismo to power. Political conflict intensified in the twenty-first century as Santa Cruz's local elites sought "autonomy" from the central government to keep the state's hands off hydrocarbons in that region.

Thomas Grisaffi completes the geographical breath of this volume with an examination of the Yungas in north-central Bolivia, the most important valleys for coca cultivation since pre-Hispanic times, compared with coca growing in the more recently settled Chapare district east of Cochabamba. Grisaffi documents how the Spaniards turned the coca leaf into an instrument of social control and oppression, but it was its transformation into the raw material for cocaine that turned the plant into a global commodity. Incurring the wrath of the United States in the twentieth century, coca then became a banned plant, the focus of an American "War on Drugs" that has inflicted great damage on the valleys by drenching the land in herbicides and systematic violence on the peasantry who have few other economic alternatives to cultivating coca.

That is what history grounded in extraction looks like in Bolivia: it leaves little national territory untouched. Although this group of scholars did not set out to prove that thesis, it emerges from their work and, as such, invites comparisons with other Latin American countries. Has extractivism poked and invaded all the territories, geographies, ecologies, and landscapes of "Our America," as José Martí called it, or is this a phenomenon sui generis to Bolivia? Can we say the same thing of Bolivia's neighbors, Peru and Chile, with similar centuries-long histories of mining? And what about countries like Argentina or the Central American nations where plantation and hacienda agriculture for export has been the dominant economic activity for much of their history too? As scholars re-examine agriculture and find it extractivist in nature—similar to the way that Grisaffi's contribution points to in this volume—a whole host of other questions arise, in fact.[8] Latin America is left to consider what centuries of extractivism means in terms of environmental degradation, contamination of land, water, air, and bodies, in addition to the possibilities of remediation and, ultimately, resilience in equity for the long term. How can Bolivians repair the social, political, and environmental damage that extractivism has wrought to so much of the country, now under the gun of climate change not of their own doing? Clearly, the challenges elucidated by this collection are enormous.

What the authors did intend to do is to demonstrate that extractivism has been a constant in Bolivia's history since the conquest. Taking with wanton abandon—a simplistic definition of "extractivism" compared to more formal ones of appropriation and commodification of nature and human beings and their labor—jumps off these pages. The essays show that extractivism survived, adapted, even thrived through the great upheavals in Bolivia's history: from colonialism to independence; through capitalism and social revolutions; through liberalism, revolution, neoliberalism, socialism, and back. The historical continuities across economic and political systems and ideologies are striking indeed, especially because Bolivia has two moments in the twentieth century where there were promises and possibilities of alternative praxis: the 1952 revolution and the Movimiento al Socialimo (MAS), in power from 2006 to the present (with the exception of 2019).[9] What happened?

Collectively, the authors in this volume make evident that the 1952 revolution made a difference in people's lives, but not in escaping the extractivist mode. A revolution in the classic tradition of changing the world for workers and peasants, the 1952 revolutionary government made significant changes in land reform, water access, working conditions in the mines, and the quota of power miners could exercise in the country's most important economic sector. The revolution also expanded the franchise to universal suffrage, including women who now had the right to express themselves at the voting booth to complement their active participation in social mobilizations.

Soliz, Hines, and Grisaffi show that the Movimiento Nacional Revolucionario broke the back of the latifundio that had grown on the altiplano and the valleys as a result of the Republican disentailment law of 1874 that annihilated communal lands in favor of individual private property. The MNR redistributed that land among the peasantry in La Paz, Oruro, Potosí, Cochabamba, Tarija, and Chuquisaca, at the same time that it dismantled various forced labor schemes that had been critical to the hacienda. Clamor for water had begun in earnest in the 1940s, so the MNR had to take access to water into account when they forged the 1953 land reform law. Thus, those communities that gained land also gained water, which went from being considered an "accessory" to being a necessity for effective land tenure. Farmers, ranchers, and consumers thus won greater access to water under the revolutionary government. A shift in coca production took place as a result of these reforms as well. Grisaffi explains how breaking up the hacienda system in the Yungas meant that the peasantry took over cultivation of the coca leaf, giving birth to a strong movement of small producers. They were to play a very important role in the twenty-first century when they would stage a "coca war."

The nationalization of the tin mines and the oil industry deepened the preference for workers and peasants embedded in the 1952 revolution, as Barragán and Young demonstrate. Miners were the driving force behind the revolution, so it is no great surprise that they should be its beneficiaries. Immediate benefits for miners included growth in employment and improved working conditions. Most importantly, though, were the gains the organized miners made in exercising control over the industry itself; that is, tangible political power on the shop floor and in the country both. In the fossil fuel sector, nationalization had come earlier, in 1937 and 1938, on the heels of the Chaco War. As would be the case with lithium in the twenty-first century, oil gave rise to dreams reminiscent of El Dorado as governing elites showed unbridled enthusiasm for oil extraction, pinning their hopes on the national oil company, Yacimientos Petrolíferos Fiscales Bolivianos, to resolve the country's problems in very explicit ways, as Young details. The earnings from fossil fuels were meant for investment in education, health care, housing, and other social benefits, a complete shift from all the profits going to foreign oil companies. To the degree possible, the YPFB delivered. But as all the authors agree, the good times did not last.

The 1952 revolution was not able to break Bolivia free from extractivism. Contradictions plagued the policies the MNR implemented. Land reform and water access were limited and their benefits unevenly distributed. Certain populations and regions did not experience the reforms, particularly the eastern lowlands. Water reform generated a demand for the damming of rivers and other practices that turned out to be environmentally unsound in the long run. The tin mines the government nationalized were in serious decline and required a level of investment the state could not afford. Likewise, the YPFB lacked the necessary resources to fulfill its promises. Furthermore, the MNR felt compelled to acquiesce to American demands, including approving the 1955 petroleum law, which was "Made in the USA." At the same time, leaning on the extractive economy meant that the revolutionary government ignored the more challenging issues of deep structural reform in Bolivian society—a phenomenon that happened in Mexico certainly, after the nationalization of oil. Ultimately, our authors argue convincingly, the revolution failed to challenge the model of development itself, chaining the state and the nation to extractivism further.

Perhaps one can argue that the best that the revolutionary government was able to do was to articulate an idea and a practice of extraction for the common good. That was certainly the case for land reform and mining. But that notion could apply to other commodities, the other "commodified natures," addressed in this volume, depending on the period examined. Foreign companies and national elites had to make room for workers and peasants and small farmers at least for a moment in history. The wealth that Bolivia's nature represented could not only go to the rich. But as brief as that moment was, it justified people's movements well after a military dictatorship ended the MNR experiment in 1964. The fact that the military did not undo land reform, for instance, points to the strength of civil organizations and the fact that the men with guns needed the peasantry on their side to stay in power. Hines's chapter unequivocally shows, for instance, that people's belief in the use of natural resources for the common good detonated the "water wars" that followed the neoliberal government decision to privatize water in the 1980s. The same applies to fossil fuels. Young relates that nationalization of oil companies remained a viable idea even within the military, which acted against Gulf Oil in 1969 to try to satisfy a militant social movement. Eventually a new movement critical of neoliberal government policies that privatized fossil fuels led to the 2003 "gas war" that did its part to lead Bolivians to the second moment in modern Bolivian history when the dream of alternatives to a tired El Dorado imaginary held sway.

The Movimiento al Socialismo in power was the second moment in Bolivia's national history where extractivism could have been ditched. Our authors document the core of the changes that did take place during the time the MAS governed: a shift in discourse combined with a flurry of new legislation, including constitutional principles, and the development of some infrastructure. The discourse became anti-imperialist and nationalist as it had been in 1952, but now it had a pronounced pro-environmentalist and pro-Indigenous tilt, keeping up with the emergence of strong Indigenous identities that had not been articulated in 1952. Likewise, the MAS spoke about "Vivir Bien" as an idea that took ecology into account, in contrast to capitalist consumerism, at the very least. The MAS also promised to roll back privatization and to make operational community participation. The latter pointed to strengthening democracy and alternatives to extractivism if carried out. Hines makes clear that such was the case in the debates on control over water, for instance.

On the legal front, the changes were wide-ranging. A new round of agrarian reform in 2006 gave *colonos*, Indigenous communities, and peasant farmers access to land still controlled by latifundistas (although these three actors did have conflicting claims as Soliz notes). Article 33 of the new constitution established the right to a livable environment that should be sustainable for the long run. The 2010 legislation that granted rights to Mother Earth (Pachamama) caught the attention of the world, just as Bolivia successfully bade the United Nations to declare water a human right, which happened that same year. Within the legal changes, the hydrocarbon sector saw a major shift in regard to who would gain from its exploitation. The government imposed the highest tax or royalty rates ever on gas production, in addition to giving YPFB more control over commercialization and business decisions. In addition, the MAS government gave legal protection to coca cultivation and won an exemption from draconian anti-drug policies for coca at the UN, which, in turn, led to the lowering of violence in the "war on drugs" and a "best practice" label from the OAS on the question of coca farming.

Legal changes allowed the Bolivian state to build some infrastructure. The MAS government, for instance, returned the wealth it captured from hydrocarbons back to the population as direct cash payments to vulnerable populations: mothers, the elderly, and families with children. One could make the case that this signified a Bolivian version of Brazil's "zero fome" program carried out when the Workers' Party was in power, at least, or that it might have been a late echo of the welfare state experienced in other countries, at best. The state also used those earnings on projects: a hydroelectric plant, road construction, railways, cable car transport in La Paz, and upgrades to the two refineries that supply the country's oil needs.[10] Social spending indeed lifted a significant portion of Bolivians out of poverty. The much maligned "resource nationalism" yielded concrete results as a means for poverty reduction in the hands of a socially minded government. It also effectively defeated, as Young explains, right-wing demands for "autonomy" in the lowlands that would have kept gas fields and their wealth totally out of the hands of the state. Thus, the MAS did use extraction for the common good. And that is as far as it went.

The MAS could not break free from extractivism. On the contrary, Young tells us that the MAS government was open to deepening the extractive economy by considering fracking, a risky technology that has caused great environmental harm and grave health problems among populations subjected to it in the United States. The MAS was conscious, of course, of Bolivia's historic role as solely a provider of raw materials for the metropolises of the world and tried to move to the next stage in the traditional pattern of capitalist modernization: industrialization. Thus, the MAS government built the first petrochemical plants in the country, in a kind of very late program of state-led import substitution industrialization, as Mexico had done with its own state oil company.

Amplifying that model of development was the intent as well when lithium entered the picture. This was no El Dorado mirage, however. In the twenty-first century, the government's assessment was much more sober about the pitfalls of extractivism, even within the MAS. A treasure like lithium could not be simply taken and sold abroad and leave nothing but contaminated holes behind, like so many puncture wounds on the face of Pachamama. At the very least, Evo Morales's government hoped that lithium would be industrialized in Bolivia and the state would capture all that added value. Certainly that was the impression that Vice President Alvaro García Linera left before the audience who heard him speak at the Latin American Studies Association conference in 2016, as I recall from listening to him then. The contradictions of MAS governing were blatant on all fronts. The state-run mines under the Morales government, for instance, had to coexist with transnational mining companies and the small size, independent cooperatives—without placing any effective breaks on the environmental devastation that they signified.

Reality is difficult and complicated as every one of our authors points out. Having gained a little room for political maneuvering and redistribution of wealth through its control of hydrocarbon royalties and facing ferocious opposition from the right on every proposal and project, the MAS ultimately resigned itself to "neo-extractivism," to Margaret Thatcher's dictum that "there is no alternative" to savage capitalism. The list of MAS shortcomings is long. The latifundio increased in the lowlands. Soybean extractivism razed forests. The state loosened logging controls and approved a road through the Isiboro Sécure Indigenous Territoy and National Park in Beni. The Tariquía National Flora and Fauna Reserve opened to hydrocarbons too, while open-pit mining spread out in Potosí. The rich paid as little in taxes as possible and the government made no demands on them to do otherwise. Without knowledge or technology, the state was at the mercy of foreign companies when it came to extracting and processing lithium, and the MAS government made ruinous deals on that front as well. We know how the story ended, with President Evo Morales fleeing for his life after a right-wing coup in 2019. Even meager redistribution attempts were too much for his neoliberal and racist adversaries. And yet. The people of Bolivia did not resign themselves to losing what they had gained by bringing the MAS to power, just like they had never resigned themselves to extractivism as the only option.

If there is something that I emphasize in my history classes to undergraduates, it is the example that ordinary Latin Americans set for us in terms of resistance and combativeness. This collection of essays adds abundant evidence to my case studies. The reservoir of courage, determination, and *espíritu de lucha* (roughly, "fighting spirit") in Bolivians is at least as rich as the richest silver veins and as deep as the deepest hydrocarbons. Five hundred years of colonialism, capitalism, and imperialism have not blunted that spirit. On the contrary, to wit the population returned the MAS to power in October 2020 in a landslide election after the 2019 coup and its brutal repression of popular protests. As this volume demonstrates, Bolivia's social movements have been heterogeneous, diverse, and creative over the course of history. They have involved ample sectors of Bolivian society, including mine workers, *k'ajchas*, peasant producers, labor unions, urban neighborhood organizations, *piqueros*, women, Indigenous groups, colonos, *cocaleros*, and at times radical students and "petty bourgeois" allies.[11] They have been active across the national territory, and they have used every tactic available to them. Although they are partial to direct action—blockading roads, organizing strikes, marching for miles and miles and days and days, going on hunger strikes, taking over haciendas, taking over a slow water project, organizing payment strikes, protest caravans, occupying government offices, and mobilizing the entire country—they have also used the courts and have not shied from the electoral path to make their claims on the state and propose alternatives to oppression and marginalization.

As a whole, Bolivia's social movements have achieved significant legal victories. Each chapter in this book documents the gains different or overlapping movements have made in the areas of land reform, access to water, constitutional recognition of collective rights and prior consultation, labor codes, international conventions, local control of processes, grassroots democracy, and, of course, the nationalization of extractive industries. Time and time again, the common people of Bolivia stopped bad things from happening, like privatizing water or giving away lithium for a song. All those victories happened because Bolivians mobilized successfully, even when the triumphs did not go far enough, even when the enforcement of the law was weak or nonexistent, the implementation of programs was short-lived or inadequate, or the changes were simply discursive. To the degree that change that favors the poor and the dispossessed has taken place at all over time, the credit goes to Bolivia's social movements, and that is, at least to me, admirable.

There is no question, however, as all the authors point out, that the kind of structural change that those same social movements have demanded has not happened. Extractivism runs deep in Bolivia's past and present; it underpins the economic model of the past five hundred years, an El Dorado nightmare the country cannot seem to wake up from. More than one scholar in this volume points out that the reason for that terrible continuity is because all Bolivian governments have been afraid of revolution, even the revolutionary ones. That assertion leads to the question: What did the social movements want?

As is typical of all sociopolitical movements, Bolivian protests were often defensive in nature. That is, the list of what people were against was long: no road through the TIPNIS, no forced labor systems, no price hikes, no deep-water well drilling, no latifundio, no coca eradication, no repression, no privatizations, no gas exports, no foreign control over national resources, no neoliberalism. Yet a closer reading of this book also shows that the Bolivian people made many more affirmative, concrete demands. I identified over twenty across these six chapters. And some were, indeed, radical. They clustered around certain principles: collective rights; local and communal control, ownership, and management of the natural resources studied in this volume; priority for local economies and food sovereignty over exports; and less state and more people power. Taken together, they could point toward a wholesale reordering of society, away from extractivism and toward direct democracy, possibly posing a direct challenge to capitalism itself, certainly chasing away El Dorado from the deep history of Bolivia. At the tipping point of climate change, that would be an ambitious agenda indeed.

In "Our America," José Martí urged the nineteenth-century criollo elite to stop looking to Europe and start looking to native America and Afro-America for the future of the continent. In these chapters, the lower classes of Bolivia offer a blueprint for such alternative actionable imaginaries. Will those remarkably vibrant social movements be able to flourish and experiment? Bolivia is such a small country, after all: only twelve million people. I only know one thing for sure: If history is our guide, they will not stop trying.

NOTES

1. López de Gómara, *Cortés*, 58.
2. Schlesinger, *In the Wake of Columbus*, 2.
3. Cook, *Born to Die*, 13.
4. Rogers, *Mourning El Dorado*, 28.
5. Rogers, *Mourning El Dorado*, 1.
6. Rogers, *Mourning El Dorado*, 33.
7. See, for example, Robinson, *Gold, Oil, and Avocados*.
8. See for instance, McKay, Alonso-Fradejas, and Ezquerro-Cañete, *Agrarian Extractivism in Latin America*.
9. It is worth noting that in 2020 Bolivia entered a non-MAS interregnum that lasted one year. The current administration is aligned with the MAS Party.
10. McNelly, "The Highs and Lows of Bolivia's Rebel City," 338–40.
11. See, for example, Webber, "Rebellion to Reform in Bolivia," 23–58.

COMMODITY FRONTIERS IN HISTORICAL PERSPECTIVE

Lessons from Bolivia

Ulbe Bosma

Bolivia's landscape is one of the most diverse in the world, ranging from the high Andes mountains, the tropical Amazonian rain forests, to the dry valleys of Cochabamba. The country harbors tremendous subsoil riches and is remarkably thinly populated. And yet most people are poor and Bolivia's society is marked by sharp inequalities, particularly between the original populations and the descendants of the Spaniards, the creoles. Throughout the past five centuries the country has been utterly dependent on commodity exports such as silver, tin, lithium, rubber, natural gas, and cocaine. Over time, the production of these commodities has spread over the country, resulting in many conflicts but also in accommodations between local communities and colonial and global interests.

Lacking competitive industrial or service sectors that cater to an international market, oil, gas, metals, and soybeans dominate the exports of this country. One of the reasons that Bolivia has failed to diversify its economy might have been that it has a much smaller population than countries such as Mexico, Brazil, or Argentina. With a large internal market, it makes sense, after all, to put up tariff walls to develop an industry for domestic consumption, a policy known as import substitution. Meanwhile, Bolivia's oil, gas, minerals, and soy are all shipped off with very limited industrial processing. This severe dependency on primary products with little added value is a situation that has been termed extractivism. It is also conceptualized as unequal ecological exchange, meaning that the flows of resources go one-sidedly from poor to rich countries.

Among commodity exports, those from mining tend to constitute the most extreme form of extractivism as these now require relatively little labor and usually concentrate the processing of raw ores (or fossil fuels) in so-called core countries. This allows firms to siphon off subsoil riches unless governments insist on a fair share in the revenues and succeed in obtaining a processing capacity themselves. In spite of Bolivia having an extensive artisanal mining sector dominated by mining cooperatives, these miners' living conditions continue to be poor as their income is determined by the world market price of the raw material they can extract. Moreover, the government of Bolivia, like other governments of the Global South, has been under severe pressure to privatize mining operations, which further reduces options to stop a massive outflow of mining profits.

At present, countries such as Bolivia are subjected to the "commodity consensus," a scramble for increasingly limited resources fueled also by rising new economies, most notably China's.[1] The word "consensus" refers to the Washington consensus or neoliberal doctrine that propelled privatizations worldwide since the 1980s. In the case of Bolivia, key export sectors such as oil and gas were privatized in the 1990s and early 2000s. The stated aim was to attract foreign direct investment and technical know-how and arguably to rein in internal bureaucracies and corruption. Under President Evo Morales (2006–2019) privatization was stopped, but he could not change the fact that powerful transnational corporations monopolize the technical wherewithal to extract mineral resources. Moreover, even in those circumstances where La Paz succeeded in replacing transnational corporations with national mining companies, it was often not enough to stop the dispossession of local populations and prevent ecological destruction.

The current wave of extractivism is definitely not the first one for Bolivia. The country experienced, for instance, a true scramble for tin, oil, and rubber a century ago.[2] These "commodity rushes" were attended by death and destruction at a mass scale. This episode in turn was part of a longer story, a five-hundred-year history of exploitation and dispossession. This history reaches right back to the sixteenth century when the mines of Potosí produced sixty percent of the world's silver, greasing the wheels of globalization. It is a history of communities immensely contributing to the rise of global capitalism, without sharing in its benefits. The reader of the six contributions that make up this book can hardly avoid the impression that the people of Bolivia have struggled not to become prisoners of their natural wealth. They actually show the lived experiences of people under a regime of extractivism. This book therefore offers a pertinent invitation to reflect on how national and sub-national economies have been integrated into the global economy over the several centuries.

The essays in this book in a way revive Dependency Theory, introduced in part by Raúl Prebisch, the first secretary general of the United Nations Conference on Trade and Development (UNCTAD). UNCTAD was established in 1964 as an intergovernmental organization to promote the interests of the Global South—or in the terms of those days, "developing states"—in world trade. UNCTAD reflected opinions then widely shared among development economists that a long history of core countries imposing the role of commodity exporters upon the world's periphery had caused the latter's underdevelopment. In the age of neoliberalism this notion of structural and historically rooted impediments to the economic development of peripheral countries was discarded by the powers that be. But this book is among those studies that provide a strong argument for the validity of Dependency Theory. It does so by offering solid historical contextualization of contemporary notions of extractivism and linking it to a commodity frontiers approach (understood as processes of dynamic incorporation of new sites of natural resources and labor in the world economy). Each author applies the same long-term time frame as development economists such as Raúl Prebisch and also Celso Furtado—who traced 350 years of resource exploitation in north-eastern Brazil.[3]

Yet this book also moves well beyond classic Dependency Theory. The conceptual lens applied by its contributors shows us a deep entanglement of global systemic forces and local transformations. At the systemic level, we see that raw commodity producers are in a weak position as they are often only one among many producers facing an oligarchy of transnational corporations dominating the markets. And even when they possess very rare commodities, producer nations often lack the know-how to extract let alone to process them. At the local level, social inequalities prevent export wealth from reaching subaltern groups. In fact, it is precisely the long history of extractivism that has deepened social inequalities along ethnic lines. Extraction results in a process of triple marginalization along global, local, and historical vectors that mutually reinforce each other, posing huge challenges to governments of countries such as Bolivia to turn national natural resources into a source of wealth benefiting the entire population. Yet there is still another crucial side to the story: this book sets its gaze on different subaltern actors in Bolivia and how they have adapted, resisted, and produced counter-movements. Over time, alliances forged between different groups have challenged unequal access to resources and brought about political change.

Although not explicitly, the essays in this book also critically engage with New Institutional Economic History, and particularly with the work by Daron Acemoglu, Simon Johnson, and James A. Robinson, who distinguish between "extractive" institutions, which concentrate power and wealth in the hands of a few, versus "inclusive" institutions that secure pluralism and the rule of law while also fostering development.[4] Mines and plantations are arguably dependent upon extractive institutions to siphon off wealth from the world's periphery. As Barragán has pointed out in several of her publications, Acemoglu et al. rely too heavily on a stereotypical dichotomy between Spanish colonialism that was mercantilistic and predatory versus a North American egalitarian settler colonialism.[5] Actually, one could also argue that the same institutions that have created the legal underpinnings of market economies, which crucially fostered development in Europe and its settler colonies, turned out to be extractive in most colonized countries in the Global South. The enclosures, the commodification of land and of precious irrigation water in Bolivia's dry Cochabamba Valley, for instance, were the result of the introduction of European legal institutions, which were arguably inclusive. And what happened in Bolivia occurred throughout the Global South and actually followed patterns set in the core countries. Dispossession of rural populations happened in eighteenth-century Britain and it was perpetrated upon Native Americans in the United States, just to mention two examples.

The crux of the matter is that the dichotomy between "inclusive" and "extractive" institutions tends to obscure the mechanisms of exclusion, the creation of subalterns, so to speak, that underlie extraction or economic marginalization. In the nineteenth century, when voting rights were expanding, inclusion and exclusion were two sides of the same process. When in western European countries and the United States voting rights for men had become more or less universal at the turn of the twentieth century, exclusionist mechanisms were fully exposed. The voting rights of African Americans in the US South in the late nineteenth century, for instance, were practically nullified by Jim Crow laws, and we see in many Latin American countries at that time only a highly limited suffrage confined to a wealthy creole elite. Until 1938, Indigenous Bolivians were excluded from the franchise and only when the MNR (Movimiento Nacionalista Revolucionario) came to power in 1952 were universal voting rights established. This long struggle over voting rights highlights the exclusionist policies of the creole elites as well as, let us not forget, the resistance and resilience of the subaltern sectors. This book makes an important contribution to debates on extractivism by showing how local and subaltern counter-movements have forged institutional change and tried to make capitalism work for national development.

At this point, it is apposite to introduce the notion of a *commodity regime*, a concept developed by the Commodity Frontiers Network referred to in the introduction and of which I am a part. In this usage, a commodity regime is an analytical device used to explain how the expansion of commodity frontiers in many different parts of the world is linked to successive configurations of global capitalism. Each commodity frontier is also a site for a variety of contestations and adaptations. Through the lens of the commodity regime we can differentiate scales and distinguish successive historical phases.[6] While on the one hand the history of capitalism is marked by long-term continuities, it has also experienced systemic ruptures emanating from the core countries (e.g., the Industrial Revolution) as well as from the periphery or semi-periphery (e.g., the revolutions in Haiti, Russia, Mexico, and Bolivia). The counter-movements discussed in the contributions to this book are both local and systemic in the sense that they are part of a broader, pan–Latin American and even global pattern of resistance. What unites the approach of this book to the commodity frontiers network is that each author attributes a crucial role to disturbances and counter-movements in calling a commodity regime into crisis, which ultimately reshapes global capitalism.

As Beckert has emphasized, capitalism is a historical phenomenon with a singular adaptability.[7] Hence, moments of social and/or ecological crisis did not lead to its collapse, but to the introduction of fixes, each one creating a new capitalist commodity regime. For example, Caribbean slave rebellions at the turn of the nineteenth century did not end plantation production but led to a worldwide expansion of commodity frontiers, first in Asia and subsequently in Africa. Beckert and others argue that we have seen three, and perhaps four, successive commodity regimes. First, there was a regime before the Industrial Revolution that put its mark on the world. This Pre-Industrial Commodity Regime ran from the Iberian overseas conquests, went through a systemic crisis during the age of revolution (including the slave rebellions and wars of independence in Latin America), until it gave way to what Beckert et al. termed the Industrial Commodity Regime. This second regime started in the second half of the nineteenth century when Bolivia experienced a run on tin, oil, and rubber. It was during this time period that the Global South increasingly became the provider of commodities feeding industrial growth and urbanization in so-called core countries. Indeed, the Industrial Commodity Regime paradoxically led to a stagnation or decline in manufacturing sectors in many parts of the world. It should be noted, however, that commodity regimes are defined at the global systemic level and have different, and even contradictory, effects at different scales. The Industrial Commodity Regime produced counter-movements throughout the Global South and in the case of Bolivia an increasing involvement of its government both in facilitating and engaging with commodity production in order to shore up state revenue, culminating in a series of nationalizations.

From the mid-1980s we can discern a third regime, often dubbed as neoliberal but termed corporatist by Beckert et al. This Corporatist Commodity Regime was marked by massive expansion and concentration of big business, accompanied by privatization of resources and waves of land grabbing. Then, in the early 2000s, the tide turned toward finding a balance between state, local communities, and global corporations, which in the case of Bolivia coincided with Evo Morales becoming head of state. His government and that of his successor have faced the tremendous challenges of promoting ecological and social justice while turning the economy away from extractivism, hoping to diversify it toward industry and services. Below, I briefly discuss each of these successive commodity regimes, how they shaped Bolivia's commodity frontiers, and how they incited counter-movements. These in turn were part of broader movements in the Global South calling successive commodity regimes, and particularly the industrial and corporate regimes, into crisis. Bolivia obviously followed its own historical trajectory, but we can clearly see how its history is entangled with these successive regimes.

BOLIVIA UNDER THE PRE-INDUSTRIAL COMMODITY REGIME (EARLY 1500S TO THE MID-NINETEENTH CENTURY)

As stated in the introduction to this book, the dispossession and oppression of Bolivia's native population started five hundred years ago and was part of a continental-scale land grab. This process extended well beyond Spanish America, as the same policies were implemented in the Philippines. Facing dramatic population decline both in the Americas and the Philippines, Spanish colonizers struggled to mobilize labor and extract revenue to maintain their colonial apparatus.

Control over peasantries allowed for new systems of tributary labor and forced cultivation or, in the case of Bolivia, requisitioning labor for the silver mines of Potosí. In the Philippines, Spanish colonial authorities enforced rice and later, tobacco production. Other Europeans followed suit. In Java, Dutch colonizers requisitioned deliveries of coffee, rice, and cotton yarn, and later indigo and sugar. Since forced production relied on cooperative local heads, export agriculture and mining almost invariably strengthened the power of local communities over individual peasants and sometimes even increased communal land holdings. This was definitely the case in Bolivia, where colonial authorities respected the *pueblos reales*' remaining land and water holdings in exchange for tribute and labor payment, what anthropologist Tristan Platt has called the colonial "pact of reciprocity."

From the early nineteenth century, the notion of tributary labor ran counter to emerging liberal ideas about taxation on land, the so-called land rent, for which individual land property was however a prerequisite. This again was a trend found throughout the colonial world, as well as in parts of Europe. Just as Stamford Raffles tried in Java and Thomas Munro in Madras, Simón Bolívar strove to replace the colonial tribute system by individual property in Bolivia. In Java, imposition of the land rent on an individual basis proved to be technically impossible given the bureaucratic capabilities of the colonial state. Likewise, Bolívar's successor in Bolivia, José Antonio de Sucre, had to turn back the clock in Bolivia. Until the 1860s, Bolivia's conservatives blocked privatization (commodification) of land—which also happened in Java incidentally—primarily because the communal village was the source of labor and revenue, which sustained the colonial apparatus. Old extractive structures proved surprisingly resilient.

BOLIVIA UNDER THE INDUSTRIAL COMMODITY REGIME (MID-NINETEENTH CENTURY TO THE 1970S)

During the Industrial Commodity Regime, mining replaced tribute as Bolivia's main source of revenue. This shift in balance opened the door to several new attempts to convert communal land into individualized private property and thus integrate it in a land market.[8] The first attack on communal property came in 1866 and was based on the fiction that all land was state property—which actually harked back to the time immediately after the Spanish conquest. The government required peasant communities to buy the land, which their families had been working for centuries. A revolt forced the Bolivian government to withdraw. But in 1874, a new attempt to privatize communal land and create a land market was more successful, resulting in a sharp fall in the share of cultivable land in the hands of Indigenous peoples.

This process of "legal dispossession" occurred throughout the Global South. Here, we see the adverse effect of the imposition of the European inclusive institution of legally enshrined individual property rights on deeply unequal societies. Mexicans experienced massive dispossession during the regime of Porfirio Díaz (c. 1876–1911). Javanese communities also suffered dispossession when the Dutch colonial government introduced the 1870 Agrarian Law, which allowed western plantation firms to acquire so-called waste land for seventy-five-year terms. The grants were complemented by disowning the living space of the swiddeners, with the false argument that they were engaged in predatory forms of exploitation.[9] Land grabbing and extractivism are terms used by contemporary, action-oriented, and critical researchers, but they definitely have their historical precedents. For example, historians speak of enclosures, a term that was born in eighteenth-century England when common fields were turned into private parcels. In sum, throughout history we can see the same processes of privatization of communal land and the creation of land markets not for rural community economies but for the benefit of the nation's elites, the large landholders. Often, legalized dispossession was brute land grabbing.

Under the Industrial Commodity Regime, as Soliz and Barragán pointed out, not only land policies changed but also the processing of raw materials moved out of the country. While silver smelting in Spanish colonial times was still done in Potosí, this was neither the case with tin smelting nor with the processing of rubber and oil refining. These were all products underpinning industrial growth in the world's core countries, while they did little or nothing to promote industrialization in Bolivia.

In the late nineteenth century, Bolivia experienced a predatory frenzy of forest rubber gathering. In the Bolivian Amazonian region—at that time still at the fringes of the country's state control—rubber barons sent out hunters to kidnap workers. It was far from an exceptional situation. The same enslaving for rubber happened in Congo as well as in Kalimantan for the harvesting of gutta-percha (a tough latex substance used to insulate telegraph cables). What James Francis Warren describes for Kalimantan, namely enslavement for modern capitalism, happened at the same time in eastern Congo and in the western Amazon basin.[10]

The rubber frontiers of Southeast Asia, the Congo, and Amazonia attracted huge migration flows of hundreds of thousands of workers. Extraction also brought about the rapid spread of diseases and the threat of famines caused by the desertion of food farming. The depopulation of Bolivia's Beni Department, in the hot tropical northeast, took on such alarming proportions that the Bolivian government forbade emigration to the rubber frontier in 1882.[11] Since the Bolivian state was only feebly present at the rubber frontier, much Bolivian latex went eastward to be marketed as Brazilian rubber. The establishment of customs houses along the river was therefore a largely futile attempt to extract government revenue from the rubber boom. Predatory rubber extraction in the western Amazon did not evolve into a consolidated complex of plantations and smallholders as in Southeast Asia, and never contributed to a processing industry as happened in Singapore. Bolivian latex was (and still is) extracted, but there was no successive upgrading of rubber production as happened in postwar Malaysia.[12]

While rubber was transported out of the Amazon without yielding much revenue for the Bolivian state, the same happened with its rich tin arteries. When canned beef, vegetables, fruits, and milk became mass consumption articles, Bolivia became the tin provider for the world together with Malaysia and the Netherlands Indies. Most of the revenues ended up with the tin barons Patiño, Hochschild, and Aramayo, leaving the Bolivian state in permanent debt. This happened in spite of the fact that the world's most important tin baron, Simón Patiño, who controlled half the world's tin processing, was of humble Bolivian descent. However, his tin smelters were located in Europe and Malaysia and not in Bolivia. The crux of the matter was that the wealth of Bolivia was in private hands, as it was in British Malaya, a colony that could only balance its budget through opium sales. Only in the Netherlands Indies was a substantial portion of tin production found in the hands of the colonial government.[13]

In response to this global wave of privatized extractivism, governments began to legislate nationalization of subsoil wealth. Postcolonial Latin American states were particularly active in this regard, as they were obviously in a better position to do so than still-colonized nations like Malaysia or Indonesia. When in 1907 the first oil reserves were found in Argentina, its government decided to have the oil industry organized as state enterprise. By 1922, Argentina had developed a strong national industry with its own retail network of pump stations.[14] In 1917, Mexico's new revolutionary government reversed the Porfirian policies that had left oil reserves to the landowners and enacted that all underground wealth belonged to the state. An even bolder step was taken by the country's president, Lázaro Cárdenas (1934–1940), who nationalized all oil reserves and facilities in Mexico in 1938. This was a big deal because at that time Mexico was the second-largest oil producer after the United States. Venezuela did not embark on nationalization but introduced the 50-50 rule in 1948 for each new contract ensuring for itself half of the revenues, which became a model for other oil exporters.

Other Latin American nations likewise turned oil production and refining into state monopolies, with or without private participation. Brazilian president Getúlio Vargas established the state oil company Petrobras in 1953. And of course Latin America was part of a wider world. The Indonesian government nationalized Royal Shell in 1957 to turn it into Permina (Pertamina), which like Petrobras still functions as a state-owned company today. Less fortunate was Iran's Prime Minister Mohammad Mossadeq, who nationalized the Anglo-Iranian Oil Company in 1952. The British, who held the monopoly on oilfield technical know-how, resisted nationalization with tooth and nail, a major cause of Mossadeq's downfall.

The extractivist surge of the industrial commodity regime impelled states to take control of commodity frontiers also to preserve their political legitimacy. From the late 1930s to the 1970s, successive Bolivian governments took drastic measures to make natural resources work for the entire population. In 1937, Bolivia nationalized the possessions of Standard Oil on its territory and established the state oil company, Yacimientos Petrolíferos Fiscales Bolivianos (YPFB). Moreover, since the late 1930s, land reform had become a political project of progressive governments across Latin America. Each aimed to address the extremely skewed land distribution and to dismantle large landholdings, the latifundia. Bolivia's agrarian reform of 1953 put an end to these large landholdings, eliminated personal service of peasants to their landlords, and redistributed land among smallholders. Furthermore, after decades of struggle peasants formally regained access to water that had been hoarded by the landlords. This was again a worldwide project in post-colonial times, one even encouraged by the US Kennedy Administration that saw moderate land reform as an essential tool to restore peace and order to the countryside and neutralize an ideal breeding ground for communist insurrections.

While land reform was something international agencies might have applauded, oil nationalization was a different matter. Bolivia's government had to bow to US pressure and allow American oil companies to start exploiting Bolivian oil fields amid conditions that violated the country's interests. For most of the 1950s it was unthinkable to ignore the dictates of the United States. A frustrated Federación Sindical de Trabajadores Petroleros de Bolivia (FSTPB) called upon the government in 1958 to tighten regulations, close tax loopholes, expand exploration efforts by

Bolivia's state oil company (YPFB), and finally, to accept loan offers from the Soviet Union. Soviet-US competition, indeed, made oil producing countries across the globe less fearful of corporate America, and in the late 1960s a new wave of measures arose in Latin America, securing both production and refining in state hands.[15] In 1969, the Bolivian army staged a coup against a democratically elected government to prevent the selling out of fossil fuel riches to US companies. The result was nationalization of Gulf Oil. The year before, in 1968, the military men's Peruvian colleagues had deposed a democratically president when it became clear that his government had contracted the country's oil fields to a subsidiary of Standard Oil on highly unfavorable conditions for Peru.

THE NEOLIBERAL OR CORPORATE COMMODITY REGIME (1970S TO THE EARLY 2000S)

The first Pre-Industrial Commodity Regime was attended by massive land grabbing, which then intensified during the Industrial Commodity Regime and was moreover joined by a predatory frenzy at the world's commodity frontiers. It was heavily resisted, however; a resistance that led to a growing role of the state to use revenue from a wider range of primary goods to enhance its distributive capacities, underpinning the formation of a national identity. Nationalizations were an obvious instrument in this endeavor. But the clock was turned back during the era of neoliberalism, which aimed at reducing the state's redistributive role in the economy. As a concomitant, the pendulum swung back in favor of each country's economic elites, while neoliberal "austerity" policies produced growing inequality. This turn may have instead put a brake on economic growth, the professed objective of the neoliberal agenda. Moreover, commodity prices fell in the 1980s, forcing a further retreat of the state in favor of corporate capitalism. The Corporate Commodity Regime had begun.

During the structural adjustment policies of the 1980s and 1990s, coca leaves became one of the few natural resources bringing added value to Bolivia's economy. Raw leaves were processed into cocaine paste for export. Cocaine production in Bolivia soared during the austerity policies of the mid-1980s, when the country suffered from droughts and the tin mines became depleted. Moreover, the collapse of prices for sugar and cotton also encouraged large landholders to engage with cocaine production and export. Coca generated employment, plus investment and secondary markets. Moreover, it provided modest yet dignified livelihoods for tens of thousands of people suffering from the hardships brought on by the neoliberal economic regime. The cocaine economy boomed, employing about ten percent of the population, which not surprisingly invoked the wrath of the United States government. US officials demanded total eradication of coca and the cocaine economy. The tragedy is that this tremendous commodification of what was once a traditional habit, simply chewing coca leaves, became a cocaine industry, fueled by the Corporate Commodity Regime.

The Corporate Commodity Regime culminated in the early twenty-first century commodity boom. China's state-backed companies have emerged as the most important buyers of Bolivia's mineral resources. Their operations are no less detrimental to the social and ecological conditions of local communities than the European and American corporations or the rubber and tin barons of the nineteenth and early twentieth centuries. What we see is a repetition of the same dispossession of livelihood combined with environmental destruction. The auctioning of national resources such as water and gas in the early 2000s led to massive protests and violent clashes between the Bolivian army and protesters. The relentless privatization, and concomitant impoverishment as well as the violent suppression of the coca-cocaine economy touched every sinew of Bolivian society. It created an enormous backlash and explains how coca could be invoked as the symbol of Bolivia's national identity against Yankee arrogance. It brought the leftist government under President Evo Morales, a coca farmer, to power.

CAPITALISM AND ENVIRONMENTAL JUSTICE

Over time, various commodity frontiers emerged and disappeared, but the general trend was that more and more of Bolivia's natural resources, labor, and production became commodified. Beckert and others have pointed out that the succession of commodity regimes and the way in which capitalist expansion overcomes crises have a cumulative effect on the reach and depth of capitalist incorporation. In addition, commodity frontiers tend to spread as inkblots to other economic activities: there are no commodity frontiers without auxiliary, or "secondary" frontiers. This term was introduced by Sabrina Joseph to describe today's grain frontiers that feed the oil industry of the Gulf States, but it is pertinent to Bolivia as well.[16] Bolivia's regional hacienda economy, for instance, provided the grain for the booming sixteenth-century Potosí silver mines to feed fourteen thousand coerced migrant workers with their families. Llama raising became another secondary frontier, because without these animals, silver would never have reached Europe and Asia. The transition from coca leaf chewing as traditional habit to cocaine as major industry serves as another example. Commodity frontiers rely on local communities, which have nevertheless demonstrated their resilience in the face of liberal and neoliberal onslaughts.

Since natural resources become scarcer over time, and local communities continue to resist the sale of the nation's natural wealth, Bolivia's five hundred–plus years of struggle over commodity frontiers will only intensify. This will likely be true even if a government is committed to serve the entire nation and not just the elite. As in other nations, Bolivian elites continue to resist more equitable access to land and water. Some subaltern groups are better positioned than others to benefit from their interaction with the global capitalist economy. Conflicts of interest emerge across many sections of society, as well as between them and various branches of government. The interests of artisanal miners, local governments, and the national government may conflict as well. States usually find it difficult to draw tax revenues from small-scale artisanal miners, tending to prefer contracts with transnational corporations. This brings less income into the country overall but perhaps generates more revenue for the central government.[17] On the other hand, commodity frontiers can also unite the country against external powers such as the United States or powerful transnational corporations, even though such battles are hard-won. President Evo Morales's policies to keep lithium mines and the processing of lithium ore entirely in state hands have been faltering because of a lack of technological know-how. Moreover, the whole mining process of Bolivia's extensive lithium resources is organized in such a way that it causes maximum environmental damage, which leads to conflicts between the national government and local communities. Obviously, Bolivia is far from unique in this respect. The Environmental Justice Atlas shows that there are hundreds of conflicts over mining across the globe and that the Andean region in particular is littered with environmental conflicts surrounding the extraction of minerals.[18] As the Bolivian example amply shows, finding environmental justice in a capitalist world dominated by the Corporate Commodity Regime is a fierce uphill battle and a tremendous global challenge.

NOTES

1. See Svampa, *Neo-Extractivism in Latin America*.
2. Cottyn, "Making Cheap Nature on High Altitude," 16.
3. Furtado, *The Economic Growth of Brazil*.
4. See Acemoglu, Johnson, and Robinson, "The Colonial Origins of Comparative Development."
5. Barragán, "Extractive Economy and Institutions?", 201–11.
6. For a more extensive discussion about the successive commodity regimes see Beckert et al., "Commodity Frontiers and the Transformation of the Global Countryside."
7. Beckert, *Empire of Cotton*, 440.

8. Platt, "Simón Bolívar, the Sun of Justice and the Amerindian Virgin," 161.
9. See Bankoff, "Coming to Terms with Nature."
10. See Warren, *The Sulu Zone.*
11. Van Melkebeke and Cardoso de Mello, "From the Amazon to the Congo Valley," 161.
12. See for instance McHale, *Rubber and the Malaysian Economy*.
13. Booth, *Colonial Legacies*, 69.
14. Sterner, "The Development of State Oil Companies in Latin America," 116.
15. Sterner, "The Development of State Oil Companies in Latin America," 119.
16. Joseph, "Introduction," 4.
17. See Verbrugge, "Undermining the State?"
18. Environmental Justice Atlas, https://ejatlas.org/.

The Struggle for Natural Resources

BIBLIOGRAPHY

INTRODUCTION

Acosta, Alberto. "Extractivism and Neoextractivism: Two Sides of the Same Curse." In *Beyond Development: Alternative Visions from Latin America*, edited by M. Lang and D. Mokrani, 61–86. Amsterdam: Transnational Institute, 2013.

———. "Aporte al debate: El extractivismo como categoría de saqueo y devastación." Accessed April 15, 2021. http://interamerica.de/wp-content/uploads/2016/09/02_fiar-Vol.-9.2-Acosta-25-33.pdf/.

Acosta, Alberto, E. Gudynas, F. Houtart, L. Macas, J. Martínez Allier, H. Ramírez Soler, and E. Siliprano. *Colonialismo del siglo XXI: Negocios extractivos y defensa del territorio en América Latina*. Barcelona: Antrazit, 2011.

Anievas, Alexander, and Kerem Nisanciougl u. *How the West Came to Rule: The Geopolitical Origins of Capitalism*. London: Pluto Press, 2015.

Bebbington, Anthony. "Underground Political Ecologies: The Second Annual Lecture of the Cultural and Political Ecology Specialty Group of the Association of American Geographers." *Geoforum* 43 (2012): 1152–62.

Bebbington, Anthony, Abdul-Gafaru Abdulai, Denise Humphreys Bebbington, Marja Hinfelaar, and Cynthia Sanborn. *Governing Extractive Industries*. Oxford: Oxford University Press, 2018.

Bebbington, Anthony, and Jeffrey Bury, eds. *Subterranean Struggles: New Dynamics of Mining, Oil and Gas in Latin America*. Texas: University of Texas Press, 2013.

Beckert, Sven, Ulbe Bosma, Mindi Schneider, and Eric Vanhaute. "Commodity Frontiers and the Transformation of the Global Countryside: A Research Agenda." *Journal of Global History* (2021), 435–50.

Bunker, Stephen G. "Exchange, and the Progressive Underdevelopment of an Extreme Periphery: The Brazilian Amazon, 1600–1980." *American Journal of Sociology* 89, no. 5 (1984): 1017–764.

Chodor, Tom. *Neoliberal Hegemony and the Pink Tide in Latin America: Breaking Up with TINA?* New York: Palgrave Macmillan, 2015.

Coney, Paul. "Reprimarization: Implications for the Environment and Development in Latin America, The Cases of Argentina and Brazil." *Review of Radical Political Economics* 48, no. 4 (2016): 553–61.

Cúneo, Martín. "Andres Soliz Rada: El presidente más habiloso para hacer daño a los países chicos de América Latina fue Lula, te metía el puñal mientras te sonreía." *Observatorio de Multinacionales en América Latina*, November 1, 2011. https://omal.info/spip.php?article590.

Cypher, J. M. "South America's Commodities Boom: Developmental Opportunity or Path Dependent Reversion?" *Canadian Journal of Development Studies* 30, nos. 3–4 (2010): 635–62.

Ellner, Steve. *Latin America's Radical Left: Challenges and Complexities of Political Power in The Twenty-First Century*. Lanham, Maryland: Rowman & Littlefield, 2014.

Ferraro, Vincent. "Dependency Theory: An Introduction." In *The Development Economics Reader*, edited by Giorgio Secondi, 58–64. London: Routledge, 2008.

Frankenhoff, Charles A. "The Prebisch Thesis: A Theory of Industrialism for Latin America." *Journal of Inter-American Studies* 4, no. 2 (1962): 185–206. www.doi.org/10.2307/165226.

Godoy, Ricardo. *Mining and Agriculture in Highland Bolivia: Ecology, History, and Commerce Among the Jukumanis*. Tucson: University of Arizona Press, 1990.

Gómez, Alicia. "Financial Sovereignty or a New Dependency? How China Is Remaking Bolivia." Asociación Ambiente y Sociedad, Inversiones Chinas en América Latina. Accessed February 2, 2022. https://nacla.org/blog/2017/08/11/financial-sovereignty-or-new-dependency-how-china-remaking-bolivia.

Gudynas, Eduardo. "Development Alternatives in Bolivia: The Impulse, the Resistance, and the Restoration." *NACLA Report on the Americas* 46, no. 1 (2013): 22–26.

———. "Neo-Extractivismo y crisis civilizatoria." In Guillermo Ortega, *América Latina: Avanzando hacia la construcción de alternativas*, 29–54. Asunción: BASE IS, 2017.

Harten, Sven. *The Rise of Evo Morales and the MAS*. London: Zed Books, Bloomsbury Publishing, 2010.

Hopkins, Terence, and Immanuel Wallerstein. "Commodity Chains in the World Economy Prior to 1800." *Review* 10, no. 1 (1986): 157–70.

Joseph, Sabrina, ed. *Commodity Frontiers and Global Capitalist Expansion: Social, Ecological and Political Implications from the Nineteenth Century to the Present Day*. London: Palgrave, 2019.

Kozloff, Nikolas. *Revolution! South America and the Rise of the New Left*. New York: Palgrave Macmillan, 2009.

Killoran, Sonja-McKibbin, and Anna Zalik. "Rethinking the extractive/productive binary under neoliberalism." In *The Handbook of Neoliberalism*, edited by Simon Springer, Kean Birch, and Julie MacLeavy, 537–48. New York: Routledge, 2016.

Levitsky, Steven, and Kenneth M. Roberts. *The Resurgence of the Latin American Left*. Baltimore: Johns Hopkins University Press, 2011.

Muhr, Thomas. *Counter-Globalization and Socialism in the 21st Century*. London: Routledge, 2015.

Langer, Erick. *Expecting Pears from An Elm Tree: Franciscan Missions on the Chiriguano Frontier in the heart of South America, 1830–1949*. Durham: Duke University Press, 2009.

Lee, Jonkoo. "Global Commodity Chains and Global Value Chains." *International Studies Association and Oxford University Press Encyclopedias* (2010–2017), 2–24. https://doi.org/10.1093/acrefore/9780190846626.013.201.

Marques, Leonardo. "Colonial America and Commodity History: The Plurality of times of Historical Capitalism." *Esboços: Histórias Em Contextos Globais* 28, no. 49 (2021): 772–812.

Moore, Jason. "The Modern World System as Environmental History? Ecology and the Rise of Capitalism." *Theory and Society* 32 (2003): 307–77.

———. *Capitalism in the Web of Life: Ecology and the Accumulation of Capital*. London: Verso, 2015. https://www.archivochile.com/Portada/bol_elecciones05/boleleccioneso009.pdf.

Prebisch, Raúl. "The Economic Development of Latin America, and Its principal Problems." Economic Commission for Latin America. Santiago: United Nations, 1950.

"Programa de gobierno." Movimiento al Socialismo (MAS). May 4, 2006. https://www.archivochile.com/Portada/bol_elecciones05/boleleccioneso009.pdf.

Schneider, Mindi. "Editorial Introduction." *Journal Commodity Frontier: Capitalism, Contestation and the Transformation of the Global Countryside* 1 (2020): i–iii.

Sábato, Hilda. *Republics of the New World: The Revolutionary Political Experiment in Nineteenth-Century Latin America*. Oxford: Princeton University Press, 2018.

Sanders, James. *The Vanguard of the Atlantic World: Creating Modernity, Nation, and Democracy in Nineteenth-Century Latin America*. Durham: Duke University Press, 2014.

Santiago, Myrna. *The Ecology of Oil: Environment, Labor, and the Mexican Revolution, 1900–1938*. Cambridge: Cambridge University Press: 2006.

Svampa, Maristella. "'Consenso de las commodities' y lenguaje de valoración en América Latina." *Nueva Sociedad* 244 (March–April 2013): 30–46.

———. *Las fronteras del Neo-extractivismo: Conflictos socio-ambientales, giro eco-territorial y nuevas dependencias*. Bielefeld: Bielefeld University Press, 2019.

Topik, Stevek, Carlos Marichal, and Frank Zephyr. *From Silver to Cocaine: Latin American Commodity Chains and the Building of the World Economy, 1500–2000*. Durham: Duke University Press, 2006.

Veltmeyer, Henry, and James Petras. *The New Extractivism: A Post-Neoliberal Development Model or Imperialism of the Twenty-First Century?* London: Zed Books, 2014.
Webber, Jeffrey. *The Last Day of Oppression and the First of the Same. The Politics and Economics of the New Latin American Left*. London: Pluto Press, 2017.
Webber, Jeffery R., and Barry Carr. *The New Latin American Left: Cracks in the Empire (Critical Currents in Latin American Perspective)*. Lanham: Rowman & Littlefield Publishers, 2012.

CHAPTER ONE

Newspapers

El Deber (Santa Cruz)
Página Siete (La Paz)
La Razón (La Paz)
Los Tiempos (Cochabamba)

Selected Legislation on Land

Law September 28, 1868.
Supreme Decrees 318, 319, and 320, May 1945, Ministerio de Asuntos Campesinos, *Gaceta Campesina*, no. 1 (August 1952): 38–44. Gaceta Oficial de Bolivia.
Decree-Law 3464 of Agrarian Reform, Aug. 2, 1953. Gaceta Oficial del Bolivia.
Supreme Decree 3464, 2 Aug. 1953, art. 12. Gaceta Oficial de Bolivia.
Supreme Decree 13830 and 12401, signed June 1976.
Supreme Decree 22609, 24 Sept. 1990. Gaceta Oficial de Bolivia.
Supreme Decree 22610, 24 Sept. 1990. Gaceta Oficial de Bolivia.
Supreme Decree 22611, 24 Sept. 1990. Gaceta Oficial de Bolivia.
ILO 169 Convention on Indigenous and Tribal Peoples Convention, June 1989.
Supreme Decree 23331, November 24, 1992. Gaceta Oficial de Bolivia.
Law 3545 de Reconducción Comunitaria November 28, 2006. Gaceta Oficial de Bolivia.
Decree 727, Dec. 6, 2010, Gaceta Oficial del Bolivia.
Constitución Política del Estado, approved Feb. 7, 2009, article 395.
Decree-Law 3973, July 10, 2019.
Law 337, Jan. 11, 2013, Ley de Apoyo a la Producción de Alimentos y Restitución de Bosques.
Law 741, Sept. 29, 2015.
Law 952, May 26, 2017.

Published Works Cited

Albó, Xavier. *Achacachi: Medio siglo de lucha campesina*. La Paz: Centro de Investigación y Promoción del Campesinado, 1979.

———. "Andean People in the Twentieth Century." In *The Cambridge History of the Native Peoples of the Americas*, vol. 3, part 2, edited by Frank Salomon and Stuart B. Schwartz, 756–872. Cambridge: Cambridge University Press, 2008.

———. *¿Bodas de plata? O, réquiem por una reforma agraria*. La Paz: Centro de Investigación y Promocion del Campesinado, 1979.

———. "Etnias y pueblos originarios: Diversidad etnica cultural y linguística." In *Bolivia en el siglo XX. La formación de la Bolivia contemporánea*, edited by Fernando Campero, 451–82. La Paz: Harvard Club Bolivia, 1999.

———. "From MNRristas to Kataristas to Katari." In *Resistance, Rebellion, and Consciousness in the Andean Peasant World, 18th to 20th Centuries*, edited by Steve Stern, 379–419. Madison: University of Wisconsin Press, 1987.

Antezana Ergueta, Luis, and Hugo Romero Bedregal. *Historia de los sindicatos campesinos: Un proceso de integración en Bolivia*. La Paz: Consejo Nacional de Reforma Agraria, Departamento de Investigaciones Sociales, 1973.

Barragán, Rossana. *Asambleas constituyentes: Ciudadanía y elecciones, convenciones y debates 1825–1971*. La Paz: Muela del Diablo Editores, 2006.

———. "Los títulos de la corona de España de los indígenas. Para una historia de las representaciones políticas, presiones y negociaciones entre Cádiz y la república liberal." *Boletín Americanista* 65 (2012): 15–37.

Becker, Marc. "The Stormy Relations between Rafael Correa and Social Movements in Ecuador." *Latin American Perspectives* 40, no. 3 (May 2013): 43–62.

Bridikhina, Eugenia, Silvia Arze, Ximena Medinacelli, and Pablo Quisbert. *Bolivia, su historia: La experiencia colonial en Charcas s. XVI-XVII*, Vol. 2. La Paz: Plural, 2015.

Calla, Ricardo, and Ramiro Molina R. "Los pueblos indígenas y la construcción de una sociedad plural." In *Movimientos indígenas y pactos de género*, 13–38. La Paz: Programa de Naciones Unidas, 2000.

Chirif, Alberto. *La normativa sobre territorios indígenas y su implementación en Bolivia*. Quito: Cooperación Alemana, 2014.

Choque Canqui, Roberto. "República de indios y república de blancos." *Diálogo andino* 49, (March 2016): 249–59. https://dx.doi.org/10.4067/S0719-26812016000100024, 250.

Choque Canqui, Roberto, and Esteban Ticona Alejo. *Sublevación y masacre de Jesús de Machaqa de 1921*. La Paz: Diálogos, 1998.

Colque Fernández, Gonzalo, Efraín Tinta, and Esteban Sanjinés. *Segunda reforma agraria: Una historia que incomoda*. La Paz: Fundación Tierra, 2016.

Condori Chura, Leandro, and Esteban Ticona Alejo. *El escribano de los caciques apoderados: Kasikinakan purirarunakan qillqiripa*. La Paz: Hisbol, 1992.

Easterling, Stuart. *The Mexican Revolution: A Short History, 1910–1920*. Chicago: Haymarket Books, 2012.

Eaton, Ken. *Territory and Ideology in Latin America, Policy Conflicts between National and Subnational Governments*. Oxford: Oxford University Press, 2017.

Fundación Tierra. *Reconfigurando territorios, reforma agraria, control territorial y gobiernos indígenas en Bolivia*. La Paz: Fundación Tierra, 2010.

García Linera, Álvaro. *Geopolítica de la Amazonía: Poder Hacendal patromonial y acumulación capitalista*. La Paz: Vicepresidencia del Estado Plurinacional, 2012.

Gotkowitz, Laura. *A Revolution for Our Rights: Indigenous Struggles for Land and Justice in Bolivia, 1880–1952*. Durham, NC: Duke University Press, 2008.

Grieshaber, Erwin P. "Survival of Indian Communities in Nineteenth-Century Bolivia: A Regional Comparison." *Journal of Latin American Studies* 12, no. 2 (November 1980): 223–69.

Hylton, Forrest. "Tierra Común: Caciques, artesanos, e intelectuales radicales y la rebelión de Chayanta." In *Ya es otro tiempos el presente: Cuatro momentos de insurgencia*, edited by Forrest Hylton, Félix Patzi, Sergio Serulnikov, and Sinclair Thomson. La Paz: Muela del Diablo, 2003: 127–87.

Klarén, Peter F. *Peru: Society and Nationhood in the Andes*. New York: Oxford University Press, 2000.

Klein, Herbert S. *A Concise History of Bolivia*. Cambridge: Cambridge University Press, 2011.

———. *Orígenes de la revolución nacional boliviana: La crisis de la generación del Chaco*. Mexico City: Editorial Grijalbo, 1968.

———. "'Social Constitutionalism' in Latin America: The Bolivian Experience of 1938." *The Americas* 22, no. 3 (January 1966): 258–76.

Langer, Erick. *Economic Change and Rural Resistance in Southern Bolivia, 1880–1930*. Stanford, CA: Stanford University Press, 1989.

Larson, Brooke Larson. *Trials of Nation Making: Liberalism, Race, and Ethnicity in the Andes, 1810–1910*. Cambridge: Cambridge University Press, 2008.

Lavaud, Jean Pierre. *El embrollo boliviano: Turbulencias sociales y desplazamientos políticos, 1952–1982*. Lima: Instituto de Estudios Francés, 1998.

Loayza, Román. "La visión de un diputado campesino." *Revista Umbrales* 9 (May 2001): 50–55.

Lora, Guillermo. *Historia del movimiento obrero boliviano*, Vol. 4. La Paz-Cochabamba: Los Amigos del Libro, 1980.

Malloy, James. *Bolivia: The Uncompleted Revolution*. Pittsburgh, PA: University of Pittsburgh Press, 1970.

Malloy, James, and Richard S. Thorn. *Beyond the Revolution: Bolivia since 1952*. Pittsburgh, PA: University of Pittsburgh Press, 1971.

Mamani, Carlos, Esteban Ticona Alejo, and Leandro Condori Chura. *El escribano de los caciques apoderados*. La Paz: Hisbol/Taller de Historia Oral Andina, 1993.

Mariátegui, José Carlos. *Seven Interpretive Essays on Peruvian Reality*. Austin: University of Texas Press, 1971.

McCreery, David J. "Coffee and Class: The Structure of Development in Liberal Guatemala." *Hispanic Historical American Review* 56, no. 3 (August 1976): 438–60.

Ministerio de Asuntos Campesinos y Agropecuarios, Instituto Nacional de Estadística, Organización de las Naciones Unidas para la Agricultura y la Alimentación. *Censo Agropecuario 1950*. La Paz: Instituto Nacional de Estadística, 1985.

Peloso, Vincent C., and Barbara A. Tenenbaum. *Liberals Politics and Power: State Formation in Nineteenth-Century Latin America*. Athens: University of Georgia Press, 1996.

Piel, Jean. *Capitalismo agrario en el Perú*. Lima: Institut Français d'Etudes Andines, 2014.

Platt, Tristan. "The Andean Experience of Bolivian Liberalism, 1825–1900s." In *Resistance, Rebellion, and Consciousness in the Andean Peasant World, 18th to 20th Centuries*, edited by Steve Stern, 280–326. Madison: University of Wisconsin Press, 1987.

———. *Estado boliviano y ayllu andino: Tierra y tributo en el norte de Potosí*. Lima: Instituto de Estudios Peruanos, 1982.

———. "Simón Bolívar, the Sun of Justice and the Amerindian Virgin: Andean Conceptions of the Patria in Nineteenth-Century Potosí." *Journal of Latin American Studies* 25 (1993), 159-85.

Postero, Nancy. *The Indigenous State: Race, Politics, and Performance in Plurinational Bolivia*. Oakland, University of California Press, 2017.

———. *Now We Are Citizens*. Stanford: Stanford University Press, 2006.

"Pronunciamiento ante el tráfico de tierras en la gestión de Jeanine Áñez." Fundación Tierra, November 3, 2020. https://ftierra.org/index.php/tema/tierra-territorio/964-pronunciamiento-2020-ante-el-trafico-de-tierras-en-la-gestion-de-jeanine-anez.

Ramírez, Shirley Orozco, Álvaro García Linera, and Pablo Stefanoni. *No somos juguete de nadie: Análisis de la relación de movimientos sociales, recursos naturales, estado y descentralización*. Cochabamba: Swiss National Centre of Competence North-South, JACS-Sud América, 2006.

Rivera Cusicanqui, Silvia. "La expansion del latifundio en el altiplano boliviano. Elementos para la caractarización de una oligarquía regional." *Avances* 2 (1978): 95–117.

Robins, Nicholas A. *Mercury, Mining, and Empire: The Human and Ecological Cost of Colonial Silver Mining in the Andes*. Bloomington: Indiana University Press, 2011.

Robins, Nicholas A. *Santa Bárbara's Legacy: An Environmental History of Huancavelica, Peru*. Leiden: Brill, 2017.

Saignes, Thierry. "Caciques, Tribute and Migration in the Southern Andes: Indian Society and the 17th Century Colonial Order (Audencia de Charcas)." London: University of London, 1985.

Sanchez-Albornóz, Nicolás. *Indios y tributos en el Alto Perú*. Lima: Instituto de Estudios Peruanos, 1978.

Sandóval, Carmen Dunia. *Santa Cruz: Economía y poder, 1952–1993*. La Paz: PIEB, 2003.

Schelchkov, Andrey. "En los umbrales del socialismo boliviano: Tristán Marof y la Tercera Internacional Comunista," *Revista Izquierdas* 3, no. 5 (July 2009). https://www.redalyc.org/pdf/3601/360133445005.pdf.

Semo, Enrique. *Historia del capitalismo en México: Los orígenes 1521–1763*. Mexico City: Era, 1973.

Soliz, Carmen. "Agrarian Reform in Bolivia in the 20th and 21st Centuries." *Oxford Research Encyclopedia of Latin American History*. August 28, 2018. https://oxfordre.com/latinamericanhistory/display/10.1093/acrefore/9780199366439.001.0001/acrefore-9780199366439-e-508?rskey=waJlAW&result=1.

———. *Fields of Revolution: Agrarian Reform and Rural State Formation in Bolivia, 1935–1964*. Pittsburgh, PA: University of Pittsburgh Press, 2021.

———. "'Land to the Original Owners': Rethinking the Indigenous Politics of the Bolivian Agrarian Reform." *Hispanic American Historical Review* 97, no. 2 (2017): 259–96.

Soruco, Ximena, Wilfredo Plata, and Gustavo Medeiros. *Los barones del oriente: El poder en Santa Cruz ayer y hoy*. Santa Cruz: Fundación Tierra, 2008.

Taller de Historia Oral Andina. *El indio Santos Marka T'ula: Cacique principal de los ayllus de Qallapa y apoderado general de las comunidades originarias de la República*. La Paz: Taller de Historia Oral Andina, 1988.

Thiesenhusen, Wiliam C. *Broken Promises: Agrarian Reform and the Latin American Campesino*. Boulder: Westview Press, 1995.

Urioste, Miguel, Rossana Barragán, and Gonzalo Colque. *Los nietos de la reforma agraria: Acceso, tenencia y uso de la tierra en el altiplano de Bolivia*. La Paz: Fundación Tierra, 2007.

Vergara-Camus, Leandro, and Cristóbal Kay. *Agronegocio, campesinos, estado y gobiernos de izquierda en América Latina: Introducción y Reflexiones Teóricas*. Buenos Aires: CLACSO, 2018.

Wagner, Lucrecia S. "Defendiendo la biodiversidad: Resistencia a megaproyectos en América Latina." *Ecología Política* 46 (July 2013), 80–84.

Webber, Jeffery. "Evo Morales, El 'Transformismo' y la consolidación del capitalismo agrario en Bolivia." In *La cuestión agraria y los gobiernos de izquierda en América Latina: Campesinos, agronegocio y neodesarrollismo,* edited by Kay Cristóbal. Buenos Aires: Consejo Latinoamericano de Ciencias Sociales, 2018.

Wesz, Valdemar João. "Expansión de la soya en el Cono Sur y sus impactos en Brasil," *Memoria: Conferencia. Repensando El Modelo Agrario Boliviano.* La Paz: Fundación Tierra, 2017.

CHAPTER TWO

Primary published and unpublished sources

Acosta, Joseph de. *Natural and Moral History of the Indies.* Edited by Jane E. Mangan. Durham: Duke University Press, [1590] 2002.

Arzáns de Orsúa y Vela, Bartolomé. *Historia de la Villa Imperial de Potosí.* Edited by Lewis Hanke and Gunnar Mendoza L. 3 vols. Providence: Brown University Press, 1965.

Bolivia, Ministerio de Minería y Metalurgia. *Anuario Estadístico y coyuntura del sector minero metalúrgico* (La Paz, 2016). http://www.mineria.gob.bo/revista/pdf/20170817-10-14-39.pdf.

Bolivia, Convención Nacional. *Redactor de la Convención de 1938*, T.I. Bolivia: 1938.

Capoche, Luis. *Relación general de la villa imperial de Potosí: Un capítulo inédito en la historia del Nuevo Mundo.* Madrid: Biblioteca de Autores Españoles, Atlas, 1959.

Coeur d'Alene Mines. *San Bartolomé Technical Report*, January 1, 2013. Prepared by Donald J. Birak, Senior Vice President, and Keith R. Blair, Manager.

———. *San Bartolomé Technical Report*, January 1, 2015.

Coeur Mining. *Technical Report for the San Bartolomé Mine, Potosí, Bolivia.* NI 43–101. Prepared by W. David Tyler and Raul Mondragon, 2015.

———. *2014 Annual Report.* Moving Forward. 2014.

Estatutos del sindicato de Ckacchas libres y Palliras de Potosí. Potosí: Imprenta y Papelería Nacional. 1940.

Moritz Hochschild Collection 1881–2002. Memoria del consejo de Administración y Balance General al 31 de Diciembre 1952. Cia. Huanchaca de Bolivia. S.A. 81 (Valparaíso: Imprenta, Valparaíso), in Moritz Hochschild Collection 1881–2002.

Recopilación de leyes de los reinos de las Indias, Vol. 2. Madrid: Imprenta de la viuda de don Joaquín Ibarra, 1791.

Toledo, Francisco de. *Disposiciones gubernativas para el Virreinato del Perú, 1569–1574*. CSIC: Sevilla, 1986.

Toledo, Francisco de. "Ordenanzas de Minas" In *Relaciones de los Virreyes y Audiencias que han gobernado el Perú. T. I. Memorial y Ordenanzas de Francisco de Toledo*, 267–348. Lima: Imprenta del Estado, 1867.

Weiß, Sandra. "Litio: acuerdo con Alemania 'era desventajoso para Bolivia.'" Deutsche Welle. Accessed July 3, 2023. https://p.dw.com/p/3jp5J.

Newspapers

Alas: October 11, 1938; February 14, 1937; July 4, 1937

Bocamina

La Calle: March 21, 1937; June 14, 1938

La Izquierda Diario: July 23, 2015. "Bolivia: Crece la tensión por el conflicto en Potosí"

El Pueblo: May 23, 2021. "Litio: el gran salto boliviano a la industrialización"

United States Congressional Record. Senate, 88 Congress. Vol 109 Part 15. 20457–63, 20463. https://www.govinfo.gov/content/pkg/GPO-CRECB-1967-pt15/pdf/GPO-CRECB-1967-pt15-6-1.pdf.

Published Works Cited

Abercrombie, Thomas. "Q'aqchas and La Plebe in rebellion: Carnival vs. Lent in 18th. Century Potosí." *Journal of Latin American Anthropology* 2, no. 1 (1996): 62–111.

Absi, Pascale. "Q'aqchas y obreros: apuntes sobre la organización del trabajo minero." *Anuario Estudios Bolivianos Archivísticos y Bibliográficos* 20 (2014): 221–46.

Albarracín, Juan. *El poder financiero de la gran minería boliviana (Los Republicanos en la Historia de Bolivia* 2). La Paz: Akapana, 1995.

Alec, Lucas. "Lithium Market Update: Elevated Prices Are Creating Favorable Dynamics for Miners." Global X. November 4, 2022. https://www.globalxetfs.com/lithium-market-update-elevated-prices-are-creating-favorable-dynamics-for-miners/.

Almaraz, Sergio. *El Poder y la caída: El estaño en la historia de Bolivia*. Cochabamba-La Paz: Los Amigos del Libro, 1967.

Anderson, Steven T. "The Mineral Industry of Bolivia." In *2008 Minerals Yearbook*. USGS. US Geological Survey Minerals, 2010.

Ayub, Mahmood Ali, and Hideo Hashimoto. *The Economics of Tin Mining in Bolivia*. Washington, DC: A World Bank Publication, 1985.

Bakewell, Peter. *Miners of the Red Mountain: Indian Labor in Potosí, 1545–1650*. Albuquerque: University of New Mexico Press, 1998.

Barragán, Rossana. "Extractive economy and institutions? Technology, Labour, and Land in Potosí, the Sixteenth to the Eighteenth Century." In *Colonialism, Institutional Change and Shifts in Global Labour Relations*, edited by Karin Hofmeester and Pim de Zwart, 207–38. Amsterdam: Amsterdam University Press, 2018.

———. "Inclusions and Exclusions: From Labor Legislation in the Andean Nations to the Formation of Labor Courts in Bolivia (1900–1952)." In *Labor Justice across the Americas*, edited by M. Leon Fink and Juan Manuel Palacios, 164–90. Illinois: University of Illinois Press, 2018.

———. "K'ajchas, trapiches y plata en el cerro de Potosí en el período colonial." *Anuario: Estudios Bolivianos Archivísticos y Bibliográficos* 20 (2014): 273–320.

———. "Los k'ajchas y los proyectos de industria y nación en Bolivia." *Revista Mundos do Trabalho* 9, no. 18 (2017): 25–48. https://doi.org/10.5007/1984 9222.2017v9n18p25.

———. "Working Silver for the World: Mining Labor and Popular Economy in Colonial Potosí." *Hispanic American Historical Review* 97, no. 2 (2017): 193–222.

Barrett, Ward. "World Bullion flows, 1450–1800." In *The Rise of Merchant Empires, Long-distance Trade in the Early Modern World, 1350–1750*, edited by James D. Tracy, 224–54. Cambridge: Cambridge University Press, 1990.

Bartels, Christoph. "The Administration of Mining in Late Medieval and Early Modern Europe." In *Mining, Monies and Culture in Early Modern Societies*, edited by Nanny Kim and Keiko Nagase-Reimer, 115–30. Leiden: Brill, 2013.

Bentancor, Orlando. *The Matter of Empire: Metaphysics and Mining in Colonial Peru*. Pittsburgh: Pittsburgh Press, 2017.

Bieber, León. *Dr. Mauricio Hochschild: Empresario minero, promotor e impulsor de la inmigración judía a Bolivia*. Santa Cruz de la Sierra: El País, 2015.

Bocangel, Danilo. *Small Scale Mining in Bolivia: National Study Mining Minerals and Sustainable Development*. England: International Institute for Environment and Development and World Business Council for Sustainable Development No. 71, 2001.

Bos, Vincent, and Marie Forget. "Global Production Networks and the Lithium Industry: A Bolivian Perspective." *Geoforum* 125 (October 2021): 168–80.

Bridge, Gavin, and Erika Faigen. "Towards the Lithium-Ion Battery Production Network: Thinking beyond Mineral Supply Chains." *Energy Research & Social Science* 89 (2022): 1–19.

Buechler, Rose Marie. *Gobierno, Minería y Sociedad: Potosí y el Renacimento Borbónico, 1776–1810*, 2 vols. La Paz, 1989.

Burke, Melvin. *The Corporación Minera de Bolivia (COMIBOL) and the Triangular Plan: A Case Study in Dependency*. School of Economics Faculty Scholarship, 1987. http://digitalcommons.library.umaine.edu/eco_facpub/16.

Calla, Ricardo. "Impactos de la producción industrial del carbonato de litio y del cloruro de potasio en el salar de Uyuni." *Un presente sin futuro: El proyecto de industrialización del litio en Bolivia*. La Paz: CEDLA, 2014.

Campbell, Maeve. "In Pictures: South America's 'Lithium fields' Reveal the Dark Side of Our Electric Future," Euronews. November 21, 2022. https://www.euronews.com/green/2022/02/01/south-america-s-lithium-fields-reveal-the-dark-side-of-our-electric-future.

Carrasco, Manuel. *Simón I. Patiño, un prócer industrial*. Paris: Jean Grassin Editeur, 1960.

Cherico Wanger, Thomas. "The Lithium Future—Resources, Recycling, and the Environment." *Conservation Letter* 4, no. 3 (2011): 202–6.

Cole, Jeffrey. *The Potosí Mita, 1573–1683: Compulsory Indian Labor in the Andes*. Stanford: Stanford University Press, 1985.

Contreras, Manuel. *The Bolivian Tin Mining Industry in the First Half of the Twentieth Century*. London: University of London, Institute of Latin American Studies, 1993.

———. "Debt, Taxes, and War: The Political Economy of Bolivia, c. 1920–1935." *Journal of Latin American Studies* 22, no. 2 (1990): 265–87.

———. "Mano de obra en la minería estañífera de principios de siglo." *Historia y Cultura* 8 (1985): 97–134.

———. "Simón I. Patiño Empresario: Minero, banquero y ferroviario." In *Simón I. Patiño y Albina Rodríguez: Una pareja fundadora*, edited by Michela Pentimalli, 185–215. La Paz: Fundación Simón I. Patiño, 2022.

Crabtree, John, Gavan Duffy, and Jenny Pearce. *The Great Tin Crash: Bolivia and the World Tin Market*. London: Latin American Bureau, 1987.

Fawthrop, Andres. "Lilac Solutions Attracts Major Backers for Lithium Extraction Technology." NS Energy. February 20, 2020. https://www.nsenergybusiness.com/news/lilac-solutions-lithium-funding/.

———. "Top Six Countries with the Largest Lithium Reserves in the World." NS Energy. November 19, 2020. https://www.nsenergybusiness.com/features/six-largest-lithium-reserves-world/.

Flores, Franz. "Regionalismo nacionalista: El conflicto por la explotación del salar de Uyuni en 1989." *Ecuador Debate* 105 (2018): 182–97.

Flynn, Dennis, and Arturo Giráldez. "Cycles of Silver: Global Economic Unity through the Mid-Eighteenth Century." *Journal of World History* 13, no. 2 (2002): 391–427.

Garavaglia, Juan Carlos. "Plata para el Rey: Tecnología y Producción en el Potosí colonial." In *Potosí, plata para Europa*, edited by Juan Marchena, 125–40. Sevilla: Universidad de Sevilla, 2000.

Garner, Richard. "Long-Term Silver Mining Trends in Spanish America: A Comparative Analysis of Peru and Mexico." *American Historical Review* 93, no. 4 (October 1988): 898–935.

Geddes, Charles. *Patiño: Rey del Estaño*. Madrid: AG Grupo SA, 1984.

Giraldez, Arturo. "Born with a 'Silver Spoon': The Origin of World Trade in 1571." *Journal of World History* 6, no. 2 (1995): 201–21.

Gunder Frank, André. *ReOrient: Global Economy in the Asian Age*. California: University of California Press, 1988.

Guzmán, Juan Carlos. "Introducción: Elementos para encarar el debate." *Un presente sin futuro, El proyecto de industrialización del litio en Bolivia*. La Paz: CEDLA, 2014.

Hillman, John. "The Emergence of the Tin Industry in Bolivia." *Journal of Latin American Studies* 16 (1984): 403–37.

Hollender, Rebecca, and Jim Shultz. *Bolivia and Its Lithium: Can the 'Gold of the 21st Century' Help Lift a Nation out of Poverty?* Cochabamba: A Democracy Center Special Report, 2010.

Ingulstad, Mats, Andrew Perchard, and Espen Storli. *Tin and Global Capitalism: A History of Devil's Capitalism*. London: Routledge, 2015.

Klein, Herbert. "La formación del Imperio del estaño de Patiño." *Historia Boliviana* 3, no. 2 (1983): 237–52.

Lane, Kris. *Potosí: The Silver City That Changed the World*. California: University of California Press, 2019.

López Calva, Luis Felipe. "Lithium in Latin America: A New Quest for 'El Dorado'?" UNPD. May 26, 2022. https://www.undp.org/latin-america/blog/graph-for-thought/lithium-latin-america-new-quest-el-dorado.

Lora, Guillermo. *Historia del Movimento Obrero Boliviano (1900–1923)*. Cochabamba: Los Amigos del Libro, 1969.

Malloy, James. *The Uncompleted Revolution*. Pittsburgh: University of Pittsburgh Press, 1970.

Mata P., Josep, Gerardo Zamora E., and Carlos Serrano B. "Riesgos de estabilidad física en el Cerro Rico de Potosí, patrimonio cultural de la humanidad." *Revista de Medio Ambiente Minero y Minería* 4, no. 1 (2019): 43–54.

Michard, Jocelyn. *Cooperativas mineras: Formas de organización, producción y comercialización*. Cochabamba: CEDIB, 2008.

Ministerio de Minería y Metalurgia. *Anuario Estadístico y Coyuntura del sector minero metalúrgico* (La Paz, 2016). http://www.mineria.gob.bo/revista/pdf/20170817-10-14-39.pdf.

———. *Boletín Informativo Institucional del Viceministerio de Cooperativas Mineras Año* 10, no. 11, 2021.

Mitre, Antonio. *El enigma de los hornos: La política económica de la fundición de estaño: El proceso boliviano a la luz de otras experiencias*. La Paz: Asociación Nacional de Mineros Medianos, Biblioteca Minera de Bolivia, ILDIS, 1994.

———. *Los Patriarcas de la plata: Estructura socioeconómica de la minería boliviana en el siglo XIX*. Lima: Instituto de Estudios Peruanos, 1981.

Molina Martínez, Miguel. "Legislación minera colonial en tiempos de Felipe II." In *XIII Coloquio de Historia Canario-Americana: VIII Congreso Internacional de Historia de América* (AEA), edited by Francisco Morales Padrón, 1014–29. Canarias: Cabildo Insular de Gran Canaria, 1998.

Mondaca, Gonzalo. "El litio en Bolivia: Un cambio radical de tecnología y mucha incertidumbre." La Paz: CEDIB, 2021. https://cedib.org/publicaciones/tecnologialitioenbolivia/.

Montenegro, Juan Carlos. "El modelo de industrialización del litio." *Revista de Ciencias Sociales* 34 (2018): 69–82.

———. "La estrategia nacional para la industrialización del litio y otros recursos evaporíticos de Bolivia." *Reporte Metalúrgico y de Materiales* 7 (2010). https://www.academia.edu/34399501/LA_ESTRATEGIA_NACIONAL_PARA_LA_INDUSTRIALIZACIÓN_DEL_LITIO_Y_OTROS_RECURSOS_EVAPORÍTICOS_DE_BOLIVIA.

Olivera Andrade, Manuel. *La industrialización del litio en Bolivia: Un proyecto estatal y los retos de la gobernanza, el extractivismo histórico y el capital internacional*. La Paz: UNESCO/CIDES, 2016.

———. "Salares altoandinos: Mundos de agua y litio." *Iqueique: La Revista del Norte Grande* 10, no. 1: 53–61.

Platt, Tristán. "Producción, tecnología y trabajo en la Rivera de Potosí durante la República temprana." *El Siglo XIX. Bolivia y América Latina*. Lima: Travaux de l'Institut Francais d'Etudes Andines, 1997.

Querejazu, Roberto. *Llallagua: Historia de una montaña*. Cochabamba-La Paz: Editorial Los Amigos del Libro, 1977.

Ramos, Demetrio. "Ordenación de la minería en Hispanoamérica durante la época provincial (siglos XVI, XVII y XVIII)." In *La minería hispana e iberoamericana: contribución a su investigación histórica: Estudios, fuentes, bibliografía, T. I.*, 373–450. León: Cátedra de San Isidro, 1970.

Ribera Arismendi, Marco Octavio. "Análisis general del caso Uyuni-litio (minería)." La Paz: LIDEMA 2001.

Robb, Kathryn, Mark Moran, Victoria Thom, and Justin Coburn. *Indigenous Governance and Mining in Bolivia*. Queensland: International Mining for Development Centre, World Vision and Institute for Social Science Research, 2015.

Robins, Nicholas. *Mercury, Mining and Empire: The Human and Ecological Cost of Colonial Silver Mining in the Andes*. Indiana: Indiana University Press, 2011.

Rodríguez, Gustavo. "Kajchas, trapicheros y ladrones de mineral en Bolivia (1824–1900)." *Revista de Historia* 4, no. 8 (1989): 125–39.

Rodríguez Ostria, Gustavo. *Capitalismo, modernización y resistencia popular, 1825–1952*. La Paz: CIS, 2014.

———. "Los mineros de Bolivia en una perspectiva histórica." *Revista Convergencia. Revista de Ciencias Sociales* 8, no. 24 (2001), 271–98.

Sempat Assadourian, Carlos. *El Sistema de la economía colonial. Mercado interno, regiones y espacio económico*. Lima: Instituto de Estudios Peruanos, 1982.

Smale, Robert. *I Sweat the Flavor of Tin: Labor Activism in early Twentieth-Century Bolivia*. Pittsburgh: University of Pittsburgh Press, 2010.

Solón, José Carlos. *Espejismos de abundancia, los mitos del proceso de industrialización del litio en el Salar de Uyuni*. La Paz: Plural, 2022.

Ströbele-Gregor, Juliana. *Litio en Bolivia: El plan gubernamental de producción e industrialización del litio, escenarios de conflictos sociales y ecológicos, y dimensiones de desigualdad social*. Santiago de Chile: Fundación Heinrich Böll, Oficina Regional para Conosur, 2012.

Tandeter, Enrique. "Forced and Free Labor in Late Colonial Potosí." *Past and Present* 93 (1981): 98–136.

Tenorio, Carlos. *Mauricio Hochschild, sus emprendimientos en Bolivia y su crecimiento económico en Potosí (1921–1939)*. La Paz: Círculo Israelita, Carrera de Historia, Facultad Humanidades y Ciencias de la Educación, Universidad Mayor de San Andrés, 2019.

"Two new ways of extracting lithium from brine. How to increase the supply of an increasingly valuable metal." The Economist. February 26, 2022. https://www.economist.com/science-and-technology/two-new-ways-of-extracting-lithium-from-brine/.

Velasco Murillo, Dana. "Laboring above ground: Indigenous Women in New Spain's Silver Mining District, Zacatecas, Mexico, 1620–1770." *Hispanic American Historical Review* 93, no. 1 (2013): 3–32.

Waszkis, Helmut. *Dr. Moritz (Don Mauricio) Hochschild, 1881–1965: The Man and His Companies. A German Mining Entrepreneur in South America*. Madrid: Verbuert-Iberoamericana, 2001.

Wood, Lucinda, and Jack Zhang. "Getting More Value from Brines: Tech Improvements, Reduce Costs, Increase Recoveries for Lithium." Saskatchewan Research Council. July 16, 2018. https://www.src.sk.ca/blog/getting-more-value-brines-tech-improvements-reduce-costs-increase-recoverieslithium?gclid=EAIaIQobChMIpPzvjNqY_QIVDGuRCh2TvQ42EAAYAyAAEgKV8vD_BwE.

Zondag, Cornelius. *The Bolivian Economy, 1952–1964: The Revolution and Its Aftermath*. New-York: Prager, 1966.

Zulawski, Ann. *They Eat from Their Labour: Work and Social Change in Colonial Bolivia*. Pittsburgh: Pittsburgh University Press, 1995.

CHAPTER THREE

Aceituno, Patricio, María del Rosario Prieto, María Eugenia Solari, Alejandra Martínez, Germán Poveda, and Mark Falvey. "The 1877–1878 El Niño Episode: Associated Impacts in South America." *Climatic Change Climatic Change* 92, nos. 3–4 (2009): 389–416.

Ari Chachaki, Waskar. *Earth Politics: Religion, Decolonization, and Bolivia's Indigenous Intellectuals*. Durham: Duke University Press, 2014.

Assies, Willem. "David versus Goliath in Cochabamba: Water Rights, Neoliberalism, and the Revival of Social Protest in Bolivia." *Latin American Perspectives* 30, no. 3 (2003): 14–36.

Baer, Madeline. "From Water Wars to Water Rights: Implementing the Human Right to Water in Bolivia." *Journal of Human Rights* 14, no. 3 (2015): 353–76.

Bakker, Karen J. *Privatizing Water: Governance Failure and the World's Urban Water Crisis*. Ithaca: Cornell University Press, 2010.

Ballestero, Andrea. *A Future History of Water*. Durham: Duke University Press, 2019.

Basadre, Jorge. *Historia de la República del Perú*, Vol. 8. Lima: Historia, 1963.

Bjork-James, Carwil. *The Sovereign Street: Making Revolution in Urban Bolivia*. Tucson: University of Arizona Press, 2020.

Bollaín, Icíar. *También la Lluvia*. Madrid: Morena Films, 2011.

Borsdorf, Axel, and Christoph Stadel. *The Andes: A Geographical Portrait*. New York: Springer, 2015.

Botton, Sarah, Sabastien Hardy, and Franck Poupeau. "Water from the Heights, Water from the Grassroots: The Governance of Common Dynamics and Public Services in La Paz-El Alto." Washington, DC: The World Bank, 2017.

Boyer, Christopher R. *Becoming Campesinos: Politics, Identity, and Agrarian Struggle in Postrevolutionary Michoacan, 1920–1935*. Stanford, CA: Stanford University Press, 2003.

Buckley, Eve E. *Technocrats and the Politics of Drought and Development in Twentieth-Century Brazil*. Chapel Hill: The University of North Carolina Press, 2017.

Butrón Mendoza, Julio. *Eran solo unos indios: Pasajes de la cara india de una revolución*. Bolivia: Weinberg, 1992.

Cárdenas, Victor Hugo. "'La lucha de un pueblo.'" In *Raíces de América: El Mundo Aymara*, compiled by Xavier Albó, 495–534. Madrid: Alianza Editorial, 1988.

Choque Canqui, Roberto. *Sublevación y masacre de Jesús de Machaqa de 1921*. La Paz: Fundación Diálogo, 1998.

Cochabamba, Departamento de Cultura. *Repartimiento de tierras por el Inca Huayna Capac*. Cochabamba: UMSS, Departamento de Arqueología, 1977.

Crespo Flores, Carlos. "El derecho humano al agua en la práctica: La política de agua y recursos naturales del gobierno de Evo Morales." Cochabamba, Bolivia: UMSS-CESU/CISO, 2010.

Crespo Flores, Carlos, Omar Fernández, and Carmen Peredo. *Los regantes de Cochabamba en la guerra del agua: Presión social y negociación*. Cochabamba, Bolivia: Memoria, 2004.

Cushman, Gregory T. *Guano and the Opening of the Pacific World: A Global Ecological History*. New York: Cambridge University Press, 2014.

Davis, Mike. *Late Victorian Holocausts: El Niño Famines and the Making of the Third World*. New York: Verso, 2001.

Escobar, Arturo. "Latin America at a Crossroads." *Cultural Studies* 24 (2010): 1–65.

Fernández Quiroga, Fredy Omar. "La relación tierra agua en la economía campesina de Tiquipaya." Undergraduate Thesis, Universidad Mayor de San Simón, 1996.

Finnegan, William. "Leasing the Rain." *New Yorker*, April 1, 2002.

First Inter-American Conference on Indian Life, Pátzcuaro, Mexico, 14–24 April 1940. "Final Act." Washington, DC: Bureau of Indian Affairs, 1941.

Francovich, Guillermo. *El pensamiento boliviano en el siglo XX*. La Paz: Los Amigos del Libro, 1985.

Garcés, Fernando. *El Pacto de Unidad y el proceso de construcción de una propuesta de constitución política del estado: Sistematización de la experiencia*. La Paz: Preview Gráfica, 2010.

García Orellana, Luis Alberto, Fernando García Yapur, and Luz Quitón Herbas. "La crisis política: La 'Guerra del Agua' en Cochabamba." La Paz: PIEB, 2003.

Goldman, Michael. *Imperial Nature: The World Bank and Struggles for Social Justice in the Age of Globalization*. New Haven: Yale University Press, 2008.

Goldstein, Daniel M. *The Spectacular City: Violence and Performance in Urban Bolivia*. Durham, NC: Duke University Press, 2004.

Gordillo Claure, Jose M. *Arando en la historia: La experiencia política campesina en Cochabamba*. La Paz: Plural, 1998.

———. *Peasant Wars in Bolivia: Making, Thinking, and Living the Revolution in Cochabamba (1952–64)*. Calgary: University of Calgary Press, 2022.

Gordillo, Jose M., and Robert H. Jackson. "Mestizaje y proceso de parcelización en la estructura agraria de Cochabamba (El caso de Sipe-Sipe en los Siglos XVIII–XIX)." *HISLA* 10 (1987): 15–37.

Gotkowitz, Laura. *A Revolution for Our Rights: Indigenous Struggles for Land and Justice in Bolivia, 1880–1952*. Durham: Duke University Press, 2008.

Grandin, Greg. *The Blood of Guatemala: A History of Race and Nation*. Durham: Duke University Press, 2000.

———. *The Last Colonial Massacre: Latin America in the Cold War*. Chicago: University of Chicago Press, 2011.

Gustafson, Bret. *Bolivia in the Age of Gas*. Durham: Duke University Press, 2020.

Hailu, Degol, Rafael Guerreiro Osorio, and Raquel Tsukada. "Privatization and Renationalization: What Went Wrong in Bolivia's Water Sector?" *World Development* 40, no. 12 (2012): 2564–77.

Heath, Dwight B., Hans C. Buechler, and Charles J. Erasmus. *Land Reform and Social Revolution in Bolivia*. New York: Praeger, 1970.

Hines, Sarah T. "The Power and Ethics of Vernacular Modernism: The Misicuni Dam Project in Cochabamba, Bolivia, 1944–2017." *Hispanic American Historical Review* 98, no. 2 (2018): 223–56.

———. *Water for All: Community, Property, and Revolution in Modern Bolivia*. Oakland, CA: University of California Press, 2022.

Hylton, Forrest. "Reverberations of Insurgency: Indian Communities, the Federal War of 1899, and the Regeneration of Bolivia." PhD Diss., New York University, 2011.

Jackson, Robert H. "The Decline of the Hacienda in Cochabamba, Bolivia: The Case of the Sacaba Valley, 1870–1929." *Hispanic American Historical Review* 69, no. 2 (1989): 259–81.

———. *Regional Markets and Agrarian Transformation in Bolivia Cochabamba, 1539–1960*. Albuquerque: University of New Mexico Press, 1994.

Jackson, Robert H., and Jose Gordillo Claure. "Formación, crisis y transformación de la estructura agraria de Cochabamba: El caso de la hacienda de Paucarpata y de la comunidad del Passo, 1538–1645 y 1872–1929." *Revista de Indias* 53, no. 199 (1993): 723–60.

Kiddle, Amelia M. *Mexico's Relations with Latin America during the Cárdenas Era*. Albuquerque: University of New Mexico Press, 2016.

Klein, Herbert S. *A Concise History of Bolivia*. 2nd ed. New York: Cambridge University Press, 2011.

———. *Parties and Political Change in Bolivia, 1880–1952*. New York: Cambridge University Press, 1969.

Kohl, Benjamin, and Linda C. Farthing. *Impasse in Bolivia: Neoliberal Hegemony and Popular Resistance*. New York: Zed Books, 2006.

Komives, Kristin. "Designing Pro-Poor Water and Sewer Concessions: Early Lessons from Bolivia." Washington, DC: World Bank, 1999.

Kruse, Thomas. "La Guerra del Agua en Cochabamba, Bolivia: Terrenos complejos, convergencias nuevas." In *Sindicatos y nuevos movimientos sociales en América Latina*, edited by Enrique de la Garza Toledo, 121–61. Buenos Aires: CLACSO, 2005.

Langer, Erick. *Economic Change and Rural Resistance in Southern Bolivia 1880–1930*. Stanford, CA: Stanford University Press, 1989.

Larson, Brooke. *Cochabamba, 1550–1900: Colonialism and Agrarian Transformation in Bolivia*. Durham: Duke University Press, 1998.

———. *Trials of Nation Making: Liberalism, Race, and Ethnicity in the Andes, 1810–1910*. New York: Cambridge University Press, 2004.

Mallon, Florencia. *The Defense of Community in Peru's Central Highlands: Peasant Struggle and Capitalist Transition, 1860–1940*. Princeton, NJ: Princeton University Press, 1983.

———. *Peasant and Nation: The Making of Postcolonial Mexico and Peru*. Berkeley, CA: University of California Press, 1995.

Marvin, Simon, and Nina Laurie. "An Emerging Logic of Urban Water Management, Cochabamba, Bolivia." *Urban Studies* 36, no. 2 (1999): 341–57.

Meyer, Michael C. *Water in the Hispanic Southwest: A Social and Legal History, 1550–1850*. Tucson: University of Arizona Press, 1996.

Mumford, Jeremy Ravi. *Vertical Empire: The General Resettlement of Indians in the Colonial Andes*. Durham: Duke University Press, 2012.

Murra, John V. *Formaciones económicas y políticas del mundo andino*. Lima: Instituto de Estudios Peruanos, 1975.

Navarro, Gonzalo, and Mabel Maldonado. *Geografía ecológica de Bolivia: Vegetación y ambientes acuáticos*. Cochabamba, Bolivia: Centro de Ecología Simón I. Patiño, 2002.

Olivera, Oscar, and Tom Lewis. *¡Cochabamba! Water War in Bolivia*. Cambridge, MA: South End Press, 2004.

Orellana Aillón, Lorgio. "El proceso insurrecional de abril: Estructuras materiales y superestructuras organizativas de los campesinos regantes en el Valle Central cochabambino." In *Ruralidades Latinoamericanas: Identidades y luchas sociales*, edited by Norma Giarracca and Betina Levy, 477–550. Buenos Aires: CLACSO, 2004.

Orellana Halkyer, Rene. "Agua, saneamiento y riego." In *Modelos de gestión del agua en los Andes*, edited by Franck Poupeau and Claudia González, 81–91. La Paz: PIEB, 2010.

Pentimalli de Navarro, Michela, and Gustavo Rodríguez Ostria. "Las razones de la multitud (Hambruna, motines y subsistencia: 1878–79)." *Estado y Sociedad* 5 (1988): 15–33.

Platt, Tristan. *Estado boliviano y ayllu andino: Tierra y tributo en el norte de Potosí*. Lima: Instituto de Estudios Peruanos, 1982.

Postero, Nancy Grey. *The Indigenous State: Race, Politics, and Performance in Plurinational Bolivia*. Oakland: University of California Press, 2017.

Querejazu Calvo, Roberto. *Guano, salitre, sangre: Historia de la Guerra del Pacífico*. La Paz: Los Amigos del Libro, 1979.

Razavi, Nasya. "'Social Control' and the Politics of Public Participation in Water Remunicipalization, Cochabamba, Bolivia." *Water* 11, no. 7 (2019): 1–19.

Rivera Cusicanqui, Silvia. *Ch'ixinakax Utxiwa: Una reflexión sobre prácticas y discursos descolonizadores*. Buenos Aires: Tinta Limón, 2010.

———. *Oprimidos pero no vencidos: luchas del campesinado aymara y qhechwa de Bolivia, 1900–1980*. Instituto de Investigaciones de las Naciones Unidas para el Desarrollo Social, 1986.

———. *Violencias (re)encubiertas en Bolivia*. Santander: Otramérica, 2012.

Rodriguez Ostria, Gustavo. "Entre reformas y contrareformas: Las comunidades indígenas en el Valle Bajo cochabambino (1825–1900)." In *Los Andes en la encrucijada: Indios, comunidades y estado en el Siglo XIX*, edited by Heraclio Bonilla, 277–334. Quito: Libri Mundi, 1991.

Saavedra Antezana, Carlos. "Ideas generales sobre obras de irrigación en Bolivia." *Irrigación en México* 27, no. 1 (1946): 10–18.

Sanjinés G., Alfredo. *La reforma agraria en Bolivia*. 2nd ed. La Paz: Universo, 1945.

Sater, William F. *Andean Tragedy: Fighting the War of the Pacific, 1879–1884*. Lincoln: University of Nebraska Press, 2009.

Scott, James C. *The Art of Not Being Governed: An Anarchist History of Upland Southeast Asia*. New Haven: Yale University Press, 2009.

———. *The Moral Economy of the Peasant: Rebellion and Subsistence in Southeast Asia*. New Haven: Yale University Press, 1976.

Solares Serrano, Humberto. *Historia, espacio y sociedad: Cochabamba, 1550–1950: Formación, crisis y desarrollo de su proceso urbano*. Cochabamba: CIDRE, 1990.

Soliz, Carmen. *Fields of Revolution: Agrarian Reform and Rural State Formation in Bolivia, 1935–1964*. Pittsburgh: University of Pittsburgh Press, 2021.

———. "'Land to the Original Owners': Rethinking the Indigenous Politics of the Bolivian Agrarian Reform." *Hispanic American Historical Review* 97, no. 2 (2017): 259–96.

Spain and Consejo de Indias. *Recopilación de leyes de los reynos de las Indias*. Madrid: Boletín Oficial del Estado, [1791] 1998.

Spronk, Susan. “Roots of Resistance to Urban Water Privatization in Bolivia: The ‘New Working Class,’ the Crisis of Neoliberalism, and Public Services.” *International Labor and Working-Class History*, no. 71 (2007): 8–28.

Thornton, Christy. “‘Mexico Has the Theories’: Latin America and the Invention of Development in the 1930s.” In *The Development Century: A Global History*, edited by Stephen J. Macekura and Erez Manela, 263–82. New York: Cambridge University Press, 2018.

Wachtel, Nathan. “The Mitimas of the Cochabamba Valley: The Colonization Policy of Huayna Capac.” In *Inca and Aztec States, 1400–1800: Anthropology and History*, edited by George Collier, Renato I. Rosaldo, and John D. Wirth, 199–235. New York: Academic Press, 1982.

Webber, Jeffery R. “From Left-Indigenous Insurrection.” In *The New Latin American Left: Cracks in the Empire*, edited by Jeffery R. Webber and Barry Carr, 149–90. New York: Rowman and Littlefield, 2013.

Zimmerer, Karl S. “Rescaling Irrigation in Latin America: The Cultural Images and Political Ecology of Water Resources.” *Ecumene* 7, no. 2 (2000): 150–75.

———. “The Origins of Andean Irrigation.” *Nature* 378 (1995): 481–83.

CHAPTER FOUR

Acker, Antoine. *Volkswagen in the Amazon: The Tragedy of Global Development in Modern Brazil (Global and International History)*. Cambridge: Cambridge University Press, 2017.

Aguirre Achá, José. *De los Andes al Amazonas: Recuerdos de la campaña del Acre*. La Paz: Tipografía Artística Velarde, Aldazosa y Co., 1902.

Armentia, Nicolás. *Diario de sus viages: A las tribus comprendidas entre el Beni y Madre de Dios y en el arroyo de Ivon en los años de 1881 y 1882*. La Paz: Tipografía Religiosa, 1883.

———. “Navegación del Madre de Dios, viaje del Padre Nicolás Armentia (1887).” In *Exploraciones de los ríos del sur*, by William Miller et al., 461–620. Iquitos: Monumenta amazónica, Centro de Estudios Teológicos de la Amazonía, 2006.

Ballivián, Manuel Vicente. *Diario del viaje de la Delegación Nacional a los territorios del Noroeste de la República y el departamento del Beni*. La Paz: Ministerio de Instrucción Pública y Colonización, 1896.

Ballivián, Manuel Vicente, and Castro F. Pinilla. *Monografía de la industria de la goma en Bolivia*. La Paz: Dirección General de Estadística y Estudios Geográficos, 1912.

Balzan, Luigi. *A carretón y canoa: La aventura científica de Luigi Balzan por Sudamérica (1885–1893)*, 269. Lima: Instituto Francés de Estudios Andinos, 2008.

Barclay, Frederica. *El estado federal de Loreto, 1896: Centralismo, descentralización y federalismo en el Perú, a fines del siglo XIX*. Lima: Instituto Francés de Estudios Andinos; Centro de Estudios Regionales Andinos Bartolomé de Las Casas, 2009.

Barham, Bradford, and Oliver Coomes. "Wild Rubber: Industrial Organisation and the Microeconomics of Extraction During the Amazon Rubber Boom (1860–1920)." *Journal of Latin American Studies* 26, no. 1 (1994): 37.

Bonilla, Heraclio. "El caucho y la economía del oriente peruano." *Historia y Cultura* 8 (1974): 69–80.

Cardoso, Antonio Alexandre Isidio. "O Eldorado dos Deserdados: Indígenas, escravos, migrantes, regatões e o avanço rumo ao oeste amazônico no século XIX." PhD diss., Universidade de São Paulo, 2018.

Colonization and Commercial Co. of Bolivia. *Bolivian Colonization: Being prospectus of the Colonization and Commercial Co. of Bolivia*. San Francisco: Alta California Printing House, 1870.

Comisiones mixtas. *Informes de las Comisiones mixtas peruano-brasileras encargadas del reconocimiento de los ríos Alto Purús i Alto Yuruá*. Lima: Oficina tipográfica de "La Opinión Nacional," 1904.

Coomes, Oliver T., and Bradford L. Barham. "The Amazon Rubber Boom: Labor Control, Resistance, and Failed Plantation Development Revisited." *Hispanic American Historical Review* 74, no. 2 (1994).

Córdoba, Lorena I. "Barbarie en plural: Percepciones del indígena en el auge cauchero boliviano." *Journal de la Société des Américanistes* 101, no. 1/2 (2015): 173–202.

———. "El boom cauchero en la Amazonía boliviana: encuentros y desencuentros con una sociedad indígena." In *Las tierras bajas de Bolivia: miradas históricas y antropológicas*, edited by Diego Villar and Isabelle Combès, 125–56. Santa Cruz de la Sierra: El País, 2012.

Coronil, Fernando. *The Magical State: Nature, Money, and Modernity in Venezuela*. Chicago: University of Chicago Press, 1997.

Da Cunha, Euclides. *Um Paraíso Perdido: Reunião de Ensaios Amazônicos*. Brasilia: Senado Federal, 2000.

Domínguez, Camilo, and Augusto Javier Gómez López. *La economía extractiva en la Amazonía colombiana 1850–1930*. Bogotá: Council of the Americas, 1990.

Espinosa, Oscar. "Los asháninkas y la violencia de las correrías durante y después de la época del caucho." *Bulletin de l'Institut Français d'Etudes Andines* 45, no. 1 (2016): 137–55.

Fawcett, Percy Harrison. *Lost trails, Lost Cities*. New York: Funk & Wagnalls, 1953.

Flores Marín, José A. *La Explotación del caucho en el Perú*. Lima: Universidad Nacional Mayor de San Marcos, 1987.

Gamarra Téllez, María del Pilar. *Amazonía norte de Bolivia: Economía gomera (1870–1940): bases económicas de un poder regional: la casa Suárez*. Biblioteca del Bicentenario de Bolivia. La Paz: Centro de Investigaciones Sociales, 2018.

———. *Barraca gomera y dominio amazónico el conflicto del acre (1899–1903): Geopolítica en la cuenca amazónica Bolivia - Brasil - Perú*. La Paz: Centro de Estudios para la América Andina y Amazónica, 2018.

———. "La frontera nómada: Frentes y fronteras económicas en el proceso cauchero ecuatoriano (1870–1920)." *Procesos* (1996): 39–78.

García Jordán, Pilar. *Cruz y arado, fusiles y discursos: la construcción de los Orientes en el Perú y Bolivia, 1820–1940*. Lima: Instituto Francés de Estudios Andinos, Instituto de Estudios Peruanos, 2001.

———. *Fronteras, colonización y mano de obra indígena, Amazonia andina (siglo XIX–XX): La construcción del espacio socio-económico amazónico en Ecuador, Perú y Bolivia (1792–1948)*. Lima: Pontificia Universidad Católica del Perú, Fondo Editorial, Universitat de Barcelona, 1998.

———. *Relatos del proyecto civilizatorio en Guarayos: Para la representación de guarayos y sirionós, 1825–1952*. La Paz: IFEA, 2019.

García Jordán, Pilar, and Anna Guiteras Mombiola. "The Construction of a Frontier Space. Inter-Ethnic Relations in Northern Bolivia." In *The Oxford Handbook of Borderlands of the Iberian World*, 691–716. UK: Oxford University Press, 2019.

Gómez López, Augusto Javier, ed. *Putumayo: La Vorágine de Las Caucherías: Memoria y Testimonio*. Bogotá: Centro Nacional de Memoria Histórica, 2014.

Guiteras Mombiola, Anna. *De los llanos de Mojos a las cachuelas del Beni 1842–1938: conflictos locales, recursos naturales y participación indígena en la Amazonía boliviana*. Cochabamba: Instituto de Misionología, Editorial Itinerarios, 2012.

Heath, Edwin R. "Exploration of the River Beni in 1880–1." *Proceedings of the Royal Geographical Society and Monthly Record of Geography* 5, no. 6 (1883): 327–41.

Hecht, Susanna B. *The Scramble for the Amazon and the "Lost Paradise" of Euclides Da Cunha*. Chicago: University of Chicago Press, 2013.

Hecht, Susanna, and Alexander Cockburn. *The Fate of the Forest: Developers, Destroyers, and Defenders of the Amazon*. Chicago: University of Chicago Press, 2011.

Hoelle, Jeffrey. *Rainforest Cowboys: The Rise of Ranching and Cattle Culture in Western Amazonia*. Austin: University of Texas Press, 2015.

Ijurra, Manuel. "Resumen de los viajes a las montañas de Mainas, Chachapoyas, i Pará por Manuel Ijurra, presentado i dedicado al Excemo. señor don Ramon

Castilla, presidente del Perú." In *Colección de leyes, decretos, resoluciones y otros documentos oficiales referentes al departamento de Loreto*, 276–410. Iquitos: Centro de Estudios Teológicos de la Amazonía, Gobierno Regional de Loreto, 2007.

Joseph, Gilbert Michael, and Daniel Nugent. *Everyday Forms of State Formation: Revolution and the Negotiation of Rule in Modern Mexico*. Durham: Duke University Press, 1994.

Junta de Vías Fluviales. *El Istmo de Fitscarrald*. Lima: Imp. Torres Aguirre, 1903.

———. *Nuevas Exploraciones en la Hoya del Madre de Dios*. Lima: Litografía y Tipografía de Carlos Fabrri, 1904.

———. *Últimas exploraciones ordenadas por la Junta de Vías Fluviales a los ríos Ucayali, Madre de Dios, Paucartambo y Urubamba. Informes de los señores Stiglich, Von Hassel, Olivera y Ontaneda*. Lima: Oficina tipográfica de "La Opiníon Nacional," 1907.

———. *Vías del Pacífico al Madre de Dios*. Lima: Imprenta de "El Lucero," 1902.

Justiniano Tonelli, Oscar. *El caucho ignorado*. Santa Cruz de la Sierra: Editorial País, 2010.

Labre, Antonio R. P. "Viagem exploradora do rio Madre de Dios ao Acre." *Revista de Geografía do Rio de Janeiro* 4, no. 2 (1888): 102–16.

La Gaceta del Norte. *El rio Orton y su colonizacion. Datos Tomados de la Sección "Noticias de Ayer" de La Gaceta del Norte de Orton*. La Paz: Imprenta y Litografia de "El Nacional," 1894.

Leal, Davi Avelino. *Direitos e processos diferenciados de territorialização: Os conflitos pelo uso dos recursos naturais no rio Madeira (1861–1932)*. PhD Diss., Universidade Federal do Amazonas, 2013.

Lema, Ana María. *El sentido del silencio: La mano de obra chiquitana en el oriente boliviano a principios del siglo XX*. Santa Cruz de la Sierra: Editorial El País, Universidad para la Investigación Estratégica en Bolivia, 2009.

Leutenegger, Ernst. "Gente en la selva: Vivencias de un suizo en Bolivia." In *Dos suizos en la selva. Historia del auge cauchero en el Oriente Boliviano*, edited by Lorena Córdoba, 171–371. Santa Cruz de la Sierra: Solidar Suiza, Centro de Investigaciones Históricas y Antropológicas, 2015.

Maccheti, Jesualdo. *Diario del viaje fluvial del padre fray Jesualdo Maccheti, misionero del Colegio de la Paz, desde San Buenaventura y Reyes hasta el Atlántico en 1869*. La Paz: El Siglo Industrial, 1886.

Mallon, Florencia E. *Peasant and Nation: The Making of Postcolonial Mexico and Peru*. Berkeley: University of California Press, 1995.

———. "The Promise and Dilemma of Subaltern Studies: Perspectives from Latin American History." *American Historical Review* 99, no. 5 (1994): 1491–515.

Mariaca, Timoteo. "Exploracion al río Acre." *Colección de Folletos Bolivianos de Hoy* 3, no. 19 (1987): 3–32.

Mercier, Víctor. "Diario de una expedición del Madre de Dios al Acre." *Colección de Folletos Bolivianos de Hoy*, no. 3 (1894): 3–16.

Miller, William. "Notice of a Journey to the Northward and Also to the Eastward of Cuzco, and among the Chunchos Indians, in July, 1835." *Journal of the Royal Geographical Society of London* 6 (1836): 174–86.

Ministerio de Hacienda. *Informes y documentos referentes al departamento del Beni*. La Paz: Imprenta de "La Razón," 1882.

Ministerio de Hacienda Bolivia. *Anexos al Informe del Ministro de Hacienda e Industria al Congreso Ordinario de 1887*. La Paz: Imprenta de "El Diario," 1887.

Moore, Jason W. *Capitalism in the Web of Life: Ecology and the Accumulation of Capital*. New York: Verso, 2015.

National Bolivian Navigation Company. *La Empresa Church en sus relaciones con Bolivia y sus complicaciones en Europa. Exposición detallada de todas la operaciones de la Compañía Nacional de Navegación Boliviana y de todas las cuestiones pendientes que embarazan su pronta realizción [sic]. Por Juan Francisco Velarde. Contiene además todos los contratos relativos a la Empresa i la correspondencia cambiada entre los Comisionados Bolivianos en Londres i el Coronel Church*. Cochabamba: Imprenta del Siglo, 1874.

Nordenskiöld, Erland. *Exploraciones y aventuras en Sudamérica*. La Paz: Apoyo para el Campesino Indígena del Oriente Boliviano, 2001.

Nugent, Stephen L. *The Rise and Fall of the Amazon Rubber Industry: An Historical Anthropology*. London: Routledge, 2018.

Nystrøm, Juan Guillermo. "Informe al Supremo Gobierno del Perú sobre una expedición al interior de la república." In *Exploraciones de los ríos del sur*, by William Miller et al., 225–312. Iquitos: Monumenta amazónica, Centro de Estudios Teológicos de la Amazonía, 2006.

Orsag Molina, José Octavio. *Circuitos económicos durante el auge de la goma en Bolivia (1880–1912)*. La Paz: Centro de Investigaciones Sociales, 2021.

Orsag Molina, José, and Nohely Guzmán Narváez. "Tecnología, modernidad, y desplazamiento del conflicto social: El continuo avance de la frontera agraria en la Amazonia sur. Brasil y Bolivia (1960-2020)." In *Amazonía y expansión mercantil capitalista como nueva frontera de recursos en el siglo XXI*, 137-95. Buenos Aires: CLACSO-CEDLA, 2021.

Palacios, José Agustín. *Exploraciones de Don José Agustín Palacios. Realizadas en los ríos Beni, Mamoré y Madera y en el lago Rogo-aguado, durante los años 1844 al 47. Descripción de la provincia de Mojos*. La Paz: Imprenta "El comercio," 1893.

Pando, José Manuel. *Viaje á la region de la goma elástica (N.O. de Bolivia)*. La Plata: Museo de La Plata, 1894.

Paredes Pando, Oscar. *Explotación del caucho-shiringa: Brasil–Bolivia–Perú: Economías extractivo -mercantiles del Alto Acre–Madre de Dios*. Cusco: JL Editores, 2013.

Pierini, Francisco. *Informe Anual que presenta al Supremo Gobierno el R.P. Prefecto Francisco Pierini. Sobre el movimiento de las Misiones de su cargo*. Tarata: Tipografía del colegio San José, 1911.

———. *Informe Anual que presenta al Supremo Gobierno el R.P. Prefecto sobre el movimiento de las Misiones de su cargo*. Tarata: Imprenta del Colegio Apostólico de S. José, 1910.

Pineda Camacho, Roberto. *Holocausto en el Amazonas: Una historia social de la Casa Arana*. Bogotá: Espasa, 2000.

Posnansky, Arthur. *Campaña del Acre: La Lancha "Iris": Aventuras y peregrinaciones . . .* La Paz: Tipografía El Diario, 1904.

Roca, José Luis. *Econnomía y sociedad en el Oriente boliviano: siglos XVI–XX*. Santa Cruz de la Sierra: Cotas, 2001.

Rodríguez Ostria, Gustavo. *Poder central y proyecto regional: Cochabamba y Santa Cruz en los siglos XIX y XX*. Cochabamba: ILDIS-IDAES, 1993.

Roller, Heather. *Amazonian Routes: Indigenous Mobility and Colonial Communities in Northern Brazil*. Stanford: Stanford University Press, 2014.

Sanabria Fernández, Hernando. *En busca del Dorado*. Santa Cruz de la Sierra: La Hoguera, 2009.

Santos, Roberto. *História econômica da Amazônia (1800–1920)*. São Paulo: Taqueiroz, 1980.

Santos-Granero, Fernando. *Selva Central: History, Economy, and Land Use in Peruvian Amazonia*. Washington, DC: Smithsonian Institution Press, 1998.

———. *Slavery and Utopia: The Wars and Dreams of an Amazonian World Transformer*. Austin: University of Texas Press, 2018.

Scott, James C. *Seeing Like a State: How Certain Schemes to Improve the Human Condition Have Failed*. New Haven: Yale University Press, 2008.

Suárez, Nicolás. *Anotaciones y documentos sobre la campaña del Alto Acre 1902–1903*. La Paz: Centro de Investigaciones Sociales, 2018.

Taussig, Michael T. *Shamanism, Colonialism, and the Wild Man: A Study in Terror and Healing*. Chicago: University of Chicago Press, 1991.

Ugarte, Auxiliomar Silva. "Alvores da conquista espiritual do alto Amazonas (século XVI–XVII)." In *Rastros da memória histórias das populações indígenas na Amazônia*, edited by Patricia Melo Sampaio y Regina de Carvalho Erthal, 13–47. Manaus: EDUA, 2006.

Vallvé, Frederic. "The Impact of the Rubber Boom on the Bolivian Lowlands (1850–1920)." PhD diss., Georgetown University, 2010.

Van Valen, Gary. *Indigenous Agency in the Amazon the Mojos in Liberal and Rubber-Boom Bolivia, 1842–1932*. Tucson: University of Arizona Press, 2013.

Villar, Diego, Lorena Córdoba, and Isabelle Combès. *La reducción imposible: Las expediciones del padre Negrete a los pacaguaras (1795–1800)*. Cochabamba: Instituto de Misionología, 2009.

Weinstein, Barbara. *The Amazon Rubber Boom, 1850–1920*. Stanford: Stanford University Press, 1983.

Wolff, Cristina Scheibe. *Mulheres da floresta: Uma história: Alto Juruá, Acre, 1890–1945*. São Paulo: Editora Hucitec, 1999.

Zárate Botía, Carlos Gilberto. *Amazonía 1900–1940: El conflicto, la guerra y la invención de la frontera*. Leticia: Universidad Nacional de Colombia, Instituto Amazónico de Investigaciones, Grupo de Estudios Transfronterizos, 2019.

Zeitum, Said. *Amazonía boliviana*. La Paz: Vision, 1991.

CHAPTER FIVE

Achtenberg, Emily. "Morales Greenlights TIPNIS Road, Oil and Gas Extraction in Bolivia's National Parks." North American Congress on Latin America, June 15, 2015. https://nacla.org/blog/2015/06/15/morales-greenlights-tipnis-road-oil-and-gas-extraction-bolivia%E2%80%99s-national-parks.

Almaraz Paz, Sergio. *Petróleo en Bolivia*. La Paz: Juventud, 1958.

Álvarez España, Waldo. *Los gráficos en Bolivia: Historia de la organización y luchas de los trabajadores de este sector social*. La Paz: Renovación, 1977.

Anaya Giorgis, Juan José. *Estado y petróleo en Bolivia (siglos XX–XXI)*. Cochabamba: ASDI/UMSS, 2018.

Andersen, Lykke, and Rubén Mamani Paco, eds. *La economía del cambio climático en el Estado Plurinacional de Bolivia*. Banco Interamericano de Desarrollo, 2014.

Anthias, Penelope. *Limits to Decolonization: Indigeneity, Territory, and Hydrocarbon Politics in the Bolivian Chaco*. Ithaca, NY: Cornell University Press, 2018.

Arauz, Andrés, Mark Weisbrot, Andrew Bunker, and Jake Johnston. *Bolivia's Economic Transformation: Macroeconomic Policies, Institutional Changes, and Results*. Washington, DC: Center for Economic and Policy Research, 2019. https://cepr.net/report/bolivia-s-economic-transformation-macroeconomic-policies-institutional-changes-and-results/

Behrends, Andrea, Stephen P. Reyna, and Günther Schlee, eds. *Crude Domination: An Anthropology of Oil*. New York: Berghahn Books, 2011.

Campanini, Jorge. "El Decreto 2366 dicta la sentencia a las Áreas Protegidas en Bolivia." Centro de Documentación e Información Bolivia, May 25, 2015. https://cedib.org/post_type_documentos/el-decreto-2366-dicta-sentencia-a-las-areas-protegidas-en-bolivia/.

Candia, Fernando, and Napoleón Pacheco, eds. *El péndulo del gas: Estudios comparativos de la política de hidrocarburos*. La Paz: Fundación Milenio, 2009.

Canelas O., Amado. *Petróleo: Imperialismo y nacionalismo*. La Paz: Librería Altiplano, 1963.

Chacón, Gustavo. "Prologue." In *Mito y realidad del petróleo boliviano*, by Enrique Mariaca Bilbao, 3–8. La Paz: Los Amigos del Libro, 1966.

Comisión Económica para América Latina y el Caribe (CEPAL). *Anuario estadístico de América Latina y el Caribe, 2005*. Santiago: United Nations, 2006.

Comité Ejecutivo de la Universidad Boliviana. *Convenciones nacionales universitarias, 1928–1929*. La Paz: CEUB, 1982.

Coronil, Fernando. *The Magical State: Nature, Money, and Modernity in Venezuela*. Chicago, IL: University of Chicago Press, 1997.

Cote, Stephen C. *Oil and Nation: A History of Bolivia's Petroleum Sector*. Morgantown: West Virginia University Press, 2016.

Dennis, Elissa. "Keep It in the Ground." In *Real World Latin America*, 2nd ed., edited by Fred Rosen and Alejandro Reuss, 83–88. Boston, MA: Economic Affairs Bureau, 2013.

Dunkerley, James. *Rebellion in the Veins: Political Struggle in Bolivia, 1952–82*. London: Verso, 1984.

Farah H., Ivonne, and Luciano Vasapollo, eds. *Vivir bien: ¿Paradigma no capitalista?* La Paz: Plural, 2011.

Farthing, Linda C. "An Opportunity Squandered? Elites, Social Movements, and the Bolivian Government of Evo Morales." In *Latin America's Pink Tide: Breakthroughs and Shortcomings*, edited by Steve Ellner, 193–215. Lanham, MD: Rowman and Littlefield, 2020.

Farthing, Linda C., and Thomas Becker. *Coup: A Story of Violence and Resistance in Bolivia*. Chicago, IL: Haymarket, 2021.

Farthing, Linda C., and Benjamin H. Kohl. *Evo's Bolivia: Continuity and Change*. Austin: University of Texas Press, 2014.

Grandin, Greg. "The Liberal Traditions in the Americas: Rights, Sovereignty, and the Origins of Liberal Multilateralism." *American Historical Review* 117, no. 1 (2012): 68–91.

Gudynas, Eduardo. "Beyond Varieties of Development: Disputes and Alternatives." *Third World Quarterly* 37, no. 4 (2016): 721–34.

Guevara Arze, Wálter. *Plan inmediato de política económica del gobierno de la revolución nacional*. La Paz: Ministerio de Relaciones Exteriores y Culto, 1955.

Gustafson, Bret. *Bolivia in the Age of Gas*. Durham, NC: Duke University Press, 2020.

Gutiérrez Aguilar, Raquel. *Rhythms of the Pachakuti: Indigenous Uprising and State*

Power in Bolivia. Translated by Stacey Alba D. Skar. Durham, NC: Duke University Press, 2014.

Haglund, Christina. "A River Turns Black: Enron and Shell Spread Destruction across Bolivia's Highlands." In *Dignity and Defiance: Stories from Bolivia's Challenge to Globalization*, edited by Jim Shultz and Melissa Crane Draper, 45–75. Berkeley: University of California Press, 2008.

Hindery, Derrick. *From Enron to Evo: Pipeline Politics, Global Environmentalism, and Indigenous Rights in Bolivia*. Tucson: University of Arizona Press, 2013.

Jiménez, Georgina. "Territorios indígenas y áreas protegidas en la mira: La ampliación de la frontera de industrias extractivas." *Petropress* 31 (2013): 4–18.

Kaup, Brent Z. *Market Justice: Political Economic Struggle in Bolivia*. New York: Cambridge University Press, 2013.

Klein, Herbert S. *Parties and Political Change in Bolivia, 1880–1952*. Cambridge, UK: Cambridge University Press, 1969.

———. "'Social Constitutionalism' in Latin America: The Bolivian Experience of 1938." *The Americas* 22, no. 3 (1966): 258–76.

Kohl, Benjamin H., and Linda C. Farthing. *Impasse in Bolivia: Neoliberal Hegemony and Popular Resistance*. London: Zed Books, 2006.

Krenn, Michael L. *US Policy toward Economic Nationalism in Latin America, 1917–1929*. Wilmington, DE: Scholarly Resources, 1990.

Langer, Erick D. *Expecting Pears from an Elm Tree: Franciscan Missions on the Chiriguano Frontier in the Heart of South America, 1830–1949*. Durham, NC: Duke University Press, 2009.

López, Pedro N. *Bolivia y el petróleo*. La Paz: Arno Hermanos, 1922.

———. *Política petrolífera*. La Paz: Boliviana, 1929.

Mao, Zedong. "On Contradiction." In *Selected Works of Mao Tse-Tung*, vol. 1, 311–47. Peking: Foreign Languages Press, 1967.

Marof, Tristán. *La tragedia del altiplano*. Buenos Aires: Claridad, 1935.

Ministerio de Economía y Finanzas Públicas (Bolivia). *Memoria de la economía boliviana 2017*. La Paz, 2018.

Mitchell, Christopher. *The Legacy of Populism in Bolivia: From the MNR to Military Rule*. New York: Praeger, 1977.

Mitchell, Timothy. *Carbon Democracy: Political Power in the Age of Oil*. London: Verso, 2011.

Molina, Fernando. *El pensamiento boliviano sobre los recursos naturales*. La Paz: Pulso, 2009.

Montenegro, Carlos. *Frente al derecho del estado: El oro de la Standard Oil (El petróleo, sangre de Bolivia)*. La Paz: Trabajo, 1938.

O'Brien, Thomas F. *The Century of U.S. Capitalism in Latin America*. Albuquerque: University of New Mexico Press, 1999.

Orgaz, Marcos, Miguel Calderón, José Rocabado, and Telmo Melgares. "Exposición de motivos." *El Petrolero* (February 1959): 3–5.

Orgáz García, Mirko. *El poder de la nacionalización: Economía, política y geopolítica de la 3ra. nacionalización de los hidrocarburos en Bolivia: La falsa nacionalización de Evo Morales y la venta de gas a Chile*. 3rd ed. La Paz: n.p., 2008.

———. *La guerra del gas: Nación versus Estado transnacional en Bolivia*. La Paz: Ofavin, 2002.

Ortiz Mercado, José. "La histórica 'Estrategia socio-económica del desarrollo nacional, 1971–1991.'" *Patria Grande: Revista Mensual de la Izquierda Nacional (Tercera Época)* 1, no. 8 (2008): 1–67.

Paz Estenssoro, Víctor. *Discursos parlamentarios*. La Paz: Canata, 1955.

Perreault, Thomas. "Extracting Justice: Natural Gas, Indigenous Mobilization, and the Bolivian State." In *The Politics of Resource Extraction: Indigenous Peoples, Multinational Corporations, and the State*, edited by Suzana Sawyer and Edmund Terence Gómez, 75–102. Houndmills, UK: Palgrave Macmillan, 2012.

Philip, George. *Oil and Politics in Latin America: Nationalist Movements and State Companies*. Cambridge, UK: Cambridge University Press, 1982.

Pruden, Hernán. "Las luchas 'cívicas' y las no tan cívicas: Santa Cruz de la Sierra (1957–59)." *Ciencia y Cultura* 29 (2012): 127–62.

Quiroga Santa Cruz, Marcelo. *Desarrollo con soberanía: La desnacionalización del petróleo*. Cochabamba: Universitaria, 1967.

República de Bolivia. *Redactor de la Convención Nacional, 1945*. Vol. 4. La Paz: n.p., n.d.

Rodman, Kenneth A. *Sanctity versus Sovereignty: The United States and the Nationalization of Natural Resource Investments*. New York: Columbia University Press, 1988.

Romero Loza, José. *Temas económicos de actualidad*. La Paz: Universo, 1952.

Rosales, Antulio. "Resource Nationalism: Historical Contributions from Latin America." In *Handbook of Economic Nationalism*, edited by Andreas Pickel, 155–70. Cheltenham, UK: Edward Elgar, 2022.

Royuela Comboni, Carlos. *Cien años de hidrocarburos en Bolivia (1896–1996)*. La Paz: Los Amigos del Libro, 1996.

Solón Pablo. *¿Es posible el Vivir Bien?* La Paz: Fundación Solón, 2016.

Soruco, Ximena, Wilfredo Plata, and Gustavo Medeiros. *Los barones del oriente: El poder en Santa Cruz ayer y hoy*. Santa Cruz: Fundación Tierra, 2008.

Tahbub, Marwan. *Las transnacionales no son socias: Por una política nacional de hidrocarburos*. Cochabamba: CEDIB, 2010.

Tinker Salas, Miguel. *The Enduring Legacy: Oil, Culture, and Society in Venezuela*. Durham, NC: Duke University Press, 2009.

Unión Boliviana de Defensa del Petróleo. *¡Defendamos el petróleo! Manifiesto de la Unión Boliviana de Defensa el Petróleo*. La Paz: Universidad Mayor de San Andrés, 1996 [1941].

United States Economic Mission to Bolivia. *Plan Bohan (Bolivia)*. Vol. 1 [1942]. Translation by G. V. Bilbao la Vieja. La Paz: Carmach, 1988.

Villegas Quiroga, Carlos. *Privatización de la industria petrolera en Bolivia: Trayectoria y efectos tributarios*. 2nd ed. La Paz: Plural, 2004.

Watts, Michael J. "Oil Worlds: Life and Death in Nigeria's Petro-State." In *Handbook on the Geographies of Energy*, edited by Barry D. Solomon and Kirby E. Calvert, 341–55. Cheltenham, UK: Edward Elgar, 2017.

Webber, Jeffery. *Red October: Left-Indigenous Struggle in Modern Bolivia*. Chicago, IL: Haymarket, 2012.

Weisbrot, Mark, and Luis Sandoval. "The Distribution of Bolivia's Most Important Natural Resources and the Autonomy Conflicts." Center for Economic and Policy Research, Issue Brief, July 2008.

Weston, Charles H. Jr. "An Ideology of Modernization: The Case of the Bolivian MNR." *Journal of Inter-American Studies* 10, no. 1 (1968): 85–101.

Weyland, Kurt. "The Rise of Latin America's Two Lefts: Insights from Rentier State Theory." *Comparative Politics* 41, no. 2 (2009): 145–64.

Wolff, Jonas. "Business Power and the Politics of Postneoliberalism: Relations Between Governments and Economic Elites in Bolivia and Ecuador." *Latin American Politics and Society* 58, no. 2 (2016): 124–47.

Yacimientos Petrolíferos Fiscales Bolivianos (YPFB). *Código del petróleo: Edición oficial*. La Paz: YPFB, 1955.

———. "Información financiera: Contratos de servicios petroleros" (2019). Accessed June 29, 2023. https://landmatrix.org/media/uploads/publicacin-pagina-web-ypfb-a-oct-2019-final.pdf.

Young, Kevin A. *Blood of the Earth: Resource Nationalism, Revolution, and Empire in Bolivia*. Austin: University of Texas Press, 2017.

———. "From Open Door to Nationalization: Oil and Development Visions in Bolivia, 1952–1969." *Hispanic American Historical Review* 97, no. 1 (2017): 95–129.

Zavaleta Mercado, René. *Clases sociales y conocimiento*. Cochabamba: Los Amigos del Libro, 1988.

Zelada Aprili, Raul. "Resource Rents, Public Investment and Economic Development: The Case of Bolivia." PhD diss., University of Massachusetts Amherst, 2018.

Zook, David H. Jr. *The Conduct of the Chaco War*. New Haven, CT: Bookman Associates, 1960.

CHAPTER SIX

Absi, Pascale. *Los Ministros del Diablo: el trabajo y sus representaciones en las minas de Potosí*. La Paz: Institut Français d'Etudes Andines, 2005.

Agreda, Evelin, Norma Rodriguez, and Alex Conteras. *Mujeres cocaleras: Marchando por una vida sin violencia*. Cochabamba - Bolivia: CEDIB, 1996.

Albó, Xavier. *Coripata: tierra y cocales*. La Paz: CIPCA, 1976.

———. "From Mnristas to Kataristas to Katari." In *Resistance, Rebellion and Consciousness in the Andean Peasant World, 18th to 20th Centuries*, edited by S. Stern, 13–34. Madison: University of Wisconsin, 1987.

———. *Movimientos y poder indígena en Bolivia, Ecuador y Perú*. La Paz: CIPCA: Cuadernos de Investigacion, 2008.

———. *Pueblos Indios en La Política*. Cuadernos de Investigacion. La Paz: CIPCA, 2002.

Alderman, Jonathan. "Unpacking Disavowals of Indigeneity in Bolivia." *Latin American and Caribbean Ethnic Studies* 15, no. 4 (2020): 430–38.

Allen, Catherine. *The Hold Life Has: Coca and Cultural Identity in an Andean Community*. Smithsonian Series in Ethnographic Inquiry. London: Smithsonian Institute Press, 1988.

———. "To Be Quechua: The Symbolism of Coca Chewing in Highland Peru." *American Ethnologist* 8, no. 1 (1981): 157–71

Andrews, George, and David Solomon. "Coca and Cocaine: Uses and Abuses." In *The Coca Leaf and Cocaine Papers*, edited by George Andrews and Solomon David. New York: Harcourt Brace Jovanovich, 1975.

Anria, Santiago. *When Movements Become Parties: The Bolivian MAS in Comparative Perspective*. Cambridge: Cambridge University Press, 2018.

Anthias, Penelope. *Limits to Decolonization: Indigeneity, Territory, and Hydrocarbon Politics in the Bolivian Chaco*. Ithaca: Cornell University Press, 2018.

Arias, Desmond Enrique, and Thomas Grisaffi, eds. *Cocaine: From Coca Fields to the Streets*. Durham NC: Duke University Press, 2021.

Arnold, Denise, and Alison Spedding. *Mujeres en los movimientos sociales en Boliva 2000–2003*. La Paz: CIDEM/ILCA, 2005.

Ballvé, Teo, and Kendra McSweeney. "The 'Colombianisation' of Central America: Misconceptions, Mischaracterisations and the Military-Agroindustrial Complex." *Journal of Latin American Studies* (2020): 1–25.

Biondich, Amy, and Jeremy Joslin. "Coca: The History and Medical Significance of an Ancient Andean Tradition." *Emergency Medicine International* 16 (2016): 1–5.

Bjork-James, Carwil. *Mass Protest and State Repression in Bolivian Political Culture: Putting the Gas War and the 2019 Crisis in Perspective*. Harvard Law School (Boston: 2020).

http://hrp.law.harvard.edu/wp-content/uploads/2020/05/CBjork-James_20_003-1.pdf.

Blanes, Jose. "Cocaine, Informality, and the Urban Economy in La Paz, Bolivia." In *The Informal Economy: Studies in Advanced and Less Developed Countries*, edited by Alejandro Portes, M. Castells, and L. Benton. Baltimore: John Hopkins University Press, 1989.

———. *De los valles al Chapare*. Cochabamba: CERES, 1983.

Blanes, Jose, and Gonzalo Flores. *Campesino, migrante y colonizador: Reproducción de la economia familiar en el Chapare tropical*. La Paz: CERES, 1982.

Blanes, José, and H. Mansilla. *La percepción social y los hechos reales del complejo Coca/Cocaína, implicaciones para una política nacional*. La Paz: SEAMOS, 1994.

"Bolivia: El avance de la coca más allá del polígono 7 del Tipnis." Mongabay/El Deber, 2018. Accessed March 3, 2021. https://es.mongabay.com/2018/08/bolivia-coca-poligono-7-tipnis-deforestacion/.

"Bolivian Coca Growers Cut Ties with Usaid." Andean Information Network, Andean Information Network, 2008. Accessed January 2, 2008. http://ain-bolivia.org/2008/06/bolivian-coca-growers-cut-ties-with-usaid/.

"Bolivian Police Arrest Colombian and Coca Growers: U.S Suggests FARC and ELN Presence." Andean Information Network Memo, 2003.

"Bolivia Reverses Years of Progress with Draconian Cocaine Policy, Supported by the EU." The Conversation, 2020.

"Bolivia: USAID out, Morales in for Re-Election Bid." NACLA, 2013. Accessed November 23, 2016. https://nacla.org/blog/2013/5/11/bolivia-usaid-out-morales-re-election-bid.

Bolton, Margaret. "Doing Waki in San Pablo De Lípez: Reciprocity Between the Living and the Dead." *Anthropos* (2002): 379–96.

Bourgois, Philippe. *In Search of Respect: Selling Crack in El Barrio*. Cambridge: Cambridge University Press, 1995.

Brewer-Osorio, Susan. "Turning over a New Leaf: A Subnational Analysis of 'Coca Yes, Cocaine No' in Bolivia." *Journal of Latin American Studies* 53 (2021): 573–600.

———. "Uniting the Opposition: Reform, Repression, and the Rise of the Cocaleros in Bolivia." *The Latin Americanist* 64, no. 3 (2020): 257–79.

Brown, Emma. "Investigating the Use of Coca and Other Psychoactive Plants in Pre-Columbian Mummies from Chile and Peru." PhD diss., University of Bradford, 2012.

"Business as Usual? Cocaine Seizures on the Rise at Bolivia-Brazil Border." Insight Crime, 2020. Accessed March 4, 2021. https://insightcrime.org/news/brief/cocaine-seizures-rise-bolivia-brazil/.

Buxton, Julia. "Drug Control and Development: A Blind Spot." In *Drug Policies and Development Conflict and Coexistence*, edited by Julia Buxton, Mary Chinery-Hesse, and Khalid Tinasti, 13–42. Nijhoff: Brill, 2020.

Camacho Balderrama, Natalia. "La marcha como táctica de concertación política (Las marchas cocaleras de 1994 y 1995)." In *Empujando la concertación. Marchas campesinas, opinión pública y coca*, edited by Roberto Laserna, Natalia Camacho, and Eduardo Córdova, 5–64. Cochabamba: CERES-PIEB, 1999.

Canessa, Andrew. "'Todos somos Indígenas': Towards a New Language of National Political Identity." *Bulletin of Latin American Research* 25, no. 2 (2006): 241–63.

Carter, William, ed. *Ensayos cientificos sobre la coca*. La Paz: Editorial Juventud, 1996.

Carter, William, and Mauricio Mamani. *Coca en Bolivia*. La Paz: Editorial Juventud, 1986.

Cintron, Myrna. "Coca: Its History and Contemporary Parallels." In *Drugs in Latin America*, edited by E. Morales, 25–51. Williamsburg, VA: College of William and Mary, 1986.

Clawson, Patrick, and Rensselaer Lee. *The Andean Cocaine Industry*. New York: Palgrave Macmillan, 1996.

"Coca and Cocaine in Latin American History." Oxford Research Encyclopedia, Oxford University Press, 2020. Accessed February 8, 2020. https://oxfordre.com/view/10.1093/acrefore/9780199366439.001.0001/acrefore-9780199366439-e-754.

"Cocaine: Falling Coffee Prices Force Peru's Farmers to Cultivate Coca." The Conversation, 2021. https://theconversation.com/cocaine-falling-coffee-prices-force-perus-farmers-to-cultivate-coca-154754.

CONALTID. *Gobierno presenta resultados del Estudio integral de la hoja de coca*. Secretaria de Coordinación Consejo Nacional de Lucha contra el Tráfico Ilícito de Drogas (CONALTID), Ministerio de Gobierno. La Paz: Ministerio de Gobierno, November 2013.

Contreras, Alex. *La Marcha Histórica*. Cochabamba, Bolivia: CEDIB, 1995.

Conzelman, Caroline. "Coca Leaf and Sindicato Democracy in the Bolivian Yungas: The Andeanization of Western Political Models and the Rise of the New Left." PhD diss., University of Colorado at Boulder, 2007.

———. "Coca: The Leaf at the Center of the War on Drugs." In *Dignity and Defiance. Stories from Bolivia's Challenge to Globalization*, edited by Jim Shultz and Melissa Draper, 181–210. Berkeley, CA: University of California Press, 2008.

Crabtree, John. *The Great Tin Crash: Bolivia and the World Market*. London: Latin American Bureau, 1987.

Csete, Joanne, Adeeba Kamarulzaman, Michel Kazatchkine, Frederick Altice, Marek Balicki, Julia Buxton, Javier Cepeda, et al. "Public Health and International Drug Policy." *Lancet* 387, no. 10026 (2016): 1427–80.

De Franco, Mario, and Ricardo Godoy. "The Economic Consequences of Cocaine Production in Bolivia: Historical, Local, and Macroeconomic Perspectives." *Journal of Latin American Studies* 24, no. 2 (1992): 375–406.

Dillehay, Tom, Jack Rossen, Donald Ugent, Anathasios Karathanasis, Víctor Vásquez, and Patricia J. Netherly. "Early Holocene Coca Chewing in Northern Peru." *Antiquity* 84, no. 326 (2010): 939–53.

Duke, James, David Aulik, and Timothy Plowman. "Nutritional Value of Coca." *Botanical Museum Leaflets, Harvard University* 24, no. 6 (1975): 113–19.

Dunkerley, James. "Bolivia at the Crossroads." *Third World Quarterly* 8, no. 1 (1986): 137–50.

———. *Political Transition and Economic Stabilisation: Bolivia, 1982–1989. Institute of Latin American Studies Research Paper* 22. London: Institute of Latin American Studies, 1990.

———. *Rebellion in the Veins: Political Struggle in Bolivia, 1952–82*. London: Verso, 1984.

———. *Warriors and Scribes: Essays on the History and Politics of Latin America*. London: Verso, 2000.

Dunkerley, James, and Rolando Morales. "Crisis in Bolivia." *New Left Review* 155 (1986): 86–106.

Durand Ochoa, Ursula. "Coca, Contention and Identity: The Political Empowerment of the Cocaleros of Bolivia and Peru." PhD diss., London School of Economics, 2012.

Eastwood, David, and Harry Pollard. "The Development of Colonisation in Lowland Bolivia: Objectives and Evaluation." *Boletin de Estudios Latinoamericanos y del Caribe* 38 (1985): 61–82.

Ehrinpreis, Andrew. "Coca Nation: Labor, Indigeneity, and the Politics of the Coca Leaf in Bolivia, 1900–1962." PhD diss., State University of New York at Stony Brook, 2018.

———. "Green Gold, Green Hell: Coca, Caste, and Class in the Chaco War, 1932–1935." *The Americas* 77, no. 2 (2020): 217–45.

Escárzaga, Fabiola. "Comunidad indígena y revolución en Bolivia: El pensamiento Indianista-Katarista de Fausto Reinaga y Felipe Quispe." *Política y Cultura* 37 (2012): 185–210.

Escóbar, Filemon. *De la Revolución al Pachakuti. El aprendizaje del respeto recíproco entre blancos e indianos*. La Paz: Garza Azul, 2008.

Farthing, Linda. "Bolivia Sees Coca as a Way to Perk up Its Economy—but All Everyone Else Sees Is Cocaine." *The Guardian*, March 15, 2017. https://www.theguardian.com/world/2017/mar/15/coca-production-farming-bolivia-law.

———. "Social Impacts Associated with Anti Drug Law 1008." In *Coca, Cocaine, and the Bolivian Reality*, edited by B. Léons and H. Sanabria, 253–70. Albany, NY: State University of New York Press, 1997.

Farthing, Linda, and Benjamin Kohl. "Conflicting Agendas: The Politics of Development Aid in Drug-Producing Areas." *Development Policy Review* 23, no. 2 (2005): 183–98.

———. *Evo's Bolivia: Continuity and Change*. Austin: University of Texas Press, 2014.

Farthing, Linda, and Kathryn Ledebur. "The Beat Goes On: The U.S. War on Coca." *NACLA Report on the Americas* 38, no. 3 (2004): 34–39.

———. *Habeas Coca: Bolivia's Community Coca Control*. Open Society Foundations (New York: 2015).

Farthing, Linda, and Thomas Becker. *Coup: A Story of Violence and Resistance in Bolivia*. Chicago: Haymarket, 2021.

Flores, Gonzalo, and Jose Blanes. *¿Donde va el Chapare?* Cochabamba: Centro de Estudios de la Realidad Económica y Social CERES, 1984.

Freud, Sigmund. "Uber Coca." *Journal of Substance Abuse Treatment* 1, no. 3 (1984): 206–17.

Gagliano, Joseph. *Coca Prohibition in Peru: The Historical Debate*. Tucson: University of Arizona Press, 1994.

García Linera, Álvaro, Marxa Chávez, and Patricia Costas. *Sociología de los movimientos sociales en Bolivia: Estructuras de movilización, repertorios culturales y acción política*. La Paz: Plural, 2004.

García-Yi, Jaqueline. "Social Control and as Supply-Side Harm Reduction Strategies. The Case of an Indigenous Community in Peru." *Iberoamerican Journal of Development Studies* 3, no. 1 (2014): 58–82.

Giacoman, Diego. "Drug Policy and the Prison Situation in Bolivia." In *Systems Overload: Drug Laws and Prisons in Latin America*, edited by Pien Metaal and Coletta Youngers, 21–29. Amsterdam/Washington: TNI & WOLA, 2011.

Gill, Lesley. *Peasants, Entrepreneurs, and Social Change: Frontier Development in Lowland Bolivia*. Boulder: Westview, 1987.

———. *School of the Americas: Military Training and Political Violence in the Americas*. Durham: Duke University Press, 2004.

Gillies, Allan. "Contesting the 'War on Drugs' in the Andes: US-Bolivian Relations of Power and Control (1989–1993)." *Journal of Latin American Studies* 52, no. 1 (2020): 77–106.

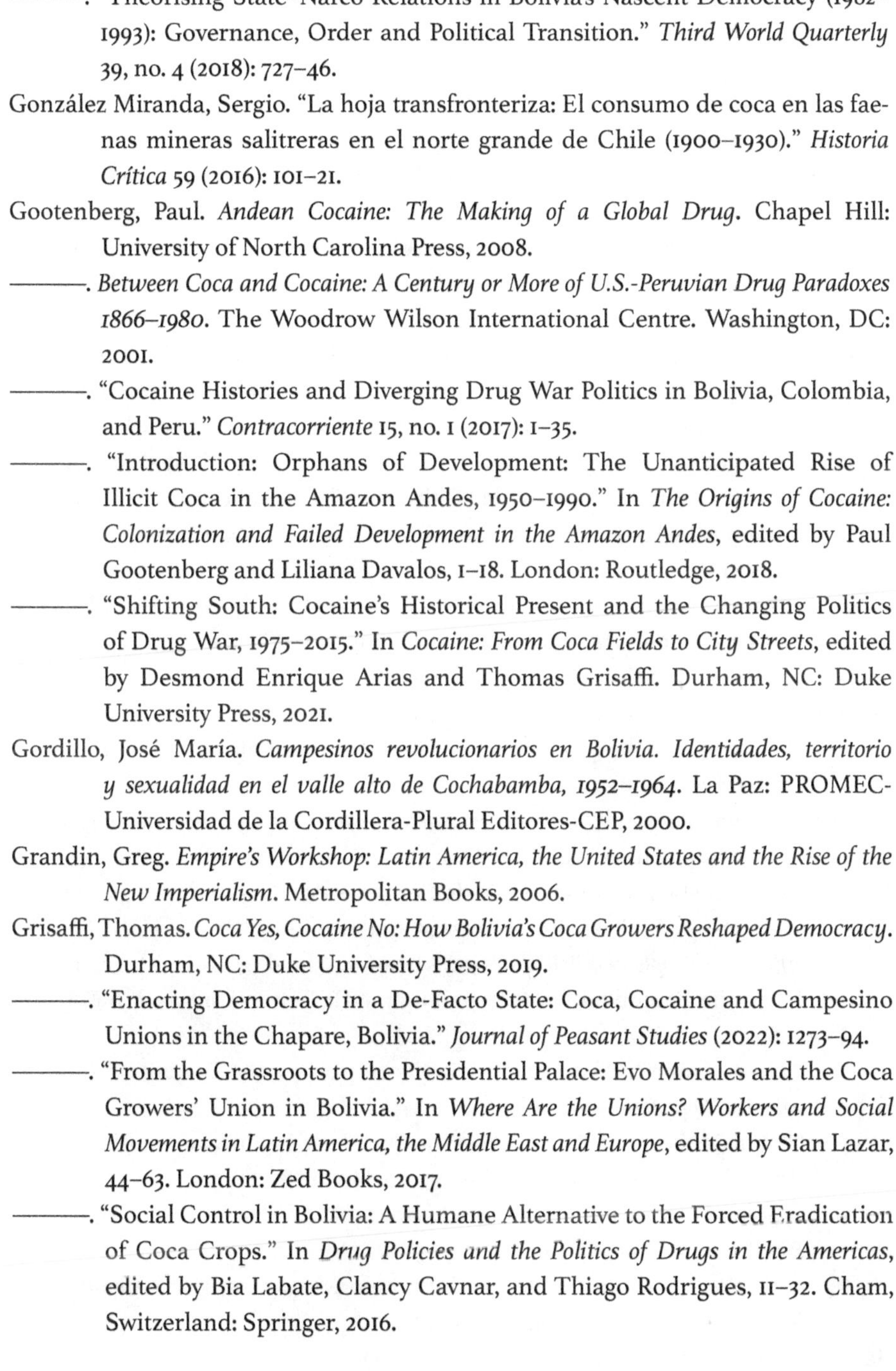

———. "Theorising State–Narco Relations in Bolivia's Nascent Democracy (1982–1993): Governance, Order and Political Transition." *Third World Quarterly* 39, no. 4 (2018): 727–46.

González Miranda, Sergio. "La hoja transfronteriza: El consumo de coca en las faenas mineras salitreras en el norte grande de Chile (1900–1930)." *Historia Crítica* 59 (2016): 101–21.

Gootenberg, Paul. *Andean Cocaine: The Making of a Global Drug*. Chapel Hill: University of North Carolina Press, 2008.

———. *Between Coca and Cocaine: A Century or More of U.S.-Peruvian Drug Paradoxes 1866–1980*. The Woodrow Wilson International Centre. Washington, DC: 2001.

———. "Cocaine Histories and Diverging Drug War Politics in Bolivia, Colombia, and Peru." *Contracorriente* 15, no. 1 (2017): 1–35.

———. "Introduction: Orphans of Development: The Unanticipated Rise of Illicit Coca in the Amazon Andes, 1950–1990." In *The Origins of Cocaine: Colonization and Failed Development in the Amazon Andes*, edited by Paul Gootenberg and Liliana Davalos, 1–18. London: Routledge, 2018.

———. "Shifting South: Cocaine's Historical Present and the Changing Politics of Drug War, 1975–2015." In *Cocaine: From Coca Fields to City Streets*, edited by Desmond Enrique Arias and Thomas Grisaffi. Durham, NC: Duke University Press, 2021.

Gordillo, José María. *Campesinos revolucionarios en Bolivia. Identidades, territorio y sexualidad en el valle alto de Cochabamba, 1952–1964*. La Paz: PROMEC-Universidad de la Cordillera-Plural Editores-CEP, 2000.

Grandin, Greg. *Empire's Workshop: Latin America, the United States and the Rise of the New Imperialism*. Metropolitan Books, 2006.

Grisaffi, Thomas. *Coca Yes, Cocaine No: How Bolivia's Coca Growers Reshaped Democracy*. Durham, NC: Duke University Press, 2019.

———. "Enacting Democracy in a De-Facto State: Coca, Cocaine and Campesino Unions in the Chapare, Bolivia." *Journal of Peasant Studies* (2022): 1273–94.

———. "From the Grassroots to the Presidential Palace: Evo Morales and the Coca Growers' Union in Bolivia." In *Where Are the Unions? Workers and Social Movements in Latin America, the Middle East and Europe*, edited by Sian Lazar, 44–63. London: Zed Books, 2017.

———. "Social Control in Bolivia: A Humane Alternative to the Forced Eradication of Coca Crops." In *Drug Policies and the Politics of Drugs in the Americas*, edited by Bia Labate, Clancy Cavnar, and Thiago Rodrigues, 11–32. Cham, Switzerland: Springer, 2016.

———. "We Are *Originarios* . . . We Just Aren't from Here: Coca Leaf and Identity Politics in the Chapare, Bolivia." *Bulletin of Latin American Research* 29, no. 4 (2010): 425–39.

———. "The White Factory: Coca, Cocaine and Informal Governance in the Chapare, Bolivia." In *Cocaine: From Coca Fields to Streets*, edited by Enrique Desmond Arias and Thomas Grisaffi, 41–68. Durham, NC: Duke University Press, 2021.

———. "Why Is the Drug Trade Not Violent? Cocaine Production and the Embedded Economy in the Chapare, Bolivia." *Development & Change* 53, no. 3 (2022): 576–99.

Grisaffi, Thomas, Linda Farthing, and Kathryn Ledebur. "Integrated Development with Coca in the Plurinational State of Bolivia: Shifting the Focus from Eradication to Poverty Alleviation." *Bulletin on Narcotics* 61 (2017): 131–57.

Grisaffi, Thomas, Linda Farthing, Kathryn Ledebur, Maritza Paredes, and Alvaro Pastor. "From Criminals to Citizens: The Applicability of Bolivia's Community-Based Coca Control Policy to Peru." *World Development* 146 (2021): 1–14.

Grisaffi, Thomas, and Kathryn Ledebur. "Citizenship or Repression? Coca, Eradication and Development in the Andes." *Stability: International Journal of Security and Development* 5, no. 1 (2016).

Gutierrez, Eric Dante. "The Paradox of Illicit Economies: Survival, Resilience, and the Limits of Development and Drug Policy Orthodoxy." *Globalizations* 17, no. 6 (2020): 1008–26.

Gutierrez Aguilar, Raquel. *Rhythms of Pachakuti: Indigenous Uprising and State Power in Bolivia*. Durham, NC: Duke University Press, 2014.

Healy, Kevin. "The Boom within the Crisis: Some Recent Effects of Foreign Cocaine Markets on Bolivian Rural Society and Economy." In *Coca and Cocaine: Effects on People and Policy in Latin America*, edited by Deborah Pacini and Christine Franquemont. Peterborough, NH: Cultural survival, Inc. LASP, 1986.

———. "The Cocaine Industry in Bolivia: Its Impact on the Peasantry." *Cultural Survival Quarterly* 9, no. 4 (1985).

———. "Political Ascent of Bolivia's Peasant Coca Leaf Producers." *Journal of Inter American Studies and World Affairs* 33, no. 1 (1991): 87–121.

Hemming, John. *The Conquest of the Incas*. London: Macmillan, 1970.

Henkel, Ray. "The Bolivian Cocaine Industry." In *Drugs in Latin America: Studies in Third World Societies*, edited by Edmundo Morales, 53–80. Williamsburg, VA: College of William and Mary, 1986.

Henman, Anthony. *Mama Coca*. La Paz: Hisbol, 1992.

Hope, Jessica. "Losing Ground? Extractive-Led Development Versus Environmentalism in the Isiboro Secure Indigenous Territory and National Park (Tipnis), Bolivia." *The Extractive Industries and Society* 3, no. 4 (2016): 922–29.

Hylton, Forrest, and Sinclair Thomson. *Revolutionary Horizons: Popular Struggle in Bolivia*. London: Verso Books, 2007.

Jabin, David. "Nómadas en la ciudad: La apropiación yuqui del espacio urbano." Amazonía, política indígena y ciudad: La dimensión urbana de la política indígena en la Amazonía. Seminario del GRDI APOCAMO, Pontificia Universidad Católica, Lima, Perú, October 4, 2014.

Jelsma, Martin. "UNGASS 2016: Prospects for Treaty Reform and UN System-Wide Coherence on Drug Policy" *Journal of Drug Policy Analysis* 10, no. 1, 2017, 181–95.

Klein, Herbert. "Coca Production in the Bolivian Yungas in the Colonial and Early National Periods." In *Coca and Cocaine: Effects on People and Policy in Latin America*, edited by Deborah Pacini and Christine Franquemont. Peterborough, NH: Cultural Survival Inc., LASP, 1986.

Kohl, Benjamin, and Linda Farthing. *Impasse in Bolivia: Neoliberal Hegemony and Popular Resistance*. London: Zed Books 2006.

———. "Less Than Fully Satisfactory Development Outcomes." *Latin American Perspectives* 36, no. 3 (2009): 59–78.

———. "The Price of Success: Bolivia's War against Drugs and the Poor." *NACLA Report on the Americas* 35, no. 1 (2001): 35–41.

Komadina, Jorge, and Céline Geffroy. *El poder del movimiento político: Estrategia, tramas organizativas e identidad del MAS en Cochabamba (1999–2005)*. La Paz: PIEB, 2007.

Laing, Anna. "Re-Producing Territory: Between Resource Nationalism and Indigenous Self-Determination in Bolivia." *Geoforum* 108 (2020): 28–38.

Larson, B. *Colonialism and Agrarian Transformation in Bolivia: Cochabamba 1550–1900*. Princeton, NJ: Princeton University Press, 1988.

Laserna, Roberto. "Desarrollo alternativo en Bolivia. Análisis preliminar de una experiencia inconclusa." Seminario Internacional, Bogotá, Colombia, Pontificia Universidad Javeriana, August 12, 2000.

———, ed. *Empujando la Concertación. Marchas campesinas, opinión pública y coca*. La Paz: PIEB-CERES, 1999.

———. "Information and Illegality: The Case of Coca Production in Bolivia." *Berkeley Planning Journal* 7, no. 1 (1992): 124–31.

———. *Las Drogas y el ajuste en Bolivia: economía clandestina y políticas públicas*. La Paz: CEDLA, 1994.

Ledebur, Kathryn. "Bolivia: Clear Consequences." In *Drugs and Democracy in Latin America: The Impact of US Policy*, edited by Coletta Youngers and Eileen Rosin, 143–84. Boulder: Lynne Rienner, 2005.

Ledebur, Kathryn, and Coletta Youngers. "From Conflict to Collaboration: An Innovative Approach to Reducing Coca Cultivation in Bolivia." *Stability: International Journal of Security and Development* 2, no. 1 (2013): 1–11.

Lema, Ana María. "The Coca Debate and Yungas Landowners During the First Half of the 20th Century." In *Coca, Cocaine, and the Bolivian Reality*, edited by B. Léons and H. Sanabria, 99–116. Albany, NY: State University of New York Press, 1997.

———. "Production et Circulation de la coca en Bolivie: 1780–1840." EHESS, 1988.

Léons, Barbara, and William Léons. "Land Reform and Economic Change in the Yungas." In *Beyond the Revolution: Bolivia since 1952*, edited by James Malloy and R. Thorn, 269–300. Pittsburgh: University of Pittsburgh Press, 1971.

Léons, Barbara, and Harry Sanabria. "Coca and Cocaine in Bolivia: Reality and Policy Illusion." In *Coca, Cocaine, and the Bolivian Reality*, edited by B. Léons and H. Sanabria, 1–46. Albany, NY: State University of New York Press, 1997.

Madrid, Raul. *The Rise of Ethnic Politics in Latin America*. Cambridge: Cambridge University Press, 2012.

Marconi, Reinaldo. *El drama del Chapare. La frustración del desarrollo alternativo*. La Paz: CEDLA, Centro de Estudios para el Desarrollo Laboral y Agrario, 1998.

Marston, Andrea, and Amy Kennemore. "Extraction, Revolution, Plurinationalism: Rethinking Extractivism from Bolivia." *Latin American Perspectives* 46, no. 2 (2019): 141–60.

Mayer, Enrique. *The Articulated Peasant: Household Economies in the Andes*. Oxford: Westview, 2002.

———. "Coca Use in the Andes." In *Drugs in Latin America*, edited by Edmundo Morales, 25–52. Williamsburg, VA: College of William and Mary, 1986.

McNeish, John Andrew. "Extraction, Protest and Indigeneity in Bolivia: The TIPNIS Effect." *Latin American and Caribbean Ethnic Studies* 8, no. 2 (2013): 221–42.

Medina, Samuel Doria. *La economia informal en Bolivia*. La Paz: Offset Boliviana, 1986.

Menzel, Sewall. *Fire in the Andes: U.S. Foreign Policy and Cocaine Politics in Bolivia and Peru*. New York: University Press of America, Inc., 1996.

Mesa, Jose, Teresa Gisbert, and Carlos Mesa. *Historia de Bolivia*. La Paz: Editorial Gisbert, 2003.

Metaal, Pien. "Coca in Debate: The Contradiction and Conflict between the UN Drug Conventions and the Real World." In *Prohibition, Religious Freedom, and Human Rights: Regulating Traditional Drug Use*, edited by Beatriz Labate and Clancy Cavnar, 25–44. Berlin: Springer, 2014.

Metaal, Pien, Martin Jelsma, Mario Argandona, Ricardo Soberon, Anthony Henman, and Ximera Echeverria. *Coca Yes, Cocaine, No? Legal Options for the Coca Leaf*. Amsterdam: Transnational Institute, 2006.

Midgette, Gregory, Steven Davenport, Jonathan Caulkins, and Beau Kilmer. *What America's Users Spend on Illegal Drugs, 2006–2016*. Santa Monica, CA: RAND Corporation 2019.

Millington, Andrew. "Creating Coca Frontiers and Cocaleros in Chapare: Bolivia, 1940 to 1990." In *The Origins of Cocaine: Colonization and Failed Development in the Amazon Andes*, edited by Paul Gootenberg and Liliana Dávalos. London: Routledge, 2018.

Mintz, Sidney. *Sweetness and Power: The Place of Sugar in Modern History*. Harmondsworth, England: Penguin, 1986.

Mortensen, Thomas, and Eric Gutierrez. "Mitigating Crime and Violence in Coca-Growing Areas." *Journal of Illicit Economies and Development* 1, no. 1 (2019): 63–71.

Murra, John. *The Economic Organization of the Inka State*. Greenwich: JAI Press, 1979.

———. "Notes on Pre-Colombian Cultivation of Coca Leaf." In *Coca and Cocaine Effects on People and Policy in Latin America*, edited by Deborah Pacini and Christine Franquemont. Peterborough, NH: Cultural survival, Inc. LASP, 1986.

Nash, June. "Interpreting Social Movements: Bolivian Resistance to Economic Conditions Imposed by the International Monetary Fund." *American Ethnologist* 19, no. 2 (1992): 275–93.

———. *We Eat the Mines and the Mines Eat Us: Dependency and Exploitation in Bolivian Tin Mines*. New York: Columbia University Press, 1979.

OAS. *Scenarios for the Drug Problem in the Americas 2013–2025*. Washington, DC: Organization of American States General Secretariat, 2013. http://www.oas.org/documents/eng/press/Introduction_and_Analytical_Report.pdf.

Oikonomakis, Leonidas. *Political Strategies and Social Movements in Latin America: The Zapatistas and Bolivian Cocaleros*. Cham: Palgrave Macmillan, 2019.

O'Phelan, Godoy Scarlett. *La gran rebelión en los Andes: de Túpac Amaru a Túpac Catari*. Cusco: Perú - CBC Centro de Estudios Regionales Andinos Bartolomé de las Casas, 1995.

Painter, James. *Bolivia and Coca: A Study in Dependency*. Boulder, Colorado: Lynne Rienner, 1994.

Paley, Dawn. *Drug War Capitalism*. Oakland, CA: AK Press, 2014.

Paoli, Letizia, Victoria Greenfield, and Peter Reuter. "Change is Possible: The History of the International Drug Control Regime and Implications for Future Policymaking." *Substance Use and Misuse* 47, no. 8–9 (2012): 923–35.

Pearson, Zoe. "Bolivia, Coca, Culture and Colonialism." In *Research Handbook on International Drug Policy*, edited by David Bewley-Taylor and Khalid Tinasti, 285–302: Edward Elgar Publishing, 2020.

———. "Coca Sí, Cocaína No? The Intimate Politics of International Drug Control Policy and Reform in Bolivia." PhD diss., Ohio State University, 2016.

Pellegrini, Alessandra. *Beyond Indigeneity: Coca Growing and the Emergence of a New Middle Class in Bolivia*. Tucson: University of Arizona Press, 2016.

Perez-Crespo, Carlos. *Why Do People Migrate? Internal Migration and the Pattern of Capital Accumulation in Bolivia*. Institute for Development Anthropology: Clark University, 1991.

"Peru and Bolivia Are Unlikely Allies in the War on Drugs." The Economist, 2018. https://www.economist.com/the-americas/2018/08/18/peru-and-bolivia-are-unlikely-allies-in-the-war-on-drugs.

Pielemeier, John. *Interview with David Cohen: Foreign Affairs Oral History Project*. Washington, DC: The Association for Diplomatic Studies and Training, 2018. https://adst.org/wp-content/uploads/2018/06/Cohen-David.pdf.

PNUD. *Bolivia: Atlas Estadístico de Municipios*. La Paz: Programa de las Naciones Unidas para el Desarrollo. El Instituto Nacional de Estadística, 2005.

Postero, Nancy. *The Indigenous State: Race, Politics, and Performance in Plurinational Bolivia*. Berkeley: University of California Press, 2017.

Prest, Stuart. "Rough Peace: Understanding the Avoidance of Armed Conflict in Bolivia." University of British Columbia, 2015.

Quiroga, José Antonio. "El Desarrollo alternativo como alternativa al desarrollo." *Nueva Sociedad* 130 (1994): 144–51.

Ramos, Beatriz, Jean Paul Benavides, María Alejandra Vélez, Gilda Jauregui, and David Restrepo. Control social de la coca: Lecciones del trópico de Cochabamba (Bolivia) para Colombia. La Paz: Instituto Investigaciones Socio-Económicas (IISEC), 2023.

Ramos Salazar, Sandra Rosemary. "Las Federaciones del Trópico de Cochabamba en el proceso de construcción de un instrumento Político (1992–1997)." UMSA, 2011.

———. "Nueva ley de la coca: Efectos sociopolíticos en productores de Yungas." *Temas Sociales* 23 (2018): 39–65.

"Regulation: The Responsible Control of Drugs." Global Commission on Drugs Policy, 2018, http://www.globalcommissionondrugs.org/wp-content/uploads/2018/09/ENG-2018_Regulation_Report_WEB-FINAL.pdf.

Reinaga, Fausto. *La Revolucion India*. La Paz: Ediciones Fundacion Amautica "Fausto Reinaga," 1969.

Reiss, Suzanna. *We Sell Drugs: The Alchemy of US Empire*. Berkeley: University of California Press, 2014.

Restrepo, David, Ernesto Saenz, Orlando Jara-Muñoz, Iván Calixto-Botía, Sioly Rodríguez-Suárez, Pablo Zuleta, Benjamin Chavez, Juan Sanchez, and John D'Auria. "Erythroxylum in Focus: An Interdisciplinary Review of an Overlooked Genus." *Molecules* 24, no. 3788 (2019): 1–25.

Rivera, Mario, Arthur Aufderheide, Larry Cartmell, Constantino Torres, and Odin Langsjoen. "Antiquity of Coca-Leaf Chewing in the South Central Andes: A 3,000 Year Archaeological Record of Coca-Leaf Chewing from Northern Chile." *Journal of Psychoactive Drugs* 37, no. 4 (2005): 455–58.

Rivera, Silvia. "Coca: An Indigenous Commodity and Its Paradoxes." *ReVista: Harvard Review of Latin America* (Fall 2011): 21–25.

———. *Las fronteras de la coca*. La Paz: Aruwiyiri IDIS-UMSA, 2003.

Sachs, Jeffrey. "The Bolivian Hyperinflation and Stabilisation." *American Economic Review* 77, no. 2 (1987): 279–83.

Salazar, Fernando, Silvano Arancibia, Luis Cutipa, and Delfin Olivera. *Kawsachun Coca: el costo humano de las políticas de erradicación de cultivios de Coca en el trópico—de Cochabamba - Bolivia 1980–2004. Tomo 1*. La Paz: UMSS/UDESTRO, 2008.

Salazar Ortuño, Fernando. *De la coca al poder: políticas públicas de sustitución de la economía de la coca y pobreza en Bolivia, 1975–2004*. Buenos Aires: Consejo Latinoamericano de Ciencias Sociales (CLACSO), 2008.

Sanabria, Harry. "Coca, Migration and Social Differentiation in the Bolivian Lowlands." In *Drugs in Latin America*, edited by Edmundo Morales, 81–124. Williamsburg, VA: College of William and Mary, 1986.

———. *The Coca Boom and Rural Social Change in Bolivia*. Ann Arbor: University of Michigan Press, 1993.

———. "Consolidating States, Restructuring Economies, and Confronting Workers and Peasants: The Antinomies of Bolivian Neoliberalism." *Comparative Studies in Society and History* 41, no. 3 (1999): 535–61.

Schwaller, John Frederick. *The Church in Colonial Latin America*. Wilmington, DE: Scholarly Resources Books, 2000.

Shakow, Miriam. *Along the Bolivian Highway: Social Mobility and Political Culture in a New Middle Class*. Philadelphia: University of Pennsylvania Press, 2014.

Soux, Maria Luisa. *La coca liberal: Producción y circulación a principios del Siglo XIX*. La Paz: CID, 1993.

Spedding, Alison. "The Coca Field as a Total Social Fact." In *Coca, Cocaine, and the Bolivian Reality*, edited by B Léons and H Sanabria, 47–70. Albany: State University of New York Press, 1997.

———. *En defensa de la hoja de coca*. La Paz: Pieb/Editorial Mama Huaco, 2003.

———. *Wachu Wachu: cultivo de coca e identidad en los Yungas de La Paz*. La Paz: Hisbol, 1994.

Spedding, Alison, and David Fernandez. "Testimonios: así erradicaron mi cocal!" *Bolivian Studies Journal* 4, no. 2 (2004): 18–26.

Stearman, Allyn Maclean. *Yuqul: Forest Nomads in a Changing World*. New York: Holt, Rinehart and Winston, 1989.

Stefanoni, Pablo. *Qué hacer con los indios: Y otros traumas irresueltos de la colonialidad*. La Paz: Plural Editores, 2010.

Stippel, Jörg, and Juan Serrano-Moreno. "The Coca Diplomacy as the End of the War on Drugs: The Impact of International Cooperation on the Crime Policy of the Plurinational State of Bolivia." *Crime, Law and Social Change* 74 (2020): 361–80.

Sturtevant, Chuck. "'Some Time from Now They'll Be Good Farmers': Rethinking Perceptions of Social Evolution in an Area of Interethnic Contact in Lowland Bolivia." *Latin American and Caribbean Ethnic Studies* 10, no. 2 (2015): 180–98.

"The 100 Largest Companies in the World Ranked by Revenue in 2019." Statista, 2020. Accessed February 28, 2021. https://www.statista.com/statistics/263265/top-companies-in-the-world-by-revenue/.Ticona, Esteban, Gonzalo Rojas, and Xavier Albó, eds. *Votos y Wiphalas: campesinos y pueblos originarios en democracia*. La Paz: CIPCA; Fundación Milenio, 1995.

"Trump Bets on Closer Ties with Bolivia." NACLA, 2020, https://nacla.org/bolivia-trump-anez

UNDP. *Development Dimensions of Drug Policy: Innovative Approaches*. New York: United Nations Development Program, 2019. https://www.undp.org/content/dam/undp/library/people/health/Development_Dimensions_of_Drug_Policy.pdf.

———. *Reflections on Drug Policy and Its Impact on Human Development: Innovative Approaches*. Vienna: United Nations Development Program, 2016. http://www.undp.org/content/dam/undp/library/HIV-AIDS/ReflectionsOnDrugPolicyAndImpactOnHumanDevelopment.pdf.

UNODC. "Drug Supply: Book 3." In *World Drug Report 2020*, 1–96. Vienna: United Nations, 2020.

———. *Estado Plurinacional de Bolivia: Monitoreo de cultivos de coca: 2019*. La Paz: Oficina de las Naciones Unidas contra la droga y el delito, 2020.

———. *Estado Plurinacional de Bolivia: Monitoreo de cultivos de coca: 2020*. La Paz: Oficina de las Naciones Unidas contra la droga y el delito, 2021.

———. *Estado Plurinacional de Bolivia: Monitoreo de cultivos de coca: 2021*. La Paz: Oficina de las Naciones Unidas contra la droga y el delito, 2022.

———."Principales hallazgos del Informe de la Unodc sobre la destrucción de drogas ilegales incautadas en Bolivia, entre enero y julio de 2020." UN, 2020. https://www.unodc.org/documents/bolivia/200827_Folleto_Hallazgos_de_la_destruccion_de_drogas_Ene-Jul_2020.pdf.

———. *World Drug Report 2021: Book 4*. Vienna: UN Office on Drugs and Crime, 2021.

———. *World Drug Report 2022: Book 4*. Vienna: UN Office on Drugs and Crime, 2022.

Urioste, Miguel. *Resistencia Campesina: Efectos de la politica econmica neoliberal del decreto supremo 21060*. La Paz: CEDLA, 1989.

Van Cott, Donna Lee. "From Exclusion to Inclusion: Bolivia's 2002 Elections." *Journal of Latin American Studies* 35, no. 4 (2003): 751–75.

Vazualdo, Diego Mattos. "Coca y representación: la hoja de coca en la constitución de la nación boliviana en la época neoliberal." *Latin American Research Review* 49, no. 1 (2014): 23–38.

Warren, Adam. "Collaboration and Discord in International Debates About Coca Chewing, 1949–1950." *Medicine Anthropology Theory* 5, no. 2 (2018): 35–51.

Weil, Andrew. "The Therapeutic Value of Coca in Contemporary Medicine." *Journal of Ethnopharmacology* 3, no. 2–3 (1981): 367–76.

Wiedemann, I. "The Folklore of Coca in the South American Andes: Coca Pouches, Lime Calabashes and Rituals." *Zeitschrift für Ethnologie* 104, no. 2 (1979): 278–309.

Wolff, Jonas. "Negotiating Interference: US Democracy Promotion, Bolivia and the Tale of a Failed Agreement." *Third World Quarterly* 38, no. 4 (2017): 882–99.

Yampara, Simón. "Cosmovivencia Andina: Vivir y convivir en armonía integral – Suma Qamaña." *Bolivian Studies Journal* 18 (2011): 1–22.

Yashar, Deborah. *Contesting Citizenship in Latin America: The Rise of Indigenous Movements and the Postliberal Challenge*. Cambridge: Cambridge University Press, 2005.

Youngers, Coletta. "The US And Latin America after 9–11 and Iraq." Foreign Policy in Focus. Updated June 2003. http://fpif.org/the_us_and_latin_america_after_9-11_and_iraq/.

Youngers, Coletta, and Eileen Rosin, eds. *Drugs and Democracy in Latin America: The Impact of US Policy*. Boulder: Washington Office on Latin America; Lynne Rienner Publishers, 2005.

Zuazo, Moira. *¿Cómo Nació el MAS? La Ruralización de la política en Bolivia*. La Paz: Friedrich Ebert Stiftung, ILDIS, 2009.

Zurita, Leonilda. "La Organización de las mujeres cocaleras en el Chapare." In *Movimiento indígena en América Latina: Resistencia y proyecto alternativo*, edited by Fabiola Escárzaga and Raquel Gutiérrez, 85–94. Mexico, DF: UACM, CEAM, 2005.

EPILOGUE ONE

Cook, Noble David. *Born to Die: Disease and New World Conquest, 1492–1650*. Cambridge: Cambridge University Press, 1998.

López de Gómara, Francisco. *Cortés: The Life of the Conqueror by His Secretary*. Translated and edited by Lesley Byrd Simpson. Berkeley: University of California Press, 1966.

McKay, Ben M., Alberto Alonso-Fradejas, and Arturo Ezquerro-Cañete, eds., *Agrarian Extractivism in Latin America*. New York: Routledge, 2021.

McNelly, Angus. "The Highs and Lows of Bolivia's Rebel City." *NACLA Report on the Americas* 51, no. 4 (2019): 338–40.

Robinson, Andy. *Gold, Oil, and Avocados: A Recent History of Latin America in Sixteen Commodities*. Brooklyn: Melville House, 2020.

Rogers, Charlotte. *Mourning El Dorado: Literature and Extractivism in the Contemporary American Tropics*. Charlottesville: University of Virginia Press, 2019.

Schlesinger, Roger. *In the Wake of Columbus: The Impact of the New World on Europe, 1492–1650*. 2nd ed. Wheeling, IL: Harlan Davidson, Inc., 2007.

Webber, Jeffrey R. "Rebellion to Reform in Bolivia. Part I: Domestic Class Structure, Latin-American Trends, and Capitalist Imperialism." *Historical Materialism* 16 (2008): 23–58.

EPILOGUE TWO

Acemoglu, Daron, Simon Johnson, and James A. Robinson. "The Colonial Origins of Comparative Development: An Empirical Investigation." *American Economic Review* 91, no. 5 (2001): 1369–401.

Bankoff, Greg. "Coming to Terms with Nature: State and Environment in Maritime Southeast Asia." *Environmental History Review* 19, no. 3 (1995): 17–37.

Barragán, Rossana. "Extractive Economy and Institutions? Technology, Labour, and Land in Potosí, the Sixteenth to the Eighteenth Century." In *Colonialism, Institutional Change, and Shifts in Global Labour Relations*, edited by Karin Hofmeester and De Zwart Pim, 207–37. Amsterdam: Amsterdam University Press, 2018.

Beckert, Sven. *Empire of Cotton: A Global History*. New York: Alfred A. Knopf, 2014.

Beckert, Sven, Ulbe Bosma, Mindi Schneider, and Eric Vanhaute. "Commodity Frontiers and the Transformation of the Global Countryside: A Research Agenda." *Journal of Global History* (2021): 435–50.

Booth, Anne. *Colonial Legacies: Economic and Social Development in East and Southeast Asia*. Honolulu: University of Hawaii Press, 2007.

Cardoso de Mello, and Louise Van Melkebeke Sven. "From the Amazon to the Congo Valley: A Comparative Study on the Violent Commodification of Labour During the Rubber Boom (1870s-1910s)." In *Commodity Frontiers and Global Capitalist Expansion: Social, Ecological and Political Implications from the Nineteenth Century to the Present Day*, edited by Sabrina Joseph, 137–82. Cham, Switzerland: Palgrave Macmillan, 2019.

Cottyn, Hanne. "Making Cheap Nature on High Altitude: A World-Ecological Perspective on Commodification, Communities and Conflict in the Andes." In *Commodity Frontiers and Global Capitalist Expansion Social, Ecological and Political Implications from the Nineteenth Century to the Present Day*, edited by Sabrina Joseph, 15–56. Cham, Switzerland: Palgrave Macmillan, 2019.

Furtado, Celso. *The Economic Growth of Brazil: A Survey from Colonial to Modern Times*. Los Angeles, CA: California University Press, 1963.

Joseph, Sabrina. "Introduction." In *Commodity Frontiers and Global Capitalist Expansion Social, Ecological and Political Implications from the Nineteenth Century to the Present Day*, edited by Sabrina Joseph, 1–14. Cham, Switzerland: Palgrave Macmillan, 2019.

McHale, T. R. *Rubber and the Malaysian Economy*. Singapore: Sendirian Berhad, 1967.

Platt, Tristan. "Simón Bolívar, the Sun of Justice and the Amerindian Virgin: Andean Conceptions of the Patria in Nineteenth-Century Potosí." *Journal of Latin American Studies* 25, no. 1 (1993): 159–85.

Sterner, Thomas. "The Development of State Oil Companies in Latin America: From Conflict to Collaboration." *Journal of Energy and Development* 15, no. 1 (1989): 111–23.

Svampa, Maristella. *Neo-Extractivism in Latin America: Socio-Environmental Conflicts, the Territorial Turn, and New Political Narratives*. Cambridge: Cambridge University Press, 2019.

Verbrugge, Boris. "Undermining the State? Informal Mining and Trajectories of State Formation in Eastern Mindanao, Philippines." *Critical Asian Studies* 47, no. 2 (2015): 177–99.

Warren, James Francis. *The Sulu Zone: The Dynamics of External Trade, Slavery, and Ethnicity in the Transformation of a Southeast Asian Maritime State*. Singapore: Singapore University Press, 1981.

CONTRIBUTORS

Rossana Barragán is a senior fellow researcher at the International Institute of Social History in Amsterdam (2011–2022) and a professor at CIDES-UMSA La Paz. She was the director of the La Paz Historical Archive (2004–2011). Her research focuses on ethnicity and citizenship and more recently on mining. Her publications include "Working Silver for the World: Mining Labor and Popular Economy in Colonial Potosí" (*Hispanic American Historical Review* 97, no. 9, 2017) and "Women in the Silver Mines of Potosí: Rethinking the History of 'Informality' and 'Precarity'" (*International Review of Social History* 65, no. 2, 2019). She is a coauthor of *Potosí in the Early Global Silver Age* (2023).

Ulbe Bosma is a senior researcher at the International Institute of Social History in Amsterdam. From 1993 to 2007 he acted as coordinator of the Sephis program, sponsoring historical research in the Global South. He is a professor of international comparative social history at the Vrije Universiteit Amsterdam. His most recent books are *The Making of a Periphery* (2019), *The Sugar Plantation in India and Indonesia* (2019), and *World of Sugar: How the Sweet Stuff Transformed Our Politics, Health, and Environment over 2,000 Years* (2023).

Thomas Grisaffi is currently a professor of Latin American studies at the University of St. Gallen. Trained as an anthropologist, Grisaffi works on topics including coca and cocaine production, alternative development, agricultural unions, and democracy in both Bolivia and Peru. He is the author of *Coca Yes, Cocaine No: How Bolivia's Coca Growers Reshaped Democracy* (2019) and co-editor of *Cocaine: from coca fields to the streets* (2021), both published by Duke University Press.

Sarah T. Hines is an assistant professor of Latin American history at the University of Oklahoma. She received her PhD in Latin American history from the University of California, Berkeley, in 2015. She is the author of "The Power and Ethics of Vernacular Modernism: The Misicuni Dam Project in Cochabamba, Bolivia, 1944–2017" (*Hispanic American Historical Review* 98, no. 2 [May 2018]) and *Water for All: Community, Property, and Revolution in Modern Bolivia* (University of California Press, 2022). She previously taught at Smith College and the University of Maine at Machias before joining the faculty at University of Oklahoma in 2018.

José Octavio Orsag Molina is a PhD candidate from New York University. His main interest is the history of the Amazon, from the rubber boom to the more contemporary expansion of the agrarian frontier. His previous work is centered around the colonization of the Bolivian Amazon during the rubber boom and the fate of the Indigenous population. He also researched the trading circuits in eastern Bolivia connected to the rubber boom and the emergence of the eastern internal market in opposition to the mining market in the west. Now his main interest is to understand the expansion of the rubber boom in the western Amazon as a continental process rather than isolated national teleologies through an environmental history perspective.

Myrna Santiago is a professor of history at Saint Mary's College of California, where she teaches Latin American studies and world history. She is also director of the Women's and Gender Studies Program and an affiliate of the Institute for Latino and Latin American Studies. Her research has focused on the environmental and social history of petroleum in Mexico. She is the author of *The Ecology of Oil: Environment, Labor, and the Mexican Revolution, 1900–1938* (2009). She is currently working on an environmental history of the 1931 and 1973 earthquakes that destroyed the city of Managua, Nicaragua.

Carmen Soliz is an associate professor of Latin America history at the University of North Carolina at Charlotte. She is the author of "'Land to Its Original Owners': Rethinking the Indigenous Politics of the Bolivian Agrarian Reform" (*Hispanic American Historical Review* 97, no. 2) and *Fields of Revolution: Agrarian Reform and Rural State Formation in Bolivia, 1935–1964*. She received a master's degree in political science from the Universidad de Salamanca (Spain) and a PhD in Latin American history from New York University.

Kevin A. Young is an associate professor of history at the University of Massachusetts Amherst. He has written and edited several books, among them *Blood of the Earth: Resource Nationalism, Revolution, and Empire in Bolivia* (2017), *Making the Revolution: Histories of the Latin American Left* (2019), and *Abolishing Fossil Fuels: Lessons from Movements That Won* (2024). His articles on twentieth-century Bolivia have appeared in *Hispanic American Historical Review*, *Latin American Perspectives*, *Diplomatic History*, and other journals.

INDEX

www.ingramcontent.com/pod-product-compliance
Lightning Source LLC
Chambersburg PA
CBHW030639270326
41929CB00007B/130

* 9 7 8 0 8 2 6 3 6 6 1 7 7 *